Native English:
A Guide from Down Under

Kujong Jung
Bernard Rowan

ISBN: 978-0-578-45647-8 (Ebook)
ISBN: 978-1794240360 (Paperback)

<u>**Table of Contents**</u>

Preface

I have been in Oz since 1970. I started this project since I wish to provide something to benefit future generations. Even though I studied English for eight years in Korea before migrating to Australia, I picked up about 90% of my English in Australia.

I have been writing *Native English* since 2006 to help others learn English faster. My initial interest was in English idioms. If foreigners try to understand what individual idioms mean with only literal meanings of words, it is totally a waste of time. **The emphasis of my book is practical usage of vocabulary.**

There are several books published for phrases, idioms, basic words, abbreviations, international English, proverbs, quotations and grammar. I have yet to find a book similar to what I have written. My book is a bit of everything. What I can attest to is that I have been listening to native speakers for over 45 years. I have screened and selected important phrases, idioms, proverbs, quotations, abbreviations, and words of international English so that anyone can master basic English faster. Potential readers are intermediate and advanced learners of English as a second language.

There's a bit of everything here, including grammar, foreign words, phrases and origins, and nationality vocabulary. Unusual expressions in a grammatical sense and short sentences have not been taken from references but are my footprint throughout the pages. I also share a number of thoughts and impressions about Korea and Australia along the way – among other subjects.

I thought that there is need for this type of book so that people can improve their English faster other than by studying for and passing exams. As far as I know, no English books have been published to cover so many areas of popular usage, i.e. many different types of words, slang, abbreviations, proverbs, short sentences, foreign words, and sayings in American, British and Australian English.

I have called this unique book *Native English* as I place more emphasis on the way native speakers from the United States, the United Kingdom, Ireland, Canada, Australia and New Zealand write and speak. They use more idioms, colloquial expressions, slang, informal language, and proverbs than non-native speakers.

Since 2015, I have collaborated with Professor Bernard Rowan of Chicago State University to complete this work. Professor Rowan is listed as an author since he contributed substantially to several chapters as well as edited the entire work prior to publication.

Key Abbreviations

adj./adjective
adv./adverb
cl./clause
Cel./Celtic
conj./conjunction
Czech./Czechoslovakia
D./Dutch
F./French
Ger./German
Gr./Greek
Hun./Hungarian
Interject./interjection
Interrog./interrogative
It./Italian
L./ Latin
n./noun
phr./phrase
pl./plural
prep./preposition
pron./pronoun
Rus./Russian
Sp./Spanish
v./verb.
W./Welsh

I. Some Definitions Plus

1.1. Formality, informality, slang and taboo

There are four main types of expressions:

    i.   Formal: words and phrases used in a serious way, for example in business documents, serious newspapers and books, lectures, and news broadcasts. Formal language is often used when people want to appear polite. For example: *She is anxiously awaiting* (=waiting for) *the results of the medical test. Guests are requested to comply with* (=obey) *all the fire and safety rules.*

    ii.   Informal: used with friends, family, or familiar people in relaxed situations. Informal words are more common in speech than in writing. *He works as an admin assistant* (= administration assistant). *He always stops for a cuppa* (=a cup of tea) *at 10 o'clock.* It might be considered impolite to use informal language in formal situations.

    iii.   Slang: informal language that might include words which are not polite. Slang is often used between members of a particular group when speaking together and might stay in use only for a short time. *That's a load of crap* (=nonsense). *The fuzz* (= The police) *have searched my flat three times this year.* Very informal words and phrases are more common in speech than in writing. I have been in Australia for more than 45 years and important Australian slang words are listed below. Some of these words also are used in the United Kingdom:

    iv.   Taboo: words that are likely to offend someone and are not used in formal situations. Taboo words may refer to sex or sexual organs, excretion and people's nationality or race. Taboo words can be particularly offensive. Strong swear words are also marked taboo.

1.2 Simple English

Absence of/no.
Acquaint/tell or inform.
Adjacent/beside.
Ahead of schedule/early.
A large proportion of/many.
A number of/some; many.
A percentage of/many.
Appreciate your informing me/please write to me; please tell me.
As a result of; on account of; owing to/because of.
At an earlier date/soon.
At this time/now; at present.
Attached please find/attached.
At the earliest possible moment/soon; immediately.
At the present time/now.

At this point of time/now.
At your earliest convenience/soon.
By means of/with; by.
Commence/start; begin.
Concerning/about, on.
Demonstrate/show.
Despite the fact that/although.
Determine/decide; find out.
Discontinue/stop.
Dispatched/sent.
Draw the attention of/show; remind; point out.
Due to the fact that/because.
Effectuate/effect.
Enclosed herewith/enclosed.
Endeavour/try.
En route/on the way.
Expedite/hasten; hurry.
Facilitate/ease; help
Filled to capacity/full.
Finalize/end; conclude.
For the month of June/for June.
For the purpose of/for.
For the reason that/since; because; as.
From my point of view/for me; to me.
Fullest possible extent/fully.
Furnish/give.
Give consideration to/consider.
Give rise to/cause.
Heretofore/before; until now.
If you desire/if you wish; if you want.
Implement/carry out; fulfil; do.
In accordance with/with; by.
In addition to/besides; as well as; also.
In advance of/before.
In a satisfactory manner/satisfactorily.
In all times/always.
In attendance/present; there.
Inasmuch as/as; since; because.
In conjunction with/and; or.
In connection with/about; in.
In consequence of/because of.
Initiate/begin; start.
In order to/to.
In regard to/about.
In short supply/scarce.
In spite of the fact that/despite; although.

In case of/if; in.
In the course of/during; in; while.
In the direction of/towards.
In the event of/in; if.
In the field of/in; with.
In the majority of instances/mostly; usually.
In the near future/soon.
In the school situation/in schools.
In the time/during.
In the vicinity or region or neighborhood/about; near; around.
In view of the fact that/since; as.
Is of the opinion/believes.
It cannot be denied that/undeniably.
Materialize/happen; come about; appear.
Necessitate/force.
Notwithstanding the fact that/although or even though.
Occasioned by/caused by.
On account of the fact that/because.
On a few occasions/occasionally.
On behalf of/for.
On the part of/by.
Owing to the fact that/because.
Previous or prior/before.
Prove beneficial/benefit.
Provided that/if; only if.
Regarding/about; on.
Reiterate/repeat.
Render assistance to/aid; help.
Submitted/sent.
Subsequent to/after.
Terminate/end.
This is to thank you/thank you.
To date/so far.
Under preparation/being prepared.
Under the circumstances/in this or that case.
Wish to apologize or advise/we apologize.
With reference to/on; about.
With the exception of/except.
With the minimum of delay/quickly.

1.3. Type of language

   i. Formal English

Formal English is more common in writing than speaking and is used in notices, business letters and legal English. There are some examples in spoken English, e.g. airport announcements.

   ii. Informal English

Informal English is more common in spoken English. For example:
- most uses of the word *get* are informal.
- many phrasal verbs are informal as in *find out* or *run around*.
- most shortened words are informal as in.

Formal English	**Informal English**
Apprehend	catch
Arrange or make	fix up
Arrive or reach	get to
Bicycle	bike
Children	kids
Collect	pick up
Commence	start
Contact	get in touch with
Further assistance	more help
I regret to inform you	I'm sorry to say
Intelligent	bright
Man	guy
Marvelous	terrific
Obtain or receive	get
Pounds	quid
Purchase	buy
Proceed to	go to
Quite	pretty
Require	need
Resume	start again
Speak to	have a word with
Stupid	thick
Think	reckon
Toilet	loo
Thus	so
What's the matter?	What's up?

iii. Slang

Slang is very informal language. It includes words used by particular groups of people, e.g. young people often refer to "drugs" as dope, and also words which many people think are impolite and unacceptable in most situations. While many are quite common, they are not used in polite speech or writing. For example, the word "piss" is a slang word meaning to urinate or go to the toilet, and it is also used in a number of other slang expressions with different meanings, including "to make angry" or to tell to "go away" as in to *piss off*.

II. International English

English is spoken in many parts of the world. Consequently, there are many varieties of English:

    i.   British English
    ii.   Scottish English
    iii.   Irish English
    iv.   American English
    v.   Canadian English
    vi.   Australian English
    vii.   New Zealand English
    viii. South African English
    ix.   Indian English
    x.   Filipino English

It is not possible to cover all these English-speaking nationalities and variants of English in one book. Attempt will be made to have good coverage of British, American and Australian English excluding pronunciations. However, other English variants will be mentioned briefly.

2.1. Varieties of English

There are no important differences in written form between the English of Great Britain and that of Australia, New Zealand, or South Africa. Brief examples of differences between American English and British are as follows. There are differences in pronunciation between American and British English. However, I have avoided writing anything about this area due to lack of my expertise.
Australian English uses words from both British and American English.

2.2. American English with British English

2.2.1. Differences in Grammar

   i.   In many situations, British English uses the present perfect of the verb while American English may use the simple past.
   ii. The past forms of some verbs differ.
   iii. The past simple is used more widely.
   iv. Different prepositions are used.
   v. Nouns referring to groups are usually followed by a singular verb,
   vi. In American English, no preposition is needed with some verbs that definitely require them on in British English

American
The present perfect or past simple may be used:
I've lost my purse. Have you seen it?

British
The present perfect is used for an action in the past with a result now:
I've lost my purse. Have you seen it?

Anne isn't here.   She's gone out.

The present perfect or simple past can be used:

I'm not thirsty. I've just had water.
I just had water.

A: What time is Sally leaving?
B: She has already left.
B: She already left.

Have you finished your work yet?
or Did you finish your work yet?

American speakers say:
Take a bath   take a shower
Take a break   take a vacation

Shall is unusual:
I will be late this morning.

Should I…? and should we…?
are more usual to ask advice etc.:
Which way shall we go?

Needn't is unusual. The usual form is
need to:
Don't need to: We don't need to hurry

The subjunctive is normally used. Should is
unusual after demand, insist etc.:
She demanded that he apologize.
They insisted that something be done about
the problem.

American speakers generally use You have?

A: Jenny isn't feeling well.
B: She isn't? What's wrong with her?

Accommodation can be countable:
There aren't enough accommodations.

Anne isn't here. She's gone out.

The present perfect is used with
just, already and yet:
I'm not thirsty. I've just had water.

A: What time is Sally leaving?
B: She has already left.

Have you finished your work yet?

British speakers usually say:
have a bath   have a shower
have a break   have a holiday

Will or shall can used with I/we:
I will/shall be late this morning.

Shall I…? and shall we…? Are
used to ask for advice:
Which way shall we go?

You can use needn't or don't:
We needn't hurry.
We don't need to hurry.

After demand, insist etc. you can
use should:
She demanded that he should apologise.
They insisted that something
should be done about the problem.

British speakers generally use Have you/
Isn't she?

A: Jenny isn't feeling well.
B: Isn't she? What's wrong with her?

Accommodation is usually uncountable:
There isn't enough accommodation.

To/in the hospital:
Two people were injured and taken to the hospital.

Nouns like government/team/family, etc. take a single verb in American English:

The team is playing well.

On the weekend/on weekends:
Will you be here on the weekend?

In the front/ in the back (of a group etc.):
Let's sit in front (of the movie theatre).

Different from or different than:
It was different from /than what I'd expected.

Write (to) somebody (with or without to):
Please write (to) me soon.

American speakers use around (not usually round)
She turned around.

American speakers use fill out:
Can you fill out this form?

American speakers do not use "get on" this way.

Get along (with somebody):
David gets along well with his new neighbours.

Do over a room:
The kitchen looks great now it's been done over.

The verbs in this section are normally regular (burned, spelled etc.)

The past principle of get is gotten:
Your French has gotten much better.

---

to/in hospital (without the):
Two people were injured and taken to the hospital.

These nouns can have a singular or plural verb:

The team is/are playing well.

At the weekend/weekends:
Will you be here at the weekend?

At the front/ at the back (of a group):
Let's sit at the front (of the cinema).

Different from or different to:
It was different from/to what I'd expected.

Write to somebody:
Please write to me soon.

British speakers use both round and *around:*
She turned round or She turned around.

British speakers use both fill in and fill out:
Can you fill in this form? or Can you fill out this form?

Get on/progress
How are you getting on in your new job?
Get on (with somebody):
David gets on well with his new neighbours.

Do up a room etc.:
The kitchen looks great now it has been done up.

The verbs in this section (burn spell etc.) can be regular or irregular (burned or burnt, spelled or spelt etc.).

The past principle of get is got:
Your French has got much better. (= has become much better)

Have got = have (as in British English):   Have got is also an alternative to have:
I've got two brothers.   *I've got two brothers.* (= I have two brothers.)

The best that ever lived.   The best that has ever lived.
Check something out   Check something
Did you open my letter yet?   Have you opened my letter yet?
Do something over   Do something again
Do you have…?   Have you--? Or Have you got--?
Does he have a problem?   Has he got problem?
Dollhouse   Doll's house
Driver's license   Driving licence
Emily spelt the word correctly.   Emily spelled the word correctly.
Fill in or out a form   Fill in a form
Friday through Sunday   Friday to Sunday
General Motors has declared a dividend.   Ross Royce have cancelled their dividend.

He has gotten a place at university.   He's got a place university.
He's always leaving his clothes around.   He's leaving his clothes about.
(on the telephone) Hello, is this Matthew?   Hello, is that Matthew?
I always have thought.   I have always thought.
I already ate.   I've already eaten.
I got a seat reserved at the restaurant.   I have got a seat reserved at the restaurant.

I just ate   I have just eaten
I should leave ten of eight.   I should leave by ten to eight...
I think he's lost his camera.   I think he lost his camera.
I've gotten a new automobile/   I've got a new car.
     Ill-gotten gains (plural)
It's important that she be told.   It's important that she should be told.
I've never really gotten to know her   I've never really got to know her.
Jacob has gotten really fat.   Jacob has got really fat.
Meet with somebody   Meet somebody
Most   Almost
Notre Dame plays Michigan.   Oxford play Cambridge.
Rowboat   Rowing boat
She dove into the pool.   She dived into the pool.
She just went home.   She's just gone home.
She looked at me real strange.   She looked at me really strangely.
Some   To some extent
Stay home   Stay at home
Swinging door   Swing door
A tempest in a teapot   A storm in a teacup
Two hundred fifty   Two hundred and fifty
The U.S. Congress adjourns.   The House of Commons rise.
Visit with somebody   Visit somebody

What took you so long?   What has taken so long?
You never can tell.   You can never tell.

With or without prepositions

Agreed to the price	Agreed on the price
Apart from or except for	Aside from
As of	As from
Cater a party	Cater for a party
Effective today	With effect from today
He wrote his MP.	He wrote to his MP.
Mondays	On Mondays
Protest	Protest against
Protest the war	Protest against the war

Parallel prepositions

Aside from	Apart from
Back of	Behind
Half the cash goes for clothes.	Half the cash goes on clothes.
He moved toward the car.	He moved towards the car.
He's in heat.	He's on heat.
In school	At school
It caters to all tastes.	It caters for all tastes.
It looks like it's going to rain.	It looks as if it's going to rain.
It's ten of three.	It's ten to three.
It's ten after seven.	It's ten past seven.
It's in back of the building.	It's behind the building.
I'll see you over the weekend.	I'll see you at the weekend.
I haven't seen him in ages.	I haven't seen him for ages.
Monday through Friday.	Monday to Friday inclusive.
She looked out the window.	She looked out of the window.
She's got a new lease on life.	She's got a new lease of life.
This shop is open Monday through Friday.	This shop is open from Monday to Friday.
Through	Up to and including
We live on X street.	We live in X street.
You're on the firing line.	You're in the firing line.

2.2.2. Vocabulary

2.2.2.1. Equivalent lexical items

Some big differences in vocabulary for the same objects:

American	**British**
Baby carriage	pram
Cotton	cotton wool

American	British	Australian
Crib	cot	
Diaper	nappy	
Pacifier	dummy	
Quint	quin	
Stroller	pushchair	

Cars, Trains and Roads

American	British	Australian
Automobile	car	
Baggage car	luggage van	
Beltway	ring road	
Cab	taxi/cab	
Car (railroad)	carriage (railway)	
Curb (sidewalk)	kerb (pavement)	
Defog(v)	demist(v)	
Divided highway	dual carriageway	
Eighth note	quaver	
Electric cord	flex	
Elementary school	primary school	
Elevator	lift	
Emergency cord	communication cord	
Engineer	engine driver	
Eraser	rubber	
Exhaust fan	extractor fan	
Expressway/freeway (in city)	motorway	
Fender (of a car)	bumper	
Fender	wing (car)	mudguards
Flat(n)	puncture(n)	
Freight car	truck (properly a wagon)	
Funnel/smokestack	funnel	
Gas or gasoline	petrol	petrol
Gear shift	gear lever	
Highway	main road	
Hood (of a car)	bonnet	
Intersection	junction	
License plate	number plate	
Main street	high street	
Median strip	central reservation	
Mobile home	motor caravans	
Moving van	removal van	
Muffler	silencer	muffler
One-way ticket	single ticket	
Overpass	flyover	
Parking lot	car park	
Railroad	railway(s)	
Round-trip ticket	return ticket	

Sedan	saloon	sedan
Sidewalk	pavement; footpath	
Station wagon	shooting brake/estate care	station wagon
Streetcar	tram	tram
Subway	underground	
Switches	(railway) points	
Taxi stand	taxi rank	
To shift gear	to change gear	
Traffic circle	roundabout	
Trailer	caravan	
Truck	bogie	
Truck	lorry	truck
Truck stop	transport cafe	
Turnpike, toll road	toll road	
Trunk	boot	
Windshields	windscreens (car)	

Clothing

American	**British**	
Backpack	rucksack	
Bowler(hat)/derby	bowler(hat)	
Fanny pack	bumbag	
Jumper	pinafore dress	
Knickers	plus-fours	
Panties	knickers(England)	pants
Pants	trousers	
Raincoat	mackintosh	
Running shoes	trainers	
Shorts	(under)pants	
Sneakers	plimsolls	
Suspenders	braces	
Sweater	jersey/ jumper	
Thread	cotton	
Tuxedo	dinner jacket	
Underpants	pants/underpants	
Undershirt	vest (England)/singlet	
Underwear, shorts	pants	
Vest	waistcoat	
Waistcoat	singlet	
Zipper	zip	

Food, Fruit and Vegetables

American	**British**
All-purpose flour	plain flour
Beer	lager (= a light beer)
Blueberry	bilberry

American	British
Can	tin
Candy	sweets
Cookie	biscuit
Corn	maize
Cornstarch	cornflour
Dessert/sweet	pudding
Eggplant	aubergine
Fish stick	fish finger
French-fries	chips (= part of a meal)
Ground meat	mince
Jelly	jam
Jell-O/(trademark) Jell-O	jelly
Molasses	treacle
Potato chips	crisps (= a cold snack)
Romaine lettuce	cos lettuce
Rooster	cock
Seltzer	soda water
Snow peas	mange tout
Zucchini	courgette

Games and Sports

American	British
Deck	pack (of cards)
Field hockey	hockey
Hockey	ice hockey
Push-up	press-up
Solitaire	patience
Tic-tac-toe	noughts and crosses

House and Building

American	British
Apartment	flat
Bathroom; the John	loo, toilet, WC
Closet or cabinet	cupboard
Clothes pin	clothes peg
Drapes	curtains
Dry goods	drapery
Elevator (for people)	lift
First floor	ground floor
Garbage or trash	rubbish
Garbage can or trash can	dustbin
(trademark) Laundromat	launderette
Second floor	first floor
Soft goods	soft furnishings
Yard	garden

Kitchen

American	British
Broil	grill
Faucet	tap
Frying pan/skillet	frying pan
Grill/broil	grill (v)
Pitcher	jug
Plastic wrap	cling film
Stove/range	cooker
Stovetop	hob
Tin	can

Telephone and postal service

American	British
Area code	dialing code
Busy	engaged
Collect call	reverse charge call
Mass mailing	mailshot
Mail (n,v)	post (n,v)
Mailbox	post box
Long-distance call	trunk call
Unlisted number	ex-directory number

Tools and Electrical

American	British
Blowtorch	blowlamp
Electric outlet	power point
Ground	earth
Hardware	ironmongery
Jackhammer	pneumatic drill
Kerosene	paraffin
Motor	engine
Wrench	spanner

Work and Money

American	British
Attorney	barrister, solicitor
Banknote	bill
Bill	bank note (note)
Check	bill (restaurant)
Current account	cheque account
Drugstore/pharmacy	chemist (shop) or chemist's
Industrial park	industrial estate
Mail carrier; mailman	postal worker
Pay envelope	pay packet

Raise (in pay)	rise (in pay)
Rent	let
Resume	curriculum vitae
Roster	rota
Seed capital	seed money
Substitute teacher	supply teacher
Unit trust	mutual fund
Vacation	holiday

Complete list

American	British	Australian
Absorbent cotton	cotton wool	
Administration	Government	
Airplane	aeroplane or plane	
Aisle	gangway or corridor	
Allowance	pocket money	
Antenna or aerial	aerial	
Anyplace	anywhere	
Apartment	flat	flat
Apartment building	block of flats	
Apartment house	block	
Ashcan	dustbin	
Attorney	lawyer	
Automobile	car	
Baby carriage or stroller	pram	pram
Backpack	rucksack	
Backside	bottom, or buttocks	
Backyard	garden	
Back-up	tailback	
Baggage	luggage	
Baggage car	guard's van	
Ball park	playing field	
Baggage checkroom	left luggage	
Ballpoint pen	biro or ballpoint	
Band	ring	
Band-Aids	sticking plaster, Elastoplast	
Barber or barbershop	hairdresser or barber	
Barkeeper	barman	
Baseboard	skirting board	
Base plug	power point	
Bathtub	bath	
Bawl out	tell off	
Beauty parlor	ladies hairdresser	
Beet	beetroot	
Bill (money)	bank note	
Billboard	hoarding	

Billfold	wallet	
Bird dog	gun dog	
Biscuit	scone	
Blooper	blunder	
Blow	to get out; to wreck	
Blowout	puncture	puncture
Blue jeans	jeans (blue denim)	
Bobcat	North American lynx	
Bobby pin	Kirby grip; hair grip	
Bookstore	bookshop	
Boondock	rough country	
Booth	telephone box	
Boxcar	roofed railway wagon	
Braids	plaits	
Broil	grill	
Buck	quid	
Bug	insect	
Building permit	planning permission	
Bulletin board	notice board	
Bumper car	dodgem	
Bureau	chest of drawers	
Business suit	lounge suit	
Busy line (telephone)	engaged	
Buzz saw	circular saw	
Cab	taxi	
Cabana	beach hut	
Cabin	cottage	
Caboose	guard's van	
Calaboose	jail	
Calling card	visiting card	
Can	tin	
Can opener	tin opener	
Candy	sweets	
Candy store	sweet shop	
Cane	walking stick	
Call-in (program)	phone-in (programme)	
Can	tin	
Candy	sweets	
Car; automobile	motorcar	
Car (on a train)	carriage; wagon	
Carfare	bus or train fare	
Car park	parking lot	
Cart	trolley	
Carnival	fair	
Carryall	holdall	

Carryout restaurant	take-away restaurant	
Casket	coffin	
Catalogue	catalogue	
Catsup	ketchup	
Cattle rustling	cattle doffing	
Cause to fail	scupper	
Cell phone	mobile phone	
Center	centre	
Charge account	credit account	
Check	bill for food	
Check (drawn on a bank)	cheque	
Checkers	draughts	
Checking account	current account	
Checkroom or coatroom	cloakroom	
Chief executive officer	managing director	
Chips	potato crisps	
City desk	news desk	
City hall	town hall	
Cleaning woman	daily help, or a char	
Clerk	shop assistant	
Clipping (newspaper)	cutting	
Closet	cupboard	wardrobe
Clothespin	clothes peg	
Cloverleaf	motorway intersection	
Coat	jacket	
Color	colour	
Comfort station	public convenience	
Comforter	eiderdown or duvet	
Commuter ticket	season ticket	
Conductor (railroad)	guard or ticket collector (on a train)	
Confectioner's sugar	icing sugar	
Conservatory	school of music	
Conspicuous fool	wally	
Cookies	sweet biscuits	
Cookie sheet	baking tray	
Corn	maize; sweet corn	
Corner (of a street)	turning	
Cornstarch	cornflour	
Corn syrup	golden syrup	
Costumes	fancy dress	
Cot	camp bed	
Cotton ball	cotton wool	
Cotton candy	candyfloss	
Councilman	councillor	
Counter clockwise	anti-clockwise	
County seat	country town	

Cozy	cosy	
Cracker	cheese biscuit	
Crazy	mad; barmy	
Crepe	pancake	
Crib	cot	
Cross walk	zebra or pedestrian crossing	
Crosstie; tie (railway)	sleeper	
Crossing guard	lollipop man or woman	
Cuffs (on trousers or pants)	turn-ups	
Curb	kerb	
Cute	pretty or clever	
Cut-off	by-pass	
Dead-end street	cul-de-sac	
Deck of cards	pack of cards	
Depot	station (railway)	
Derby hat	bowler	
Dessert	sweet, pudding or dessert	
Detour (road sign)	diversion	
Dial tone	dialing tone	
Diaper	nappy	nappy
Dicker	haggle	
Dinky	small and inconsequential	
Dipper	ladle	
Difficult situation	sticky wicket	
Directory assistance	directory enquiries	
Dish towel	tea towel	
Disk	disc	
Divided highway	dual carriageway	
Do the dishes	wash up	
Dormitory	hall of residence	
Downspout	drainpipe	
Downtown, city center	town centre or city centre	
Draft	draught	
Draft	call-up; conscript	
Drapes	curtains	curtains
Dresser	dressing table	
Driver's license	driving licence	
Drug store or druggist	chemist, pharmacist, general store	
Drummer	commercial traveller	
Drunk	tanked up	
Drunk driving	drink driving	
Dry goods	drapery; soft goods	
Dumb	stupid	
Dumbwaiter	food lift or food trolley	

Dump truck	tipper lorry	
Duplex house	semi-detached	
Eggplant	aubergine	
Eighth note	quaver	
Electric cord	flex	
Elementary school	primary school	
Elevator	lift	lift
Emergency cord	communication cord	
Endive	chicory	
Engineer (railroad)	engine driver	
Enjoin	forbid	
Eraser	rubber	
Excuse me	sorry	
Exhaust fan	extractor fan	
Expiration date	expiry date	
Expressway or freeway	motorway	
Fall	autumn	autumn
Faucet	tap	tap
Favorite	favourite	
Fender (of a car)	bumper or wing	
Ferris wheel	big wheel	
Field	field	paddock
Field hockey	hockey	
To figure	calculate	
Fill out (a form)	fill in	
Fire department	fire brigade	
Fireplug	hydrant	
Fish dealer	fishmonger	
Flashlight	torch	
Flat (tire)	puncture (tyre)	
Flatware	table cutlery	
Flier	circular (in the post)	
Flavor	flavour	
Float valve	ballcock	
Floor lamp	standard lamp	
Flutist	flautist	
Football	American football	
Freeway; highway	motorway	
French doors	French windows	
French-fries	chips (= a part of meal)	
Fresh	cheeky; impudent	
Freight car	truck (properly a wagon)	
Freight train	goods train	
Friend	mate	

Front desk	reception
Frying pan/skillet	frying pan
Funeral director	undertaker
Funnel/smokestack	funnel
Funnies	comic paper
Furnace	boiler
Game	match
Garbage	rubbish; refuse
Garbage can, trash can	dustbin, rubbish bin
Garbage dump	rubbish tip
Garbage pail	pedal bin, or rubbish bin
Garage sale	jumble sale
Garbage truck	dustcart
Garden	vegetable patch
Garters	sock suspenders
Gas or gasoline	petrol
Gas gauge (car)	petrol gauge
Gas pedal (car)	accelerator
Gas pump	petrol pump
Gas tank door	petrol cap
Gauze	swindle
Gear-shift (car)	gear lever
Generator (car)	dynamo, or alternator
German shepherd	Alsatian
Get fired	get the chop
Gimpy	lame
Gingersnaps	ginger nuts
Girl Scout	Girl Guide; Guide
Given name	Christian name
Gizmo	gadget
Glasses (for the eyes)	spectacles, or glasses
Go-slow	slow-down
Grab bag	lucky dip
Grade	year
Grade crossing	level crossing
Grade school	primary school
Graham crackers	digestive biscuits
Grain	corn
Green beans	French beans
Green thumb	green finger
Gridiron	football field
Grinder	mincer
Grip	suitcase
Grippe	flu; influenza
Ground meat	mince

Ground wire	earth wire
Guess	imagine
Half note	minim
Harbor	harbour
Hash	shepherd's pie
Hayseed	yokel
Head	bonce
Head nurse	Sister
To hire	to employ
Hobo	tramp
Hogpen	pigsty
Home	house
Home maker	home help
Homely	ugly; plain (in looks)
Homework	prep
Hogpen	pigsty
Hood (car)	bonnet
Hoosegow	jail
Horse sense	common sense
Horseback riding	riding
Hot water heater	immersion heater
Huckster	salesman or fairground trader
Humid	close
Humor	humour
Hurricane	cyclone
Icebox	refrigerator
Ice cream	ice
In your behalf	on your behalf
Internal Revenue Service	Inland Revenue
Inning	innings
Inquiry	enquiry
Install	fix
Installment plan	hire purchase
Intermission (of a play)	interval
Intersection (road)	junction
Intern	houseman
Inventory	stock
Jack (cards)	knave
Jackrabbit	large hare
Jackass	male donkey
Jacket, parka	anorak
Jacklight	lantern

Jail	gaol
Jalopy	old banger (car)
Janitor	caretaker
Jellyroll	Swiss roll
Jellybean	jelly baby
Jewelery	jewellery
Jumper	sleeveless dress or pinafore
Jumping rope	skipping-rope
Kerosene	paraffin
Kitchen sideboard	dresser
Kilometer	kilometre
Knee pants	short trousers
Kook	an eccentric person
Labor union	trade union
Ladybug	ladybird
Laid-back	relaxed
Lawn party	garden party
Lawyer, attorney	solicitor (notary), barrister (advocate), or lawyer
Leash	lead
Legal holiday	bank holiday
Lemon soda	lemonade
Lettuce, iceberg	web lettuce
Lettuce, romaine	cos lettuce
Liability insurance	third-party insurance
License plate (car)	number-plate
Life preserver	lifebelt
Lightning bug	glow-worm
Lima bean	rare or broad bean
Line	queue queue
(hard) liquor	spirits
Liquor store	off-licence
Liter	litre
A little hungry	puckish
Lockup	jail
Long-sighted	far-sighted
Longshoreman	docker or stevedore
Lookalike	double
Lost and found	lost property
Lowboy	dressing table
Lox	smoked salmon
Lumber	timber
Lunch	tiffin

Mackinaw	short woollen coat
Maid of honor	chief bridesmaid
Mailman	postman
Make tea	brew up; brew a cupper
Marketing	shopping
Math (colloq.)	maths/math
Mean	nasty
Men's room	Gents
Mom	mum
Mopboard	skirting-board
Mortician	undertaker
Motorcycle	motorbike
Movie	cine film or film
Movies, movie theater	cinema
Moving van	removal van
Mucilage	gum (adhesive)
Muffler (car)	silencer
Mulligan stew	Irish stew
Muslin	calico
Mustang	brumby
Mutt	mongrel

Nail polish	nail varnish
Narcotic	drug
Native American	American Indian
Nauseated	sick
Neighbor	neighbour
Nervy	impudent
News dealer	newsagent
Newsstand	bookstall
Nightgown	nightdress
Nothing; zero	nil
Notions	haberdashery

Oarlock	rowlock
Oatmeal	porridge
Odd	rum
On the weekend	at the weekend
One-way ticket	single ticket
Open house	open day
Operating room	operating theatre
Orchestra; orchestra seats	front stalls
Outhouse	outdoor privy or closet
Outlet	electric power socket
Overpass	flyover

Pacifier	baby's dummy
Panhandler	beggar
Pantry	larder
Pants	trousers
Pants suit	trouser suit
Panty hose	tights
Parakeet	budgerigar
Parcheesi	ludo
Parka	anorak
Parking brake	hand brake
Parking lights (car)	sidelights
Parking lot	car park
Patrolman	police constable
Pavement	road way
Pay station	telephone call box
Pea jacket	duffel coat
Peddler	stallholder
Peek	glimpse
Penitentiary	prison
Pen pal	pen friend
Penpoint	nib
Period	full stop
Phone booth	phone box
Phonograph	gramophone
Pit (fruit)	fruit-stone or pip
Pitcher	jug
Pocketbook	purse; wallet
Port warden	harbormaster
Popsicle; ice	ice lorry
Pot holder	oven glove or kettle holder
Potato chips	crisps
Powdered sugar; icing sugar	powdered sugar
Pram	baby carriage
Present or gift	prezzy
Presently	now
Prime rate	base rate
Principal	headmaster, head teacher
Private room in a hospital	private ward
Private school	public school
Program	programme
Pry	prise
Public school	state school
Pullover sweater	jumper, pullover or sweater
Punk	trashy or worthless
Purse or pocketbook	handbag or bag
Pushcart	barrow

| Quarter note | crotchet |
| Quotation marks | inverted commas, quotation marks |

Racetrack (horses)	racecourse
Racket	racquet
Railroad	railway
Railroad crossings	level crossing
Railroad tie	sleeper
Raise (salary)	rise
Raisin	sultana
Ramp	slip road
Ranch	station
Realtor	estate agent
Redcap	railway porter
Rent	hire
Reserve(a table)	book
Retroactive	retrospective
Robe	dressing gown
Roller coaster	big dipper
Renter	roomer
Roundabout	merry-go-round
Round trip (ticket)	return trip (ticket)	return trip (ticket)
Row house	terraced house
Rubber boots	wellies, or wellington boots
Rubbing alcohol	surgical spirits
Rugged	sturdy
Run (in stocking; hosiery)	ladder
Rutabaga	swede

Sailboat	sailing boat
Salary increase	rise
Sales clerk	shop (or sales) assistant
Saloon	pub
Saltines; crackers	water biscuits
Saltshaker	salt cellar
Sanitary napkins	sanitary towels
Santa Claus	Father Christmas
Sassy	cheeky
Scallion	spring onion
Schedule	timetable
Scientist	boffin
Scofflaw	habitual law-breakers
Scotch	whisky
Second floor	first floor
Second-guess	be wise after the event
Sedan (car)	saloon car (car)

Semester	term
Serial killer	mass murderer
Sewage plant	sewage farm
Shade	window-blind
Sheep muslin	muslin
Sherbet	water-ice or sorbet
Shingle	sign
Shrimp	prawn
Shoestring	shoelace
Shopping cart	shopping trolley
Shopping mall	shopping centre
Shorts	pants
Shrimp	shrimp (small); prawns (medium); and scampi (large)
Shrimp cocktail	prawn cocktail
Sick (with a cold)	ill
Side mirror (car)	wing mirror
Sidelight	parking light
Sidewalk	pavement or footpath footpath
Signal tower	signal box
Sirloin	rump
Skillet	frying pan
Skipping rope	jumping rope
Sleeper (railroad)	sleeping car
Slingshot	catapult
Slowpoke	slowcoach
Slipcovers	loose covers
Small dairy truck	milk float
Smart	clever
Snap (bargain)	snip
Snap fastener	press-stud
Snaps	press studs, or poppers
Snarl	tangle
Sneakers; tennis or gym shoes	training shoes. plimsolls
Soccer	football
Soda	soft drink
Soda biscuit	cream cracker
Soda cracker	cream cracker
Solitaire (cards)	Patience
Someplace	somewhere
Soon	soon or presently
A spare room for storage	lumber room
Specialist (medical)	consultant or specialist
Speedway	motorway

Splash guard (car)	mud flap
Spool of thread	reel of cotton
Sporting events	fixtures
Squash (vegetable)	marrow
Stand in line	to queue
Stingy	mean
Stock	share
Stoop	veranda
Store	shop
Storekeeper	shopkeeper
Stove	cooker
Streetcar	tram
String beans	French beans
Strip of bacon	rasher
Stroller	push-chair
Study something intensely	mug up
Subway	underground, tube
Substitute	make-do
Sucker (candy)	lollipop
Squash	marrow
Sundown	sunset
Sunup	sunrise
Supply teacher	substitute teacher
Suspenders	braces
Sweater	jumper; jersey; pullover
Swimsuit	bathing costume
Switch (railroad)	points
Taffy	toffee
Tag	label
Tag day	flag-day
Take out	take away
Talk show	chat show
Tallow turnip (rutabaga)	swede
Tape needle	bodkin
Teacart	tea trolley
Telephone	ring up
Telephone boot	telephone box; kiosk
Telephone booth	call-box
Telephone pole	telegraph pole
Theater	theatre
Throughway	motorway
Thumbtack	drawing-pin
Tick-tack-toe	noughts and crosses
Tie (railroad)	sleeper
Tire	tyre

Tired	fagged-out	
To bathe	to bath	
To call	to ring	
To fill out	to fill in	
To line up	to queue	
To rent	to hire	
To set the table	to lay the table	
Topcoat	overcoat	
Toque	woolen hat	
Track (railway)	line	
Track meet (school)	sports	
Traction	tramway	
Trade	swap	
Traffic circle, rotary	roundabout	
Trailer	caravan	
Transom	fanlight	
Trash	rubbish	
Trash can, garbage can	dustbin	
Travelled	travelled	
Trolley	tram	
Truck	van (panel truck), lorry (large truck), or truck	
Truck farm	market garden	
Truck stop	transport cafe	
Trunk (car)	boot	boot
Tube	subway	
Turn signal lever (car)	indicator switch	
Turtle neck	popo neck	
Tuxedo	dinner-jacket	
Twister	tornado	
Two weeks	fortnight	
Underpants (women)	pants; panties, knickers, or briefs	
Underpass; tunnel	subway	
Undershirt	vest	
Undershorts (men)	pants	
Unlisted telephone	ex-directory	
Uptight	anxious	
Vacation	holiday	
Vacuum cleaner	hoover	
Valance	pelmet	
Valise	hand luggage	
Valve	stopcock	
Vest	waistcoat	

Vegetable market	greengrocer's
Vine	creeper
Warden (prison)	governor
Wash up	to wash
Washcloth	flannel
Weenie; hot dog	hot dog
Whine	grizzle
Window roller (car)	window winder
Windshield	windscreen
Wrench	spanner (a wrench is a plumber's spanner)
Yam	sweet potato
Yard	back garden
Yard sale	jumble sale
Zip code	post code
Zipper	zip
Zucchini	courgette
Zwieback	rusk

Preference

American	**British**
Defog	demist
Rooster	cock
Store	shop
Visor	peak

	American English	**British English**
Bomb	to fail	to succeed
Cheap	something of poor quality	inexpensive
Pissed	an expression of anger	someone very drunk
Scheme	something that is a bit sly and slick	plan
Sharp	the person is quick, intelligent, and able.	a devious and unprincipled person

	American English	**British English**
Mad		angry
Emergency room		casualty (department)
Silverware, flatware		cutlery
Driver's license		driving licence
Fire department		fire brigade
Overpass		flyover
Give someone a ride		give someone a lift
Purse		handbag

Sick	ill
Bug	insect
Jelly	jam
Highway	main road
Buddy; friend	mate, pal
Math	Maths
License plate	number plate
Deck of cards	pack of cards
Grade school	primary school
Real estate	property
Swimsuit	swimming costume
Closet	wardrobe

2.2.2.2. Origin

American: belittle, boost, coverage, fall for, fly off the handle, hitchhike, off-beat, punch line, quiz (as a noun), round trip, round-up, snoop

Foreign: American words (some taken from French, Spanish and Dutch):
bartender, boss, caribou, canyon, chowder, commuter, cookie, coyote, dime, disc jockey, dollar, gas station, gopher, hickory, a high-riser, hype, junk food, laid-back, moccasin, newscaster, no way, OK, plaza, poison ivy, prairies, raccoon, skunk, sleigh, soap opera, tepee, tomahawk, tornado, totem, waffle, wigwam

2.2.2.3. Spelling

i. There are few absolute rules: words ending in –ize (American)/-ise (British) and –yze (American)/-yse (British). –yse Retains the 's' form in British English. The American form is mostly 'z'.

American	**British**
Apologize	apologise
Analyze	analyse
Breathalyze	breathalyse
Civilize	civilise
Criticize	criticise
Emphasize	emphasise
Equalize	equalise
Organize	organise
Organization	organisation
Ostracize	ostracise
Paralyze	paralyse
Publicize	publicise
Realize	realize or realize
Recognize	recognise

Exceptions: advertise, advise(v), apprise, arise, chastise, circumcise, comprise, compromise, demise, despise, devise, disguise, enfranchise, enterprise, excise, exercise, improvise, incise, merchandise, premise, prise, revise, supervise, surmise, surprise and televise.

The following verbs end with –ize in British English: authorize, familiarize, symbolize, agonize, dogmatize, sterilize, appetize, baptize, recognize, capsize

ii. words ending in –er (American)/ -re (British)

American	British	America/British
Accounter	accountre	
Caliber	calibre	
Center	centre	
Centering	centring	
Fiber	fibre	
Goiter	goitre	
Liter	litre	
Louver	louver	
Luster	lustre	
Meager	meagre	
Meter	metre	
Reconnoitrer	reconnoitre	
Sepulcher	sepulchre	
Somber	sombre	
Specter	spectre	
Theater		theatre

iii.   British English generally doubles the –l where further syllables are added to a stem word (label/ labelled), while American English does not (label/labeled). However, a final l is not doubled when adding an ending that begins with a vowel in American English. American English usually does not double words ending with –l for compounds of two-syllable or longer words. The British use -ll only:

American	British	America/British
Canceled	cancelled	
Carburetor	carburettor	
Combated	combatted	
		controller
		controlled
Councilor	councillor	
Counselor	counsellor	
Crueler	crueller	
Cruelest	cruellest	
Dueling	duelling	
Hosteler	hosteller	
Jeweler	jeweller	

Jewelry	jewellery
Labeled	labelled
Libeled	libelled
Libeling	libelling
Libelous	libellous
Marvelous	marvellous
Modeled	modelled
Modeling	modelling
Panelist	panellist
Quarreled	quarrelled
Quareling	quarrelling
(un)rivaled	(un)rivalled
Tasseled	tasselled
Teetotaler	teetataller
Tranquillity	tranquillity
Traveled	travelled
Traveler	traveller
Traveling	travelling
Tunneled	tunnelled
Tunneling	tunnelling
Woolen	woollen
Wooly	woolly
Worshiping	worshipping
Yodeler	yodeller
Yodeling	yodelling

iv. However, for the following words, Americans double the –l, while British do not:

American	British
Appall	appal
Appalling	appaling
Distill	distil
Enroll	enrol
Enrollment	enrolment
Enthrall	enthral
Enthralling	enthraling
Enthrallment	enthralment
Fulfill	fulfil
Fulfillment	fulfilment
Install	instal
Installment	instalment
Instill	instil
Skillful	skilful
Skillfully	skillfully
Skullduggery	skulduggery
Willful	wilful

Exceptions: annul   annulment
               extol   extolment

v.   American use –se for nouns and verbs while British use -ce for nouns and –se for verbs.
However, American use –ce for nouns and verbs:

   a. nouns:

American	British
License	licence
Defense	defence
Offense	offence
Practise	practice
Pretense	pretence

   b. verbs –ize, -yze (American) and –ise and -yse (British):

American	British	American/ British
Analyze	analyse	
Apologize	apologise	
Breathalze	breathalyse	
Emphasize	emphasise (also –ize)	
Energize	energise	
Finalize	finalise	
Defense	defense	
		license
Paralyze	paralyse	
Practice	practise	
Recognize	recognise (also –ize)	
Standardize	standardise	

Exceptions: advertise, advise, analyse, arise, chastise, circumcise, compromise, despise, devise,
excise, exercise, improvise, paralyse, promise, revise, supervise, surmise, surprise.

American uses practice for both nouns and verbs. Exception: fence.

vi.   Words ending in –or (American)/-our (British):

American	British
Ardor	ardour
Armor	armour
Behavior	behaviour
Candor	candour
Color	colour
Endeavor	endeavour

Favor	favour
Favorite	favourite
Flavor	flavour
Glamor	glamour
Harbor	harbour
Honor	honour
Humor	humour
Labor	labour
Neighbor	neighbour
Odor	odour
Parlor	parlour
Rancor	rancour
Rumor	rumour
Vapor	vapour
Vigor	vigour
Succor	succour

Exceptions: glamour, saviour. In Australia, the Australian Labor Party has been using American style of spelling in labor.

Exceptions: Error, horror, languor, liquor, pallor, savior, squalor, stupor, terror, torpor, tremor.

vii. The digraphs -ae and -oe. In most cases American spelling uses simple -e rather than -ae or -oe:

American	**British**	**American/British**
		aerial
		aesthete
		aesthetic
		aestheticism
Ameba	amoeba	
Anemia	anaemia	
Anesthesia	anaesthesia	
Anesthetic	anaesthetic	
Anesthetize	anaesthetize	
Archeology	archaeology	
Cesarian	caesarian	
Diarrhea	diarrhoea	
Edema	oedema	
Encyclopedia	encyclopaedia	
Eon	aeon	
Esophagus	oesophagus	
Estrogen	oestrogen	
Ether	aether	
Fecal	faecal	
Feces	faeces	

Fetal	foetal
Fetus	foetus
Gonorrhea	gonorrhoea
Gynecology	gynaecology
Hematology	haematology
Hemoglobin	haemoglobin
Hemophilia	haemophilia
Hemophiliac	haemophiliac
Hemorrhage	haemorrhage
Hemorrhoids	haemorrhoids
Homeopath	homoepath
Leukemia	leukaemia
Maneuver	manoeuvre
Maneuverable	manoeuvrable
Medieval	mediaeval
Orthopedics	orthopaedics
Orthopedist	orthopaedist
Pediatrician	paediatrician
Pedophile	paedophile
Pharmacopeia	pharmacopoeia
Phoenix	phoenix
Primeval	primaeval
Pyorrhea	pyorrhoea
Septicemia	septicaemia

viii. words ending in –able. American spelling consistently drops the –e of the root word. –able nouns ending in -e in adjective form often drop the -e in American:

American	British	American/British
Aging	ageing	
		eyeing
Likable	likeable	
Livable	liveable	
Movable	moveable	
Salable	saleable	
Sizable	sizeable	
Unshakable	unshakeable	

ix. –ge American normally drops the –e:

America	British
Judgment	judgement

x. –ou A few English words using ou are found just o in American:

American	British
Donut	doughnut
Mold	mould
Molt	moult
Plow	plough
Smolder	smoulder

xi. American: -ection; British: -ection, -exion:

American	British
Connection	connexion
Inflection	inflexion

xii. American: -og; British: –ogue:

American	British	American/British
Analog		analogue
Catalog		catalogue
Dialog		dialogue
Pedagog		pedagogue
Prolog		prologue
Travelog		travelogue

xiii. American: -am; British: –amme:

American	British	American/British
Aerogram	aerogramme	
Gram	gram(me)	
Kilogram	kilogramme	
Program	programme	
Program (computer)		program
		telegram

In British English, they refer to a 'TV programme', but a 'computer program' (software). In America, the spelling of programme is program in all cases.

xiv. Some small differences in spelling:

American	British	American/British
Accommodations	accommodation	
Aluminum	aluminium	
Alternate or alternative	alternative	
Anymore	any more	
Ax(e)	axe	

Ay(e)	ay
Airplane	aeroplane
Annex(e)	annex
Bail out	bale out
	baritone
Battleax	battleaxe
Behoove	behove
Baloney	boloney
Busses	buses
Caldron	cauldron
	calisthenics
Cantalope	cantaloupe
Carburetor	carburettor or carburetter
Carry-on	hand
Catsup (tomato)	ketchup
Check (money)	cheque
Checkers	chequers
Chili	chilli
Cigaret	cigarette
Clarinetist	clarinettist
Coach class	economy class
Cozy	cosy
Curb	kerb
Deplane	disembark
Disc (in computing)	disk
Disk	disc
Distention	distension
Draft (wind)	draught
Draftsman	draughtsman
Drafty	draughty
Draught	draft (military party)
Dumpster	skip
Epilog	epilogue
Faucet	tap
Fill out	fill in
Flotation	floatation
Flutist	flautist
Font	fount (typeface)
Furor	furore
Gage	gauge
Ga(u)ntlet	gauntlet
Garrote	garotte
Glycerin	glycerine
Gray	grey
Ground	earth
Gypsy	gipsy

Imbed   embed
Inclose   enclose
Inflection   inflexion
Inquire   enquire
Insure   ensure
Jail   gaol, jail
Jeweler   jeweller
Jewelry   jewellery
Jibe   gybe (nautical)
Karat (gold)   carat
Kidnaped   kidnapped
Kidnaper   kidnapper
Kidnaping   kidnapping
Largess   largesse
Licorice   liquorice
Math   maths (mathematics)
Milage   mileage
Mollusk   mollusk
Mom; mommy   mum; mummy
Mustache   moustache
Naught   nought
Omelet   omelette
Organdy   organdie
Pajamas   pyjamas
Paillaise   pailliasse
Peddler or pedler   pedlar
Percent   per cent
Plow   plough
Racket   racquet
Renege   renegue
Sanitorium   sanatorium
Scalawag   scallywag
Sissy   cissy
Skeptic   sceptic
Skeptical   sceptical
Skillet   frying pan
Skullduggery   skulduggery
Specialty   speciality
Specialties   specialities
Story   storey (building)
Stove   cooker
Sulfur   sulphur
Thruway   throughway
Tidbit   titbit
Tire   tyre (on a car)
Trademark   trade mark.

Undefinable	indefinable
Vise (clam tool)	vice
Whisky	whiskey
Wiskey (Irish)	wisky (Scottish)
Zipper	zip

xv. Hyphenation

There is a tendency in American English to conjoin terms that, currently, are written as two words in English, occasionally hyphenated:

American	British
Nonprofit	non-profit
Nonscientific	non-scientific
Preexist	pre-exist

xvi.   Verb forms

Verb form in present, past and past participle in American English generally follow regular ones except get and spit while those in British English follow irregular ones The past forms of some verbs can be different for some irregular verbs:

American			**British**		
Present	**Past**	**Past Participle**	**Present**	**Past**	**Past Participle**
Burn	burned	burned	burn	burnt	burnt
Dive	dove	dove	dive	dived	dived
Dream	dreamed	dreamed	dream	dreamt	dreamt
Dwell	dwelled	dwelled	dwell	dwelt	dwelt
Get	got	gotten (not all senses)	get	got	got
Knell	knelled	knelled	knell	knelt	knelt
Lean	leaned	leaned	lean	leant	leant
Leap	leaped	leaped	leap	leapt	leapt
Learn	learned	learned	learnt	learnt	learnt
Prove	proved	proved	prove	proved	proved
Shine	shined	shined	shine	shone	shone
Smell	smelled	smelled	smell	smelt	smelt
Sneak	sneaked	sneaked	sneak	snuck	snuck
Spell	spelled	spelled	spell	spelt	spelt
Spit	spit	spit	spit	spat	spat
Spoil	spoiled	spoiled	spoil	spoilt	spoilt
Swell	swelled	swelled	swell	swelled	swollen
Thrive	thrived	thrived	thrive	throve	throve

xvii.   Compound words

American   **British**
Nonprofit   non-profit
Nonscientific   non-scientific
Percent   per cent
Preexist   pre-exist
Trademark   trade mark

xviii. Abbreviations, acronyms and hyphenation

In America, they tend to put a dot after abbreviated word. However, they tend not to use dots in Britain these days:

American   **British**
B.S.   B.Sc.
Jr.   Jnr.
Mr.   Mr.
M.S.   M.Sc.
Sr.   Snr.
U.N. or UN   UN
U.S.A.   USA

2.5   Australian English to American and British English

2.3.1. Introduction

Australian English and British English spelling are generally identical. Australian English grammar is comparable to general usage in both USA and Britain. Australian English has a large and distinctive home-grown vocabulary that include:

    i.   Extensions meaning of everyday words:
                To feel crook/to feel ill
                To farewell someone/to give someone a farewell party
                Mob/a flock or group (of sheep, kangaroos, etc.)
                Station/ a ranch, as in sheep station
    ii.   Extensions or shifts in the meaning of British dialect words:
                Dinkum/reliable, genuine
                Dunny/a lavatory
                Wowser/ a spoilsport, prude
    iii.   Distinctive informal word endings, e.g. –o in abbreviations and -ie in names for
                workers:
                Arvo/afternoon
                Journo/ journalist.
                Truckie/truck driver
                Wharfie/stevedore

2.3.2   Australian

ABC, or Aunty/n. the Australian Broadcasting Corporation.
About right/ adj. phr. means that the statement or fact is absolutely correct.
Ace/adj. excellent; brilliant; great; fabulous; wonderful; exciting; outstanding; terrific;
        something really good. ("They have had an ace time swimming in the shipwreck this
        morning.").
Aerial ping pong/ n. The Sydneysiders' contemptuous name for Melbourne's passion,
        Australian Rules Football.
Air guitar/n. the pretence of playing an imaginary guitar.
Akubra/n. broad-brimmed Australian bush (rural towns) hat made from rabbit fur; brand name
used for a hat.
Alice/n. an abbreviation for a place called Alice Springs.
All right/adj. phr. used to describe that everything's okay.
Ambo/n. an ambulance or an ambulance officer.
And so on/phr. and other things.
Ankle-biter/n. a small child; child, esp. one not yet walking erect.
ANZAC/n. Members of the Australian and New Zealand Army Corps in World War I;
        soldiers who fought at Gallipoli.
The Apple Isle/n. The home of Tasmanians.
Arbor Day/n. tree planting day.
Arvo/n. afternoon: "He's going to spend this arvo exploring the reef."
Argy-bargy/n. argument.
Arse/n. buttocks, anus.
Arse end of the world/n. a thoroughly hideous place; a hole.
Arse licker/n. a sycophant.
Arvo/n. afternoon.
As scarce as hen's teeth/adj. phr. non-existent.
ASAP/adv. as soon as possible.
Assembly/n. a weekly gathering of the entire school.
Aunty or Auntie/n. an affectionate moniker for the Australian Broadcasting
        Corporation.
Aussie/n. Australian.
Aussie battler/n. a typical member of Australian working class who has to struggle
        hard to make a decent living.
Aussie Rules/n. Australian Rules Football.
Aussie salute/n. the back and forth waving of hands before the face to shoo away the
        flies; hand going up to brush a fly away.
Average/adj. pretty bad.
Ay?/inter. Literally it means "I beg your pardon?"

Babe/n. a familiar term of address to a woman or a girl: "Hey, babe. How've you been?"
Back of a truck/n. Australia's commercial vehicles are neither less robust, nor more
        badly driven than those of the rest of the world, but their loads are notoriously
        insecure.
Back off/v. phr. Order to relax, or to stop arguing.

Backburner/n. deferred; postponed; not in high priority.

Backchat/n. insolent answering back.

Bagging/n. the act of criticizing someone or something quite severely. Film critics, for instance, often give a bad movie a "good bagging"--- which is a bit of a contradiction in terms.

Bar/n. having nothing to do whatsoever with another person or thing.

Barbie/n. a barbecue meal, cooked on a hotplate or over hot coals.

Balmain boy/ n. A dry-eyed, street-wise urchin who has battled his way to the top and can thus face adversity without sobbing on shoulders.

Barbie/b. abbreviation of barbecue, cook-out; a barbecue meal, cooked on a hot plate or over hot coals.

Bargain!/n. excel general expression of approval or joy.

Bash/v. to hit; to beat.

Bash up/v. phr. to hit, often a bigger or older child hitting a weaker one.

Basket case/ n. somebody in a state of mental exhaustion and on the brink of collapse.

Bastard/ n. mainly used as an insult, can also be affectionate; an unpleasant or despicable person. A term of abuse, but it can also be one of male endearment. As in, "G'day ya silly old bastard."

Battler/n. someone who struggles hard to make ends meet; somebody who works very hard against insurmountable odds but never seems to get anywhere. Working–class Australians are known as "little Aussie batters". Hard-working person.

B.B.Q./n. abbreviation for barbecue.

Be at the cutting edge/v. phr. to be involved with the most advanced or recent developments.

Be in it/v. phr. to be actively involved. Appeal to join an activity.

Be looking at/v.phr., expect a certain amount.

Beach inspector/n. A municipal officer, employed to safeguard the decency of Sydney bathers when bikinis first became fashionable.

Beat/v. to win; to defeat another in competition.

Beaut or beauty/ n. very good or excellent; an exclamation of approval; beautiful; Great!

Beauty/n. "you beauty" expressing happiness.

Beg the question/v. phr. raise or invite the question.

Belt/v. if someone receives a belt, it's not to hold the trousers up --- but s/he has been punched or whipped! If punched continuously, the person is said to have received a "belting"!

Belt/v. to hit someone, especially to hit repeatedly.

Belting/n. a beating, usually administered by an adult as punishment.

Betcha/excl. a lazy way of saying "Bet you!"

Better half/n. generally one's wife or husband.

Between you and me/phr. confidentially.

Bible bash/v. phr. To attempt to force Christian beliefs on others who are not interested.

Bible basher/n. generally a person of Christian persuasion. In particular, a person who attempts to force Christian beliefs on others.

Bickie/n. biscuit.

Big/adj. popular.

Big ask/n. a request or expectation that is difficult to fulfill; a major imposition on one's generosity.

Big deal/n. expression of scorn or dismissal, "So what?"

Big gun/n. a powerful or influential people.

Big mob/n. a large number; a large group (cattle, people); a lot.

Big smoke/n. a country expression for any large city; the city, or any built-up area, as opposed to the countryside; any metropolis.

Big time/adv. phr. to a great degree.

Big wet/n. the monsoon season in tropical north Queensland.

Billabong/n. a water hole in a dry river bed; a pond in an otherwise dry stream; a water hole, orig. part of a river, formed when the channel connecting it to the river dries up. A water hole in the bush.

Billy/n. container for boiling water; a metal can, usually tin, enamel ware, or aluminum used for making tea over an open fire; a tin can with a wire handle generally suspended over a camp-fire for the purpose of boiling water to make tea. Can for boiling water over a fire to make tea.

Billy cart or go-cart/n. a small, homemade cart used by children as a downhill racer.

Bimbo/n. 1. an attractive but empty-headed woman. 2. insult, a stupid person

Binge/n. a bout of indulgence: 1. over-indulgence in food 2. a bout of heavy drinking of alcohol. Drinking party.

Bingo! /excl. used when someone is correct.

Bird/n. a derogatory word for a woman or girl.

Bitch/n. a disagreeable or malicious woman; an insult for a woman or girl when she is really ugly, mean or horrible.

Bite the bullet/v. phr. to make an important or difficult decision.

Black eye/n. bruised eye, often resulting from a blow.

Blind Freddy or blind Freddie/n. An imaginary blind person; a person with little perception; contemptuous phrase who cannot find something or who 'cannot see for looking'. "Even blind Freddy could see it."

Bloke/n. man; a male; a guy in charge; a guy; a complimentary term for the average Australian male and usually preceded by the adjectives "good", "nice" or "fair dinkum". "Lachlan and Ethan are my best mates. They're great blokes."

Blood brother/n. fellow member of a gang from US English; one who has sworn lifeline brotherhood to, and mingled his blood with that of another.

Blood sucker/n. someone who uses other people for their own ends.

Bloody/adj. commonly known as the Great Australian Adjective. It is often used to emphasize either approval or disapproval: "That's a bloody lovely car" Or "What a terrible bloody game that was!"

Blow it/v. to make a serious error of judgment.

Blowie/n. blowfly.

Blow torch/n. Parliamentary weapon for the purpose of payback, e.g. by pitilessly exposing an opponent's rorts, sorts, torts and forgeries in return for his asking too many questions.

Bludge/v. 1. to do very little work. 2. to laze around. 3. to waste time. 4. to live off someone else.

Bludger/n. someone who is lazy; someone who imposes on others, evades responsibility, or does not do their fair share of work; someone who doesn't pull (his or her) weight at work and sponge on others. A person who lives off someone else, or doesn't pay his or her way.

Bogey/n. something or someone scary lurking in the dark.
Bogus/adj. very bad; unfair; no good.
Boil the billy/v. phr. make tea or coffee.
Bomb/n. an old car in poor condition. An old car or a second-hand in need of repair.
Bombed out/adj. drunk, high on drugs.
Bombshell/n. a sudden or devastating action.
Boomerang/n. curved throwing implement. A curved piece of wood. It was made by the
        Aborigines for hunting.
Bookworm/n. a person who reads a lot.
Boot/n. 1. Not only something worn on the feet, but a sacking or when fired from a job:
        "Poor old John got the boot yesterday." 2. Australian and British expression for car trunk.
Boots and all/adj. phr. completely, whole-heartedly; with all one's strength or resources.
        Originally it meant "no holds barred' in a fight, but the meaning is now generalized.
Booze/n. alcoholic drink.
Booze bus/n. bus used by police for random breath testing.
Boozer/n. pub. When going off to the boozer, what one really means is that s/he's off to the
        pub for a drink!
Born-again/n. a Christian who has been 'born again', especially a zealous or evangelical one.
Born loser/n. an unsuccessful person; someone who seems destined to misfortune and failure.
Boss over/v. to dominate.
Bottom line/n. the basic truth.
Bottom of the harbor/n. a tax-evasion practice of the seventies.
Bottle shop/n. a liquor store.
Bowser/n. petrol pump. Petrol reservoir; either a tanker-truck or the pedestal-pump at a
        service station.
Box seat/n. the premier or best position; the best seat.
Brainless/adj. insult, stupid.
Break up/v. phr. To end relationship; to stop going out with someone.
Brekkie/n. breakfast.
Brickie/n. bricklayer.
Bro/n. friend; a brother; a close male friend; a member of one's gang.
Broke/adj. having little or no money.
Brothel/n. a house of prostitution.
Brumby/n. a wild horse.
Brush up on/v. phr. To revise or review or practise.
Buck/n. a dollar.
Buck's night /n. a stag party; an exclusively male get-together, held before the wedding for
        the bridegroom by his mates; What Americans call a stag or bachelor party to initiate a
        bloke into marriage. "I'll never forget my buck's night – the hotel manager still can't
        figure how we smuggled 25 cheerleaders past the front desk!"
Buck's party/n. pre-wedding party given to the groom by his friends.
Buckley's chance/n. little or no chance of success.
Buddy/n. a good friend; a mate.
Bugger/n. a contemptible or despicable person; a merely annoying person.
Bugger all/n. nothing; as in "There was bugger all to do."
Bugger me!/excl. damn me! "Well, I'll be damned!"

Bugger off/v. get lost, scram! To order to go away.
Buggered/adj. tired out; exhausted.
Bulb/n. electric light bulb.
Bull bar/ n. a protective metal grille extending from the front of a vehicle.
Bullshit/n. nonsense; rubbish; crap; expression of disbelief, used when someone says a lie.
Bully/n. a person who is known to torment or physically attack others, especially those who
    are weaker or smaller.
Bunch/n. a group of people.
Bungalow/n. a small self-contained dwelling in the grounds of a house.
The Bush/n. natural vegetation; a place covered by forest; unspoiled land beyond the city
    with natural vegetation.
Bush/ n. country area in Australia.
Bushie/n. a person who lives in the country (bush).
Bushranger or bush ranger/n. an outlaw in early colonial days. Ned Kelly was one of
    Australia's most notorious bushrangers. Term used for a thief – from the early days in
    Australia when bushrangers roamed the country on horseback. People who robbed others.
    They hid in the bush. Also an escaped convict; an outlaw who lives by robbery.
Bush tucker/n. native food such as berries, roots, and foodstuffs, such as edible insects; the
    food eaten when traveling through the bush: "Chloe and Jessica lived off bush tucker
    during their trip to Sydney Harbor."
Bust/v. to break; to destroy.
Buying back the farm/n. buying back anything Australian from overseas investors.
Bye-bye/a form of saying goodbye.
BYO/v. "bring your own" liquor to a party or restaurant; if going to a party or restaurant and
    requested to BYO , it simply means one is required to bring one's own liquor. Many
    restaurants in Australia do not have a license to sell liquor on their premises, but it is
    quite legal to B.Y.O.

Call names/v. phr. to insult.
Call the shots/v. phr. to be in charge.
Canteen/n. there appears to be no distinctively Australian name for shop at school which sells
    food.
Captain Cook/n. British navigator and explorer who mapped the east coast of Australia in
    1976.
Carry the can/v.phr. bear the responsibility; take the blame.
Cashed-up/adj. having ready money; having plenty of money; in funds; recently paid and
    therefore with ready money.
Casual day/n. a day on which uniforms and suits can be discarded in favor of casual
    clothes.
Cat-fight or Cat fight/n. a fight between two women.
Catch up/v. to reach or achieve the required level.
Chap/n. a bloke or fellow.
Chatterbox/n. a talkative person.
Cheap/adj. worthless, degrading, especially of behaviour.
Cheap as chips/adj. extremely cheap.

Check out/v. phr. To look at or examine something; to appraise someone or something.
Cheerio/form of saying good-bye.
Chemist/n. a pharmacy or drugstore.
Chick/n. a young woman.
Chicken feed/n. a meager or insignificant sum of money.
Chill out/v. to relax; to calm down.
Chip/n. Aussie equivalent of the American French Fries or crisps.
Chippie/n. a carpenter or someone who works with wood.
Chook/n. a fowl; a domestic chicken, hen or rooster. Sometime term for a woman.
Chocoholic/n. a person suffering chocolate addiction.
Chopper/n. a helicopter.
City slicker/n. a person living the slick, fast moving lifestyle of a large city.
Classic/adj. excellent; brilliant; unreal; of a very high standard.
Clobber/v. to hit aggressively.
Coat hanger/n. The Sydney Harbor Bridge.
Cocky/adj. self-confident, arrogant; a cockatoo. Farmer.
Combo/n. any combination of things.
Come in handy/v. phr. to be useful.
Come in, spinner!/ v. phr. in two-up, a call made to signify that all the bets are laid and it is
    time to spin the coins.
Compo/n. workers' compensation.
Computer geek/n. a person with a passion and talent for using computers.
Con artist/n. a person who fools another; someone who is false or misleading.
Con man/n. a man who swindles by gaining the victim's confidence.
Cool/adj. excellent; radical; unreal; great; fashionable; popular; an up-to-date thing in
    fashion; looking better than everyone else; expression of approval.
Cop/n. police officer.
Cop out/v. phr. to withdraw; to avoid; to escape; to opt out in gutless way, as by giving some
    feeble justification.
Cop shop/n. a police station.
Cop the lot/v. phr. to bear the brunt of some misfortune; to suffer multiple misfortunes at once.
Copper/n. a policeman.
Cordial/n. soft drink.
Couch potato/n. a dull and inactive person, generally found plonked in front of the telly.
Cover up/v. phr. to conceal the truth, usually on a friend's behalf.
Crack a tinnie/v. phr. to open a can of cold beer.
Crack it/v. succeed in doing something.
Cranky/adj. irritable, in a bad mood; bad-tempered, mad or both.
Crap/adj. 1. worthless; of poor quality. 2. nonsense; rubbish; bad; awful
Chrissie/n. Christmas.
Cocky/n. cockatoo (a type of native parrot), also a farmer.
Crook/adj. 1. unwell; irritable; sick or no good; broken down also angry; bad; dishonest; if
    one feels unwell, s/he is feeling crook; bad; irritable; ill.; not feeling well: "He had to
    cancel the meeting last night because he was feeling a bit of crook." 2. n. thief, robber;
    lawbreaker.
Crooked/adj. dishonest; criminal; illegal.

Crunch time/n. the time for a critical decision to be made or for critical action to take place.
Cuppa/n. abbreviation for "cup of tea: "Let's sit down for a minute and have a cuppa"; short for cup of tea: "Benjamin and I stopped for a cuppa before heading to the Coral Sea." Cup of tea or coffee.
Cut out/v. phr. to stop.
Cute/adj. pleasing or attractive; gorgeous; endearing.

Daddy/adj. unfashionable; ugly; dull, used both of clothes and more generally of overall personal style.
Damn!/excl. expression of disappointment, frustration or annoyance.
Damper/n. a type of bread made in the outback; primitive form of bread, made in the bush from flour and water and cooked on the coals of a camp-fire; a flat loaf of flour, water (and baking soda), originally baked in the ashes. It is rather heavy, with close consistency. Early form of bread, flour and damper water cooked in hot ashes.
Dead/ adj. completely; totally.
Dead set/adj. absolute; genuine; completely; totally.; This word is used to emphasize what a speaker means: "He's a dead-set genius!"
The Deep North/n. Queensland.
Deli/n. delicatessen shop or a shop selling cold meat and cheeses.
Demo/n. abbreviation of demonstration: "If you want to protest about the government policies, you stage a demo."
Didgeridoo/n. An aboriginal wind instrument.
Digger/n. originally a miner in the goldfields, now used to refer to an Australian soldier. Gold miner or Australian soldier.
Dingo/n. The Australian wild dog; a wild dog.
Dinkum/adj. 1. adj. genuine; true; authentic; reliable 2. adv. Really, genuinely
Ditch/v. to abandon.
Dob in/v. to inform or tell tales about someone; to incriminate someone.
Dog's breakfast/n. a mess; a confused state of affairs; a real mess: "Charlotte told Ella to clean up the room because it was like a dog's breakfast in there." Untidy presentation of something.
Dole bludger/n. a person who makes no attempt to get a job and is content to live off Social Welfare payments. Someone drawing unemployment benefits when work is available.
Donkey vote/n. an election vote that is not expressing any preference among candidates at all; a random choice; choice of candidate at top of ballot paper. Vote by numbering candidates in order they appear on a ballot paper.
Dorothy Dixer/n. a pre-arranged question asked in Parliament specially to allow a propagandist reply by a minister.
Dossier/n. swimming costume.
Double whammy/n. a double blow, or any problem or difficulty that has a two-pronged effect two bad things happening at once, or one right after the other; a stroke of amazing bad lucks, or two strokes of bad luck coming together.
Down the gurgler or down the drain/adj. irretrievably lost or destroyed; things have turned out for the worse.
Down Under/n. Down Under is what the rest of the world calls Australia.
Drag/n. a car drive for fun; a bit faster than is sensible.

Drag race/n. a vehicle race from a standing start.

Drop a bombshell/v. phr. to make a startling announcement.

Drop it/v. imp. order to change the subject of conversation.

Drop out/v. quit or stop participating.

Drover's dog/n. someone of absolutely no importance. Canine exemplar of doggedness; a
faithful follower.

Dude/n. a person; friend; mate; a bloke or fellow.

Dumb/adj. stupid.

Dumb down/v. to act dumber than one is.

Dummy bid/n. real estate term for bid taken from an imaginary bidder by the auctioneer at
house auctions. A dummy bidder is generally disguised as a letterbox or a tree!

Dummy, to spit the /v. to throw a tantrum or get very irate. Relating to baby spitting out dummy
and crying loudly.

Dump/v. to break off a romantic relationship. n. waste depot or garbage tip.

Dunno/v. disclaiming knowledge: "I don't know."

Dunny/n. outdoor toilet; lavatory; originally an unsewered toilet at the bottom of the garden,
now used generally for the toilet; an outside toilet; a lavatory. Outside toilet.

Eastern States/n. South Australia, Victoria, New South Wales and (sometimes) Queensland.

Easy mark/n. underworld slang for a victim who is easily duped or conned.

Enlarge on something/v. explain in more detail.

Emerald City or Sin City/n. Sydney.

Emergency teacher/n. a relief teacher.

Emu/n. a very large bird. They cannot fly but they run fast.

Esky/n. portable ice box for drinks or food; a cooler to carry drinks and food to barbies and
parties; trademarked name for a portable icebox or car fridge. Found frequently at
football or cricket matches---- ideal for putting "coldies" in or standing on; insulated box
used as a portable cooler for drinks or food; a portable icebox.

Ex/n. term used to describe an ex-wife or husband: "Darling, I would like you to meet my ex!"

Faceless men/n. the policymakers of the A.L.P. unelected by the community, and by implication,
unrepresentative of its opinion and a threat to its well-being.

Failing off/adj. decreasing.

Fair dinkum/adj. 1.something true, genuine; real; an assertion of truth or genuineness; genuine
opposed to phoney or correct; reliable: "That Jack is a fair dinkum friend the way he
saved Joshua and Ethan from being eaten by the sharks." 2. fair and equitable. 3. in
earnest 4. showing typical Australian honesty, guts, directness and the like. 5. adv.
really; genuinely; well and truly. 5. excl. expression of surprise or affirmation. 6. really,
honestly.

Fair go/ 1. n. a chance, equal opportunity; a fair or reasonable opportunity; just treatment; 2.
excl., call for fair treatment; an appeal for fairness or reason. Equivalent to "Be fair!"

Fall off the back of a truck/v. phr. to be obtained by questionable or illegal means.

Farewell someone/v. give someone a farewell party.

Fat cat/n. overpaid and underworked public service mandarin.

Fat chance/n. little chance; if someone has no hope of becoming a multi-millionaire s/he has "a
fat chance".

Feather duster/n. a descriptive term normally confined to the future of politicians as in, " This week he's top rooster but next week he'll be nothing but a bloody feather duster."
Feel crook/v.phr. feel ill.
Feisty/adj. high-spirited and volatile.
Fella/n. boy; man.
Fire up/v. phr. to become excited or aroused.
Fit the bill/v.phr. to be exactly the right person or thing for the job.
Flat out/adv. really busy; if a car is driven to its maximum speed, it is said to be "going at flat out."
Flogging/n. a reprimanding, especially by parents.
Flying doctor/n. a medical practitioner operating in connection with an aerial service, and providing medical aid to remote parts of Australia.
Folding/n. failing or closing business.
Fool around/v. to flirt or engage in sexual play; to have an affair.
Footpath/n. pavement.
Footie or footy/n. abbreviation for football; Rugby League, Rugby Union or Australian Rules football.
Forget it!/excl., expression of dismissal or disdain.
Found out/v. phr. learnt or discovered or heard about.
Freak/v. to get extremely upset or angry.
Freddie, blind/n. mythical person used to accentuate the blatantly obvious: "Even blind Freddie could've told you that your marriage wouldn't last!"
Fringe dweller/n. a person who lives, in miserable condition, on the fringe of a town or settlement.
Frock/n. dress.
From time to time/adv. sometimes.
Full Monty/n. everything; the lot; the whole kit and caboodle.

Garbage/n. rubbish/adj. poor quality.
Garbo/n. someone who collects the garbage; garbage collector.
Gas guzzler/n. a car that consumes an inordinate amount of fuel.
Gay/n. homosexual.
G'day/imp. good day. "Hi there: G'day Daniel!" Good to see ya! Hi, Hello
Get a life!/excl., expression of disgust, displeasure or rejection; "You must be joking"; "No way!"; "Stop being so hopeless!"
Get lost/ v. imp. expression of rejection; order to go away.
Get my head around/v. phr. understand or accept
Get real/excl. expression of disbelief; tell the truth.
Get stuck into/v. phr. encourage one's mates to work hard. Try or work hard.
Get the axe/v. phr. to be dismissed from work; to get the sack.
Get the ball rolling/v. phr. start the project or activity.
Get through/v. phr. to pass or complete.
Girlie/n. a girl or young woman.
Girl's night out/n. an evening on which a group of women have a night out together.
Give a damn/v. phr. to care, usually used negatively.
Give away/v.phr. to stop doing something.

Give it a go/ v. phr. to have a go or try.

Give it away/v. phr. to give up on

Give the game away/v. phr. to abandon whatever one is doing.

Globe/n. light globe.

Go along with/v.phr. to agree with.

Go bananas/v.phr. to have become really angry.

Go for it/v. phr. to encourage someone to do something.

Go gangbusters/v.phr. to go along terrifically.

Go for/v. phr. to get or seek or show interest in something.

Go over something/v phr. to review or discuss.

Go steady/v. phr. to be romantically committed to another person.

Go under/v. phr. to fail.

Go with the flow/v. phr. to accept changes (in life).

Goer/n. a useful or successful project.

Goggles/n. glasses, especially strong ones.

Gold-digger/n. a person who marries for financial gain.

Goner/n. anyone who is beyond help or dead: "The tree fell right on top of her, Mr. Jones. I'm afraid he's a goner."

Goodday/excl., hello.

Good-looking/adj. attractive; pretty; handsome.

Good one!/excl. expression of approval; well done.

Good on ya! /excl., Well done, mate! Bravo! Well done.

Government school/n. state school.

Granny flat/n. a partially or fully self-contained dwelling at the rear of a house.

Granny Smith/n. a variety of green apple grown in Sydney.

Greengrocer/n. a retailer of fruit and vegetables.

Greenie/n. conservationist who supports bans on demolishing old buildings or excess tree felling. a mildly derogatory term for a conservationist; an environmentalist.

Grog/n. a term for booze or alcohol. Any alcoholic drink. When someone spends too much at the hotel drinking, s/he is in fact "grogging in"!

Grog shop/n. bottle shop

Grow up/v. phr., to mature; to become an adult.

Gum tree/n. Eucalyptus tree.

Gurgler/n. a drain; something that has gone terribly wrong. a pushhole. If something has failed, it is said to have "gone down the gurgler". "I hope this book doesn't go down the gurgler!"

Gutsy/adj. great; excellent.

Guy/n. boy or man.

Guy thing/n. something that only males are supposed to be concerned with or know about.

Hack/v. to illegally gain access to someone else's computer.

Hang around/v.phr., to loiter; to do nothing.

Hang out/v. phr. to do nothing; usually in company with friends.

Hangout/n. a place where young people can spend time in a relaxed fashion.

Hang with/v. spend time with someone.

Hanky/n. a handkerchief.

Happy pill/n. an anti-depressant drug.

Hard rubbish collection/n. periodic, often annual, collection of large items of rubbish (broken appliances, furniture etc.) by a local council.

Hard yakka/n. hard work.

Hard yards/n. exacting work that is necessary in order to achieve some desired end.

Hen's teeth /n. phrase, extremely rare, as in "scarce as hen's teeth."

Have a go/v. phr. 1. to make a gutsy effort; to make an attempt; to try 2. to tease; criticize or fight someone.

Have a shot at/v. phr. to attack verbally; to attempt to take the piss out of someone else verbally as in, " The bastard had a shot at me."

Having open slather/n. phr. free to do anything one wants.

Headless chicken/n. phr. to act without rhyme or reason.

Heaps/adv. many; lots: "He loves Port Phillip Bay. There are heaps of seals there."

Hen's night/n. a party, exclusively for women, thrown for a bride-to-be before the wedding day.

Hey?/int. What?: "Hey, Grace! I'm over here!"

Hi!/imp. A greeting or hello.

Highway robbery/n. the act of extracting an exorbitant amount of money for goods or services and getting next to nothing in return.

Hip pocket nerve/n. located adjacent to the buttocks and where one keeps one's wallet. It tends to jump with every price or tax hike.

Hit the nail on the head/v. phr. to get to the nub of the matter.

Hit the road/v. phr. to begin a journey; to set out.

Hoist/n. rotary clothes-line.

Hold our own/v.phr. to keep or defend our position.

Hold the line/v. phr. to wait a minute.

Homestead/n. main house on a farm.

Hoon/n. a noisy or aggressive adolescent showing off a car.

Hooray or hurrah/excl. a form of saying goodbye; Cheerio.

Hostie/n. shortened version of air hostess.

Hot/adj. fashionable and exciting; cool.

How're you going?/int. phr. a typical Aussie form of greetings

How's going?/int. phr., a form of greeting or hello.

Hubbie or hubby/n. abbreviation for husband.

Huge/adj. great; wonderful.

Humbug/n. nonsense.

Hut/n. holiday house.

Icy pole/n. a frozen flavoured confection on a stick.

Idiot/n. insult, frequently coupled with stupid; an utterly foolish; senseless person.

Idiot box/n. television set.

I'm all right, Jack./phr. an expression of selfish complacency on the part of the speaker.

I may as well./phr. I should.

I wouldn't count on it./phr. don't expect to happen or rely on it.

In the bag/expr., as good as done.

In-ground-pool/n. domestic swimming pool set into the ground.

It just so happens/phr. by chance.

Jackaroo or Jilleroo/n. young male working on a farm to gain experience; a trainee on a
    sheep or cattle station; young apprentice stockman or cowboy, generally found on
    outback ranches. Young female working on a farm to gain experience. The female
    equivalent is known as a jillaroo.
Jap/n. Japanese person.
Jeez!/excl. an expression of pleasure, surprise, annoyance, horror or amazement.
Joey/n. a baby kangaroo carried around in its mother's pouch.
Joy-ride/1. n. a drive in a stolen car 2. v. to drive a stolen car
Journo/n. a journalist.
Jumbuck/n. Aboriginal word for a sheep.
Junk/n. heroin.
Junkie/n. a drug addict, especially one addicted to hard drugs.
Jump the bandwagon/v. phr. follow the popular course.
Jumper/n. Australian word for sweater.

Kangaroo/n. any of several herbivorous marsupials of the Australian region, with
    powerful hind legs developed for leaping and very short forelimbs.
Keep going/v. phr. to continue.
Keep your finger on the pulse/v. phr., to know the latest information.
Kelpie/n. a breed of sheep dog developed in Australia from imported Scottish collies.
Kick off/v. to start.
Kick out/v. to exclude; expel.
Kick the bucket/v. phr. to die.
Kindy, kindie or kinder/n. common abbreviation for kindergarten.
King hit/n. a knockout punch; a surprise punch delivered from behind; a knock-out blow.
Kiwi/n. New Zealander; any person who comes from New Zealand. A kiwi is a nocturnal
    New Zealand bird.
Knickers/n. pl. girls' underpants or panties.
Knock/v. criticize.
Knock-back or knock back/n. a refusal or rejection; to be rejected (normally by a woman).
Knocker/n. one who knocks. A critic as in, " Every time I come up with a good idea the idiot
    knocks it."
Knock-out/n. a very attractive person.
Knocker/n. a person who's always putting others down; one that doesn't have anything good
    to say about anything.
Knock off/v. to finish up; to quit working; finishing work for the day: "He had to knock off
    early from a meeting the other day to go to the dentist."
Knock-off time/n. time to go home from your place of employment.
Knuckle down/n. work hard.
Koala n. tree-dwelling marsupial. It enjoys eating those gum leaves.
Kookaburra/n. Australian kingfishers renowned for their harsh voices and call resembling
    human laughter.
Koori or Koories/n. Australian Aboriginals.

Lady killer/n. an attractive man popular with women.
La-la/n. the toilet.

Lagoon/n. a freshwater pond.
Larrikin/n. a hooligan; an urban hooligan with a dash of style; someone who likes a bit of
        mischief. a young, mischievous male; a lout or hoon; originally a criminal, now any high
        spirited or unruly youth. Young noisy person who is apt get into mischief; a poorly
        dressed mug lair who is prone to punch ups at the drop of a hat.
Lay-by/n. hire purchase; put a deposit on an item in a shop, then pay the balance later.
Learner's permit/n. a learner driving licence.
Leftie/n. anyone who has socialist ideals.
Leg opener/n. a bottle of wine, which a certain kind of Australian male believes to be a
        female aphrodisiac.
Legacy/n. an Australian organization which cares for deceased servicemen.
Legend/ n. a person who is exceptionally good at something.
Lemon/n. anything that is no good.
Life wasn't meant to be easy/a phrase erroneously attributed to a right-wing prime minister of
        the 1970s (Malcolm Fraser), meaning that one was supposed to work for one's keep.
Little Aussie battler/n. a typical member of the working class in Australia.
Lolly/n. a sweet or candy.
Loo/n. lavatory; a toilet or bathroom.
Look out for/v. phr. to take care of; to protect; to keep an eye on someone.
Looked over something/v. phr. examined.
Lose the plot/v. phr. to no longer fully understand what is going on.
Lost cause/n. insult, hopeless; pathetic.
Lost the plot/v. phr. confused; talking rubbish.
Lost your marbles/adj. phr. mad; insane
Lousy/adj. awful; terrible; mean with money; one is "crook in the guts" or otherwise off-color.
Lousy feeling/n. not feeling very well at all.
Love machine/n. a passionate lover.
Lucky Country/n. Australia.
Lurks and perks/n. the advantages of a job or situation.

Macho-man/n. 1. a very masculine man 2. a man who puts on a display of strength.
Mad about/adj. enthusiastic.
Mad with/adj. cross; angry.
Make friends/v. phr. to start a friendship; to revive a friendship after a fight.
Make up/v. phr. to repair a friendship that has been damaged by a fight; to rekindle a romance.
Make up my mind/v. to decide.
Mate/n. a friend, usually male; buddy; informal way of addressing a male.
Mateship/n. the mysterious Australian male manifesto of solidarity.
Matilda/n. a swag; a bedroll generally carried by nomadic bushman who walked around
        Australia looking for work.
Mean/adj. cruel; nasty.
Meat market/n. (slang) a venue at which casual sexual partners are to be easily acquired.
Megabucks/n. a large amount of money.
Melbourne Cup/n. Australia's best-known horse-race.
Mercy flight/n. transporting seriously ill or injured people by plane.
Metho/n. methylated spirits.

Mickey Mouse/n. something that is a bit quirky, tricky or suspect.
Middy/n. a medium-sized glass of beer; a beer glass of 10 fluid ounces (285 ml); measure of
	beer in a glass.
Milk bar/n. a corner shop selling milk, bread, cigarette, lollies and groceries.
Mindboggling/adj. unbelievable or amazing.
Mind your own business/v phr. to order to keep away and not invade another's privacy.
Miss the boat/v. phr. to lose an opportunity.
Mixed business/n. a corner shop.
Mob/n. a group, especially of people; a crowd of people; family; tribe; a flock or group (of
	sheep, kangaroos, etc.).
Mole/n. a spy.
Mongrel/n. word of insult.
Moron/n. insult, extremely stupid person
Mozzies/n. mosquitoes.
Muck around/ v. 1. to do very little; to hang around 2. to misbehave
Muck up/ v. phr. 1. to disturb or destroy something; to make something go wrong 2. To
	misbehave.
Mucking about (or around)/v. phr. simply wasting time doing nothing in particular.
Mummy's boy/n. a male who is mollycoddled by his mother, hence, a wimp or wuss.
My word/excl. "You bet!" "Certainly!"

Nanosecond/n. a very brief period of time.
Nappies/n. diapers; napkins. Basic juvenile equipment.
Nature strip/n. a grassed strip of land between the front yard of a home and the edge of the road.
Ned Kelly/n. name of a famous Australian bushranger given to anyone dishonest.
Netizen/n. a user of the Internet.
Never-never or Never Never/ n. home of the outback Aborigines, meaning the desert regions of
Australia; remote areas of Queensland and the Northern Territory; the
	desert; a term describing the most remote and isolated areas of Australia's inland desert.
	Area of Australia far from towns and cities.
Nightie/n. a woman's night dress.
N.I.M.B.Y. (nimbly)/n. a person who is against having necessary developments such as new
	prisons, hospitals, airports, and the like, built in the vicinity of their home, although they
	would support such development elsewhere. An acronym for "Not In My Back Yard."
No hoper/n. useless person.
No problem!/excl. Everything is ok!
No questions asked/imp. without a doubt; certainly.
No show/n. an instance of not turning up for an appointment.
No way/adv. phr. Expression of emphatic refusal; no; definitely not.
No worries!/adv. phr. Yes; Fine; expression used to instill confidence in what probably is a very
	worrying situation.
Nod/n. permission; the go-ahead.
Non-starter/n. something which has no chance of success.
Not keeping up/v. phr. not progressing at the expected rate.
Not up to scratch/v. phr. not good enough or not acceptable.
Nugget/n. a lump of naturally occurring gold.

Nuke/n. a nuclear weapon.
Nuts/adj. crazy.

Ocker/n. The average Australian male usually called Norm, Alf or Bruce. Person who is not
        well-educated and does not behave in a polite way. His going-out rig consists of a T-shirt,
        shorts, thongs and an Esky full of tinnies; An uncultivated Australian; a typical,
        uncultured, chauvinistic Aussie male; boor; a person who displays aggressive, usually
        boorish, Australian characteristics. Uncouth Australian who speaks with a broad
        Australian accent.
Odds-on/adj. certain.
Off the chance/n. the slight possibility.
Off the hook/adj. safe. If one has managed to get one's self off the hook one has managed
        to avoid a difficult situation which means that usually one has told a barefaced lie.
Oh boy!/excl. an expression of apprehension, worry, excitement or pleasure.
Oh my God!/excl. expression of apprehension and concern.
Oh no!/excl. expression of worry, used when someone has done something wrong.
Okay/adj. alright; correct; fine.
Old bloke/n. father.
Old boy network/n. a system of male nepotism among old school buddies.
Old country/n. country of origin – was mainly U.K.
Old fellow or fella/n. father.
Old folks/n. parents.
Old lady or woman/n. mother.
Old man/n. father.
Oldie/n. term used for older people; a word used by one under the age of 17 for anyone over
        the age of 20.
Oldies/n. pl. both parents.
On the blink/adj. not working properly.
On the nose/adj. unpleasant; distasteful; off; literally bad smelling. Usually used in reference to a
        shady deal.
One-armed bandit/n. a poker-machine.
Open slather/n. unrestrained activity.; a situation where rules aren't observed.
Ordinary/adj. no good; nothing special.
Out of here/v. to leave; to go away
Outback/n. the vast dry area of Australia; remote inland districts of Australia: What we Aussie
        call the desolate heart of Australia, or any remote part of the country for that matter.
Outhouse/n. toilet.
Over the top/adj. 1. exaggerated; excessive. 2. wonderful; great.
Own up/v. phr. to admit to wrong-doing; to confess.
Oy/excl. hey.
Oz/n. slang name for Australia; abbreviated affectionate term for this great country of Australia!;
        short for Australia, mate! The Great!

Paddock/n. an area of land used for farming; a field of any size. Fenced area of farm-land.
Pal/n. a good friend; a mate.
Parasite/n. a person who lives off others.

Party animal/n. a person who parties hard.

Pastoralist/n. a sheep or cattle farmer.

Peanut butter/n. a paste made from finely ground roasted peanut, used as a spread, etc.

Peanuts/n. a piddling amount of money.

Pee/1. v. to urinate. 2. n. urine.

Period/n. menstruation cycle.

Perk/n. A company car or an expense account is a "perk". Politicians have many perks, but
     we mere mortals get charged a fringe benefit tax on ours. Special privilege.

Physio/n. physiotherapy or physiotherapist.

Pick on/v. to single someone out for unfriendly treatment.

Pick up/v. phr. to collect.

Picnic/n. something easy.

Piece of cake/n. an easy task.

Pigs fly/excl. retort used to express disbelief or doubt.

Pin down/v. to recognize; to remember.

Pinch/v. to steal.

Piss/1. v. to urinate. 2. n. urine

Piss off/v. imp order to go away.

Pissed off/adj. annoyed; angry; disgruntled; fed up; thoroughly discontented.

Platypus/n. an amphibious, egg-laying monotreme with webbed feet and a muzzle like the
     bill of a duck.

Play it cool/v. phr. to be cautious and shrewd; to maintain composure.

Plum/n. an exceptional person or thing.

Plus/n. an advantage: "It's a plus for him to know the course before competing.

Pocket money/n. money given to children by their parents in the form of a small regular
     allowance.

Pointing the finger/v. phr. saying the problem was caused by someone else.

Pokies/n. poker or slot machines.

Polly or Pollie or pollies/n. a parrot or a politician.

Pom or Pommy/n. Affectionate Australian term for anyone of British extraction.

Pommy bastard/n. English person; English immigrant; an English person who embodies the
     antithesis of all things Australian.

Poofter/n. an effeminate male; offensive term for male homosexual.

Portable/n. a school building consisting of one or two classrooms.

Possie/n. position or place.

Possum/n. 1. well-known Australian marsupial. 2. a term of affectionate address -- now generally
     regarded with affection; an Australian term of endearment, as in "you little possum.";
     something soft and cuddly.

Postie/n. postman or woman.

Pot/n. marijuana.

Prawn/n. a shrimp.

Prep/n. a preparatory class.

Pressie/n. present or gift.

Provisional licence/n. an initial driver's licence which stipulates a restricted speed and the use
     of P-plates.

Psycho/adj. crazy; insane; n. insane person.

Pub/n. hotel.
Pull off/v. to achieve or do.
Pull out/v. to withdraw or cancel.
Pull your socks up/v. phr., to urge improvement in attitude; to make more effort.
Punter/n. a gambler on horse or dog race.
Pusher/n. a light, collapsible chair on wheels for small children.
Put in/v. time or work invested.
Putting off/v. delaying or postponing.
Put together/v. to compose or make.
Put up or shut up/ v. to be prepared to support what one says or else remain silent.
Put you down/v. phr. to write a name on the list.
Put you through/v. phr. connect.

Quack/n. a doctor
Qantas/n. Australia's international airline, from Queensland and Northern Territories Air
     Service.
Quid/n. formerly one-pound note, still heard in the phrase " not worth a bloody quid (worthless),
     or "not the full quid" (insane); a sum of money; one pound; formerly the slang term used
     for the pound (currency). Still in use today: "He's made a few quid out of his business."

Rafferty rules/n. no rules at all; total disorganization and ad hockery.
Rag trade/n. the clothing business – either selling or manufacturing.
Rain boots/n. rubber boots for wet weather.
Raincoat/n. a condom.
Rambo/n. an aggressive, macho male.
Rare as hen's teeth/v. phr. exceedingly scarce.
Ratbag/ n. the Bush version of a rogue or troublemaker; someone who's a bit mischievous:
     "Isabella is a little ratbag the way she kills her pet fish." Stupid or odd person; insulting,
     eccentric person; foolish person.
Rattler/n. a train; any of various type of trains noted for their loud rattling.
Reality check/n. a moment of self-reflection; a bringing of oneself back down to earth.
Rave/n. a sort of late-night perambulating party involving anyone from the sun-teen acne set
     through punks and dole-bludging hippies to Yuppies.
Reckon/v. to believe; to think.
Red centre/n. Central Australia.
Red-hot/1. violent; furious: red-hot anger. 2. fresh; new; most recent: red-hot tip for a horse race.
     3. very excited or enthusiastic; unreasonable; over-priced, outlandish, totally
     unreasonable; superlative for anyone or anything of an extreme nature: "Their prices are
     red-hot."
Red rattlers/n. Sydney's aging fleet of groaning, lurching, suburban railway cars.
Red tape/n. official rules or procedures.
Rego/n. an abbreviation for registration; motor vehicle registration fee.
Rehab/n. rehabilitation.
Rellie/n. family relative (in-laws).
Reps, House of/n. the lower house of Federal Parliament ; the House of Representatives.
Right on/adv. expression of agreement or approval.

Righto/adv. all right then. This is really just another way Aussies say "okay." All right! Sure! Okay!
Rip-off/n. something excessively expensive.
Rip off/v phr. to swindle; to overcharge for a product or service.
Road-train/n. a series of linked trucks and vans for transporting stock.
Roaring/adj. if a business is doing well, it can be said to have "a roaring trade."
Rock melon/n. the edible fruit of the cantaloupe.
Romper stomper/n. a very short haircut.
Roo/n. abbreviation for kangaroo.
Rort/n. a fraudulent act; a deceptive scheme; a dishonest person. People receiving social welfare benefits under false pretences are " rorting" the system; v. to act dishonestly or fraudulently.
Rough idea/n. an estimation.
Row/n. argument; a verbal fight.
Rubbish/v. to denigrate or put down.
Rubbish bin/n. a container for the disposal of household waste.
Rubbish collector/n. a garbage collector.
Rule of thumb/n. a rule for general guidance.
Rusty/adj. weak or impaired due to lack of practice.

Sack/n. when someone is fired, s/he gets the "sack".
Sacred site/n. a place of great significance.
Sadie/n. a cleaning lady.
Salvo/n. Salvation Army.
Scab/v. to borrow items from another.
Scam/v. to get something for nothing.
Scarce as hen's teeth/adj. phr. exceedingly rare.
Schoolie/n. a school student.
Screwed/adj. ruined or wrecked.
Screw up/v. 1. to blunder. 2. to ruin or wreck.
Scum/n. contemptible people.
Scum bag/n. a strong insult; a contemptible person
Sea-changer/n. a person who has recently moved to a coastal area after having lived in the city.
See something through/v. phr. to continue; to see something to completion.
See you later/v, phr. a salutation; goodbye.
Septic/n. abbreviation of septic tank.
Set up/v. to arrange or organise.
Settle down/v. imp order to behave; calm down; not to become excited.
Sexy/adj., great; good-looking.
Shandy/n. a mixture of beer and lemonade.
She'll be alright/expr. a reassuring expression meaning "it'll be OK". Everything will be okay.
Sheila/n. a member of the female sex; girl; a woman: "Of course, Australia has the greatest Sheilas in the world"; once meant a girlfriend, then generalized to any young female: "She's a nice-looking Sheila." "He met some really nice Sheilas at the party last night."
Shifter/n. an adjustable spanner.
Shithouse/n. 1. a toilet or dunny; lavatory. 2. foul, wretchedly bad, terrible; bad; awful.

Shonky/adj. of dubious integrity or honesty; goods of poor quality or a job that has been badly done.

Shopping trolley/n. any four-wheel drive, especially one used primarily to do the shopping.

Shot, take a shot at/v. to make an attempt at something.

Shout/v. when it's someone's turn to buy a round of drinks, it's his/her turn to "shout the school"; buy drinks for others.

Show bags/n. a sample bag of goods found at agricultural shows.

Show time/n. time to begin.

Shrimp/n. what we call prawns.

Shut up/v phr. be quiet; order to be quiet

Sickie/n. a day taken off work because of illness (with the excuse of being sick).

Silly bugger/n. gullible; naïve

Silvertail/n. wealthy person.

Sin-bin/n. penalty box in some team games; a place where a sportsman is sent after being ordered off the field for appalling behaviour.

Singlet/n. a sleeveless t-shirt.

Skippy/n. a derogatory term for any Australian.

Slacker /n. anyone who avoids toil.

Sleaze/n. a person who behaves in a sexually inappropriate way, especially an older person.

Sleep with/v. to have sexual intercourse with someone.

Slug/v. to charge too much for something.

Slut/n. a promiscuous woman.

Smack/n. a slap with the open palm of the hand.

Snapped up/adj. taken.

Sneak/v. to steal.

So-so/adv. not completely satisfactory; a little disappointing.

Some pointers/n. some advice.

Something along the same lines/adv. similar to.

Son of a bitch/n. a contemptible man.

Sooner the better/adv. as soon as possible.

Spell out/v. to explain clearly.

Speed/n. amphetamines or other drugs.

Spinner/n. the person tossing coins in a game of two up, an Australian gambling game once played with two imperial copper pennies.

Spinner, come in/v. call made to person tossing two-up coins once all bets are laid and the ring is clear.

Spit the dummy/v. phr. to throw a tantrum; to lose one's temper ; to show anger; to refuse to put up with a situation and opt out.

Sponger/n. someone who lives off the efforts of others. A close relative of a bludger.

Stag party/n. a party, exclusively for men, with entertainment such as strippers, prostitutes, pornographic films, and the like.

Stand out/v. phr. to be noticeable.

Starving/adj. hungry.

Starving to death/adj. phr. exceedingly hungry.

Station/n. a ranch, as in sheep station.

Sticky tape/n. as the name suggests, adhesive tape (Scotch tape).

Stingy/adj. reluctant to spend money.

Stir/v. to provoke someone.

Stirrer/n. a person who teases or makes people angry; someone who's always poking fun at others; a person who delights in stirring up trouble then decamping when it gets out of control: "In his younger days, he was a bit of stirrer."

Stressed out/adj. overloaded; unable to cope.

Stubbie or Stubby/n. short, round little bottle of beer; squat bottle of larger; a small bottle of beer.

Stuff-up/n. a bit like an average "screw–up" or failure; the mess resulting from a mistake.

Stuff up/v. phr., to make a mistake.

Sundowner/n. itinerant worker; a swagman who arrives at a homestead at nightfall, too late for work, but obtains shelter for the night and hopefully a food handout.

Surfie/n. a devotee of surfboard riding.

Super/n. abbreviation of superannuation.

Super cool/adj. better than wonderful.

Sure thing/n. a certainty; something assured beyond any doubt.

Surfie/n. person who spends much time at the beach surfing or board riding.

Swag/n. wandering bushmen, "swagmen" carries all their belongings rolled up in a blanket. This is called a swag; a bundle of belongings carried by a

Swagman/n. a man who travels about the country on foot, carrying his possessions in a swag and living on his earnings from occasional jobs, or gifts of money or food. Person who travels carrying all his possessions.

Sweetener/n. 1. a bribe. 2. a financial or other benefit added to something on offer.

Ta ta /excl. pronounced "tah-tah", it doesn't mean saying "thanks! Twice--- but to have said "Goodbye"!.

Take for granted/v. to assume or suppose something will be known.

Take it easy/v. to relax; to do very little; order to calm down.

Take your details/v. to record one's name, address, etc.

Tall poppy n. a person who is pre-eminent in a particular field; a person with great status.

That's more like it!/phr. that's a better idea.

Tassie/n. Tasmania.

Tea/n. evening meal; the principal meal of the day.

Telly/n. abbreviation of "television".

Terrific!/adj. good; excellent; wonderful; an exclamation of approval. Variations include: "beaut!" A word that describes anything favorable.

That's the shot!/excl. That's the right way to go about it!

This arvo/n. this afternoon.

Thongs/n. casual footwear; a backless sandal; a type of bathing suit, bikini.

The Three Sisters/n. spectacular sandstone outcrop at Katoomba, in the Blue Mountains.

Ticker/n. courage; bravery; guts.

Tit/n. a female breast.

Too laid-back/adj. too relaxed.

Top end/n. the northernmost part of Australia.

Top-enders/n. Inhabitants of Australia's newest state, The Northern Territory.

Top notcher/n. a first-rate person.

Town water/n. water from the mains as opposed to tank water.

Truce!/excl. call to halt hostilities in a game or fight.

Truckie/n. truck-driver.

True blue or true-blue/adj. something that's genuine or real. Genuine, fair dinkum, spot on, etc.
Also, the highest compliment to pay an Aussie!

Tucker/n. food.

Tuck shop/n. school canteen

Tummy/n. stomach.

Turf/n. the territory belonging to a street gang.

Turn off/v. to disgust, especially sexually.

Turn on/v. to arouse or excite, especially sexually.

Turn up/v. to attend.

Turps/n. another term for alcohol. Abbreviation for turpentine.

The Twelve Apostles/n. a number of monoliths, their feet in the surf, along the coast of
southern Victoria.

Two up/n. once the national game played with a pair of pennies thrown into the air by a spinner.

U-ie or U-turn/n. a movement to turn around and drive the opposite way.

UGG boot/n. a type of winter footwear, made from sheepskin: "After seeing all his patients, Dr
Johnson likes to slip on a pair of UGG boots and relax in his chair for a while."

Unbelievable/adj. wonderful.

Under way/adv. in progress.

Undies/n. pl. underwear, especially female panties.

Uni/n. university.

Up against/phr. competing with.

Up for grabs/adj. available.

Up in air/adj. undecided.

Useless/adj. insulting, incompetent; no good for anything

Ute/n. abbreviation of utility, an open-backed small truck; utility truck or utility van.

Vegemite/ n. trademark name for a black yeast extract used as a spread on toast and sandwiches.

Veggies/n. vegetables.

Vet/n. a veterinary surgeon.

Vicious circle/n. a cycle of problems in which the solution to one problem creates more
problems.

Wacky/adj. crazy; silly; strange.

Wag/v. truant: I never "wagged" school; to deliberately stay away from school without
permission.

Wake up/v. to know exactly what is going on.

Walkabout/n. to wander the countryside; if someone goes off without any particular
destination in mind, they've "gone walkabout".

Walkover/n. a very easy victory.

Wallaby/n. a small kangaroo.

Waltzing Matilda/n. it means wandering (waltzing) the countryside as a tramp, carrying one's possessions wrapped in a blanket (Matilda).

Wanna/v. to want to.

Wannabe/n. a person who appears to be like someone else.

Watering-hole/n. a pub or bar used by a regular group.; one's favorite pub.

Wee/1. n. urine; an act of urination. 2. v. to urinate.

Weekender/n. cottage where a family can spend the week-end usually by the sea.

Well-heeled/n. a person who's got more money than sense.

Whacker/n. a person of no consequence; a fool.

Whammy/n. a supernatural spell or curse directed at a person.

Wharfie/n. dock worker; one who works on wharves; a stevedore.

What's up?/1. greeting of hello 2. What is wrong? What is happening? Or What's the problem?

Whatever/phr., it doesn't matter; as one wishes.

Wheely bin/n. large rubbish bin on wheels.

Widow tree/n. the grey gum which has a habit of shedding branches suddenly and killing timber-getters.

Winge or whinge/v. to complain or grizzle: "He got a bit sick of hearing his mum whinge about him becoming a vegetarian."

Whinger/n. an incessant complainer; complainer all the time, usually with little justification.

Whingeing Pom/n. an English person who is always criticizing and complaining about life in Australia.

Widow-maker/n. a dead tree branch which is likely to snap off and kill a person below.

Willy-nilly/adv. happening without thought or organization.

Wimp/n. a meek, spineless person, especially man.

Wimpish/adj. of the nature of a wimp; gutless, cowardly.

Wog/n. 1. a native of North Africa or the Middle East, esp. an Arab. 2 a person of Mediterranean extraction, or of similar complexion and appearance.

Wog boy/n. a young adult male "wog".

Wombat/n. a large, heavily-built burrowing marsupial with short legs and a rudimentary tail.

Wow!/excl. expression of wonder or delight.

Wowser/n. a spoilsport; prude.

Write-off/n. if a $2000 car is bingled, causing $2500 damage, it's a write-off.

Ya/pron. you.

Yabbie or yabby/n. Australian freshwater crayfish found in freshwater dams and creeks.

Yacker/n. work. Most work is "hard yacker".

Yank/n. an American.

Yarn/n. a story, usually of adventure and usually very long; a talk, chat.

Yellow peril/n. The Asian invasion which Australians have dreaded for over a century.

Yep/adv. expression of agreement.

Yes, no/phr. an expression used as a sentence starter, where only the context can determine if the positive or negative is intended.

You are joking/phr. retort that expresses displeasure and rejection of the other person's intention.

You beaut!/excl. a cry of joyful praise.

You're not wrong/The Australian way of saying, "You are right."

Your shout/n. a person's turn to buy the drinks.

You've got to be in it to win it./If one doesn't buy a ticket in the lottery one doesn't stand a show

of collecting first prize. Self-explanatory.
Yum/adj. tasting nice.

Zillion/n. an unimaginably large amount.
Zombie/n. a dull, brainless person.

2.5   New Zealand English to American English

Australia and New Zealand share many words in common usage. There is little distinctiveness in New Zealand grammar, but its vocabulary has three special features:

i.   the first being adoptions from Maori:

Pakeha/a European, also a common name for Caucasian New Zealanders generally
Haere mai/a term of greeting
Hongi/ o press noses, the Maori greeting
Kiwi/a flightless bird unique to New Zealand and by extension a New Zealander
Rahui/a sign warning against trespass.

ii. the second major vocabulary feature involves words shared with and borrowed from Australia:

larrikin/ hooligan
ocker/ boor
shanghai/ catapult
truckie/ truck driver

New Zealand	American
Arterial road	major road, trunk road
Articulated lorry	trailer truck
Assistant	salesclerk in a store
Autumn	fall
Bank holiday	legal holiday
Barman or barmaid	bartender
Barrister	trial lawyer
Beetroot	beet
Bend (in a road)	curve
Block of ice	ice cube
Brassed off	angry
Bread bin	bread box
Call box	outside public telephone
Caravan	house trailer
Caretaker	janitor, building superintendent
Car park	parking lot

Casket	jewel box, coffin
Castor sugar	finely granulated sugar
Change down	downshift in car gears
Chap	guy fellow
Cheap	reduced in price
Cheeky	rude, naughty
Chilly bin	cooler for picnics
Commercial traveller	salesperson
Company	corporation
Cooker	stove
Corporation	city, municipal government
County borough	county seat
Crib	vacation flat
Cupboard	closet
Daft	strange
Dairy	convenient store
Dear	expensive
Decorate	paint
Digs	rooms, lodging
Director (of a company)	officer
Dispenser	pharmacist
Double-glazed	storm windows
Dustbin	garbage, trash can
Enquiries	information
Entrée	appetizer
Fag	cigarette
Father Christmas	Santa Claus
Fender	bumper
First floor	second floor
Flannel	washcloth
Flex	electric cord
Fridge	refrigerator
Girl Guide	Girl Scout
Give way	yield (as in traffic)
Grammar school	college preparatory school for ages 11-19
Grease-proof paper	wax paper
Ground floor	first floor
Guillotine	paper cutter
Gum boots	high rubber boots
Head boy or girl	top boy, girl in school
Headmaster	principal of a school
Inverted commas	quotation marks
Jacket potato	baked potato
Jack up	to arrange, organize
Joiner	carpenter
Larder	pantry

Lay-by   rest area on a highway; putting a deposit on a purchase and paying in instalments

Lay-by	rest area on a highway; putting a deposit on a purchase and paying in instalments
Lay on	to provide or arrange for
Leave (school)	graduating student
Match	game
Mend	to repair
Milk float	milk truck
Mind	to watch out for
Mineral	soft drink
Motor coach	bus
Newsagent	news or magazine dealer or store
Notice board	bulletin board
Old boy or girl	alumnus or alumna
On the dole	unemployed and on welfare
Panel beater	auto body shop
Pants	panties
Reception	front office or desk
Resident	a person registered in a hotel
Ring binder	loose-leaf notebook
Rubber	eraser
School term	school semester
Shout	to buy a round of drinks
Singlet	undershirt
Smashing	terrific
Spencer	woman's undershirt
Surgery	doctor's office
Swat	to study hard or cram for an exam
Tap	faucet
Tea	usually more than just a cup of tea, possibly supper
Telly	television set
Trifle	a dessert
Trunk call	long-distance telephone call
Vacuum flask	thermos bottle
Varsity	university
Wag	to skip school

At a rate of knots/very fast
Bach/holiday house
Barnes walk/a diagonal walk at traffic lights
Chilly bin/insulated food or drink box
Chocolate fish/a type of sweet
Dwang/timber floor strut
Fizz boat/speed boat
Have the wood on/have an advantage over
Lamburger/burger made from minced lamb

Mutton/clear out
Section/building plot
Superette/small supermarket
Swannie/a type of jacket
Wopwops/a derogatory term for the suburbs

2.5   Canadian English

American spelling now predominates:

i.   adoptions from indigenous languages:
        anorak/waterproof jacket or coat
        kayak/small watercraft
        mackinaw/a bush jacket
        muskeg/mossy, swampy land
ii.   adoptions from French:
        Anglophone/English-speaking person
        Francophone/French-speaking person
        caboteur/a coastal trading vessel
iii.   British English usages adapted for local purposes
        riding/a political constituency
        prime minister/the federal first minister
        premier/the first minister of a provincial government

Canadian English to American English

Canadian English	American English
Braces	suspenders
Chesterfield	sofa
First Nations	Native Americans (Indians)
Holidays	vacation
Marks	grades
Pavement	sidewalk
Provinces	states
Spanner	wrench
Tap	faucet
Railway	railroad
Washroom	toilet
Went missing	lost

2.6   Scottish/Irish English

There are distinctive grammatical forms influenced by Irish Gaelic

i.   First, forms like these are used for emphasis and increased focus:
        It's fine woman she is.

> It was to help him I went.
> It's herself was the best player.

ii.   Second is the use of after and –ing to mark an action just completed:
> He's after helping them this very morning.

iii.   The third is the omission of yes and no in answers:
> Did you come yesterday? I did
> Can you see her now? We can.

Vocabulary

adapted from Gaelic:
banshee/fairy woman
boreen/narrow, quiet country lane
colleen/young woman
craic/fun, employment
fleadh/festival, usually of traditional music
guards or gardai/police
kitter/left-handed
messages/shopping
piece/sandwich snack
pinkie/little finger
shillelagh/a thick stick
slater/woodlouse
stay/live
Taoiseach/Prime Minister
wee/small
wiskey or wisky/water of life
youse/you (plural)

2.7 South African English

A curiosity of the grammar is the affirmative "no" , as "How are you? – No, I'm fine", probably adopted from Afrikaans.

Vocabulary

i.   With its parent Dutch, this language has provided the bulk of local borrowings:

Afrikaner/South African Caucasian of Dutch or Huguenot origin
apartheid/separate racial development, now obsolete
bakkie/pickup truck
braai/barbecue
drift/ford
trek/journey
veld/open country

ii.   With its hybrid extensions:

    highveld
    backveld

iii.   Words from African languages

    impala
    muti/medicine
    sangoma/diviner
    tshwala/sorghum beer

iv.   Distinctive English words

    the now archaic bioscope/cinema
    location/district set aside for a particular group
    robot/traffic light

v.   Others

    advocate/barrister
    arvey/afternoon
    bad friends/not on speaking terms
    bell/to phone
    bioscope/cinema
    bottle store/liquor store
    butchery/butcher's shop
    camp/paddock
    dinges/thingummay
    dorp/village
    fundi/expert
    gogga/insect
    indaga/meeting
    kloof/ravine
    lekker/nice
    putu/a type of porridge
    shebeen/illegal liquor establishment
    verkrampte/narrow-minded
    voorshot/advance payment

South African English to American   **English**

South African English	American English
Can	a glass jar
Catfish	any of several species of octopus
Christian flower	hydrangea
the Church	the Anglican Church

eye	a source/fountainhead of a spring or river
fuse	cigarette
Harley Davidson	handlebar mustache
Ink pen	fountain pen
Kraal	1. corral; 2. a cluster of huts
Meneer	Sir or Mister
Monkey's wedding	simultaneous rain and sunshine
New Year's Eve	Old Year's Night
Painted lady	a species of gladiolus
Paraffin	1. light rain; 2. gin; 3. kerosene
Pirate taxi	unlicensed taxi
School leaving	graduation
Standard	gra

III. Multi-Word Verbs

Compound and multi-word verbs

This chapter includes compound verbs and any other forms of multi-word verbs. A compound word is a combination of two words, sometimes hyphenated, sometimes not. Multi-word verbs are combinations of verbs and one or more other words. The combinations function like a single word. Compound verbs are verbs made up of two or more words. This chapter includes compound verbs (phrasal verbs, prepositional verbs, phrasal prepositional verbs), idioms and other multi-word verbs.

i. Phrasal verbs are combinations of a verb and an adverb. "Susan turned off the light." or "Susan turned the light off." They will work. However, it is not possible to have this kind of flexibility with prepositional verbs and phrasal-prepositional verbs.

1. Prepositional verbs are combinations of a verb and a preposition. He'll kook into the matter immediately.
2. Phrasal-prepositional verbs are combinations of a verb, an adverb and a preposition. He won't put up with this noise any longer.
3. Phrasal verbs can be separated in the following example.
    We called off the meeting.
    We called the meeting off.

ii. However, prepositional verbs and phrasal-prepositional verbs cannot be separated:

"Ask for " and "look at" are prepositional verbs. "Look forward to", "look down on", and "cut down on" are phrasal-prepositional verbs. "She asked for his address." However, this sentence cannot be written in following ways:
    She asked his address for.
    She asked it for.
The above rule applies to phrasal-prepositional verbs.

There are four types of compound verbs:

   i.   Phrasal verbs - Transitive verbs with an adverb: v. adv. (M) or v. adv. (T)
        Usually these are (M) "put away" (= eat): I don't know how she manages to put away so much food away. She put away an entire box of chocolates. Sometimes the adverb can go in one position. These verbs are marked (T). for example "gloss over" (= avoid considering): He glossed over the company's fall in profits, focusing instead on his plans for modernization.
   ii. Phrasal verbs - Intransitive verbs with an adverb: v. adv. (I)
        For example: When he opened the office door, he was hit on the head and passed out (= became unconscious). Diana set off down the road on her own bike. I admired the way she soldiered on (= continued although it was difficult) when his business ran into trouble.
   iii. Prepositional verbs - Verbs with a preposition: v. prep.

These are usually (T), for example: How does he intend to deal with (= manage) the problem? So, she made a mistake – don't hold it against her – I'm sure she won't do it again.

Some verbs can also be followed by –ing form of another verb: I've no idea how to set about changing a tire on a car.

iv. Phrasal prepositional verbs - Verbs with an adverb and a preposition: v. adv. prep.
v. There are (T) verbs or followed by an –ing form. Notice that they rarely have a passive form. Examples are: Can I come in on (= join) your plans for the weekend? I can't seem to get down to (= start to direct efforts to) writing this letter to Dave.

Some multi-words- verbs do not belong to the above category, i.e. to fit the bill etc.

Phrasal verb – a verb consisting of a lexical element and particle(s) (sit down)

A

Account for/give good reason for; explain satisfactorily (some action or expenditure): "She has behaved in the most extraordinary way! I can't account for her actions at all."

Act in cold blood/to do something callously.

Add insult to injury/1. to cause additional trouble to someone; to hurt someone's feelings after doing him harm: "Robert added insult to injury when he called the man a bastard after he had already beaten him up." 2. To make bad trouble worse.

Add to/to unite or join so as to increase the number, quantity, size, or importance.

Add up/1. Come to the correct amount. 2. To make sense; be understandable: "Her story didn't add up."

Add up to/1. Make a total of; amount to: "The gas bill added up to $25.55." 2. Mean; result in: "The rain, the storm, and the crowded cabin added up to a spoiled vacation."

All roads lead to Rome/there are many different ways but all reach the same goal or conclusion.

Allow for/to make provisions in advance for; take into account (usually some additional requirement, expenditure, delay etc.): "Allowing for depreciation, his car should be worth $4,000 this time next year."

Answer back/to answer a reproof imprudently: "He has answered his father back."

Apply for/to make application or request; ask: "He has applied for a job"

Approve of/to speak or think favorably: "She has approved of him." "Sally doesn't approve of smoking." "She approved of the work, but she objected to the cost." "James approves wholeheartedly of our plan."

Are you right there?/Do you need some help?

Argue with (someone) or argue by/to contend in argument; dispute.

Ask after or ask for /ask for news of; seek information about: "He phoned the hospital to ask after her mother." "I met Sally at the party; she asked after you (asked how were or how you were getting on)."

Ask one about/inquire of: "I asked him about his religious beliefs."

Ask (somebody) for (questions, the way, the time, favors)/ 1. To make (something bad) likely to happen to you; bring (something bad) upon yourself: "Daniel drives fast on worn-out tires; he is asking for trouble." 2. request; demand: "A woman stopped me and asked me for money. She asked for a loan." "She asked for her bill." "The women asked for more pay and shorter hours." 3. ask to speak to: "Go to the office and ask for my manager."

Ask for it (trouble)/to behave so as to invite trouble.

Ask one out/ask someone to go on a date; invite someone to an entertainment or a meal (usually in a public place): "He had a lot of friends and was usually asked out in the evenings, so he seldom spent an evening at home."

Ask someone over/to invite someone to your home.

Aspire to/to want or hope to do something or be something, and work towards it.

Augur well (or ill) for/to be a good (bad) sign for the future.

B

Back away/to stop or move back slowly (because confronted by some danger or unpleasantness); to act to avoid or lesson one's involvement in something; to draw or turn back; retreat: "She glared at her and he backed away." "When Jacob took a gun out everyone backed away nervously."

Back down or back off/to give up a claim; not follow up a threat: "Tom said he could beat James, but when Ronald put up with his fists Tom backed down."

Back foot/to have someone at a disadvantage.

Back out of/to withdraw from some joint action previously agreed on; to discontinue or refuse to provide previously promised help or support: "Joshua agreed to help but backed out when he found how difficult it was." "She backed out of the project when she realized what it would cost." "If I've signed the contract I can't back out of it."

Back somebody up/1. to support morally or verbally: "Please back him up in this argument." 2. to reverse course: "We'll have to back up and turn around."

Back the wrong horse/to support the wrong person or party.

Back up/1. to move backwards: "The bus was backing up." 2. to help or be ready to help; stay behind to help; agree with and speak in support of; stand by: "Ethan has joined the Boy Scouts, and his father is backing him up in this decision." "The president backs up the cabinet." "Samuel told us what has happened, and Benjamin backed him up."

Bad mouth/to say uncomplimentary or libelous things about someone; deliberately to damage another's reputation: "It is not good to bad mouth people."

Bail out/1. to secure release from prison until trial by leaving or promising money or property: "When high school students got into trouble with the police, the principal would always bail them out." 2. To relieve financially; free from trouble by giving or lending money: "Anthony started a small business, which prospered after his father had to bail her out a couple of times."

Bang into/to bump into

Bank on something/to count or depend on something: "They were banking on a change of heart."

Bark up for the wrong tree or bark up the wrong tree/to choose the wrong person to deal with or the wrong course of action; to mistake an aim: "If she thinks she can fool me, she is barking up for the wrong tree." "Anne is trying to find the lost files in the reception area, but I think she's barking up the wrong tree."

Black out/1. to darken by putting out or dimming lights. 2. to prevent or silence information or communication; to refuse to give out truthful news.

Be a good Samaritan/to help the distressed.

Be a law unto yourself/to disregard the advice and rules of others.

Be about to/1. close to; ready to: "They were about leave when the rain began."

Be acquainted/to add insult to injury; to upset someone and then deliver a second insult, or to
     make an already bad situation worse by a second insulting act or remark.
Be against/to be opposed to (often used with gerund): "He's against doing anything till the police
     arrive."
Be all years/to pay close attention.
Be all for/to agree with or approve of something.
Be all go/to be very busy or active.
Be angry about (or at) (something)/to have strong feelings of irritation about an issue or
     situation: "We were angry about the bank's decision not to extend the loan." "What is he
     so angry about? They're all angry about the new working hours." "Alexis was angry
     about what happened."
Be angry with somebody/ to have strong feelings of irritation about a person or group of
     people: "Why is he angry with me? What I have done?" "I'm pretty angry with her for
     not telling me." "Anne's very angry with you."
Be annoyed with, about/to have strong feelings of irritation about a person or group of people:
     "We were angry with the bank manager for not extending the loan."
Be in another man's shoes/to be in (or to identify with) another person's situation or
     predicament.
Be anxious about/to be worried about.
Be anxious for/to be eager for, wanting: "They're anxious for a quick solution."
Be at each other's throats/to quarrel or fight persistently.
Be at loggerheads over something/to be quarrelling; to have a bitter argument with someone.
Be at the cutting edge/to be involved with the most advanced/recent developments.
Be at the receiving end of/to be subjected to something unpleasant.
Be aware of (feel)/to know about something. He wasn't aware of the time.
Be away/to be absent or gone from home or a place temporarily: "I'm afraid he's away for the
     weekend."
Be back/to arrive back home; back to a place, a person etc.; to have returned after a long or short
     absence: "When will he back?. He'll be back in an hour."
Be blown away/to be extremely impressed.
Be born again/said of Christians who have been saved, with Christ controlling their lives and
     united to Christ's Spirit.
Be born in my blood/to be born with these characteristics.
Be born with a silver spoon in your mouth/to be born well-off; to have undeserved
     privilege; to act as if one if superior when it's all accidental.
Be bound for/travelling towards a particular place..
Be comprised of/refers to a whole unit rather than its components: "The minority government is
     comprised of four parties."
Be crazy about/to like someone or something: "He's crazy about her."
Be cut off/to be inconveniently isolated (the subject is usually a place or residents in a certain
     place); to be deprived of telephonic or telegraphic communication: "I will be completely
     cut off if I go to live in that village because there is a bus only once a week."
Be cut out for/to be fitted or suited for (used of people, usually in the negative): "Her father got
     her a job in a bank, but it soon became clear that she was not cut out for that kind of
     work."
Be disappointed with (somebody or about something)/to have one's hopes, expectations, trust, or

promises violated by another person or event: "My mother never showed it if she was disappointed with me." "He must be pretty disappointed about his exam results."

Be green with envy/to be very jealous over what someone else has.

Be familiar with/to know about something.

Be fed up with/to be unhappy; to be completely bored; to be angry and disgusted: "He's fed up with his job. He wants to do something different." "She's fed up with this wet weather."

Be fired/to get the sack; to lose one's job or employment.

Be fond of/to love, with emphasis on tender affection; to like something as in a preference: "She was fond of her youngest grandson. He reminded her of her late husband." "We are very fond of apples, all three of us."

Be for/to be in favor of (often used with gerund: "I'm all for trying harder").

Be frightened to death/to be very alarmed and fearful, though not to die; typically a form of hyperbole: "She was   frightened to death by a mouse that ran into the room."

Be in good hands/to be well looked after.

Be in/1. to agree to take part: "I'll be in a fishing trip any day." 2. to be at home or in this building: "Can I speak to Victor? He's not in."

Be in a hole/to find oneself in difficulty; have financial problem.

Be in charge of/to manage; to run.

Be in for/to be about to encounter (usually something unpleasant): "If he thinks that the work is going to be easy he's in for a shock."

Be in hot water/to be in trouble.

Be in the race/to have a chance of success.

Be in the red/the situation where one's bank account is overdrawn; to be in debt.

Be in vain/to fail.

Be laid up (of a person)/to be confined to bed through illness: "Victor was laid up for weeks with a slipped disk."

Be left in the lurch/to abandon one to one's fate, usually in circumstances of danger or difficulty.

Be mad about/to like, with an intensity or fervor characteristic of a crush: "Susan was just mad about her new love interest, James."

Be made redundant/to be fired; to be asked to leave a company because there is no longer a job; to be laid off.

Be or get mixed up with/to be involved (usually with some rather disreputable person or business): "He doesn't want to be mixed up with any illegal organization."

Be neck and neck/to tie; to be running even in the race to the finish (often a term in a horserace.

Be nuts/to be mad; to lack mental stability.

Be off/going to a place: "Tomorrow he's off to London."

Be on the fence/to be undecided.

Be on the lookout/to keep searching.

Be on the tip of one's tongue/to be almost but not quite able to bring a particular word or name to mind; to suffer from a temporary memory lapse.

Be one's own man/to be true to oneself.

Be open with/to speak frankly to; to conceal nothing from.

Be over/to be finished: "The snow is over now; we can go on."

Be pissed-off/to be disgruntled; fed up; thoroughly discontent.

Be put out/to be annoyed: "Angus was very put out when I said that his summer shirt didn't suit him."

Be run down/to be in poor health after illness, overwork etc.: "She is still run down after her illness and unfit for work."

Be running on empty/to have exhausted all one's resources or sustenance.

Be sent down/to be expelled from a university for misconduct: "She behaved so badly in college that she was sent down and never got her degree."

Be short of/to want or to not have enough: "I'm short for this month's rent."

Be sick of/to hate or to have grown tired of something.

Be sitting pretty/to be comfortably established; to be at an advantage.

Be someone's back/to nag at someone.

Be sure of/to know; to be certain or have certainty with respect to something.

Be taken for a ride/to be deceived or cheated.

Be touch-and-go/to be uncertain whether something will happen or not.

Be under the illusion/to believe mistakenly.

Be under the weather/to be ill.

Be up/to be out of bed: "Don't ring him up at eight o'clock on Sunday morning. He won't be up."

Be up against/to be in severe trouble.

Be up to/to be physically or intellectually able (to perform a certain action): "After his illness, the Principal continued in office though he was no longer up to the work."

Be up to something (some mischief, some trick, to no good)/to be occupied or busy with some mischievous act: "Don't trust her; she is up to some trick." "The girls are very quiet. I wonder what they are up to."

Be used to/to have a level of familiarity or comfort with something: "I'm used to noise. It doesn't worry me."

Be well off/to be rich.

Be well-up-on/to be well-informed and up to date about a subject.

Be worn out/to be exhausted: "She walked all night and wanted to go on working the next day, but we saw that she was completely worn out and persuaded her to stop.

Bear a resemblance/to look like someone or something else.

Beat up/to hit somebody repeatedly so that they are badly hurt; to give a hard beating to; thrash; whip: "When Sam first came, he had to beat up several neighborhood bullies before they would leave him alone."

Become aware of/to find out about; to learn of.

Beef up/1. to make stronger by adding men or equipment; to make more powerful; to reinforce 2. to increase 3. To enlarge: "The university beefed up the baseball coaching staff by adding several good assistants.

Beg the question/to evade the question skillfully; to raise the question; to assume the truth of the thing which is to be proved.

Bear out/to confirm: "This report bears out his theory."

Bear up/to support bad news bravely; to hide feelings of grief: "The news of his death was a great shock to her, but she bore up bravely and none of us realized how much she felt it."

Believe in (believe that something is real)/to have faith in: "Our son believes in Santa Claus." "Do you believe in God?"

Belly up/to go bankrupt, to cease to function; to die: "His company went belly up after the stock
        market crash."
Belong to/to bear relation as a member, adherent, inhabitant, etc.: "This book belongs to
        him." "Does this toy belong to you?"
Bet on the wrong horse/to misread the future; not to choose the winning person or solution.
Bite the bullet/to endure in a difficult situation, to show courage in facing a difficult or
        unpleasant situation.
Blame for/to find fault with; to censure.
Blow away/1. to devastate; to shock deeply, astonish or overwhelm. 2. to fly away: "He dropped
        the ticket, and it blew away in the wind."
Blow it/to fail at something.
Blow one's mind/to become enthusiastic over something as if understanding it for the first time
        in an entirely new light: "Read Shakespeare's book Hamlet; it will blow your mind."
Blow out/1. to cancel; to cut out. 2. to extinguish (a flame) by blowing: "She blew out the
        candles." 3. (of expenditure) to increase suddenly and not according to expectation. 4. to
        astonish or dazzle.
Blow out of/to depart, exceed (budget); (of expenditure) to increase suddenly and not according to
        expectation.
Blow up/1. to destroy by explosion; to break or destroy or be destroyed by explosion;
        explode. 2. to fill with air, inflate, pump up.
Bump into/to strike; to run into someone or something, perhaps unintentionally, as in a crowd.
Bog down or get bogged down/1. to stop progressing; to slow to a halt: "Work on a new hotel
        bogged down because the contractor didn't deliver the needed concrete blocks." 2. to
        become entangled with a variety of obstacles making your efforts unproductive or
        unsatisfying.
Boil away/to be boiled until all (the liquid) has evaporated.
Boil down/1. to reduce the length of; cut down; shorten. 2. to reduce carcasses of stock for
        tallow. 3. Reduce itself to; come down to; be brief or basic: "It all   boils down to money
        in the end."
Boil over/to rise and flow over the sides of the container (used only of hot liquids): "The soup
        boiled over and there was a horrible smell of burning."
Bottom drop out or bottom fall out/1. to fall below an earlier lowest price: "The bottom
        dropped out of the price of Chinese pork bellies." 2. to lose all cheerful qualities; become
        very unhappy, cheerless, or unpleasant: "The bottom dropped out of the day for Sam
        when he saw his report card."
Bottom out/after a decline, to stop falling any lower and stabilize at a low level; a leveling
        out of something that has reached its lowest point; the price of goods or difficult situation
        starts to level off or not get any worse; reach the lowest level: "The share market has now
        bottomed out and is expected to improve by the spring." House prices bottomed out."
Bounce back/to recover health, prosperity, form, etc. after a temporary setback.
Bow out/1. to give up taking part; to excuse oneself from doing any more; to quit: "Mr. Hill
        often quarreled with his partners, so finally he bowed out of the company." 2. to stop
        working after a long tenure; to retire: "John bowed out as train engineer after forty years
        of railroading."
Brag about/to boast.
Break a leg!/an expression meaning, "Good luck!"

Break down/ 1. to smash or hit (something) so that it falls; to cause to fall by force: "The firemen broke down the windows to get into the burning building." "I broke down the door." 2. to stop working; stop functioning; to go wrong; to collapse; to cease to function properly, owing to some fault or weakness; to reduce or destroy the strength or effect of; weaken; to win over: "Our marriage broke down after only a few months." "By helpful kindness the English teacher broke down the new girl's shyness." 3. to cry, or to burst into tears: "She broke down when telling me about her son's tragic death." "Under prolonged interrogation, she broke down in tears." 4. to reduce to the constituent parts; to take a total and sub-divide under various headings so as to give additional information: "You say that 5,000 people use this library. Could you break that down by age-groups?"

Break-even/the point at which one is neither gaining nor losing; to end a series of gains and losses having the same amount you started with; having expenses equal to profits; have equal gains and losses: "The storekeeper made many sales, but her expenses were so high that he just broke even."

Break free/to escape, as in from a prison or jail or captivity.

Break (new) ground/1. to begin a construction project by digging for the foundation; especially, by turning over the formal first spadeful of dirt: "New York city officials and industrial leaders were there as the company broke ground for its new plant." 2. to begin something never done before.

Break in/1. to enter by force from the outside: "The firemen broke in the window of the burning house." 2. to enter by force unlawfully: "Thieves broke in while the family was away." 3. to interrupt someone with a sudden remark: "I was telling them about China when she broke in with a story of her own." 3. to train a horse or animal for use: "We cannot ride a horse safely before he has been broken in."

Break into/1. to enter by force, often illegally; to force an entrance into; to make a rough or unlawful entrance into: "Their house was broken into last night. Thieves broke into the house and stole $1,000." 2. to succeed in beginning an endeavour (a career, business, or social life).

Break into a smile/to start smiling suddenly: "She broke into television as an actress"; to interrupt.

Break new ground/do something no one has done before.

Break off/1. to stop suddenly; to stop talking suddenly; to interrupt oneself: "John and Peter broke off discussions late last night. We were in the middle of an argument but broke off when someone came into the room." 2. End a friendship, relationship or love: "I hear that Michael and Sally have broken off." 3. detach or become detached: "She took a bar of chocolate and broke off a bit."

Break one's heart or break the heart of/1. to feel deep disappointment; to disappoint grievously in love; to grieve (or cause to grieve) very deeply, esp. through love. 2. to crush with sorrow or grief.

Break out/1. to begin (used of evils such as wars, epidemics, fires, etc.): "The Korean War broke out on 25 June 1950." 2. to escape by using force from a prison: "Sam broke out of prison on Friday night."

Break rank/to fail to maintain solidarity.

Break the ice/to ease a first meeting between people; break down social awkwardness and formality; conquer the first difficulties in starting a conversation, getting a party going, or making an acquaintance: "To break the ice, Philip spoke of his interest in mountain climbing, and they soon had a conversation going."

Break the mould/to put an end to a pattern of events or behaviour, especially one that has become rigid and restrictive, by doing things in a markedly different way.

Breakthrough/to be successful after overcoming a difficulty or bar to success: "Dr. Warren failed many times but he finally broke through to locate the black box flight recorder."

Break up/1. to break into pieces; to disintegrate, cause to disintegrate: "She broke up a piece of bread and threw the bits to the birds." 2. to end or terminate (used of school terms, meetings, parties, etc.); to disperse: "Primary schools broke up last week for the summer holidays." 3. to put to an end, especially by separation; to separate: "She broke up the party." "We broke up just a month before our wedding." 3. Stop being friends: "Alice and Patricia were good friends, and they did everything together, but they had a quarrel and broke up."4. to become overwrought emotionally: When he heard the sad news he broke up and cried.

Break with/to separate from; to end membership in; to stop friendly association with: "She had broken with some friends who had changed in their ideas." She broke up with her boyfriend."

Bring about/to cause; produce; lead to.

Bring back/1. to recall to mind; to remind oneself. 2. to return: "You can take my book but please bring it back."3. to revive. 4. to re-introduce.

Bring down/1. to lower. 2. to destroy or remove from power.

Bring home the bacon/to earn a livelihood, especially for a family; to succeed, to win a prize: "Malcolm was a steady fellow, who always brought the home the bacon."

Bring in/1. to introduce to a domicile or place: "Well, don't just stand there. Bring her in to meet us!" 2. to convey or carry something: "Could you bring in the tea."

Bring into the open/to make public: "WikiLeaks brought a lot of government secrets into the open."

Bring into force/to become law and have the force of a legal sanction.

Bring off/to succeed.

Bring on/to cause to start.

Bring out/introducing.

Bring round/1. to persuade someone to accept a previously opposed suggestion: "After a lot of argument, I brought her round to my point of view." 2. restore to consciousness: "He fainted with the pain, but a little brandy soon brought him round." 3. bring to one's house: "He has finished that book you lent him; he'll bring it round tonight."

Bring something to light/to reveal.

Bring together/to gather.

Bring up/1. to train, educate. 2. to raise children; care for a child as it grows; to take care of: "After my parents died, my grandparents brought up me." "They brought up all their children to believe in God." 3. to mention or introduce a topic; to introduce it in a conversation; begin a discussion of; speak of: "At the class, William brought up the idea of a picnic." "He brought up that subject again."

Bring up to date/to change to include the most recent information/ideas.

Brush off/to refuse to hear or believe, quickly and impatiently; not take seriously or think important: "Peter brushed off Andrew, warning that he might fall from the tree."

Brush up/to refresh one's memory or skill by practice or review; improve; make perfect: "He spent the summer brushing up on his European history as he was to teach in the Fall."

Buck the trend/the opposite of what is commonly happening.

Bucket down/to pour (as in rain).

Bugger up/to ruin, wreck or root.

Build-up/1. to make out of separate pieces or layers; construct from parts: "Joshua built up a fort out of a large ball of snow." "Olivia built up a cake of three layers." 2. to cover over or fill up with buildings: "The fields where Lachlan's father played as a boy are all built up now." 3. to increase slowly or by small amounts; grow: "Ethan built up a bank account by saving regularly." "The noise built up until Chloe couldn't stand it any longer." 4. to make stronger or better or more effective: "Samuel exercised to build up his muscles." "Ella was studying to build up her Japanese."

Bump into/to meet by chance; meet without expecting to; come upon by accident: "I bumped into Susan in John Street yesterday."

Burn down/to destroy or be destroyed completely by fire (used of buildings): "The mob burnt down the police station."

Burn the midnight oil/to study or work until late into the night.

Burn one's fingers/to get hurt from meddling with or engaging in anything: "She burned her fingers in the stock market once and didn't want to try again."

Burn out/1. to die out for want of fuel. 2. to have no energy mentally and physically; get in trouble doing something and fear to do it again; learn caution through an unpleasant experience. 3. destroy by fire or by overheating: "Mrs. Scott burned out the clutch on her car." 4. to break, tire, or wear out by using up all the power, energy and strength of something: "David burned out in the first part of the race and could not finish."

Burn rubber/to start up a car or a motorcycle from dead stop so fast that the tires leave a mark on the road.

Burn the candle at both ends/to have very little sleep (due to too much activity).

Burn the midnight oil/to stay up late, usually to study or write.

Burn your fingers/to come off badly.

Burst into tears/to start crying; to show sudden emotion by shedding tears.

Bury one's sand in the sand or one's head in the sand/to keep from seeing, knowing, or understanding something dangerous or unpleasant; to refuse to see or face something; pretend that something isn't happening: "If there is a war, we cannot just bury our heads in the sand."

Bury the hatchet/to settle an argument or quarrel; end a quarrel; cease to quarrel; settle a quarrel or end a war; make peace; restore a relationship, make up after quarrelling: "The two women had been enemies a long time, but after the flood they buried the hatchet."

Butt out/to mind one's own business and not interfere in something which is not one's proper concern.

Buy back the farm/to attempt removal of foreign ownership of domestic-based companies as government policy.

Buy out/to buy ownership of; purchase the stock of: "Emma bought out several small stockholders." 2. Buy all the goods of; purchase the merchandise of: "Mr. Smith bought out a nearby hardware store."

C

Call a spade a spade/to tell the truth about something, even if it is not very polite.

Call after/to hail; recall.

Call at (a place)/to visit or stop in: "He called at the bank and arranged to transfer some money."

Call back, phone back or ring back/to return a telephone call.

Call for/1. to need; require; demand: "The barrister called for a unanimous verdict" "She's got the job! This calls for a cerebration." 2. to visit a place to collect a person or thing: "I am going to a pop concert with Victor. He is calling me at eight so I must be ready."

Call in/1. to ask to come to an official place for a special reason; summon: "It was too late to call in a plumber." "We called in a doctor." 2. to look in. 3. to visit somebody for a short time; drop in: "Call in on your way home and tell me how the examination went."

Call in question, call into question, call in doubt/to say (something) that may be a mistake; express doubt about; question: "Richard called in question John's remark that basketball is safer than football."

Call it a day/to stop for the day; quit: "John studied hard till 10 p.m., then decided to call it a day and go to bed."

Call it quits/to decide to stop what one is doing; quit: "When Charles painted half the garage, he called it quits."

Call names/to use ugly or unkind words when speaking to someone or when talking about someone: "Richard got so mad he started calling Charles names."

Call off/to cancel something not yet started or abandon something already in progress; decide not to do something that has been arranged; stop (something planned); quit; cancel; abandon: "They called off the meeting. The race was called off because of rain."

Call on or call upon/1. to make a call on; visit: "I'll call on Dr Adams." "He called on Friday." 2. demand: "The prime minister called upon his people to make sacrifices for the good of their country." 3. ask a student a question in class.

Call out/to summon someone to leave his house to deal with a situation outside: "We called out the guard."

Call the shots/to be in command; give orders; be in charge; direct; control: "Joseph is a first-rate leader who knows how to call the shots.

Call up/1. to call on the telephone; phone: "He took the phone and called up Sandra." 2. to tell to come (as before a court). 3. to make someone think of; bring to mind; remind. 4. to bring together for a purpose; bring into action: "Nicholas called up all his strength, pushed past the players blocking him, and ran for a touchdown." 5. to summon for military service: "The marine called up its reserves when war seemed near."

Calm somebody down/to become calmer, make somebody calmer: "Calm down. There's no point in getting angry."

Can't hold a candle to/to be nowhere near as good as.

Can't turn the clock back/can't return to the past.

Cancel out/to destroy the effect of; balance or make useless: "Paul's hot temper cancels out his skill as a player."

Care about or care for/to be interested in or concerned about somebody or something; consider important: "I don't care about her problems – I've got enough of my own."

Care for/1. to like, love: "Would you care for a cup of coffee?" "She didn't much care for his manner." 2. to look after someone: "She is caring for two orphans in Vietnam." "My wife would hate to get old without anyone to care for her." 3. In the negative, it can also be a formal way of expressing disapproval: "I do not care for his sense of humor." 4. It is also used to express a polite way of offering something to someone: "Would you care for something to eat?" 5. to keep.

Carry away/to cause very strong feeling; excite or delight to the loss of cool judgement: "The music carried him away."

Carry off/to cause death of; kill: "Years ago influenza carried off tens of thousands of people."

Carry on/1. to work at; be busy with; manage; keep; last; continue along; continue doing something: "They'll take a short break and then carry on with the meeting." "Thomas and his father carried on hardware business." 2. make a fuss: "These pupils have been carrying on all afternoon."

Carry out/to do; perform (duties); obey (orders and instructions); complete an action; do something as planned or instructed; put into action; follow; execute; undertake: "Tom listened carefully and carried out the teacher's instructions." "They carried out a search for the missing child."

Carry over/1. to save for another time. 2. to transfer (as a figure) from one column, page, or book to another: "When she added up the figures, she carried over the   total into next year's account book." 3. to continue in another place.

Carry the can/to take responsibility for a misdemeanour; bear the responsibility; take the blame.

Carry the day/to win completely; succeed in one's aim; win a contest or competition.

Carry the weight of the world on one's shoulders/to feel worried or sad about things.

Carry through/1. to put into action: "Mr. Baker was not able to carry through his plans for a hike because he broke his leg." 2. do something planned; put into action: "Nancy makes good plans, but she cannot carry through with any of them." 3. Keep (someone) from failing or stopping; bring through; help: "When the tire blew out, the rules Peter had learned in driving class carried him through safely."

Carve up/to divide something.

Cash in on/1. to gain a return from. 2. to turn to one's advantage.

Cast around/to search.

Cast the first stone/to be the first to attack; to be the first to blame someone; lead accusers against a wrongdoer: "Although Kenneth saw the girl cheating, he did not want to cast the first stone."

Catch cold/to contact the common cold.

Catch fire/to begin to burn.

Catch on/1. to understand; learn about: "That boy catches on quickly." 2. to become popular; be done or used by many people.

Catch one's eyes/to attract attention: "She caught his eye as he moved through the crowd, and waved at him to come over."

Catch red-handed/to catch someone in the act of doing something bad.

Catch sight of/to see suddenly or unexpectedly: "Donald caught sight of a sparrow in a maple tree." " I caught sight of her."

Catch up/1. to take or pick up suddenly; grab (something): "He caught up the book from the table and ran out of the room." 2. to capture or trap (someone) in a situation; concern or interest very much: "The Nelson family was caught up in the war in Europe and we did not see them again till it was over." 3. to move faster so as to reach their location from behind; overtake; come even: "Bill ran hard and tried to catch up to his friends." 4. to find out about or get proof to punish or arrest: "George is always fooling in class but the teacher will catch up with him someday." 5. to finish; not lose or be behind: "Kenneth stayed up late to get caught up on his homework."

Catch up on/to make up a deficiency: "He caught up on his sleep. He'll catch up on work later."

Catch up with (someone)/to reach the same position or level as someone; overtake, not pass: "He'll soon catch up with you." "I've missed a whole term; I'll have to work hard to catch up with the rest of the class."

Cave in/1. to fall or collapse inward: "The building caved in and crushed 55 people." 2. weaken and be forced to give up: "The children begged their mother to take them to the circus until she caved in."

Center around/to be concerned primarily: "The movie centers around a group in a city squat."

Center in/it is used in the passive to refer to the place where an activity or event is concentrated: "The movie industry is still centered in Hollywood."

Center on/to focus attention on an event, situation or concern (often used in the passive): "Every fourth year global attention is centered on the World Cup."

Change hands/to become the property of a different owner.

Change horses in midstream/to change one's mind or tactics midway through a course of action.

Change the gear/to begin to move or act differently, usually more rapidly.

Chase a rainbow/to think and pursue the impossible.

Chase after/to pursue something, not necessarily in vain.

Cheat on/1. to deceive. 2. to be sexually unfaithful to (one's spouse or lover).

Check in/1. to register; sign one's name (at a hotel or convention): "He checked in at the Hilton Hotel last night." "Conference delegates have to check in at this desk." 2. to arrive: Their friends did not check in until Sunday."

Check into/to investigate.

Check on or check up/to try to find out the truth or rightness of; make sure of; examine; inspect; investigate: "They checked on Edward's age by getting his birth record." "They've checked on her story and it seems to be true."

Change one's mind/to change ideas or opinions.

Check out/1. to pay the bill and leave. 2. to go away; leave: "They hoped their guest would stay, but he had to check out before Monday." 3. to make a list or record of: "We checked out all the goods in the store." 4. to try; test: "He checked out the car battery." 5. to investigate. 6. to borrow a book from a library.

Check up/to find out or try to find out the truth or correctness of something; to make sure of something; investigate: "Mrs. Carter thought he had heard a burglar in the house, so Mr. Carter checked up but found nobody."

Cheer up/1. an exhortation to be happier; feel happy; stop being sad or discouraged; become hopeful, joyous, or glad: "Mr. Turner was sad at losing the business, but he cheered up at the sight of his daughter." 2.to make someone feel happier: "He went to the hospital to cheer up a sick friend."

Cherry-pick/to choose or take the best or most profitable of (a number of things), esp. for one's own benefit or gain.

Chicken out/to stop doing something because of fear, or decide not to do something after all: "He said he'd ride a motorcycle on the highway, but he chickened out."

Chill out/to relax; calm down.

Chip in or kick in/to contribute; give together with others: "The pupils chipped in a dime apiece for the teacher's Easter present."

Chase rainbows/to pursue an illusory goal.

Claim the life of/something that takes a person's life: "Fire claimed the lives of six people in the town last night.".

Clamp down/to put strict controls in place; to enforce the rule of laws.

Clean out/1. to take everything from; empty; strip: "Paul's friends cleaned him out when they were playing cards last night." 2. to clear and tidy up thoroughly (a room, cupboard or drawer): "She must clean out the spare room."

Clean-up/1. to clean everything (a mess, e.g. anything spilt); to put in order; make clean and orderly: "Clean up all the spilt milk." "He cleaned up the house for his party." 2. to make a lot of money; make a big profit: Brian cleaned up in the share market last year."

Clean up one's acts/to alter one's lifestyle, especially if one has purged it of what are seen as antisocial aspects.

Clear away/1. to remove articles, usually in order to make space: "Could I clear away these papers?" 2. to disperse: "The dark clouds soon cleared away."

Clear off/to go away (from an open space): "'Clear off,' said the rancher angrily." "

Clear out/1. to empty (a room, building) and take everything out; to go away: "He cleared his room out and gave his old toys away." 2. to leave suddenly; go away; depart: "John cleared out without paying his room rent." 3. to empty a space or place, usually to make room for something else: "Mum'll clear out this drawer, and you can put your things in it.

Clear the air/to eliminate dissension, ambiguity, or tension from a discussion or situation; to remove angry feelings; misunderstanding, or confusion: "The Prime Minister's statement that he would run for office again cleared the air of rumors and guessing."

Clear the deck/to prepare for action.

Clear up/1. to make plain or clear; explain; solve: "Maybe he can clear up your problem." 2. (of weather) to get better; become clear and brighter; become fine after clouds or rain: "The weather cleared up after the thunderstorm." 3. to make tidy and clean. 4. to finish (some work which still remains to be done): "He has some letters which he must clear up before he leaves tonight." 5. to solve (a mystery).

Climb on the bandwagon or jump on the bandwagon/to support a plan or cause for personal profit or advantage; join popular cause or movement: "At the last possible moment, the Congressman jumped on the winning candidate's bandwagon."

Climb out/to leave or extricate oneself from a place: "He swam up and down the pool, and then climbed out."

Climb over/to traverse or cross a boundary or summit of a place: "The wall wasn't very high, so they climbed over."

Climb the corporate ladder/to progress to a higher level in an organization, career, or society.

Close down or shut down/to stop doing business; shut permanently (a shop or business); to stop all work, as in a factory; to stop work entirely; stop operations: "The factory closed down for Easter."

Close in/to come in nearer from all sides; to approach from all sides (used of mist, darkness, enemies, vessels/craft, etc.): "They wanted the boat to reach shore before the fog closed in." "As the darkness was closing in we decided to stay where we were."

Close doors/1. to keep someone or something from entering or joining; become closed. 2. to fail as a business; go bankrupt: "Business was so poor that Tommy had to close the company's doors after sixty years."

Close ranks/1. to come together in a line, as a formation, especially in a battle maneuver. 2. to stop quarrelling and work together; unite and fight together: "The Liberal Party and Labor Party closed ranks to win the war."

Close the books/to stop taking orders; end a bookkeeping period: "The tickets were all sold, so Mary Anne said to close the books on the 25th of the month."

Close the door or shut the door/to prevent any more action or talk about a subject: "After Mac makes up his mind, he closes the door to any more arguments."

Close up/to" come nearer together (of people in a line): If you pupils closed up a bit there'd be room for another one to sit down."

Collide into/to bump into.

Come a long way/to show much improvement; make great progress: "The university has come a long way since its beginning."

Come about/to take place; happen; occur: "When Joanne woke up, she was in the hospital, but she didn't know how that had come about."

Come across /1. to find by chance; to locate someone or something unexpectedly; find or meet by chance; discover by chance: "He came across this old book in the library." 2. to make an impression: "Rachael came across well at the convention in her speech."

Come after/to follow.

Come alive/1. to brighten up and become active; become alert or attentive; wake up and look alive: "When Lily mentioned money, the girls came alive." "Joshua pushed the starter button; the engine came to life with a roar."

Come along/1. to go with someone; accompany. 2. to make progress; improve; succeed: "Matthew was coming along well after the operation." "Sonya is coming right along learning the piano."

Come around/to happen or appear again and again in regular order; regain consciousness: "I will tell Jacob when he comes around.

Come back/1. to reply; answer: "Brandon came back sharply in the defense of his client." 2. to regain a former position; reach again a place lost: "After a year off to have her baby son, the singer came back to even greater fame." 3. to return: "Anne is leaving today and coming back on Friday."

Come by/to obtain or acquire: "How did he come by that money? How did he come by such a fortune?"

Come clean/to tell all; tell the whole truth; confess: "The girl suspected of stealing the watch came clean after long questioning."

Come down/1. to reduce itself; amount to no more than: "The quarrel finally came down to a question of which girl would do dishes." 2. to land; be handed down or passed along; to descend from parent to child; to pass from older generation to younger ones: "Sally's necklace had come down to her from her mother."

Come down with/to catch: "The whole school staff came down with the flu last winter."

Come (in) first/to win: "Basai came in first in the 100m dash."

Come from/either to hail originally from a particular place or to live there at the moment: "He comes from Sydney, Australia."

Come full circle/1. to change continuously until returning to the original position; to change and develop, only to end up where one started. 2. to become totally opposed to one's own earlier conviction on a given subject: "Today's conservative politician has come full circle from her former radical student days."

Come good/to regain form, health, interest.

Come home to roost/ to reap the result of what one does, often in the sense of a misdeed or wrongdoing; to have to face the consequences; to experience karma in the negative sense.

Come in/1. to enter: "Come in and sit down." "A strange boy in black came in." 2. to finish or complete a sports contest or other competition: "She came in first in the hundred-meter-dash."

Come in for/1. to receive or reap the results of a particular line of behaviour (often negative): "Her conduct came in for much criticism."

Come in handy/"to be useful; prove useful: The Japanese language John learned in high school came in handy when he was in the army in Japan."

Come in on/to join; to interrupt; to enter a room while others are meeting (privately): "He came in on their meeting, which was not appreciated, as it was confidential."

Come in, spinners/in two-up, a call made to signify that all the bets are laid and it is time to spin the coins.

Come into/1. to enter: "Come into the lounge, and I'll show you my old photographs." 2. to receive, especially after another's death; get possession of: "She came into a lot of money when her father died."

Come into line/to conform.

Come into money/to inherit money or wealth: "If a rich member of someone's family dies, it is possible that you will come into some money."

Come into view/to appear.

Come next/to follow.

Come of age/to have fully developed; to mature.

Come off/1. to fall, usually from a horse or vehicle: "My daughter came off her bike." 2. to do well; succeed; prosper; of a plan or scheme (used in negative): "Her plans haven't come off very well." "Jack's afraid that scheme of Joshua's won't come off." 3. to take place; happen as arranged. 4. to end its run (of a play, exhibition etc.)

Come on/to be quick; hurry (often said to someone who is hesitating or delaying): "Come on! Everybody is waiting for you."

Come on stream/to start production.

Come out/1. to be revealed; exposed; to be published (a book); publish: "The new book on deep sea fishing has just come out." 2. to end; finish: "The game came out as they had hoped." 3. come out of the closet; to identify/claim one's sexuality. 4. to make an exit; leave. 4. to be removed (of stains): "Coffee stains don't usually come out."

Come around. 2. finally to accept a previously opposed suggestion: "His father at first refused to let him study abroad, but he came around to it in the end." 3. to come to someone's location: "He'll come round after dinner and tell you the plan." 4. to recover consciousness: "When we found her she was unconscious, but she came round in a half hour."

Come out of one's shelf/to become less shy and retiring.

Come to/1. to arrive at or reach: "During his years at the school, John came to know the road well." 2. to amount to: "When it is all added together, it will come to $30.53." 3. to recover consciousness; wake up, especially after being unconscious rather than asleep: "She has just come to after her operation."

Come to light/to be revealed; appear, be found; be discovered; become known; appear: "It will come to light sooner or later." "When the old man died, it came to light that he was actually rich."

Come to mind/to occur to someone; to be thought of.

Come to nothing/to end in failure; be in vain: "The dog's attempts to climb the tree after the monkey came to nothing."

Come to rest/to land.

Come to terms with something/to accept a state of affairs.

Come to the party/to contribute to or join in some venture; to assist with money; fall in with one's plan.

Come to the point/to talk about the important thing; reach the central question: "James was giving a lot of history and explanation, but his father asked him to come to the point."

Come to one's aid/to assist or to provide relief, usually in a time of distress or following an accident.

Come through (or off) with flying colors/to perform or witness something accomplished in splendid fashion: "The church bring-and-buy came off with flying colors."

Come together/to join.

Come true/to really happen; change from a dream or a plan into a fact: "It took years of planning and saving, but our seagoing vacation came true at last."

Come under attack/to face an assault; to be thrown on the defensive.

Come under the microscope/to be examined critically.

Come unstuck/when two persons or things cease to be joined, often as a result of an unusual prior situation: "The cars came unstuck following their fender bender.".

Come up/1. to be introduced in a conversation; become a subject for discussion or decision to talk about or decide about; be mentioned: "She was a good saleswoman, and price came up until the very last." 2. to provide; supply; furnish: "For years, Mr. Campbell kept coming up with new and good ideas." 3. to rise to the surface: "Dandelions are coming up everywhere." 4. to approach; come close enough to talk: "A policeman was standing a few meters away. She came up to me and said, 'You can't park here.'"

Come up to/1. to meet, satisfy, or reach: "Did the trip to Japan come up to your expectations?" 2. to approach; come close enough to talk, stressing interpersonal objective: "He came right up to me and told me he'd like to ask me out."

Come up with/to produce an idea; invent: "Sally is very creative. She's always coming up with new ideas."

Come upon/to meet; find by chance.

Compare to/to point out a resemblance between two people, things or situations: "With her small eyes and thin face, she was often compared to a rat."

Compare with/to show the similarity or dissimilarity between things that are usually in the same category: "If you compare the sound of a pigeon with that of a cuckoo, you can hear the difference immediately." "Her singing compares with that of Joan Sutherland."

Compete against/to play, oppose in a game or sport contest; to try to better in some context.

Conceive of/to invent something, like a plan or an idea.

Consist of (refers to a whole unit)/to form or to be composed of; to comprise: "The computer package consists of a PC, a 14 inch screen, a keyboard, software, and user support." "This desert consists of a few common ingredients."

Continue on/to continue.

Contrast with/to be obviously different from something else.

Cook the books/to falsify accounts.

Cool down or cool off/to lose or cause to lose the heat of any deep feeling (as love, enthusiasm, or anger); make or become calm; lose one's anger ; cooled or indifferent; lose interest: "James was deeply in love with Anne before he left for college, but he cooled down before he got back."

Cool off/1. to lower body temperature: "Cool off with a glass of cold milk." 2. to take a rest or leave off an irritation or angry moment: "I was livid, but my mother told me to cool off."

Cop out/to avoid committing oneself in situation where doing so would result in difficulties; opt out in gutless way, as by giving some feeble justification; give up.

Cop the lot/to bear the brunt of some misfortune; suffer multiple misfortunes at once.

Cope with/to accept or suffer something; to handle a situation: "He's got more work than he can cope with." "Because she could not cope with the volume of work she called on her colleagues to deal with the problem."

Cost the earth/to be very expensive.

Cross your heart/to promise.

Couldn't care less/to be indifferent; not care at all: " The pupils couldn't care less about the band; they talked all through the concert."

Couldn't help it/to avoid it; prevent it.

Count (up) on/to depend on; rely on; trust: "The team was counting on Peter to win the race."

Count out/to leave (someone) out of a plan; not expect (someone) to share in an activity; exclude: 'When the coach was planning who would play in the big game, he counted John out as John had a hurt leg."

Count on it/to expect it to happen, rely on it: I wouldn't count on it.

Count the pennies/to be careful about how much one spends.

Cover up/1. to cover completely 2. to attempt to conceal the truth. 3. to hide something wrong or bad from attention: "A crooked banker tried to cover up her stealing some of the bank's money by starting a fire to destroy the records."

Crack down/to enforce laws or rules strictly; require full obedience to a rule: "The police suddenly cracked down on the selling of cigarettes to minors."

Crack up/1. to wreck or be wrecked; smash up: "She cracked up her car." 2. burst into laughter or cause to burst into laughter.

Cracked up to be/asserted to be.

Crash and burn/1. to collapse from exhaustion. 2. to fail miserably; to flop.

Crash the gate/to enter without a ticket or without paying; attend without an invitation or permission: "Jeff got into the circus without paying. He crashed the gate."

Crop up/to appear; arise unexpectedly or by accident.

Cross one's fingers/to be hoping for luck or a happy outcome; hope that everything will work out well.

Cross one's mind/to have a sudden or passing thought; come to mind; occur to someone: "At first James was puzzled by Mary's waving, but then it crossed his mind that she was trying to tell him something."

Cross out/to rub something out; to draw a line through (writing) because it was wrong (a mistake or a word etc.): "She made a mistake so she crossed her name out. She crossed her name."

Cross the floor/to join the opposing side in Parliament; to change political parties.

Cross the Rubicon/to take an irrevocable step.

Cross the wire/to finish a race: "The Korean crossed the wire just behind the Chinese."

Crow before one is out of woods/to be glad or brag before one is safe from danger or
trouble: "Lisa nearly died during the operation; she is not out of the woods yet."
Cry foul over/to complain of an injustice, especially belatedly when other expedients have failed.
Cry over spilled milk/to cry or complain about that has already happened; be unhappy about
something that cannot be helped: "After the baby tore up Maria's picture book, Maria's
mother told her there was no use crying over spilled milk."
Cry wolf/(habitually) to sound a false alarm; give a false warning of danger.
Cut a long story short/to conclude a lengthy account of events; in lieu of a longer discussion,
to provide a brief or summary statement of the issue or point.
Cut and paste/v. in computing, to delete data or text in a document and insert it
elsewhere in the same or another document..
Cut a ribbon/to perform an opening ceremony by formally cutting a ribbon string across the
entrance to a building, road, etc.
Cut and run/to make a quick get-away, quit.
Cut both ways/1. to serve both sides of an argument. 2. to have both good and bad effects.
Cut corners/to undertake something in what appears to be the easiest, quickest, or cheapest way.
Cut down/1. to lessen; reduce in size or amount; limit: "I must cut down expenses, or I'll be
getting into debt." "I'd better cut down on fatty foods, cakes and alcohol." 2. to fell (a
tree): "If he cuts down all the trees, he will ruin the land."
Cut down on/to eat, drink or do something less often; reduce: "We cut down on our sugar."
"Even though he cut down on beer, he was still very overweight."
Cut down tall poppies/to undermine, not only another's self-importance but also any kind of
egregious distinction or achievement.
Cut in/1. to slip into a traffic lane ahead of another car when there isn't room or aggressively;
force way into a place between others in a line of cars, people, etc.; push in: "After
passing several cars, John cut in too soon and nearly caused an accident." 2. to interrupt:
"Victor was so rude. I was talking to Jackie, when he cut in."
Cut into/to make less; reduce: "The other houses got old and shabby, and that cut into the
value of her house."
Cut it out/to stop; remove.
Cut loose/1. to free from ties or connections; cut the fastenings of: "He hastily cut the boat loose
from its anchor." 2. to break away from control; get away and be free: "The girl left home
and cut loose from her parents' control."
Cut no ice/to make no impression upon someone.
Cut off/1. to separate or block: "Her rudeness cuts her off from friends she might have."
"Five villages were cut off by the heavy rain that had fallen overnight." 2. to stop;
disconnect, discontinue supply (usually of gas, water, electricity etc.): "Their water
supply was cut off while repairs were carried out." 3. to create a barrier to safety: "They
were cut off by the tide and had to be rescued by boat."
Cut out/1. to finish, especially a contracted job or a supply of something. 2. to stop an annoying
activity; stop; quit: "The engine cut out just before landing." "Chris was teasing the dog
and Daniel told him to cut it out." 3. to displace in favour: "Ronald cut Anthony out with
Deborah." 4. to cut from a piece of cloth or paper a smaller piece of a desired shape:
"When she is making a dress, she marks the cloth with chalk and then cuts it out." 5. to
omit ; leave out: "If I want to get thin, I must cut out sugar."
Cut something to the bone/to reduce something to the bare minimum.

Cut to the chase/to get to the point.
Cut up/to cut into small pieces: "She'll cut up the meat for the child." "We chopped down the
    tree and cut it up for firewood."

D
Damp down/to reduce the intensity of.
Deal in/to buy and sell.
Deal with/to handle; manage; do whatever has to be done: "Every problem that came up was
    dealt with well." "A special commission will deal with donations for the earth quake
    victims?"
Decide on (upon)/to pick: "They finally decided on holiday in Hong Kong." "Anne
    decided on the blue skirt."
Deliver the goods/1. to carry things and give them to the person who wants them: "Chris
    delivered the goods to the right house." 2. to produce the promised results, to succeed in
    doing well what is expected: "This power tool surely delivered the goods."
Depend on (or upon)/to await, to wait and see (about): "They may go sailing – it depends on
    the weather." "They may arrive late this afternoon. It depends on the traffic."
Develop into/to turn into
Die away or die down/to fade; become gradually fainter till inaudible; become gradually
    calmer and finally disappear (of riots, fires, excitements etc.); come slowly to an end;
    grow slowly less and weaker; gradually disappear; come to an end: "The music died
    away." "The clamor finally died down." "She waited until the excitement had died
    down." "Her mother's anger died away."
Die for/an informal expression meaning extremely good or desirable.
Die hard/to take a long time to change or disappear.
Die out/to become extinct (of customs, races, species of animals etc.): "Tigers would die out
    if men could shoot as many as they wished."
Dig deep/to give money; in sports, to use energy reserves and courage to make an effort.
Dig in/1. to prepare ditches for protection against an enemy attack. 2. to go seriously to work;
    work hard: ""Peter dug in and finished his homework.
Dig up/to find or get (something) with some effort: "Daniel dug up some useful material for
    his English composition." "Henry asked each boy to dig up one dollar to pay for the hot
    dogs and soda."
Dig your own grave/to make a situation bad for oneself.
Dish out/to serve (food) from large bowl or plate: "Lisa's mother asked her to dish out the
    beans." "He dished out drinks to all the kids."
Dish up/to serve from a bowl or pot: "Mother asked my sister to dish up the peas."
Dive in/to enter into the water: "Anne walked up to the edge of the pool and dived in."
Do away with/to pull down; put an end to; stop; abolish: "The city should do away with that old
    merry go round." "We should do away with that rule."
Do (my) homework/to research or investigate.
Do it easy/to make the best of it while inside.
Do it tough/to carry on through difficult times; take prison life badly.
Do one's bit/to serve one's cause or country.
Do out of/ to prevent from having by deceit.
Do over/to repeat.

Do a roaring trade/to sell large amounts of something; do very good business.

Do someone a favour/to do something for someone as act of kindness.

Do the hard yards/to carry out difficult task

Do the trick/to prove successful; bring success in doing something; have a desired result: "William was not passing in English, but he studied harder and that did the trick." "The car wheels slipped on the ice, so David put sand under them, which did the trick."

Do time/to spend time in prison as sentence for a crime.

Do up/1. (for a coat, a shoelace, buttons) to fasten; tie: "It's quite cold. Do up your overcoat before you go out."; 2. (of a building or a room) to repair and improve; redecorate: "When he does this room up he'll paint the walls cream."

Doing up/repairing or improving something.

Do with/1. to find enough for one's needs; manage: "Some boys can do with very little spending money." 2. to make use of; find useful or helpful: "After cleaning out the basement, the girl could do with a bath."

Do without/to manage in the absence of a person or thing: "I had to do without petrol during the fuel crisis." ""If there isn't any milk they'll have to do without it.

Do your best (or utmost)/to try; to do something as well as one can.

Doctor history/to record a distorted view of history to serve a particular agenda.

Don't bet on it/used to express doubt about an assertion or situation.

Don't hold your breath/don't expect something to happen immediately.

Don't mince the matter/to speak plainly and frankly.

Don't rock the boat/don't spoil things which are pleasant or comfortable.

Doom to failure/to ensure failure.

Doze off/to fall asleep.

Drag on/to pass very slowly: "The cold winter months dragged on until they thought spring would never come."

Drag one's feet/to act slowly or reluctantly: "The children wanted to watch television, and dragged their feet when their father told them to go to bed."

Draw a line or draw the line/1. to think of as different. 2. to set a limit to what will be done; say something cannot be done: "I would like to invite everybody to my party, but I have to draw a line somewhere."

Draw back/to retire; recoil; move back; back away; step backward: "When Richard spotted the rattlesnake, de drew back and aimed his shotgun." "Some juice from the grapefruit that Mother was eating squirted in her eye, and she drew back in surprise."

Draw near/to approach or come closer; to gather unto oneself.

Draw the attention of/to show, remind or point out.

Draw lines in the sand/to set limits or boundaries (law-making bodies).

Draw together/to unite.

Draw up/1. to make a written plan or agreement; write (something) in its correct form; put in writing: "The rich woman had her lawyers draw up her will so that each of her children would receive part of her money when she died." 2. Plan or prepare; begin to write out: "Plans are being drawn up for a new university next year." 3. stop (of vehicles): "The truck drew up at the kerb and the driver got out."

Dream up/to invent.

Dress up/1. to put on best or special clothes: "Charles hated being dressed up and took off his best suit as soon as he got home from church." 2. to disguise.

Dressed to kill/to wear attractive and flamboyant clothes in order to make a striking impression.

Drink up/to drink completely.

Drive a bargain or drive a hard bargain/1. to buy or sell at a good price; succeed in a trade or
      deal: "John's collie is a champion; it should be easy for John to drive a bargain when he
      sells his puppies." 2. Make an agreement that is better for oneself than the other person;
      make an agreement for one's advantage. 3. to haggle or bargain, usually in the interest of
      avarice.

Drive away or drive off/to leave from a place, a person: "Hannah got into the car and drove
      away."

Drive at/to try or want to say; mean; trying to convey: "I don't understand what she's driving at."
      "Joseph did not understand what the coach was driving at." "She had been talking for half
      an hour before anyone realized what she was driving at."

Drive someone to the wall/to force someone into a hopeless situation by circumstances.

Drop a bombshell/to disclose disturbing news or information; make a startling
      announcement: "Our golden years were just about to begin when James dropped a
      bombshell; all our married life he had been having affairs."

Drive on/to continue driving.

Drive someone crazy/to annoy.

Drop a hint/to give an indirect suggestion.

Drop dead/to go away or be quiet.

Drop a line/to write and mail a note or letter: "Deborah's friend asked her to drop a line while
      she was away on vacation." "Please drop a line to me when you get to New York."

Drop by/to visit informally.

Drop in (on)/to visit informally; make a short or unplanned visit; pay a call; make a casual visit:
"Drop in (by) to see Chris someday." "The Andersons dropped in on
      some old friends on their vacation to New York." "She dropped in for a few minutes to
      ask if she could borrow your power drill."

Drop in on/to pay a short visit: "Peter is always dropping in on us without warning."

Drop like a stone/to fall.

Drop off/1. to leave something or someone somewhere; take (someone or something) part of
      the way one is going: "Thomas asked Mrs. Williams to drop him off at the library on her
      way downtown." 2. abandon: "The lecture wasn't very interesting. In fact, he dropped off
      in the middle of it. "

Drop out (of)/to stop going to school or class; stop before one has completely finished the
      course; to quit, stop participating, stop attending; quit; stop; leave or withdraw; retire
      from a scheme or plan: "In the middle of the decade, Paul went to university but dropped
      out of it now." "John got a blister on his foot and had to drop out." "They planned to hire
      a coach for the excursion but so many people have dropped out that it will not be
      needed."

Drum up/to get by trying or asking again and again; attract or encourage by continued effort:
      "The furniture dealer tried to drum up business by advertising low prices."

Dry up/1. to become dry. 2. wither; disappear or vanish as if by evaporating: "The
      Congressman's influence dried up when he was voted out of office."

Dumb down/to act dumber than one is; to oversimplify, perhaps inappropriately.

Dummy spit/a temper tantrum.

Dust off/to get ready to use again: "Three years after he graduated from school, Paul
decided to dust off his algebra book again."
Dwell on or dwell upon/to stay on a subject; not leave something or want to leave; not stop
talking or writing about: "Donald dwelt on his mistake long after the test was
over." "Their eyes dwelled on the beautiful sunset."

E
Ease up or ease off/to make or become less nervous; relax; work easier: "When the boss realized
that George had been overworking, he eased off his load."
Eat away at/to rot, rust, or destroy, gradually reduce or damage
Eat humble pie/to be humbled; accept insult or shame; admit error and apologize; admit
one's fault, humiliate oneself while admitting wrong: "John told a lie about Kenneth, and
when he was found out, he had to eat humble pie."
Eat in /to eat at home.
Eat out/to eat at a restaurant; eat away from home: "Peter ate out often even he wasn't out of
town."
Eat up with/1. Get as a result. 2. to feel jealousy, curiosity or desire very intensely.
Embark on/to start a big, important job or a journey.
End up/1. to come to an end; be ended or finished; to stop. 2. Finally to reach or arrive; land:
"Your father hopes that you don't end up in jail." 3. Die, be killed.
End up in smoke/1. to come to nothing. 2. burn up vigorously. 3. to flare up in anger.
Enter for/to become a competitor or candidates for a contest, examination, etc.: "Ten
thousand competitors have entered for the next Boston Marathon."
Every cloud has a silver lining/bad things result in something good.
Exert yourself/to struggle.
Explain away/to explain (something) so that it does not seem true or important: "Steven
explained away his unfinished homework by showing the teacher his broken arm in a
cast."

F
Face lights up/to look happy suddenly.
Face the music/to confront the consequences of an action; approach an unenviable
situation; confront the worst; accept responsibility and criticism (for an action or
decision); accept the consequences; confront boldly and win; defy: "The girl was caught
cheating in an examination and had to face the music." "If she does, she will have to face
the music."
Face up to something/to accept a situation bravely; face; admit – there is a greater determination
to deal with or accept something unpleasant: "Let her face up to her mistakes." "I've got
to face up to my responsibilities." "The government has faced up the problem of illegal
immigrants." "He'll have to face up to the facts sooner or later."
Factor in/to include as an influencing factor.
Fade away/to disappear; become gradually fainter (usually of sounds): "The music faded away as
we left the station."
Fall apart/to break into pieces.
Fall back/to withdraw; retreat; move back; go back: "The crowd around the hurt girl fell back
when someone shouted 'Give her air!'" "As the enemy advanced, the column fell back."

Fall back on or fall back upon/1. to retreat to: "The parliamentary committee fell back on an earlier plan." 2. to go from help to; turn in time of need; use if necessary; use in the absence of something better: "If Mr. Davis can't find a job as a teacher, he can fall back on his skill as a printer."

Fall behind/to slip into the rear through inability to keep up with the others; fail to keep up an agreed rate of payments; fail to keep up with; go slower than others and be far behind them: "He fell behind in school and life." "Laura was not promoted because she dreamed too much and fell behind in her lessons."

Fall flat/to be a failure; fail: "Her joke fell flat because no one understood it."

Fall for/1. to begin to like very much: "Frank fell for baseball when he was a little boy." 2. to fall in love with; begin to love (a boy or a girl): "He has fallen for her in a big way."

Fall from grace/to lose favor; go back to a bad way of behaving; do something bad again: "The girls behaved well during the dinner until they fell from grace by eating their desert with their fingers instead of their forks."

Fall in/to get into line (of troops, etc.)

Fall in love/ a comprehensive emotional attraction to another person; to become enamoured each other; to like very much: "Robert and Sally fell in love."

Fall in with/to accept someone's plans and agree to co-operate: "They'd better fall in with her suggestion for the sake of peace."

Fall into line or fall in line/obeying or agreeing with what is right or usual; doing or being what people expect or accept; within ordinary or proper limits.

Fall off/1. to become less; decrease (of numbers, attendances etc.): "Business picked up in the stores during December, but fell off again after Christmas." 2. to be careful: "Don't fall off."

Fall off the back of a truck/to be obtained by questionable or illegal means.

Fall off the wagon/to return to the consumption of an addictive, such as alcohol or drugs: "After a period of abstinence: Poor Joshua has fallen off the wagon again – he is completely incoherent today."

Fall on/to attack violently: "The gangsters fell on the killers and clubbed them to death."

Fall on deaf ears/words spoken to people who are not listening.

Fall out/1. v. to quarrel; fuss; disagree: "The burglars fell out over the division of the stolen goods." 2. v. to leave the lines (of troops). 3. v. to stop being friends: "We used to be very good friends. We have fallen out." "Mark fell out with his father and left home."

Fall over/to fall to the ground; lose one's balance: "She fell over and hurt her knee." "He fell over because his shoes were too big for him."

Fall prey to/be vulnerable to or overcome by.

Fall short/to fail to reach (some aim); not succeed: "Her jump fell three inches short of the world record."

Fall through/to fail to materialize; fail to take place; fail; to be ruined; not happen or be done: "Sally's plans to go to college fell through at the last moment." "Mr. Brown's deal to sell his house fell through." "His plan to go to China fell through because the journey turned out to be much more expensive than I had expected."

Farm out/to have another person do (something) for you; send away to be done: "Our teachers had too many test papers to read, so he farmed out half of them to a friend."

Feel at home/one feels comfortable and relaxed in it.

Feel blue/to be melancholic or depressed; be depressed; unhappy.

Feel free/to do as you wish (Feel free to ask questions. ask questions if one wants to.)

Feel good/to be happy or in good health.

Feel like/to want; want to do or have: "He doesn't feel like running today." "She just doesn't feel like pancakes this morning."

Feel the loss of/to miss.

Feel the pinch to/ undergo hardship through lack of money.

Feel uneasy/to worry.

Feel up to/to feel strong enough (to do something): "She doesn't feel up to tidying the kitchen now. She'll do it in the morning."

Fight fire with fire/to fight back in the same way one was attacked; make a defense similar to the attack.

Fight like cat and dog/to argue all the time.

Fight tooth and nail/to fight ferociously or with determination; fight with all weapons or ways of fighting as hard as possible; fight fiercely: "When the Indian boy was captured, he fought tooth and nail to get away." "Her friends fought tooth and nail to elect her to Congress."

Figure in/1. to add to a total; remember to put down in figures: "They figured in the travel expenses but forgot the cost of the meals." 2. to have a part in; be partly responsible for: "Barbara's good grades figured in her choice as class president."

Figure out/to find the answer by logic; find an answer by thinking about (some problem or difficulty); solve: "Frank couldn't figure out the last problem on the arithmetic test."

Fill in/to complete something; complete forms etc.; write words needed in blanks; put in; fill: "She filled in the passport renewal form." "He had to fill in three forms to get his new passport." 2. to take another's place; substitute: "The teacher was sick and Miss Miller filled in for her."

Fill one's shoes/to take the place another and do as well; substitute satisfactorily for: "When Michael got hurt, the coach had nobody to fill his shoes." "William hopes to fill his father's shoes."

Fill out/1. to put on weight: "He filled out after a long summer of cream teas." 2. to complete a form; complete something: "She filled out her passport renewal form."

Fill someone's shoes/to take over someone's function or duties and fulfil them satisfactorily.

Fill up/1. to complete writing on forms. 2. to pour to capacity (in a glass); to add gasoline to a vehicle's fuel tank.

Find out/1. to discover information; get information; learn; discover; discover something either on purpose or by accident; come to know something, discover as a result of conscious effort; learn or discover (something) not known before: "He's trying to find out the name of that new hotel." "I need to find out what time the next bus leaves." 2. to discover; learn; Get the facts; get facts about: "He's trying to find out the name of that new hotel." "She wrote to find out about a job in New York." 3. to discover (someone) doing wrong; catch; to find some out means to discover that a person has not been telling the truth, or has been attempting to deceive in some other way: "The girl knew that if she cheated on the test the teacher would find her out. She had been stealing from the company for a long time before she was eventually found out." 4. to write the necessary information.

Find something heavy going/to find difficulty in making progress.

Finish something off/to do the last part of something: "I'll finish painting the kitchen off tomorrow."

Fire up/to switch on (a computer).

Fit in/the state of being happy and accepted by a group of people as similar to them.

Fit out or fit up/to give things needed; furnish: "She fitted her room up as a photographic laboratory."

Fit the bill/to be exactly the right person (or thing) for the job; to suit; be what is required.

Fix up/to arrange it; improve: "He managed to fix up an appointment for 6.30."

Flare up/1. to burn brightly for a short time especially after having died down. 2. to become suddenly angry: "The mayor flared up at the newspaper's report."

Flex one's muscles/to exercise power.

Fly a kite/to put up a suggestion or idea, usually to test the reaction of the others; to test public opinion by spreading rumours, etc.

Fly high/1. to be ambitious 2. to be in a state of euphoria, as induced by drugs.

Foist down/to avoid at others' expense: "Olivia foists all her problems on her unfortunate friends."

Fold up/to collapse; fail: "The new hotel folded up in less than a year."

Follow in someone's footsteps/to do as another person did before, especially in making a journey or following an occupation.

Follow suit/1. to play a card of the same color and kind that another player put down. 2. Do as someone else has done; follow someone's example: "When the others went swimming, he followed suit."

Follow through/to complete.

Follow up/1. to chase or follow closely without giving up. 2. Make (one person) more successful by doing something more: "After Anne sent a letter to apply for a job, she followed it up by going to talk to the personnel manager." 3. Investigate again (more news about something that has already been in the newspapers, radio or TV news): "The day after news of the fire at Wilson's store, the newspaper sent a reporter to follow up Mr. Wilson's future plans."

Follow in someone's footsteps/to do something which has been done before.

Fool around or mess around or play around or fiddle around/1. spending time playing; fooling, or joking instead of being serious or working; waste time: "He was fooling around. If he goes to college, he must work, not fool around." 2. Treat or handle carelessly: "David cut himself by fooling around with a sharp knife." "Father says she wishes Peter would quit playing around with the girls and get married."

Foot the bill/to pay for (the meal at a restaurant), often as a responsibility suffered instead of embraced: "As half the team had no money, the other half had to foot the bill for the night at the pub."

Forgive and forget/to have no bad feelings about what happened in the fast: "After the argument, the girls decided to forgive and forget." Sometimes considered the best way to resolve a conflict or injury or disagreement.

Fork out/to pay up; to give over one's money, often under an external constraint.

Fork over or fork out or fork up/to hand over, give; pay; pay out: "She had to fork over one hundred dollars to have the car repaired."

Freak out/1. to act jokingly. 2. to behave in an unconventional way (applies to many contexts).

Fulfil your full potential/to accomplish to the best of one's ability.

G

Gang up against or gang up on/to attack in a group; get together to do harm: "The older girls
ganged up against the girl who beat up a younger girl."
Get or give someone a break/to get or be given a good opportunity; be let off.
Get a life/(slang), to start living a fuller or more interesting existence.
Get a move on/to hurry.
Get about/to circulate; move or travel in a general sense: "The news got about that she had
won the first prize in the lottery and everybody began asking her for money."
Get (a point) across/1. to explain clearly, make (something) clear; make clear the meaning
of; communicate the ideas: "Mr. Moore is a good coach because he can get across the
plays." "She got her message across to her audience with great force." 2. become clear.
Get ahead/1. to make progress; become successful: "Mr. Taylor was a good lawyer and soon
began to get ahead." 2. Be able to save money; get out of debt: "In a few more years, she
will be able to get ahead." "After Mother pays all the doctor bills, maybe we can get a
little money ahead and buy a car."
Get along with/1. to manage; to try to get along with what one has/possesses. 2. Progress;
have a good relationship with; be or remain agreeable together: "The two boys get along
well." "We don't get along with each other."
Get around/to find a way of not obeying or doing; escape from: "Charles did not weigh
enough to join the Navy, but he got around that; he drank a lot of water before his
physical examination." 2. to spread information or gossip: "Bad news gets around fast."
Get at (something)/to reach; find; to express something.
Get away/to escape, leave with difficulty; be free to leave; get loose or get free; come free
from being held or controlled; succeed in leaving; escape: "As Tom was trying to catch
the bat, it got away from him." "Anne tried to catch a butterfly, but it got away from her."
Get away with/1. do something wrong without being caught; avoid the result of something
done or not done; escape punishment; do (something bad or wrong) without being caught
or punished; evade discovery of: "Not knowing that she was being observed, the student
expected to get away with her cheating." "That woman got away with murder." 2. to
steal: "The bank robbers got away   with a million dollars." "The thief managed to get
away with about $4,000 in cash."
Get back/1. to recover possession of: "If you lend her a book, she'll lend it to someone and
you'll never get it back." 2. to return from somewhere; reach home again: "I spent the
whole day in the hills and didn't get back till dark." 3. to move away.
Get back at/to take revenge.
Get back from/1. to return from somewhere. 2. receive again.
Get back into/to devote oneself to something again.
Get back to nature/1. to return to the type of life that existed before the development of
complex industrial societies. 2. to temporarily leave urban or present-day living; to
retreat to natural surroundings as an escape or therapy.
Get back to someone/1. to reply them by phone: "I sent her an email, but she never got back
to me." 2. Start doing something after an interruption.
Get back together/to restart a relationship.
Get behind/to fail to do something by a certain time.
Get by/1. to be able to go past; pass. 2. manage to cope; manage financially; satisfy a need or
demand; cope; manage: "They'll have to get by on their stores of paper until after the
strike." "Sally can get by with her old coat this winter."

Get cold feet/to feel anxious and uncertain about an undertaking, to the point of wanting to
     withdraw.
Get cracking/to hurry up; to begin vigorously; hurry; hurry up; start moving fast; hurry up;
     begin some task; move off: "Come on, Thomas! Let's get cracking!"
Get behind/to back up; to approve of; to support.
Get cracking/to hurry up.
Get down/1. to enter a state of depression. "Don't let him get you down!"
Get down to/ start to direct effort to; get started on, being on: Andrew wasted a lot of time before
     he got down on his work.
Get even or to square accounts with. 1. to owe nothing: "Mr. Thomas has a lot of debts, but
     in a few years he will get even." 2. to do something bad to pay someone back for
     something bad; get revenge; hurt back: "Paul is waiting to get even with Jack for tearing
     up his notebook."
Get even with someone/to have or accomplish one's revenge.
Get in or get into/to enter a car: "Water gets in through the cracks in the roof." 2. to arrive.
Get in(to) or out of (a car, taxi, or small boat)/to enter a vehicle or mode of transport: "When he
     got into his car this morning he found the radio had been stolen." "He picked up his case
     and got into the taxi."
Get into hot water/to be in trouble because of behaving badly.
Get in on the ground floor/to become part of an enterprise in its early stage.
Get in touch with (oneself)/phr. to understand one's inner feelings.
Get into bed with someone or get in bed with someone/to enter into a close business arrangement
     with someone; to have sexual relations.
Get into hot water/to get into trouble.
Get into shape/to become physically fitter by exercise.
Get it on (with)/to make love.
Get it over/to deal with something unpleasant and be finished with it: "If I have to go to the
     dentist, why not go at once and get it over?"
Get it right/do it correctly.
Get it wrong/do it incorrectly.
Get lost/excl. an order to go away: "Get lost, will you!"
Get nowhere/to fail to make progress: "He's trying to write an essay but he's getting nowhere."
Get off (a bus, train, plane, ship)/Get off/1. to be acquitted or receive no punishment: "She was
     tried for theft but got off because there wasn't sufficient evidence against her." 2. to leave
     any vehicle, to come down from or out of: "They'll be getting off the train in ten
     minutes." "They got off the bus at the wrong stop." 3. to finish, leave work. 4. to start a
     journey. 5. to stop talking on the phone.
Get off one's back/to leave one alone after a period in which one has given another trouble; to
     stop bothering someone; to stop criticizing or nagging someone; to cease to annoy or
     harass someone.
Get off the ground to/ make a successful beginning; get a good start; go ahead; make
     progress: "Their plans for a party didn't get off the ground because the planning
     committee never met."
Get off the hook/to free from an obligation or an uncomfortable situation; to be out of
     trouble; to find release from an awkward or embarrassing situation: "Jennifer found she

had made two dates for the same night; she asked Elizabeth to get her off the hook by going out with one of the boys."

Get off on the wrong foot/to start something badly.

Get on/1. to have a good relationship; to get along; to live and work amicably with someone: "She is a pleasant friendly woman who gets on well with nearly everybody." 2. to get on (to) (a bus, train, plane, ship): to enter any vehicle: "The train was full. I couldn't get on." 3. to make progress; progress; do; manage (in a job, at school, in an exam); be successful: "How is she getting on at school?" "How is he getting on in his new job?" 4. to continue to do: "Let's get on with this football match."

Get on my nerves/to annoy; make angry: "The girl really gets on my nerves."

Get on to/to contact: "The goods are damaged. They'll have to get on to their suppliers." "There was a mistake in Anne's bank statement, so she decided to get on to the bank immediately."

Get on top of it/to solve a problem.

Get on with/1. to advance the discussion; to proceed or continue with, continue doing something one must do, usually after an interruption; start; continue; start making: "He hasn't started packing yet. He'd better get on with it." 2. to have a friendly relationship with; have a good relationship with: I" get on well with Sally." "She doesn't get on with her parents."

Get on the bandwagon or jump on the bandwagon/to join a popular cause or movement.

Get one foot in the door/to have an opportunity.

Get one's act together/to organize oneself in the manner required in order to achieve something.

Get one's own back/to have one's revenge.

Get out (of)/1. to leave a car (a car, taxi, or small boat): "He got out of the taxi at Flinders Station." "The bus stopped and he got out." 2. to escape from; leave (an enclosed space): "Don't worry about the spider. It's in a box. It can't get out." "He's so busy that he doesn't very often get out."

Get one's act together/to gather oneself in a course of action; to take stock; to organize oneself: "After three attempts at the bar exam, John got himself together by taking a test prep course and passed!"

Get one's hand in/to become practiced in something.

Get out of (doing something)/1. to avoid doing it; lose, drop: "He promised I'd go to the wedding. He doesn't want to go, but he can't get out of it now." "He can't get out of making a decision now." 2. to avoid some unpleasant activity; free oneself from an obligation or habit: "I suspect that his backache was just a way of getting out of the housework." "She says that she smokes too much but she can't get out of the habit." 3. to leave or go away: "They got out of the haunted house as fast as they could do."

Get over/1. to recover, get better; recover from an illness; get well from; recover from (illness, distress or mental weakness): "Has Susan got over her illness yet?" "The woman returned to work after she got over her illness." 2. to accept or forget (a sorrow or surprise): "He'll never get over the shock." "It is hard to get over the death of a member of our family."

Get real/to stop being ludicrously optimistic or idealistic.

Get rid of/to throw away; shake off.

Get round/1. to coax another into doing what one wants: "Boys can usually get round their mothers." 2. to find some solution to or to evade a difficulty or regulation.

Get round to/to find time for: "I never seem to get round to actually doing lots of little   jobs."

Get rid of/to dispatch; throw away, shake off; remove; throw it away: "They should get rid of some of this stuff."

Get something across/to make something understood.

Get something down/to swallow something: "His throat was so swollen that he couldn't get the tablets down."

Get something out of something/to benefit from.

Get the ax/to be dismissed from one's work, team; get the sack; be fired from a job: "Poor Donald got the ax at the office yesterday." "She's been meaning to reply to Peter's letter, but she hasn't managed to get round to it yet."

Get/set/start the ball rolling/to start activity or action; make a beginning; initiate action begin: "George started the ball rolling at the party by telling a new joke."

Get the boot/to be dismissed; to be discharged.

Get the ball rolling/to start a project or activity.

Get the picture/to become fully informed about something.

Get through/1. to pass an examination 2. to consume: "They got through 9 liters of juice last week." 3. to complete: "They got through all the orders ahead of schedule." 4. Use up.

Get to the bottom of/to find out the real cause of: "The doctor made several tests to get to the bottom of the woman's stomach ache."

Get the feel of/to become familiar with; become used to; learn about, especially by feeling or handling; get used to the experience or feeling of; get skill in: "Kenneth had never driven a big car, and it took a while for him to get the feel of it."

Get the nod/to be given approval; to get a decision in one's favor; win selection over others.

Get the picture/to follow.

Get the sack/to be dismissed from one's job; be fired or dismissed from work: "Steven got the sack at the factory last week."

Get through/1.to pass an exam. 2. to pass; finish a piece of work; finish successfully: "He's got a lot of work to get through before Thursday." "She got through her exam all right." 3. to make contact and talk to one; get into telephone communication: "He is trying to call New York but he can't get through." "He thinks all the lines are engaged."

Get to grips with/to address a problem or understand it.

Get to the bottom of/to solve; to discover the real truth about; find out the real cause: "The principle talked with several students to get the bottom of the trouble." "The doctor made several tests to get the bottom of the woman's headaches."

Get to your feet/to rise.

Get together/1. to come to an agreement; agree: "Father says I should finish my English lesson, and Mother says I should mow the garden. Why don't you two get together?" 2. Meet up.

Get under way/to start.

Get up/1. to arise from bed, a chair etc. rise to one's feet; mount; get out of the bed: "Peter's mother told him that it was time to get up." "He gets up at seven o'clock every morning." 2. to organize; arrange; prepare; get ready: "Anne got up a picnic for her visitor." "We got up a concert in aid of cancer research." 3. to stand up; get on one's feet: "Some men think it's polite to get up when a lady comes in." 4. to succeed; win.

Get up and go/to show drive or initiative.

Get up to/to do especially something bad.

Get used to/to become adjusted to: "The new heater is very difficult to get used to."

Get your own way/to have or do what one wants.

Get up to/to do or be engaged in (an activity).

Give (one) a go/to allow (one) fair play; have a try, make an attempt

Give a hand/to help; assist.

Give a hard time/1. to give trouble by what one does or says: "Margaret gave her mother a hard time on the bus by fighting with her sisters and screaming." "Don't give him a hard time, Edward. He's doing his best on this job." 2. get in the way by teasing or playing; kid: "Don't give me a hard time, girls. I'm studying."

Give along with something/to consent or agree to.

Give an arm and a leg for/to pay a higher price for.

Give away/1. to give it to someone or anyone because one doesn't want it anymore; give as present: "I'll give this old hat away." "Mrs. Harris has several kittens to give away." 2. to forget about, give up: "Give away the idea of another job – you don't have the time." 3. to let (a secret) become known; tell the secret of: "The little girl gave away her hiding place when she coughed." 4. to betray a confidence; betray someone: "He plays his cards close to his chest – never gives anything away."

Give back/to restore (a thing) to its owner; return something to someone: "He must call at the library to give back this book." "I've got Sally's keys. I must give them back to her."

Give consideration to/to consider.

Give in/to yield; cease to resist; agree to something unwillingly; to stop fighting or arguing and do as the other person wants; give someone his own way; stop opposing someone; yield, surrender: "John kept asking another ice cream, and at last his mother gave in." "He had to give in his job because he hated his boss."

Give it a rest/to stop doing or talking about a particular thing.

Give it one's best shot/to try hard; to do one's best.

Give off/to emit; send out; let out; put forth: "Rotten fish give off a bad smell."

Give oneself up/to stop hiding or running away; surrender: "The burglar gave himself up to the police." "Mr. Martin hit another car, and his wife told him to give himself up."

Give out/1. to announce verbally; distribute; make known; let it be known; publish: "We gave out the names of winners." 2. to become exhausted (supplies); fail or collapse: "Her patience gave out, and she slapped the child hard." "Their petrol supply has given out." 3. to issue; give to people; distribute: "The barber gives out free chocolates to all the children." "No one noticed until the papers had all been given out." "Social workers were giving out bread to the hungry."

Give rise to/to be the reason for; to cause: "Michael's black eye gave rise to rumors that he had been in a fight."

Give someone a break/to stop putting pressure on someone about something

Give someone a hand/to help someone.

Give someone enough rope/to give a person enough freedom of action to bring about their own downfall.

Give someone or thing the benefit of the doubt/to concede that something or thing must be regarded as correct or justified, if the contrary has not been proved.

Give someone the cold shoulder/to make someone feel unwelcome; be deliberately unfriendly to someone; behave in an unfriendly way towards someone, snub someone; be unenthusiastic about an idea.

Give something the thumbs up/down/to show approval or disapproval for something, give a project the go-ahead or reject a project.

Give the benefit of the doubt/to believe (a person) is innocent rather than guilty when not
sure: "The money was stolen, and William was the only boy who had known where it
was, but the teacher gave him the benefit of the doubt."

Give the game away/1. to let a secret out; reveal or betray. 2. to resign, stop working at any
activity: "High taxes are forcing some foreign businessmen to give the game away."

Give the nod/to approve.

Give the green light/to encourage or allow to be proceed.

Give up/1. to stop doing something; stop something that one does; abandon (a habit or
attempt); abandon an attempt; cease trying to do something; stop doing something;
lose interest; stopped trying; stop trying to keep; surrender; yield: "He tried to climb the
wall but after he had failed three times he gave up." "After several attempts, we gave up."
"Jacob gave up smoking four years ago." 2. to stop doing or having; abandon (a habit or
attempt); quit; renounce; stop: "Have you given up drinking beer before breakfast?" "She
tried to learn Japanese but soon got tired of it and gave it up." 3. to stop hoping for;
waiting for; or trying to do: "Anthony was given up by the doctor after the accident, but
he lived just the same." 4. to surrender: "She gave herself up to despair." "She was cold
and hungry after a week on the run so she gave herself up to the police."

Give way/v. phr. 1. to go back; retreat. 2. break off; collapse; fail: "During the tunnelling
work a corner of the building gave way." "Lisa's legs gave way and she fainted." "The
balcony gave way." 3. make room; get out of the way: "The children gave way, and let
their father through the door."

Give way to/1. to make room for; allow to go or pass; yield to: "Michael gave way to the old
lady and let her pass." 2. Allow to decide: "Mrs. Robinson gave way to her husband in
buying the car." 3. Be replaced by: "When he saw the clowns, the little boy's tears gave
way to laughing."

Give your word/to promise.

Gloss over/to avoid considering.

Go about (something)/to be busy at or working on; start working on; to do: "William is going
about his homework very seriously tonight." "How will you go about building the dog
house?"

Go after/to try to get; pursue; chase; follow: "First find out what job you want and then go after
it," said Henry's father.

Go against the tide/to act in accordance against the prevailing opinion or tendency.

Go ahead/to help oneself; take it; do it; proceed; continue; lead the way; begin to do
something; not wait, continue or proceed: "The teacher told the students not to write on
the paper yet, but David went ahead and wrote his name." "While he was away she went
ahead with the work and got a lot done."

Go along/1. to move along; continue: "Uncle Richard made up the story as he went along." 2. to
go together or as company; go for fun: "Linda went along with us to Sally's house."
"David just went along for the ride to the ball game." 3. to agree; cooperate: "Barbara is
a nice girl." " I'll go along with that," said Richard. "Just because the other girls do
something bad, you don't have to go along with it."

Go ape/to become highly excited or behave in a crazy way: "Olivia went ape over the hotel and
beautiful beaches."

Go around in a circle or go around in circles/to move without making demonstrable progress;

without getting anywhere; uselessly: "She seemed to be working hard, but was just going around in a circle."

Go at/1. to start to fight with; attack: "Emma went at the MPs in a floor debate." 2. make a beginning on; approach; tackle: "How are you going to go at the job of fixing the door?"

Go away/to leave away from home; leave me; leave this place: "Olivia has gone away for a few days." "Go away and don't come back!" "Is he going away for his holiday?"

Go back/to return; retire; retreat: "We're never going back to that hotel. It is most uncomfortable." "They went out for dinner and then went back to their hotel."

Go back on/to withdraw or break (a promise); change; fail to keep: "He can't make a promise and then go back on it, can he?" "Do you think the school council are likely to go back on their previous decisions?"

Go bananas/to go wild or angry; to act berzerk or crazy.

Go belly up/to go bankrupt; to fail completely.

Go down/1. to fall; drop; become less; be reduced (of wind, sea, weight, prices etc.): "During his illness his weight went down from 70 kilos to 60." "Temperatures went down last week." 2. to go or move lower: "She walked to the stairs and went down." 3. to be received with approval (usually an idea): "She suggested that he should look for a job, but this suggestion did not go down at all well."

Go down in history or go down in the records/to be remembered or recorded for always: "The lives of great people go down in history." "The girl's straight A's for four years of college went down in the records." "The Prime Minister said that the day the war ended would go down in history."

Go down the tubes/phr. to fail, often used of commercial endeavors.

Go down with/to catch; contract; become ill with: "Half the class went down with cold."

Go Dutch/to go out for fun together but each person pay for himself; share the costs of an outing instead of allowing one's companion to pay (especially if a man invites a woman out: "High school students often go Dutch to baseball games." "Sometimes men and women go Dutch on dates." "The boy knew her girl friend had little money, so he offered to go Dutch."

Go easy or take it easy/1. to go or act slowly, carefully, and gently: " Go easy," said Joseph to the other boys carrying the table down the stairs." " Take it easy on Charles and don't scold him too much," said Mrs. Brown. 2. to avoid hard work or worry; have an easy time; live in comfort: "Elizabeth likes to take it easy."

Go flat out/to go very quickly.

Go for/1. to fall in love with: "If you were only younger, I could go for you." 2. attack: "The dog went for the cat and chased him out of the yard."

Go from bad to worse/to become worse than before.

Go from strength to strength/to grow stronger; to gain more and more success, power, etc.

Go gangbusters/to proceed very vigorously or successfully.

Go in for/1. to be especially interested in; practice; enter for (a competition); try to do it; take part in; enter; compete in; take pleasure in; prepare for an occupation, or follow a particular interest; enter for: "Mrs. Clark goes in for simple meals." "He went in for the Mastermind quiz." "He's decided to go in for the 10-km road run this year." 2. to like: "All my friends go in for basketball in a big way."

Go into/to investigate thoroughly" "'I shall have to go into this very carefully,' said the detective."

Go into smoke/to disappear, hide away: "After the wedding they went into smoke for awhile."

Go it alone/to do things oneself; do something without any help.

Go nuts/to go crazy

Go off/1. to start a journey; leave; depart: "Anne's mother told her not to go off without telling her." "She went off in a great hurry." 2. to fire (of guns, usually accidentally); explode (of ammunition or fireworks): "As Dave was cleaning his gun it went off and killed him." 3. to ring; begin to ring or buzz: "The alarm clock went off at six o'clock and woke Mother." 4. to be successful (of social occasions); happen: "The party went off without any trouble." 4. go bad: "Milk soon goes off in hot weather."

Go off the rails/to begin behaving in a strange, abnormal, or wildly uncontrolled way.

Go on/1. to walk on; drive on; keep; happen; continue going; continue a journey; not stop: "Go on till you come to the church." "The TV picture began to jump, and it went on like that until Mother turned a knob." 2. to continue any action.

Go on about/to complain, keep talking about.

Go on with/to continue any action: "Most of the audience had left in the interval, but the singers decided to go on with the show."

Go one's separate ways/to leave in a different direction from someone with whom one has just travelled or spent time.

Go out/1. to leave the house: "He is always indoors; he doesn't go out enough." "The boy went out." 2. to join in social life, leave one's house for entertainment: "Ingrid is very pretty and goes out a lot." 3. to disappear; be discontinued (of fashions). 4. to be extinguished (of lights, fires etc.): "The light went out, and they were left in the dark." 5. The car stopped and a man got out (out of the car).

Go out (of) the window/to go out of the effect; be abandoned; to lose an opportunity.

Go over/1. to review or check; examine; study or repeat carefully; think about or look at carefully: "The teacher went over the list and picked Jane's name." "She went over the plans again and discovered two very serious mistakes." 2. to repeat; do again: "They painted the house once, and then they went over it again." 3. to read again; study: "After I finish the test, go over it again to look for mistakes." 4. to cross; go to stop or visit; travel: "They went over to the other side of the street." "I'm going over to Jane's house." "They went over to the next town to the game."

Go overboard for/to be enthusiastic about something.

Go public/to reveal a plan to the public.

Go round/1. to suffice (for a number of people): "Will there be enough beer to go round?" 2. to go to a place or location: "He said that he'd go round and see her during the weekend."

Go slow/to work deliberately at a very slow rate.

Go south/for (something) to drop or begin to fail: "After Jimmy baled, the plan to rob the bank went south in a hurry."

Go strong/to continue to be healthy, vigorous, or successful.

Go through/1. to examine or think about carefully; search: "I went through the papers looking for Anne's letter." 2. to experience; endure; suffer; live through: "No one knows what he went through while he was waiting for the verdict." "I don't think that I can go through this ordeal." "He's gone through a lot lately." 3. to go or continue to the end of: "Paul went through the magazine quickly." 4. to be allowed; pass; be agreed on: "I hope the new law we want goes through the parliament."

Go through the roof/to be very angry.

Go through with/to finish; bring to a conclusion (usually in the face of some opposition or
    difficulty): "She went through with her plan although all her friends advised her to
    abandon it."
Go to bed with/to participate in; form a partnership with a group or individual
Go to the wall/to suffer failure, ruin; fail; to be ruined; collapse financially.
Go too far/to do something unacceptable.
Go under/1. to lose money; become bankrupt; 2. to fail; be defeated. 2. to be sunk: "The ship hit
    a rock and went under."
Go up/1. to rise; to go or move higher: "He walked to the stair and went up." 2. to grow in
    height while being built; be built: "The new hotel is going up on the corner." 3. to
    increase in price (of prices): "The price of bananas went up towards the end of the
    season." "Prices seem to go up all the time." 4. to burst into flames (and be destroyed);
    explode (used of entire buildings, ships, etc.)
Go up or end up in smoke/to burn up completely.
Go with/to fit; to accept; to tolerate; to permit life to sweep one along.
Go with the flow/to be relaxed, accept a situation.
Go without/to do without.
Go without saying or Goes without saying/to be too plain to need talking about; not be necessary
    to say or mention; to be self-evident: "It goes without saying that winters are cold in the
    arctic." "It goes without saying that boys should not be given knives to play with."
Gobble down/to eat hungrily or quickly; to devour a snack or meal.
Gone with the wind/to be gone completely; to disappear without a trace.
Grease the wheels/to make things smoothly, especially by paying the expenses.
Grind to a halt/to slow down and stop like a machine does when turned off: "The old lawn
    mower ground to a halt in front of the house."
Grow out of/to abandon, on becoming older, a childish (and often bad) habit: "She used to tell a
    lot of lies as a young girl but she grew up of that later on."
Grow up/1. to increase in size or height; become taller or older; reach full height: "Donald is
    growing up; his shoes are too small for him." "He grew up on a farm." 2. to develop into
    an adult; become an adult in mind or judgement; become old enough to think or decide in
    important matters: "She grew up in a city." "George wants to be a coach when he grows
    up." "'I'm going to be an actor when I grow up,' said the boy."

H
Hack into/to gain unauthorized access to (a computer).
Had better/should; must; ought to: "I had better leave now, or I'll be late."
Had it/to be exhausted, give up after much trying: "I've had it."
Hammer out/1. to write or produce by hard work: "The Prime Minister sat at his desk till
    midnight hammering out his speech for the next day." 2. to remove, change, or work out
    by discussion and debate; debate and agree on (something): "Mrs. Johnson and Mrs.
    Lewis have hammered out their difference of opinion."
Hand down/1. to bequeath or pass on (traditions, information or possessions); to   arrange to
    give or leave after death: "Kenneth will have his father's gold watch because it is handed
    down in the family." 2. to decide: "The court handed down the decision."
Hand in or turn in/to submit an assignment; give to someone; deliver to someone; given by

hand: "I want you to hand in a good history paper." "She'll have to go into college to hand her essay in." "When the football season was over, they handed in their uniforms." "She has handed in her resignation."

Hand off/to hand the football to another back.

Hand out/to give (things of the same kind) to several people; distribute: "The English teacher handed out the examination papers." "She was standing at the door of the store handing out leaflets."

Hand over/to surrender authority or responsibility to another; give control or possession of; give (something) to another person, often when one does not want to: "When the teacher saw Peter reading a comic book in study period, he made him hand over the book." "When Mr. Lee gets old, he will hand over his business to his son."

Hand round/to give or show to each person present: "The host handed round coffee and cake. Sally handed round some sweets."

Hands off/to keep your hands off or do not interfere; leave that alone: "I was going to touch the machine, but Steven cried," Hands off!" and I let it alone."

Hands up/a command to put up one's hands (at the point of a gun or other threat): "Put your hands up high and keep them there!"

Hang about or hang around/1. to wait (near); loiter; pass time or stay near without any real purpose or aim; wait idly: "She spent her days hanging about street corners." "The principal warned the pupils not to hang around the corner drug store after school." 2. to spend time or associate: "Dorothy hangs around with some girls who live in her neighborhood."

Hang back/to show unwillingness to act; hesitate: "She always hangs back when she is in his company."

Hang in the balance/to have two equally possible results: "Until Steven scored the winning touchdown, the outcome of the game hung in the balance." "He was very sick and his life hung in the balance."

Hang in (there)/to persevere; not to give up; stick to a project and not lose faith or courage; to hold on; to hang on; to maintain one's position despite the odds.

Hang loose/to be relaxed; refrain from taking anything too seriously.

Hang on/1. to hold on to something, usually tightly: "Edward almost fell off the cliff but managed to hang on until help came." 2. to continue doing something; persist; persevere: "The milk bar was losing money every day, but he hung on, hoping that business would improve." 3. to hold a lead in the race or other contest while one's opponents try to rally: "The favorite dog opened on early lead and hung on to win as two other dogs almost passed him in the final stretch." 4. to wait a minute; wait to persevere, maintain existing conditions with effort; sometimes means 'to wait'.

Hang on to/to retain; keep in one's possession: "He should hang on to that Picasso painting. It's worth a lot of money."

Hang out/1. to spend time idly or by lounging about: "The teacher complained that Jacob was hanging out in poolrooms instead of doing his homework."

Hang someone out to dry/to leave someone in a difficult or vulnerable situation.

Hang tough/to tough it out.

Hang up/1. to put up clothes a line or a hook; to place on hook, peg, or hanger. Mark hung his coat. 2. to stop a telephone conversation; to place a telephone receiver back on its hook and break connection; end a phone conversation: "We were in the middle of a chat when he just hung up on me." "Karen's mother told her she had talked long enough on the phone and made her hang up."

Hanker after/to think about something that one wants but cannot have.

Have a blast/to have a great time.

Have a crack/to try.

Have a crush on/to be infatuated with, attracted to.

Have a field-day/to enjoy oneself a great deal.

Have a finger in every pie or have finger in the pie/to have something to do with what happens; to be involved in many different activities (sometimes to excess): "When the girls got up a Christmas party, I felt sure Sally had a finger in every pie." "Ronald is a boy with a finger in every pie at school, from dramatics to football."

Have a free hand/to have too little to do.

Have a heart of gold/to be generous, kind, and sincere

Have a go/1. to find fault with: "They had a go at each other." 2. to make an attempt at something; try: "The task may be difficult, but let's have a go at it." "Brian asked John to let him have a go at shooting at the target with John's rifle."
Have a heart/to stop being mean; be kind, generous, or sympathetic; be reasonable: "Have a heart, John, and lend me three dollars." "Have a heart, Helen. And help me with this lesson."

Have a meal/to eat.

Have a mind of one's own/to be capable of independent opinion or action.

Have a seat/to sit down.

Have a shot/to try.

Have a silver tongue/to be eloquent or persuasive.

Have a thick skin/to be insensitive to criticism or insults.

Have a tiger by the tail/to have a task or situation that one is unprepared for, which is a bigger challenge that expected.

Have an axe to grind/to have an interest in something, something to gain; to have a personal or profitable interest in something; to have a selfish, usually secret motive for doing something; to insist upon one's own fixed belief or course of action.

Have been around/to have visited many places and done many things; know people; have experience and be able to take care of oneself: "Uncle Kevin is an old sailor and has really been around." "Donna likes to go out with Jason because he has been around."

Have been there before/to know all about a situation from experience: "Been there; done that!"

Have bigger fish to fry/to have more important matters to attend to.

Have blood on one's hand/to be responsible for the death of someone.

Have cold shower/to go away and think through a matter less emotionally.

Have deep pockets/to have large financial resources.

Have done with/to stop doing or using something: "Have done with that paintbrush, Jane. I would like to use it."

Have fun/to play.

Have goosebumps/to be so cold or stimulated that the skin raises up in little bumps.

Have had it/to have experienced or suffered all one can; have come to the end of one's patience or life: "I've had it," said John, " I'm resigning from the job of chairman right now." When the doctor examined the woman who had been shot, he said, "She's had it."

Have in place/to have operating or functional.

Have nerves of steel/not easily upset or frightened.

Have on/to wear.

Have one's feet on the ground/to be practical and sensible.

Have one's hands full/to have as much work as one can do; be very busy: "The electrician said that he had his hands full and could not take another job for two weeks." "With four small children to take care of, Carol's mother has her hands full."

Have shots at (someone)/to criticize; to ridicule.

Have someone on the back foot/to have someone at a disadvantage; to have something in common; to share the same interests or experiences with someone.

Have something up your sleeve/to have a secret plan which can be used in an emergency.

Have steam coming out of your ears/to be really angry about something.

Have the guts to do something/to be brave enough to do something difficult and dangerous: "Jeff wants to marry Ruth, he doesn't have the guts to pop the question."

Have the last laugh or get the last laugh/to have one's opinion justified in the end; to prove ultimately successful; to win after an earlier defeat; to make someone foolish for having laughed at you: "Other schools laughed at us when our little team entered the national championship, but we had the last laugh at them when we won it."

Have to/must: "They have to get up at seven o'clock."

Have words/to engage in a heated argument.

Haven't looked back/to have progressed or succeeded.

Head up/to lead; organize.

Help out/1. to be able to help or useful; help sometimes or somewhat: "Mr. Walker helps out with the milking on the farm." "Sally helps out in the shop after the school."

Hit home/to reach an intended target.

Hit the bulls-eye/to reach or focus on the main point of something.

Hit the ground running/to proceed at a fast pace with enthusiasm and dynamism.

Hit the jackpot/to win chief prize on gambling machine; achieve great success; to be lucky; be very lucky or successful: "Mr. Hall invented a new gadget which hit the jackpot." "Mrs. Allen hit the jackpot when she hired Anne for a maid."

Hit the mark/to be successful in an attempt or accurate in a guess.

Hit the nail on the head/to understand exactly.

Hit the road/to become a wanderer; live an idle life: "After Ronald's wife left him, he felt a desire to travel, so he hit the road."; go away: "Hit the road, Jill. Don't come back."

Hold back/1. to stay back or away; show unwillingness: "The visitor tried to get the girl to come to her, but she held back." 2. to keep someone in place; prevent from action; stop: "The police held back the mob."

Hold off/to keep at a distance; stay away (used of rain): "The snow fortunately held off till the school sports day." "Madison held off purchasing."

Hold on/1. to keep holding tightly; continue to hold strongly: "As John was pulling on the rope, it began to slip and Anthony cried, 'Hold on, John!'" 2. wait and not hang up a telephone; keep a phone for later use: "Mr. Young asked me to hold on while he spoke to his secretary." 3.persist in spite of; endure hardship or danger; keep on with a business or job in spite of difficulties: "It was hard to keep the shop going during the depression, but Daniel held on and at last met with success." 4. wait; wait a minute; stop: "Hold on!" Michael's father said, "I want the car tonight."

Hold one's breath/1. to stop breathing for a moment when you are excited or nervous: "The race was so close that William was holding his breath." 2. to endure great nervousness, anxiety, or excitement: "Kevin held his breath for days before he got the word that the college he chose had accepted him."

Hold out/1. to put forward; reach out; extend; offer: "Mr. King held out his hand in welcome." "The company held out many fine promises to Jason in order to get him to work for them." 2. persist in spite of, endure hardship or danger; keep resisting; not yield; refuse to give up; endure: "How long can the Japanese enemy hold out?" "The city held out four months under siege." 3. refuse to agree or settle until one's wishes have been agreed to: "The strikers held out for a raise of fifty cents an hour."

Hold out an olive branch/to offer a token of peace or goodwill.

Hold the line/to wait a minute during a telephone call; keep a situation or trouble from getting worse; hold steady; prevent a setback or loss: "The President held the line on taxes."

Hold the purse strings/to have control of expenditures.

Hold up/1. to raise; lift: "Jeff held up his hand." 2. support; bear; carry: "The chair was too weak to hold up Mrs. Wright." 3. rob at gunpoint; stop and rob: "The bandits held up the bank." 4. check; stop by threats or violence; delay: "There was an accident which held up all the traffic going into town." 5. keep one's courage or spirits up; remain calm; keep control of oneself: "The grieving father held up for his children's sake." 6. prove true: "The police were doubtful at first, but John's story held up." 7. delay action; defer; postpone: "The Prime Minister held up on the news until he was sure of it."

Hold water/1. to keep water without leaking. 2. stand up to close inspection; prove true; stand testing; bear examination: "David told the police a story that wouldn't hold water." That argument does not hold water."

Hold your tongue/to remain silent;

Hollow out/to cut or dig out a hole; make a cut or cave in; excavate: "Mathew's father hollowed out a pumpkin to make a jack-o'-lantern."

Home in/to make for it as though for a target.

Hook up/to connect or fit together: We could not use the gas stove because it had not been hooked up.

Hose down/to attempt to suppress.

Hunt down/to pursue and capture; look hard for an animal or person until found and caught.

Hurry up/to do something more quickly: Hurry up! Everybody is waiting for you.

I

I'd rather not go into it/I'd rather not talk about it or discuss it.

Immerse yourself/to become completely involved in it.

Impact upon/to have an effect on.

Inquire into (matter or person)/to ask or find about; to seek to understand.

Iron out/to discuss and reach an agreement (a difference); find a solution for (a problem); remove (a difficulty); resolve; solve; remove: "He has a few more problems to iron out before work can begin."

It never rains but pours/misfortunes or difficult situations tend to follow each other in rapid succession or to arrive all at the same time.

It's not on/it's impractical or unacceptable.

It takes two to tango/both parties involved in a situation or argument are equally responsible for it.

J

Jack up/1. to lift with a jack: "Michael jacked up his car to fix a flat tire." 2. make (a price)
        higher; raise: "Just before Easter, some shops jack up their prices."
Join forces or join hands/to come together for the same aim; group together for a
        purpose; unite: "The South Korean soldiers joined hands with the Americans in the war
        against North Korea."
Join in/to take part in an activity that is already going on: "They're playing a game. Why don't
        you join in?"
Join up/to enlist in one of the armed services: "When war was declared, Angus joined up at
        once."
Jump at/to accept with enthusiasm (an offer or opportunity): "Roger was offered a
        place in the Himalayan expedition and jumped at the chance."
Jump on the bandwagon or get on the bandwagon/to join the winning sides; take
        advantage of a popular movement or fashion; follow the crowd.
Jump ship/suddenly to abandon an organization, enterprise, etc.
Jump the gun/1.to be too hasty; act prematurely; to start prematurely; to start before
        the assigned time. 2. to obtain an unfair advantage 3. To start before the starter's gun in a
        race. 4. to be hasty in embarking upon a course of action; start before others in any
        activity; thus gaining an advantage; start before one should; start before anyone else:
        "The new pupils were not supposed to come before noon, but one girl jumped the gun
        and came to school at eight in the morning." "Sally didn't finish her algebra homework
        because her mind kept jumping the gun to think about the new boy in class."
Jump the queue/to push into a queue of people in order to be served or dealt with before one's
        turn.
Jump to the conclusion/to form an opinion precipitately, before one has learned or considered all
        the facts: "We don't jump to the conclusion that he's trying to kill them with his car."
Jump up and down/to be excited

K

Keep a low profile phr. to act discreetly; to keep oneself hidden from the public gaze.
Keep an eye on something or keep one's eye on/1. To mind; watch; look after; watch
        carefully; not stop paying attention; watch to make sure if something is safe: "We asked
        them to keep an eye on the house while we're away." "You must keep your eye on the
        ball when you play basketball." 2. watch and do what is needed for; mind: "Mother told
        Sharon to keep an eye on the baby while she was in the shop."
Keep at/to persist.
Keep (something or someone) at bay/to keep someone or something out or at a safe distance.
Keep away/to remain at a distance.
Keep company/1. To stay or go along with (someone) so that he will not be lonely;
        visit with (someone): "David kept Richard company while his parents went to the
        movies." 2. go places together as a couple; date just one person: "After keeping company
        for one year, Ruth and Charles decided to marry."
Keep dark about something/to keep something a secret.
Keep down/to repress; control: "What is the best way to keep down mice?" "He's trying to keep
        down expenses."
Keep from/to hold oneself back from; stop or prevent oneself from (doing something): Can you

keep from repeating rumors?" "Anne can't keep from talking about her trip." "You can't
keep from liking Jill."

Keep off/to refrain from walking on, or from coming too close.

Keep on/1. To go ahead; not stop; continue; continue doing something; do something
continuously or repeatedly: "She kept on blowing her horn." "The girl kept on talking
even though the teacher asked her to stop." 2. allow to continue working: "The new
owner kept James on as gardener."

Keep one back/to restrain; hinder; prevent from advancing: "Frequent illness kept her back."

Keep one's eye on the ball/to remain alert to what is happening nearby.

Keep one's finger crossed/to wish for good luck or success in a particular enterprise;
cross two fingers of one hand for good luck: "Carol kept her fingers crossed to bring
Donald good luck."

Keep one's head/to remain calm when there is trouble or danger; stay calm and under control:
"When Anne heard the fire alarm she kept her head and looked for the nearest exit."

Keep one's head above water/to avoid succumbing to difficulties, especially falling into debt.

Keep one's mouth shut/to remain or stay silent: "George began to tell John how to kick the ball,
when Kenneth said angrily, 'Keep your mouth shut!'"; keep one's options open/not
commit oneself.

Keep out (of)/not to enter; stay outside: "Corporal, keep out."

Keep someone in the dark/to keep information from someone.

Keep something for a rainy day/to put something aside in case you may need it later.

Keep something under wraps/conceal; be secretive about.

Keep (that) up/to continue with (that activity).

Keep the ball rolling/to keep a discussion or activity going; keep something going, keep up the
rate of progress or activity; keep up an activity or action; not allow something that is
happening to slow or stop: "Steven kept the ball rolling at the party by dancing with a
lamp shade on his head." "They keep track of all their expenses."

Keep the peace/to refrain or prevent others from disturbing civil order.

Keep track/to know about changes; stay informed or up-to-date; keep a count or record: "Mr.
Evans kept track of his business by telephone when he was in hospital." "The farmer has
so many sheep, he can hardly keep track of them all." "I keep track of all my expenses."

Keep up/1. to go on; not stop; continue; continue at the same speed or level: "The snow kept
up for two days, and the roads were blocked." 2. to go on with (something); continue
steadily; never stop: "Mrs. Collins told Brian to keep up the good work." "The teacher
asked Kevin to stop bothering Donna, but he kept it up." 3. maintain an effort; go at the
same rate as others: "Peter had to work hard to keep up." "Jason was the youngest boy on
the hike, but he kept up with the others." 4. keep (something) at the same level or rate or
in good condition: "The shortage of apples kept the prices up." "Grandmother was too
poor to keep up her house." 5. keep informed: "Jill is interested in politics and always
keep up with the news."

Keep up with/to stay at the same position or level; not to lag behind; go as fast as; remain
abreast of someone who is advancing; advance at the same pace as: "Bill was walking so
fast I couldn't keep up with him." "The students couldn't keep up with the teacher."

Key in/to enter data or write on a computer keyboard: "She keyed in the commands and
password."

Kick around/to act roughly or badly to; treat badly; bully: "James likes to kick around the little boys." "Mr. Collins is always kicking his dog around."

Kick ass/(slang) to act in a forceful or aggressive manner.

Kick back/to pay money illegally for favorable contract arrangements: "I will do it if you kick-back a few thousand dollars."

Kick in or chip in/to give together with others; contribute: "The students kicked in a dime a piece for the teacher's Christmas present." "Andrew kicked in ten points in the basketball game."

Kick off/1. to make the kick that begins the football game: "Jeff kicked off, and the football game started." 2. get started on anything; begin; launch; start: "The candidate kicked off her campaign with a speech on television." "We kick off at five o'clock with a speech from the governor."

Kick (somebody) out of or boot out/to force someone to leave; expel him; make (someone) go or leave; get rid of; dismiss: "The girls made so much noise at the movie the manager kicked them out."

Kick-start/to start (a motor) with a kick-starter; an impetus given to a process or thing started or restarted.

Kick the bucket/to die: "She kicked the bucket last Friday." "Old Mrs. Smith kicked the bucket just two days ago before her eighty-fourth birthday."

Kick the habit/to stop engaging in a habitual practice.

Kill a story/not to print a story (by a newspaper or publisher).

Kill off/to kill or end completely; destroy: "The president suggested a new law to Parliament, but many members were against the idea and killed it off." "Mother made Jill practice her dancing an hour every day; Jill got tired of dancing and that killed off her interest."

Kill the goose which lays golden eggs/to destroy a source of profit through greed; spoil something that is good or something that you have, by being greedy: "Mrs. Williams gives you an apple from her tree whenever you go by her house, but don't kill the goose that laid the golden egg by bothering her too much."

Kill time/to occupy oneself in some manner so as to make the time pass very short time.

Kill two birds with one stone/to gain two objectives with one effort; succeed in two things by one action; get two results from one effort: "Mother stopped at the supermarket to buy bread and then went to get Helen at dancing class; she killed two birds with one stone."

Kiss and make up/to reconcile.

Knock back/to reject.

Knock down/to force to the ground with a blow; demolish (a building): "We are going to knock down the school and build a new one." "A woman was knocked down by a car and taken to hospital."

Knock off/(casual) to stop work for the day: "Japanese workmen usually knock off at 5.00 or 5.30 p.m." "They knock off work in time for tea."

Knock out/to hit someone so hard that he falls unconscious; defeat; eliminate a competitor or team from a sporting contest; make helpless, unworkable, or unusable: "The boxing champion knocked out the challenger in the third round."

Knock over/to upset; topple(a cup, a glass, a person, etc.): "Be careful. Don't knock your cup over." "A woman was knocked over by a truck."

Know someone or something inside out/to know someone or something very thoroughly.

Know the ropes/to be thoroughly acquainted with the way in which something is done.

L

Lag behind/to move more slowly than all the others.

Lap up/to drink water (as animals do).

Lash out/1. to kick: "The donkey lashed out at the man behind him." 2. try suddenly to hit: "The man lashed out at the crowd with her umbrella."

Laugh all the way to the bank/to make a great deal of money with very little effort.

Laugh off/to dismiss with a laugh as not important or not serious; not take seriously: "She had a bad fall while ice skating but she laughed it off."

Lay aside/1. to put off until another time; interrupt an activity: "The Prime Minister laid aside politics to turn to foreign affairs." 2. save: "We tried to lay aside a little money each week for our vacation."

Lay by/to save, especially a little at a time; set aside goods for later acquisition, on a small deposit with interest-free payments: "The Browns laid a little money by every week till they had enough for a trip to Alaska." "The farmer laid by some of his best rice to use the next year for seed."

Lay down/1. to let (something) be taken; give up or surrender (something): "John was willing to lay down his life for his country." 2. ask people to follow; tell someone to obey; make (a rule or a principle): "The committee laid down rules about the size of basketball courts."

Lay down/to put down horizontally.

Lay down the law/1. to give strict orders: "The English teacher lays down the law about homework every afternoon." 2. speak severely or seriously about wrongdoing; scold: "The principal called in the pupils and laid down the law to them about skipping classes."

Lay in/to obtain a sufficient quantity (of stores etc.) to last for some time: "Olivia expected a shortage of dried fruit so she laid in a large supply."

Lay low/to knock down; force into a lying position; put out of action: "Jill was laid low by the flu."

Lay off/to put out of action: "The company lost the contract for making the clothes and laid off half of its workers."

Lay on/to arrange.

Lay out/1. to plan: "Come here, Jill. I have a job laid out for you." 2. plan gardens, building sites or the like; plan the building or arrangement of; design.

Lay to rest/1.to put a dead person into a grave or tomb; bury. 2. get rid of; put away permanently; stop: "The Scoutmaster's fears that John had drowned were laid to rest when John came back and said he had gone for a boat ride."

Lay up/to store carefully till needed again (used of ships, cars, etc.): "Before Fiona went to India for a year, she laid up her car, as she didn't want to sell it."

Lead by the nose/to have full control of; make or persuade (someone) to do anything whatever; dominate completely.

Lead the way/to go before and show how to somewhere; guide: "The girls need someone to lead the way on their hike."

Lead up to/to prepare the way for; introduce (figuratively): "Bella wanted to borrow my binoculars, but she didn't say at once. She led up to it by talking about bird watching."

Leave no stone unturned/to try in every way; miss no chance; do everything possible; make every effort possible to accomplish an aim; make every effort to do something.

Leave high and dry/to abandon someone: "When the time came to put up decorations, Jill was left high and dry."

Leave off/to stop (doing something): "Sam was playing his trumpet, but I told him to leave off because the neighbors were complaining about the noise."

Leave on/to allow to stay alight or keep burning or take off: "The gas fire had been left on overnight."

Leave out/to omit; decide not to do something: "When we printed the papers, we left out a page." "They'll sing their song leaving out the last ten verses."

Leave out in the cold/to be left alone or not included: "All the other children were chosen for parts in the play, but Ethan was left out in the cold." "Everybody made plans for Christmas Day, but Emily found herself left out in the cold."

Leave something out/to omit something; decide not to do something.

Left high and dry/to be stranded; be left out of things.

Lend a hand/to help.

Lend an ear/to listen sympathetically or attentively.

Lend itself to/to give a chance for or be useful for; be possible or right for: "Bill was sick and did not go to Jill's party, but his absence lent itself to misunderstanding."

Lend oneself to/to give help or approval to; encourage, assist: "Sally wouldn't lend herself to the plot to hide the teacher's chalk."

Let bygones be bygones/to let the past be forgotten: "After a long angry quarrel, the two girls agreed to let bygones be bygones and made friends again." "They should let bygones be bygones and try to get along with each other."

Let bygones be bygones/to forgive and forget past offences or causes of conflict.

Let (someone) down/1. to fail to do something that someone expected you to do; fail to do as well as (someone) expected; disappoint someone by failing to act as well as expected, or failing to fulfill an agreement: "The basketball team felt they had let the coach down." "She said she would finish the work Thursday, but she let me down." 2. to lower: "When Jackie lets her hair down it reaches her waist."

Let go/1. to stop holding something; loosen your hold; release: "The boy grabbed James's coat and would not let go." "When the child let go of her father's hand, she fell down." 2. to weaken and break under pressure. 3. to allow something to pass; do nothing about: "When James was tardy, the teacher scolded him and let it go at that."

Let in/to allow to enter; admit: "We let in the ticket-holders. I didn't have a key, but luckily someone was here to let me in."

Let off/1. to free someone who has done wrong; release: "Their teacher let them off the punishment because it was half-term." 2. refrain from punishing; forgive; excuse: "She thought that the magistrate was going to fine her, but he let her off." 3. explode; cause a firework to explode: "We let off hundreds of fireworks on New Year Eve."

Let off steam/to give full expressions to your feelings.

Let one's hair down/to behave wildly or uninhibitedly.

Let out/1. to make wider (of clothes): "That girl is growing. You'll need to let out her clothes." 2. allow to leave; release: "She opened the door and let out the cat."

Let something slip through one's fingers/to miss an opportunity.

Let the cat out of the bag/to disclose a secret; reveal secret or important news; reveal the secret motive; inform beforehand; tell something that is supposed to be a secret: "We wanted to surprise Jill with a birthday gift, but Bill let the cat out of the bag by asking her what she would like."; divulge a secret inadvertently: "She was afraid, being a little affected with wine, she would 'let the cat out of the bag'."

Let up/1. to become less or weaker or quiet; become slower or stop. 2. to do less or go
        slower or stop; relax; stop working or working hard: "Father has been working all his life.
        When is he going to let up?" "Abigail ran all the way home without letting up once."
Lie down/to recline.
Lie low/to hide; conceal one's intentions; to be in hiding. 1. stay quietly out of sight; try not
        to attract attention; hide. 2. keep secret one's thoughts or plans: "I think she wants to be
        elected president, but she is lying low and not saying anything."
Lift a finger or lift a hand or raise a hand/to do something; do your share; help: "We all
        worked hard except Andy. He wouldn't lift a finger." "The queen did not lift a hand when
        her people were hungry."
Lift one's game/to improve one's performance, often suddenly and dramatically.
Light up/to illuminate.
Line up/to take places in a line or formation; stand side by side or one behind another; form a
        line or pattern: "The girls lined up and took turns diving off the springboard."
Live and let live/to tolerate others' views and behaviour so that one's own might be tolerated
        in turn.
Live down/to live in such a manner that people will forget it (a bad refutation): "Victor has
        never quite been able to live down a reputation for drinking too much which he got when
        he was a young man."
Live from hand to mouth/to live only for today, without planning for the future; live on little
        money and spend it as fast as it comes in; live without saving for the future; have just
        enough; have very little money to live on; have hardly enough money to live on: "Mr.
        Taylor got very little pay, and his family lived from hand to mouth."
Live in/1. to live in the school you attend or the place where you work: "James decided to
        live in during his freshman year at college." 2. live in one's place of work (chiefly used
        of domestic servants): "Advertisement: Cook wanted. $300 a week. Live in." "It's a
        boring town to live in."
Live it up/to enjoy an extravagant lifestyle.
Live now, pay later/phr. The hedonistic philosophy of the early days of hire purchase, when one
        had the material things one desired at once, and paid for them at some later date.
Live off the land/to subsist on whatever fruit, animals, etc. one can find or kill.
Live on/1. to use as stable food: "We lived on next to nothing."
Live on a shoestring/to manage on very little money.
Live on borrowed time/to enjoy an unexpected extension of life; live or last longer than
        expected: "Ever since his operation, James felt he was living on borrowed time." "Mr.
        White was living on borrowed time because a year ago the doctor had told him he would
        only live six months."
Live on the edge/to live dangerously
Live out of a suitcase/to live or stay somewhere on a temporary basis and with only a limited
        selection of one's belonging.
Live together/to share the same room, apartment or house and it usually implies that there is a
        sexual relationship between the people concerned.
Live up to/to accord with or maintain (expectations and standards); maintain certain
        standards – moral, economic or behavioral; act according to; come up to; agree with;
        follow; be good as: "So far as she could, Jill had always tried to live up to the example
        she saw in Oprah." "Did the trip to America live up to your expectations?".

Live within one's means/to spend no more than one has.

Lock horns with (someone)/to get into an argument with someone.

Lock out/to prevent from entering, usually by means of a door and key: "He had no key, so he was locked out."

Lock up/1. to lock all doors (a house): "Dave locks up before he goes to bed at night." "Don't forget to lock up the house before going on holiday." 2. put in a locked place, i.e. box, safe, prison (a person or thing): "He locked up the papers in his desk."

Long for/to want something very much.

Look after or see after/1. to take care of; care for; handle; watch and take care of; watch over; attend to; take care of: "When Emma is at work, a friend of hers looks after her children." "Will you look after my dog when I am away?" "Who will look after the cat while we are on vacation?" 2. to keep; manage; mind; protect; run; keep safe: "Look after this book." "Will you look after my store while I'm at the doctor's?"

Look ahead/to consider the future so as to make provision for it: "It's time he looked ahead and Look at/1. to have a way of thinking or feeling toward; think about something in a certain way. 2. to watch; see; point one's eyes at: "He's looking at his watch." "Stop looking at me like that: it's getting on my nerves." 3. to review or analyse: "They looked at the picture on the tin." "There's so much to look at when you visit the National Museum."

Look back/1. to think about what happened in the past; consider the past; review the past; think of what has happened: "As Peter looked back, his life seemed good to him." " Andrew looked back on his early struggles as having made him feel especially alive." "When Peter applied for a job and asked the school to recommend him, the principal looked back over his records." 2. look behind: "Don't look back now but the man behind us is wearing the most extraordinary clothes."

Look back on/to consider the past; remember something from the past.

Look down on/to despise: "He thinks his neighbors look down on him a bit because he's never been abroad."

Look for/1. to think likely; expect: "They look for James to arrive any day." "John wouldn't go for a ride with the boys because he was looking for a phone call from Jill." 2. to seek; try to find; hunt; search for: "They are looking for a solution." "He's looking for his key." 3. to do things that cause (trouble); make (trouble) for oneself; provoke: "Henry often gets into fights because he is always looking for trouble." "If he says the opposite of everything that others say, he is looking for a quarrel."

Look forward to/1. to expect eagerly: "At breakfast, James looked forward to a difficult day." 2. to think with pleasure about something that is going to happen; expect something in the future with pleasure; expect with hope or pleasure; think ahead with pleasure: "She is looking forward to seeing her nephew when she visits her sister next week." "Is she looking forward to the party?"

Look in or call in/to call; pay a (often unannounced) visit: "The doctor will look in on Sara on his way home." "Roger will look in this evening to see how Melissa is doing."

Look into/to investigate; study; try to find out about; find out the facts about; examine; inspect; study the matter; investigate: "He'll look into the matter immediately." "I looked into the cave. The mayor felt he should look into the decrease of income from parking fines."

Look like a million dollars/to look great or extremely attractive.

Looks like rain/to appear as if rain is imminent: "It looks like rain."

Look on/1. to regard; consider; think of: "These students seem to look on their teachers as
their enemies." "The staff had always been looked on as a worthless company waste."
"Until the day John made the touchdown, the other boys had looked upon him as rather a
weak player." 2. to watch; to be a spectator only, not participator: "Two women were
fighting. The rest were looking on." 3. be facing: "Her house looks out on to the sea."
Look out /1. to watch to see whether anyone is coming, or whether something will happen;
watch out; take care; beware; be careful; be on guard: " Look out!" James called, as the
car came toward him." 2. be watchful; beware; be alert; keep watching: "A collector of
antique furniture asked John to look out for about 100 year old ones." "If you're going to
break the speed limit driving to work, look out for traffic wardens." 3. watch or keep (a
person or thing) and do what is needed; provide protection and care: "Anne looked out
for her brother's children one afternoon a week." "Uncle John looked out for his
brother's orphan son until the boy was through college."
Look out for/to exercise caution or be careful about: "If you're going barefoot, look out for
dangerous snakes." "We'd better watch out for kangaroo in the road."
Look out for/to be careful for another's safety; to keep one's eyes open so as to see
something if it presents itself (suggesting caution or danger).
Look out on/to be facing; to face something, as in an assembly: "Caesar Augustus looked out
over Rome's massed army."
Look round/to look behind: "Peter looked round the room."
Look over/to review or check; inspect critically; read it; read again; revise quickly: "He's going
to look over a house that he's thinking of buying." "She looked over the plan."
Look someone up and down/to review another in a manner with one's eyes: "She looked the girl
up and down disapprovingly.
Look through/1. to examine a number of things, often in order to select some of them; turn over
the pages of a book or newspaper, looking for information: "She looked through the
books and decided that he wouldn't like them." 2. look at someone without appearing to
do so as a deliberate act of rudeness: "He has to be polite to me in the office but when we
met outside he always looks through me." "In court, Marcia looked right through the
defendant, as he'd murdered her husband."
Look up/1.to improve (the subject is usually things, business, world affairs or the weather);
get brighter; improve chances in future; promise more success: "The first month was
tough, but business looked up after that." 2. look for information in a reference book;
search for a word or item in a dictionary, encyclopedia or other reference book; find the
meaning in a dictionary; look for it in the appropriate book or paper, i.e. address book,
dictionary, timetable or dictionary; consult; search for; hunt for information about; find:
"He didn't know the meaning of the word, so he looked it up in a dictionary." "It is a
good habit for students to look up new words in a dictionary." "If you don't know the
number, you can look it up in the phone book.". "He looked up the addresses and sent
out the invitations." 3. visit; seek and find: "While he was in New York, Peter looked up
a friend of college days." "He looked the addresses up and sent the invitations out."
"Anytime you come to Seoul, do look me up." 4. to look up from what one is doing; gaze
upwards: "He looked up and saw an airplane in the sky." "They looked up at the stars."
Look something up/to find information.
Look up to/to think of (someone) as a good example; to see as a mentor; honor; admire or
respect: "Mr. Brown had taught for many years, and all the students looked up to him."

Look up to someone/to respect someone highly; admire: "She had no role model to look up to." "Young students usually look up to great athletes."

Lose face/to be embarrassed or shamed by an error of failure; lose dignity, influence, reputation; lose self-respect or the confidence of others: "James' careless work made him lose face with his employer." "The banker lost face when people found out he bet on dog races."

Lose ground/1. to go backward; retreat. 2. to become weaker; get worse; not improve: "The sick woman began to lose ground when her cough grew worse." "When the Republicans are in power, the Democrats lose ground."

Lose one's marbles/to go mad.

Lose one's shirt/to lose all one's possessions, especially as the result of unwise financial transactions.

Lose one's temper/to lose control over one's anger; become angry: "She lost her temper when she broke the key in the lock."

Lose one's touch/not to show one's customary skill.

Lose out/to fail to win; miss first place in a contest; lose to a rival: "James lost out in the rivalry for Jill's hand in marriage." "John didn't want to lose out to the other salesman."

Lose sight of/1. to forget about: "Do not lose sight of your goals!" 2. to lose the view of something or someone: "I lost sight of Anne in the crowd." "I watched the ship go further and further until I lost sight of it." 2. forget; overlook: "Henry was so interested in the game he lost sight of the time." "No matter how famous and rich she became, she never lost sight of the fact that she had been born in the slums."

Lose sleep over/to worry excessively about something.

Lose the plot/to lose one's ability to understand what is happening; lose touch with reality.

Lose touch/to fail to keep in contact or communication: "I lost touch with Emily." "After he moved to another town, he lost touch with his childhood friends."

Lose track/to forget about something; not stay informed; fail to keep a count or record: "Sally lost track of her friends at camp after summer was over." "James lost track of the money he spent at the circus." "I lost track of Jenny when she changed her job."

Lose your nerve/to become afraid: "When the time came to face the gang, Jim lost his nerve and fled."

M

Make a day of it/to do something all day, usually as a matter of pleasure or enjoyment: "When we go to the beach we take a picnic lunch and make a day of it."

Make a difference or make the difference/to change the nature of something or a situation; be important; matter: "James good score on the test made the difference between his passing or failing the course." "It doesn't make a difference if he is late to my party. I just want him to come."

Make a fast buck/to earn money easily and quickly.

Make a fool of someone/to make (someone) look foolish: "The girl made a fool ofherself." "Jill's classmates made a fool of herself by telling her the party was to be a masquerade."

Make a go of something/to make a success of something; succeed at something as a result of hard work; cause to be a success; produce good results: "She was sure she could make a go of the hair salon."

Make a killing/to make a large profit.

Make a monkey out of someone/to humiliate someone by making him appear ridiculous.

Make a move/1. to take action. 2. start on a journey; leave somewhere.

Make a name for oneself/to become famous.

Make a noise/to speak or act in a way designed to attract a lot of attention or publicity.

Make a note of something/to write down somewhere and remember it.

Make a point/to try hard; make special effort: "She made a point of remembering to get her glasses fixed." "She made a point of thanking her hostess before she left the party."

Make a quid, dollar/to earn some money.

Make a song and dance about something/to make a great fuss.

Make a splash/to be noticed; make an impression on people; be successful and attract attention.

Make allowance/to judge results by the circumstances: "When a small girl is helping you, you must make allowance for her age."

Make allowance for/to take into consideration.

Make an exception/to allow someone or something not to be included in a general statement, judgement, or rule.

Make away with/to take; carry away; cause to disappear: "Three masked men held up the clerk and made away with the payroll."

Make an effort/to try.

Make believe/to act as if something is true while one knows it is not; pretend: "James made believe he didn't hear his mother calling." "If you and I don't really have a good time, let's make believe it was fun."

Make contact with/to meet

Make do with something/to use something inferior instead of something better; use a poor substitute when one does not have the right thing; manage, usually with some difficulty: "He'll do somehow, so don't worry." "Andrew did not have a hammer, and he had to make do with a heavy rock."

Make (both) ends meet/to live within one's income; keep expenditures within one's means; make the most of; fully use and enjoy; have enough money to pay one's bill; earn what it costs to live; pay one's bills, live within one's means: "Both James and his wife had to work to make ends meet."

Make every effort/to struggle, do one's best, try all means possible.

Make for/1. to head for; move in the direction of; go toward; start in the direction of: "They made for the site office." "They made sales tables." "This kind of get-together makes for good social relations." 2. provide a basis for: "His   management style doesn't make for good industrial relations." 3. travel toward.

Make friends/to become friends; form a friendship: "Mrs. Green invited Andy to her home party to play with Bill." "You can make friends with a monkey by giving him bananas."

Make fun of/to tease; joke about; laugh at; tease; mock: "John made fun of the new pupil because her speech was not like the other pupils."

Make great strides/to make good progress.

Make hay/to make good use of an opportunity while it lasts; move forward with an effort to completion; make a major push to accomplish something.

Make headway/to make progress.

Make it/to manage to arrive in time for what one wants to do; to succeed or accomplish an intention.

Make it known/to reveal information: "They made it known that they wanted to sell their car."

Make its mark/to have a lasting or significant effect.

Make love/1. to be warm, loving and tender toward someone of the opposite sex; try to get

him or her to love you too: "There was moonlight on the roses, and John made love to Jill
in the porch swing." 2. commonly, to have sexual relations with (someone): "It is
rumored that Peter tries to make love to every girl he hires as a secretary."
Make a mockery of something/to make something seem foolish or absurd.
Make a monkey out of (someone)/to make someone look foolish.
Make no bones about it/1. to have no doubts; not to worry about right or wrong; not to be
against: "James makes no bones about telling a lie to escape punishment." 2. to say
openly and without hesitation; make no secret; state something without hesitation; not
keep from talking; admit: "Andrew thinks being poor is no disgrace, and he makes no
bones about it." "Jill made no bones about her love of poetry even after some of her
friends laughed at her."
Make no mistake about it/not to be deceived into thinking otherwise.
Make of/think of: "What do you make of this newspaper article?" "What do you make of the
new teacher?" "I was unable to make anything of the scrawled message."
Make off/to leave hurriedly; run away (used of thieves etc.): "She made off when the alarm
rang." "The girls made off when they saw the policeman."
Make one's blood boil/to infuriate; to cause to be angry or indignant; make someone
very angry: "It made Jill's blood boil to see the children make fun of the crippled boy."
Make one's mouth water/1. to look or smell very good; make one want very much to eat or
drink something: "The pies in the shop window made Mark's mouth water." "The picture
of the ice cream soda made her mouth water." 2. to be attractive; make one want to have
something very much: "Jane loves cheesecake, and the strawberry one in the shop
window made her mouth water." 3. excite desire or envy.
Make one's way/1. to go forward with difficulty; find a path for yourself: "We made our way
through the crowd." 2. succeed; do many hard things to earn a living; make a life work
for yourself: "After finishing college, she made her way in the world."
Make or break/to cause success or complete failure: "The manager has the power to make or
break your career."
Make out/1. to write; write a check; spot; write facts asked for; fill out: "He made out a check
for $100." "Mrs. Green gave the clerk in the shop some money, and the clerk made out a
receipt." 2. discover the meaning of, understand, see or hear clearly; understand; see,
hear, or understand by trying hard: "She can't make out the address; he has written it so
badly." "Mr. Brown does many strange things. No one can make him out." 3. state; make
someone believe; show; prove: "John and Bill had a fight, and John tried to make out that
Bill started." "She made out that she was a student looking for a job." 4. get on: "How
is he all making out?" 5. colloq., to kiss. 6. claim: "It's not as expensive as it's made out
to be." "He always makes out that he's right."
Make over/to make something look different; change the style of: "John asks the tailor to
make over his pants. The tailor cut off the cuffs and put a belt across the back."
Make peace with/to agree to stop arguing or fighting.
Make sense/1. understandable; not difficult or strange. 2. seem right to do; sound reasonable
or practical: "Does it make sense to let little boys play with matches?
Make sense of/to understand something because you have thought after it."
Make sure/to see about something yourself; look at to be sure: "Mother makes sure that all
the lights are off before she goes to bed."
Make somebody's day/to make somebody very happy.

Make someone's blood boil/to make someone very angry.

Make something from scratch/to begin with the basic ingredients

Make something up/to invent or create something (from your imagination): "I had to make up a story."

Make sure/to check.

Make the blood boil/to make one's blood boil.

Make the most of/to do the most you can with; get the most from; use to the greatest advantage, fully use and enjoy: "He planned the weekend in town to make the most of it." "John studied hard. He wanted to make the most of his chance to learn.".

Make time/to arrange free time to do something.

Make up/1. to become friends again after a quarrel; end it (a quarrel); be reconciled; renew friendship; return to good relations: "After the row, she kissed him and asked to make up." "Isn't it time Fiona and you made up after your quarrel?" 2. invent something that is not true; create something from your imagination; invent (an answer, excuse, a story, explanation); think and say something that is new or not true: "They had to make up a story." "James makes up stories to amuse his little sisters." 3. constitute; put together; compound; compose; make things by putting things or parts together: "The women make up only 9 percent of top management." "She asked two junior players to make up the basketball team." 4. do or provide (something lacking or needed); do or supply (something not done, lost, or missed); get back; repay: "He has to make up the test he missed last week." "She wants to go to bed early to make up the sleep." 5. to do what is lacking or needed; do or give what should be done or given; get or give back what has been lost, missed, or not done; get or give instead; pay back: "They made up for lost time by taking an airplane instead of a train." "Jill had to make up for the time she missed in school when she was sick, by studying very hard." 6. apply cosmetics; use cosmetics; put on lipstick and face powder: "James watched his sister make up her face for her date."

Make up/1. to invent. 2. do past work.

Make up for/to do something good after having done something bad; compensate for: "He'll have to work very hard today to make up for the time he wasted yesterday." "I made up for the slow start."

Make up one's mind/to make a decision; come to a decision; choose what to do; decide: "We made up our minds to sell the house." "In the end she made up her mind to go by bus."

Make war on/ to oppose someone or something and do things to stop a course of action; to fight or engage in conflict.

Make waves/to cause a disturbance; make one's influence felt: "John White is the wrong man for the job; he is always trying to make waves."

Make way/to stand aside; move from in front so someone can go through; stand aside: "The people made way for the queen."

Make yourself at home/ you behave in an informal, relaxed way because you feel comfortable and welcome in a place.

Make yourself understand/ you succeed in expressing what you mean in a way that other people can understand.

Mean business/to decide strongly to do what you plan to do; really mean it; be serious: The manager said he would fire us if we didn't work harder and he means business. When he went to college to study, he meant business. She just liked the company of the other boys she dated; but this time she seems to mean business.

Measure up/to be equal; be of fully high quality; come up: Peter didn't measure up to the best
        catchers, but he was a good one. Jane's school work didn't measure up to her ability.
Meet halfway or go halfway/to give up part of what you want or to do your share in
        reaching agreement with someone: Mark wants make up after your fight and you
        should meet him halfway. James met Jill halfway after their argument.
Meet one's Waterloo/to suffer a decisive defeat
Meet up with/1. to meet (someone): "I met up with her in Paris." "In the woods, she met with
        two strangers." "They met up with us on holiday." 2. experience (as unhappiness); suffer
        (as bad luck); have (as an accident or mishap): "The farmer met with misfortune; her
        crops were destroyed by a storm." "The tourist met with an accident on the road."
Mend fences/to attempt to improve relations between opposing groups
Mend one's fences/to do something to resolve past differences; strengthen friendships or
        influence: "After their squabble over a fenceline boundary, Mr. Smith and Mr. Jones
        decided to mend their fences." "The Congressman went home from Washington to mend
        his fences with a disappointed constituency."
Mess around/1. to engage in idle or purposeless activity: "Come on, girls, start doing some work
        and don't just mess around all day!" 2. to be promiscuous, to indulge in kissing with little
        discrimination: "James needs straightening out; he's been trying to mess around with
        nearly the whole female population of his class."
Mess up/1. to cause trouble, to spoil something: "What did I have to mess up your
        accounts for?" 2. to cause someone emotional trauma: "John will never get
        married; he got messed up when he was a teenager."
Miss out/to leave out; fail to use information.
Miss the boat or miss the bus/to lose an opportunity; lost opportunity.
Mix up/to confuse; make a mistake about: "Bill doesn't know colors yet; he mixes up purple
        with blue." "The twins' father mixes them up all the time when he introduces them."
        "These two words are so similar that I keep mixing them up."
Money talks/ a saying that means money has power and influence.
Monkey around with (someone or something)/to play with or waste time with someone or
        something.
Move heaven and earth/to make every effort; do one's utmost; try every way; do everything
        you can: "James moved heaven and earth to be sent to Washington."
Move in/to move self and possessions into new house, flat, room, etc: I've rented a new
        apartment. I'm moving on Thursday."
Move mountains/to carry out a difficult task.
Move on/to continue a journey and go to a different place.
Move on or up/to advance; go higher: "Normally in high school, students move up every year."
Move out/to leave one's house, flat, etc., with possessions; vacate one's accommodation: "I
        have found a new apartment. The present tenant is moving out this weekend, and I am
        moving in on Thursday."
Move the goalposts or shift the goalposts/to change the rules: "Mary moves the goalposts of
        her partnership slightly, but Patricia abandons them entirely. For both, the effects are far-
        reaching."
Muck about/to muck around/to fool around; not get on with the job.
"My head is spinning."/expr., to have too many things to think about, inducing a dizzying effect.
"My lips are sealed."/expr., to keep a secret.

N

Nail down/to make certain; make sure; settle: "Jane had a hard time selling his car, but she
finally nailed the sale down when she got her friend, Anne, to give her $300."
Name after/to give a baby the name of someone else: "Can we name the baby after you, if it's a
girl?"
Need eyes in the back of your head/to need to observe in all directions; to have the
appearance of doing so: "Bernard seems to have eyes in the back of his head. He
always knows what I'm up to."
Need no introduction/to be well-known, famous, or familiar to one's audience.
Need one's head examined/to be foolishly irresponsible.
Not have a clue/to be unintelligent.
Not know which way to turn or not know which way to jump/to be puzzled about getting out
of a difficulty; not know what to do to get out of trouble: "When Elizabeth missed the last
bus home, she didn't know which way to turn." "After Mr. Scott died, Mrs. Scott had no
money to pay the bills. When the landlord told her to pay the rent or move out, she didn't
know which way to turn."

O

"One swallow doesn't make a summer."/expr., a single instance or indicator of something is
not necessarily significant.
Open its doors/1. to allow someone or something to enter or join; become open: "The college
was stated for men only, but a few years ago it opened its doors to women." 2. to begin
doing business; open: "Myers Department Store is having a birthday sale; it first opened
its doors ninety years ago this month."
Open one's eyes/to see or understand the truth; realize; tell a person what is really happening or
what really exists: "Jill didn't believe that her cousin could be mean until the cousin
opened Jill's eyes by scratching and biting her." "Peter's eyes were opened up to the
world of nature when he visited his grandfather's farm."
Open one's heart/1. to talk about one's feelings honestly; confide in someone: "After going
around worrying, John opened his heart to his father." "Robert felt much better after he
opened his heart to Jane." 2. to show sympathy; give concern, regard or help generously:
"Mrs. Green opened her heart to the poor little boy." "After the moving speech by Bono,
people opened their hearts to the poor of Africa."
Open the door/to allow more action or discussion; give a chance: "Raising taxes will open doors
to more help for those in need."
Open up/1. to show for the first time; make clear; reveal: "The story of Lincoln's life opened up
a whole new world for John." 2. make available; present opportunity; offer: "James
opened up a whole new section of the Scrabble board." 3. begin to talk frankly: "After
Frank learned to trust Mr. Smith, he opened up and told him how he felt." 4. become
available: "When he completed his college degree, many new jobs opened up."
Opt for/to choose something or decide to do something.
Opt out/to choose not to participate or be involved.
Order about/to give one a lot of orders: "He is a retired general and still has the habit of
ordering people about."
Own up/to confess; take the blame; admit your guilt; confess: "When Mr. Smith asked who

broke the window, Robert owned up to it." "Jill owned up to having borrowed her sister's
sweater."

P

Part with/1. to separate from; leave: "She parted with us at the end of the trip." 2. let go;
    release; give up: "We were sorry to part with the old house." "Robert had to part with his
    friend when she married."
The party's over/expr., a period of success, good fortune, etc. has come to an end.
Pass away/1. to die; pass away: "She passed away at seventy." "She passed away in her
    sleep." "Her grandmother passed away one year ago." 2. to slip by; go by; pass: "They
    had so much fun that the weekend passed away they realized it." "Thirty years had passed
    away since we had met." 3. cease to exist; end; disappear; vanish: "When motor cars
    became popular, the use of the horse passed away."
Pass off/1. to take place. 2. masquerade: "She passed herself off as a Texan millionaire."
Pass on/to give away (what has been outgrown): "As she grew up, she passed on her clothes to
    her younger sister."
Pass out/1. to lose consciousness; faint; become unconscious: "She passed out in the
    crowded, airless compartment." 2. not to consider someone for promotion: "The manager
    passed my sister over." 3. distribute.
Pass over to the other side/to die.
Pass some up/to refrain from accepting.
Pass the buck/to pass responsibility onto someone else; shift the responsibility or blame to
    another person; blame someone else; make another person decide something or accept a
    responsibility or give orders; shift or escape responsibility or blame: "Lee tried to find out
    if the goods had been sent, but everyone just passed the buck." "Mrs. Jones complained
    to the man who sold her the bad meat, but he only passed the buck and told her it was the
    farmer's fault."
Pat someone on the back/1. to clap lightly on the back in support, encouragement, or praise:
    "The tennis coach patted the player on the back and said a few encouraging words." 2.
    make support or encouragement for (someone) felt; praise: "After she won the game,
    everyone patted her on the back for days."
Pave the way/to make preparations; ease the way.
Pay back/1. to repay (money that one borrowed): "Thanks for lending me the money. I'll pay
    you back next month." "He must pay back the money that he borrowed." 2. to take
    revenge: "He'll pay you back for this. He always does when he feels wronged."
Pay for/1. to suffer because of something; to be punished or suffer because of: "When Robert
    could not get a good job, he realized he had to pay for all the year of fooling around
    instead of working in school." "Jill was very mean to James because she wanted to make
    him pay for all the years in which he had ignored her." 2. to pay somebody for
    something; pay a bill: "You haven't paid for your   orange juice." "They paid for the
    flat." "Have you paid Mark for the tickets?"
Pay one's way/to earn enough to cover one's costs.
Pay lip service to (something)/to talk about an issue without sincerity (without meaning what
    is said).
Pay off/1. to pay the wages of: "The women were paid off just before quitting time, the last

day before the holiday." 2. to pay and discharge from a job. 3. to bring a return; make profit: "At first Mr. Jones lost money on his investments, but finally one paid off." 4. prove successful, rewarding, or worthwhile: "Bill's friendship with the old man who lived beside him paid off in pleasant hours and broadened interests."

Pay one's respects/to make a polite visit to someone; to attend a funeral or wake.

Pay out/1. to pay off. 2. to revenge.

Pay your way/to live free of debt.

Pay up/to pay money owed in full; pay in full; pay the amount of; pay what is owed: "The monthly installments on the boat were paid up." "She pays her dues up promptly." "She gets behind when she is out of work but always pays up when she is working again." "Unless she pays up I shall tell my solicitor to write to her."

Pick and choose/to select with much care; choose in a fussy way; take a long time before choosing: "She was always one to pick and choose her hats." "I don't get to pick and choose who I work with."

Pick on/1. to make a habit of annoying or bothering (weaker people); do or say bad things to (someone): "Other girls picked on her until she decided to fight them."

Pick out/to choose, select, distinguish from a group: "Here are eight rings. Pick out the one you like best."

Pick up/1. to go and get someone (from their home or a location); raise or lift a person or thing, usually from the ground or from a table or chair; lift something up with your hand; take up; lift: "During the morning, Mrs. Jones picked up sticks in the yard." "Anthony picked up a coin in the yard." "He scatters toys all over the floor, and I have to pick them up." "He picked the phone up immediately." 2. collect (someone); call for; collect; take with one (in a vehicle); give someone a ride in the car: "She had to pick up the kids from school." "Henry picked John up on his way home." "There's always litter here. No one ever picks it up." 3. pay for someone else: "After lunch, in the restaurant, Uncle Robert picked up the check." 4. take on or away; receive; get: "At the next corner, the bus stopped and picked up three pupils." 5. get from different places at different times; a little at a time; collect: "She had picked up rare coins in seaports all over the world." 6. acquire cheaply; learn without effort; obtain without trying; acquire accidentally: "Pupils usually pick up foreign languages very quickly." "She picked up knowledge of radio just by staying around the radio station." 6. to gather together; collect: "The old people picked the litter up." "He dropped his keys and quickly picked them up." 7. speak to a stranger in order to invite them to start a relationship; proposition. 8. take in one's hand.

Pile up/to grow into a big heap: "She didn't go into her office for three days and her work kept piling up."

Pinch pennies/not to spend a penny more than necessary; be very saving or thrifty: "When John and Jill were saving money to buy a house, they had to pinch pennies."

Pin down/1. to keep (someone) from moving; make stay in a place or position; trap: "Mr. Brown's leg was pinned down under the car after the accident." 2. tell clearly and exactly; explain so that there is no doubt.

Piss off/to bother, annoy, irritate: "He really pisses me off when he talks like that."

Pit against/to match against; oppose to; put in opposition to; place in competition or rivalry with: "The game pits two of the best pro basketball teams in the East each other." "She pitted her endurance against the other woman's speed."

Play around/to joke; have an affair.

Play by the rules/to follow what is generally held to be the correct line of behavior

Play down/to give less emphasis to; make (something) seem less important; divert attention from; draw notice away from; give little importance to something by paying no attention to it, or be belittling its significance: "The newspaper stories played down the actress's unattractive past."

Play hard ball/to negotiate without compromise.

Play havoc with/to completely disrupt; cause serious damage to.

Play into one's hands/to be or do something that another person can use against you; help an opponent against yourself: "In the basketball game, John's foul played into the opponents' hands." "Anne and Bill both wanted the last piece of cake, but Bill played into Anne's hands by trying to grab it."

Play off/1. when two teams play against each other to decide the competition winner 2. match opposing persons, forces, or interests so that they balance each other: "The boy played off his admirers against each other." 3. settle (a tie score) between contestants by more play.

Played out/to be used up, finished, exhausted.

Play politics/to make secret agreements for your own gain; handle different groups for your own advantage: "In order to get elected, she had to play politics with both the unions and the bosses." "Anne always gets what she wants by playing office politics."

Play safe or play it safe/to be very careful; accept small gains or none to avoid loss; avoid danger of the sake of safety: "She grew tired as the game went on and began to play safe." "James didn't know what the other driver would do, so he played it safe and stopped his own car."

Play second fiddle/to take a back seat while someone else leads; act a smaller part; follow another's lead; be less noticed: "Her husband had the stronger mind, and she played second fiddle to him."

Play the game/to behave fairly and honourably; act fairly.

Play with fire/to put oneself in danger; take risks: take unnecessary risks; court danger; put oneself in danger; take risks: "Leaving your door unlocked in L.A. is playing with fire." "The Doctor told Mr. White that he must watch his diet if he doesn't want to play with fire."

Plug in/to connect (an electrical appliance) to a power wire by putting its plug into a receptacle or hole; connect to the electricity supply: "The television isn't working because you haven't plugged it in."

Plug into/to connect (an electrical appliance) to a power wire by putting its plug into a receptacle or hole: "She thought she had left the lamp plugged into the wall, and so was puzzled when it wouldn't light that night."

Point out/1. to indicate; show by pointing with the finger; point to; make clear the location: "The guide pointed out the main sights of the city." 2.call someone's attention to; draw attention to something; bring to notice; call to attention; explain: "The school administrator pointed out that the closing date for making applications had passed." "He pointed out the mistake."

Point the finger/to blame somebody else.

Poke one's nose into something/to interfere in a matter not properly one's own: "She always her noses into other people's business."

Polish off/to finish drinking something that you like.

Pop into/to go into.

Pop up/1. to appear suddenly or unexpectedly; show up; come out: "Just when the coach thought she had everything under control, a new problem popped up." "After no one had heard from him for years, Robert popped up in town again."

Pork barrel/to supply an inappropriate share of government money to, in return for political support.

Pour/throw cold water on something/to discourage, quench enthusiasm for something; dampen enthusiasm.

Pour oil on troubled waters/to quiet a quarrel; say something to lessen anger and bring peace.

Practice what you preach/a saying that says to behave as one tells others to behave.

Prepare the ground/to make it easier for something to occur or be developed.

Press on/to continue to work hard: "Regardless of all the interruptions, he pressed on with the job." "They pressed on resolutely."

Press the panic button/to respond to a situation by panicking.

Prevent (object) from/to interfere with or stop another in a particular course of action: "Their party prevented everybody from sleeping last night."

Promise the moon/to promise something impossible: "He can't promise you the moon, but he'll do the best job he can."

"Publish or perish"/referring to an attitude or practice existing within academic institutions; to have a requirement formally to document one's knowledge in a professional publication, book, or setting.

Pull back/1. to move something away or to the side with one's hand: "He pulled the child back from the edge of the road." 2. stop oneself from doing something: "She pulled back from calling me a liar." 3. withdraw.

Pull down/to demolish (used of buildings): "He'll pull down those posters and stick up new ones."

Pull off/to succeed with something; succeed in (something thought difficult or impossible); do: "Much to our surprise, she pulled off the deal." "Seri Park pulled off the impossible by winning three gold tournaments in one year."

Pull one's leg/to get someone to accept a ridiculous story as true; fool someone with a humorous account of something: "For a moment, I actually believed that her husband had royal blood. Then I realized she was pulling my leg." "He was only pulling your leg."

Pull one's socks up/to make an effort to improve one's work, performance, or behavior.

Pull one's weight/to do one's fair share of work.

Pull out of hat/to accomplish as if by magic; invent; imagine: "Let's see John pull this one out of his hat!"

Pull over/to drive to the side of the road and stop: "James pulled over to let the ambulance pass."

Pull strings/to exert influence; secretly use influence and power, especially with people in charge or in important jobs to do or get something; make use of friends to gain one's wishes: "If you want to see the President, Mr. Bush can pull strings for you."

Pull the plug on/to prevent from happening or continuing; put a stop to.

Pull the strings/to be in control of events or of other people's actions.

Pull the wool over one's eyes/to fool someone into thinking well of you; deceive; deliberately mislead someone: "Anthony tried to pull the wool over his teacher's eyes, but she was too smart for him."

Pull through/1. to help through; bring safely through a difficulty or sudden trouble; save: "A generous loan showed the bank's faith in Robert and pulled him through the business trouble." 2. recover from an illness or misfortune; conquer a disaster; escape death or failure: "In a near-miracle, she pulled through after the smash-up." "We thought he was going to die but his own will-power pulled him through."

Pull together/to join efforts with those of others; work on a task together; cooperate: "James was a good basketball captain because he always got his teammates to pull together."

Pull up/to halt; stop (of vehicles): "John pulled up his horse at the gate." "The bus pulled up at the traffic lights." "They pulled up the boards at the bottom of the boat."

Pump iron/to lift weights, as a form of exercise or as a competitive sport; to work out with weights in a gymnasium.

Punch above one's weight/to engage in an activity or contest perceived as being beyond one's capacity or abilities.

Push around/to boss; bully: "Peter is always pushing the smaller children around."

Push the envelope/phr. to go to the limit; to go beyond established limits; to do something new, to pioneer.

Push the panic button/to become very much frightened; nervous, or excited especially at a time of danger or worry: "James thought he saw a ghost and pushed the panic button."

Push yourself/to force oneself to work hard.

Put across/1. to make oneself clear; explain clearly; make oneself understood; communicate: "She knew how to put her ideas across." "She found it hard to put her ideas across to the other committee members." 2. get (something) done successfully; bring to success; make real: "She put across a big sales campaign." 3. connect: "The receptionist put him across to Mr. Brown's phone."

Put all your eggs in one basket/ risk everything on one's venture.

Put an end to or put a stop to/1. to make (something) end; stop; end. 2. destroy or kill: "The new highway took most of the traffic from the old road and put an end to Mr. Brown's motel business." "When the horse broke her leg, the farmer put an end to her."

Put aside or put by/to save for future use (usually money): "Jackie puts aside $100 per month to pay for her summer holiday."

Put away/1. to tidy; remove to an appropriate place; put it in the place where it is kept, usually out of sight; put tidily out of sight (usually in drawers, cupboards etc.); put something in the place where it is usually kept; put in the right place or out of sight: "He put away the towels." "Put your toys away, boys; it's bedtime." 2. lay aside; stop thinking about: "She put her worries away for the weekend." 3. eat.

Put back/1. to return to the original place; replace something to where it was found or where it belongs: "You can look at the dictionary, but remember put it back on the shelf." "When you've finished with the CDs, put them back on the shelf." "He read the letter and then put it back in the envelope." 2. retard the hands (of a clock or watch); return to the customs of the past.

Put down/1. to crush a rebellion or movement; stop by force; crush: "In 48 hours, the General had entirely put down the rebellion." 2. write a record of; write down: "Put down her phone number before you forget it." "She put down the story while it was fresh in her mind." 3. name as a cause; attribute: "Some people put success down to sheer luck." 4. decide the kind or class of; characterize: "James put the man as a bum." "He finished the book and put it down." 5. making someone look small: "He was her mother's least favorite child, and she always put him down." "His manager always used to put him down in front of other people." 6. the opposite of pick up: "Victor picked up the saucepan and put it down at once because the handle was almost red-hot."

Put down to/to attribute: "The children wouldn't answer her, but she wasn't annoyed as she put it down to shyness." "He hasn't been well since she came to this country; I put it down to the climate."

Put forward or put on/1. the opposite of put back; to advance the hands (of clocks and watches): "In March, Scotland put their clocks forward an hour." 2. propose: "He put my name forward to the committee."

Put in/1. to make a claim: "Dave put in a claim for compensation because he had lost his luggage in the train crash." 2. submitted. 3. installed.

Put in for/to apply for a job or a post: "They are looking for a lecturer in history. Why don't you put in for it?"

Put in place/1. to set up or install (a key element relating to a policy, program, or enterprise, etc.). 2. to implement (a policy, program, enterprise, etc.).

Put money on/to have confidence in the truth or success of something.

Put off/1. to delay; postpone an action; decide to do something later than planned; wait and have (something) at a later time; postpone it: "John put off his meeting with my parents." "He put off going to the dentist." "I'll put off my visit to Sweden till the weather is warmer." 2. feel badly about something you dislike; cause confusion in; embarrass; displease; repel; deter one: "I was put off by the shamelessness of her proposal." "She was quite put off by the way he spoke to her. Jackie wanted to see the exhibition but the queue put her off." 3. distracted.

Put on/1. to dress; the opposite of take off; dress oneself (clothes, glasses or jewelry); dress in: "It was cold, so he put on his coat." "Dave put on a black coat so that he would be inconspicuous." "Diana put on her best clothes for the interview." 2. begin to have more (body weight); gain (weight); get heavier: "Since Anne was thin from sickness, the doctor said that she must put on 4 kilograms." 3. plan and prepare; produce or perform (a play); arrange; give; stage; mount: "The junior class put on a dance." "The pupils usually put on a play at the end of the year." 4. switch it on (a light, gas or electric fire or radio): "Put on that radio."

Put on the back burner/to assign (something) a low status or priority.

Put on the line or lay on the line/1. to pay or offer to pay. 2. to take a chance of losing; risk: "Charles decided to put his job on the line and tell the boss that he thought he was wrong."

Put one's feet in it or put one's foot in one's mouth/to speak carelessly and rudely; hurt another's feelings without intending to; make a rude mistake; say the wrong thing and feel embarrassed: "She put her foot in it with her remark about self-made men, because Smith was one of them." "He put his foot in his mouth with his joke about church, not knowing that one of the guests belonged to it."

Put one's finger on something or lay one's finger on/to find exactly; see exactly what the problem is, or what the answer is: "They called in an electrician on the cause of the short circuit."

Put one's foot down/to be firm about something; to take a decided stand; be stubborn in decision; assert one's authority: "Jane didn't want to practice her piano lesson, but Mother put her foot down."

Put one's foot in one's mouth or put one's put in it/to speak carelessly and rudely; hurt another's feelings without intending to; make a rude mistake: "She put her foot her foot in it with her remark about self-made women because Brown was one of them." "He put his foot in his mouth with his joke about that church, not knowing that one of the guests belonged to it."

Put one's head in the sand or hide one's head in the sand/to keep from seeing, knowing, or understanding something dangerous or unpleasant; refuse to see or face something: "If there is a war, you cannot put your head in the sand."

Put one's house in order/to make necessary reforms.

Put one's mind to/to direct thoughts towards an object; focus intently.

Put one's money where one's mouth is/to follow through a stated intention.

Put out/1. to stop something burning; extinguish (any kind of light, cigarette or fire); make a flame or light stop burning; turn off: "Put out your cigarettes." "She put out the flames with a bucket of water." 2. leave outside: "Donald put out the rubbish." 3. to be inconvenienced or annoyed: "Sarah is very selfish. She put me out over his refusal to cooperate at work."

Put someone on notice/to warn someone of something about or likely to occur, often formally or threateningly.

Put someone's back up/to irritate.

Put something behind one/to overcome a bad experience by distancing oneself from it.

Put something in a nutshell/to state something accurately and in a few words only. Put something on the map/to make something prominent or important.

Put the cart before the horse/to get or do things the wrong way round.

Put the dampers on something/to discourage; hinder.

Put the lid on/to put a stop to.

Put or set the record straight/to correct an error or misunderstanding.

Put this behind me/to recover from (this unhappy experience.).

Put (someone) through/to connect you with telephone: He phoned reception and she put him through to customer services.

Put to sleep/to kill.

Put together/to make; mix; assemble.

Put two and two together/to draw an obvious conclusion.

Put up/1. to accommodate. 2. provide lodging for; accommodate for a short time (a visitor): "I can put him up for a couple of nights." "Could you put up my brother for three nights?" 3. get ready; prepare: "Put up my umbrella.; it's starting to rain." 4. place on sale; offer for sale: "He put the house up for sale." 5. build; erect (a building, monument, statue, etc.): "Roger put up a shed in the garden." 6. raise (prices): "When the importing of bananas was forbidden, home growers put up their prices." 7. install: "I've put up that picture you brought last week." 8. give one the idea of doing it or tell one how to do it: "Diana couldn't have thought of that trick by himself. Someone must have put her up to it." 7. display for others to see. 9. fix.

Put up or shut up/1. to be serious or withdraw; produce what's been promised or be quiet 2. prove something or stop saying it: "'Put up or shut up,'" said her partner when she argued about her share of the business."

Put up with/bear something (burden) even though it's disliked; suffer; tolerate; accept patiently; bear patiently: "I don't know how she's put up with him." "They had to put

up with a lot of noise when the children were at home." "It is so late now that they will
have to put up with this miserable hotel." "She's difficult to put up with."
Put your cards on the table/to be honest and reveal all.
Put your feet up/to rest.

R
Rain cats and dogs or rain buckets/to rain heavily; rain very hard; come down in torrents: "Jack
looked out of the window and said, 'It's raining cats and dogs, so we can't go out to play
now.'"
Raise the alarm/to warn people of danger.
Raise the bar/to lift the standard; to improve.
Raise (some) eyebrows/to shock or surprise people mildly; to shock people; cause
surprise or disapproval: "The news that the prince was engaged to a commoner raised
eyebrows all over the kingdom."
Read between the lines/to understand something which is implied; understand all of a
writer's meaning by guessing at what he has left unsaid.
Read my lips/to listen carefully.
Read out/to say.
Recharge battery or recharge one's batteries/to train or educate oneself or take time out for
relaxation.
Reckon with/to consider as changing a situation; consider (something) that will make a
difference in the results.
Rein supreme/to rule (completely or with authority).
Render assistance to/to provide help, aid, or assistance.
Resign oneself/to stop arguing; accept something that cannot be changed: "When Anne's
father explained that he could not afford to buy her a new bicycle, she finally resigned
herself to riding the old one."
Revolve around/to move in a circular orbit, like a planet around a star; treat a person or thing
as the most important element: "Her entire life revolved around one thing – LPGA."
Rewrite history/to select or interpret events from the past in a way that suits one's own
particular purpose.
Ride high/to go well.
Ride off/to move away by means of transport: "Sally got on her bike and rode off."
Ride out/to survive safely; endure: "James decided to ride out his troubles by saying that he
had made a mistake but that he had learned his lesson."
Right hand doesn't know what the left hand's doing/phr. a state of confusion or a failure of
communication within a group or organization.
Ring a bell/to recall a distant memory; remind someone of something, jog someone's
memory (of a shared experience).
Ring back/to telephone again: "He'll ring you back in ten minutes."
Ring off/to end a telephone call; end a phone conversation: "He rang off when his boss came into
the room." "She rang off."
Ring up/1. to telephone: "Jill rang up Jane and told her the news." "I rang up all the friends I had
made on the East Sea cruise the previous summer." 2. register cash in a till: "The
assistant rang up $30 for the garment."
Rip off/1. to cheat somebody; steal; pay too much: "I think you were ripped off." "The

hippies ripped off the milk bar." 2. end a telephone call by putting down the receiver: "She rang off before I could ask her name."

Rise from the ashes/to be renewed after destruction.

Rise through the ranks/to advance from a lowly position in an organization by one's own efforts.

Roar with laughter/to laugh noisily and hard.

Rob Peter to pay Paul/to pay one person at another's expense; benefit one person or enterprise at the expense of another; change one duty or need for another; take from one person or thing to pay another: "James owed John a dollar, so he borrowed another from Peter to pay John. He robbed Peter to pay Paul."

Rock the boat/to make trouble and risk losing or upsetting something; cause a disturbance that may spoil a plan: "The other boys said that Mark was rocking the boat by wanting to let the girls into their club."

Roll out the red carpet/1. to welcome an important guest by putting a red carpet down for him to walk on: "We rolled out the red carpet for the King when he arrived in Japan." 2. greet a person with great respect and honor; give a hearty welcome: "Anne's family rolled out the red carpet for her teacher when she came to dinner."

Roll up one's sleeves/to get ready for a hard job; prepare to work hard or seriously: "When Robert took his science examination, he saw how little he knew about science. He rolled up his sleeves and went to work."

Roll over/to invest a lump sum received on termination of employment in an approved deposit fund.

Rome was not built in a day/phr., a complex or ambitious task is bound to take a long time and should not be rushed.

The rot sets in /phr., a rapid succession of failures begins.

Round up/1. to drive or bring together (people, cattle or horses). 2. Collect; gather: James rounded up many names for his petition.

Rub off/to remove or be removed by rubbing; erase: "Anne thought that the good luck would rub off."

Rub out/to erase pencil or ink marks with an India-rubber: "The boy wrote down the wrong word and then rubbed it out." "I'm writing in pencils so that I can rub out my mistakes."

Rub salt in the wound/intentionally to increase someone's pain, discomfort.

Rub shoulders or rub elbows/to be in the same place (with others); meet and mix: "City people and country people, old and young, rub shoulders with people from faraway lands."

Rub shoulders with someone/to meet someone or work alongside someone.

Rub up/to revise one's knowledge of a subject: "I am going to China; I must rub up my Chinese."

Rule out/1. to say that (something) must not be done; not allow; decide against: "The principal ruled out singing on school nights." "Jill probably will not go to college, but she has not ruled it out." 2. show that (someone or something) is not a possibility; make it unnecessary to think about; remove (a chance): "They have to find a baby-sitter for tonight; Anne has a date, so that rules her out." 3. make impossible; prevent: "Father's death seems to rule out college for Anne." "Jane's date for the dance ruled out any baby-sitting that evening."

Rule the roost/to be dominant, display one's authority; be leader or boss; be in charge: "Peter is very bossy; he always wants to rule the roost."

Rule them with an iron hand/to control or supervise others with little toleration for dissent or disagreement; to possess firm control over subordinates.

Run across/to find by chance; meet someone by chance: "You ran across my brother at the airport the other day."

Run after/to pursue.

Run amuck/to be frenzied, out of control.

Run away/to escape; flee; desert (one's home or school etc.); elope; leave and not plan to come back; go out without permission; escape: "Many times James said he would run away from home, but he never did." "Sam ran away from home and got a job in a garage." "The burglar ran away (or ran off)."

Run away with/1. to become uncontrollable (in one's emotions); gallop off out of rider's control (of horses): "Her horse ran away with her, and she had a bad fall." 2. flee; desert: "The rat ran away from our cat." The girl ran away from school. 3. take quickly and secretly, especially without permission; steal: "A burglar ran away with grandpa's silver teapot." 4. go away with: "Jane said that if her parents wouldn't let her marry Peter, she would run away with him." 5. to be much better or noticeable than others; win easily: "Their team ran away with the game in the last half." 6. accept an idea too hastily: "You shouldn't run away with the idea that I am unsociable; I just haven't time to go out much."

Run down/1. to knock down with a vehicle: "She was run down by a speeding motorist." 2. speak ill of; disparage: "He loves running people down behind their backs." "She is always running down her neighbors." 3. slowly bring to a halt; become unwound or discharged (of clocks or batteries etc.): "The Coal Board has been running that mine down for the last five years."

Run dry/to be completely used up.

Run in the blood or run in the family/to be a common family characteristic; be learned or inherited from your family: "A great interest in horse breeding runs in his family."

Run into/1. to meet by chance; meet by accident; meet by chance: "I ran into Henry yesterday on Station Street." "I ran into Peter at the Flinders Station this morning." 2. add up to; reach; total: "Boat repairs might cost you an amount running into the thousands or more." "Her income runs into millions of dollars." 3. hit; collide into (of vehicles); bump; crash into; hit: "John lost control of his car and ran into a tree." 4. be affected; get into: "When I ran into a problem while making a kite, I asked Uncle Henry for help."

Run into a brick wall or run into a stone wall/to meet an unmovable force or obstacle; to face a difficulty one cannot overcome (apparently): "Trying to convince Jim was like running into a brick wall."

Run into the ground/1. to do or use (something) more than is wanted or needed: "It's alright to crack that joke once in a while, but don't run it into the ground." "The Oakleigh Senior Citizen Club is being run into the ground by poor leadership." 2. win over or defeat (someone) completely: "They lost the game today, but next year they'll run us unto the ground."

Run off/to drive away: "The boys saw a pig digging in mother's flower bed, and they ran him off."

Run on empty/to continue to work when energy reserves are used up.

Run out/1. to come to an end; be used up: "Robert almost got across the brook on the slippery stones, but his luck ran out and he slipped and fell." "They'd better do their

Christmas shopping; time is running out." 2. use all of the supply; be troubled by not having enough; use up: "Jill never runs out of ideas for clever party decorations." "The boat's run out of petrol." 3. force to leave; expel: "The Grand Army of the Republic ran out the enemy."

Run out of/to finish a supply of something; finish; having consumed all the supply; have none left: "They've run out of bread." "We ran out of money so we had to find work to pay the bills."

Run out of gas/to run out of energy; lose momentum.

Run out of steam/to become exhausted; to reach one's limit.

Run over/1. to drive over accidentally (in a vehicle); drive on top of; ride over: "The car ran over the dog." "The truck ran over the field." 2. to rehearse; check or revise quickly; try or go over (something) quickly, practice briefly: "During the lunch break, Sally ran over her history facts so she would remember them for the test." 3. overflow. "We've got a few minutes before the train goes, so I'll just run over your instructions again."

Run through/1. to rehearse; check or revise quickly. 2. consume extravagantly; waste (used of supplies or money): "She inherited a fortune and run through it in a year."

Run up/1. to make: "He can run up a dress in an hour on that machine." "Do you think Mrs. Johnson will run up a pair of curtains for me?" 2. accumulate; add to the amount of; increase: "James ran up a big bill at the bookstore." "She ran up a big bill at the hotel."

Run up against/to encounter difficulties or opposition: "If she tries to change the rules of the club, she will run up against a lot of opposition." "They ran up against difficulties."

S

Save face/to save one's good reputation, popularity, or dignity when something has happened or may happen adversely; hide something that may cause shame; protect oneself from being embarrassed: "James would not play in the game because he knew he could not do well and he wanted to save face."

Save one's skin/to escape from imminent danger or difficulty.

Save the day/to bring about victory or success: "The team was behind, but at the last minute John saved the day with a touchdown."

Save up/to put away for future use; keep as savings; save money to buy something: "Bill was saving up for a new bicycle." "Alice saved up pieces of cloth to make a quilt."

Say something off the top of your head/to say the first thing that you think of.

Scale down/to make smaller or less; decrease: "Robert scaled down each boy's share of food after a bear robbed the camp."

Scratch one's back/to return a favor; do something kind and helpful for someone or flatter in the hope that s/he will do something.

Scratch the surface/to learn or understand very little about something: "We thought we understood China, but when we made a trip there, we found we had only scratched the surface."

Screw up/1. to make a mess of; make an error which causes confusion. 2. cause someone to be neurotic or maladjusted: "His divorce screwed him up so badly that he had to go to a psychiatrist."

Search for/to look for: "The customs were searching for drugs when he came through the airport."

Search one's soul or search one's heart/to study reasons and acts; try to discover if one has been fair and honest: "The teacher searched her soul trying to decide if she had been unfair in failing Joshua."

Search out/to search for and discover; find or learn by hunting.

See about/to make inquiries; make arrangements for something to happen: "I'll see about ordering an Easter egg." "I must see about getting a room ready for her."

See eye to eye/to agree fully; hold exactly the same opinion: "Though they did not usually agree, they saw eye to eye in the matter of reducing taxes." "My mother and I hardly ever see eye to eye."

See off/to take to one's departure point or place (airport, train station, etc.); say or wave goodbye to; say goodbye to: "He saw me off from the station." "His sister went to the train with him to see him off."

See out/to accompany a departing guest, visitor, or client to the door of the house or office.

See over/to go into a home or other physical property, examine it carefully, often with a view to buying or renting: "Melissa is definitely interested in the house. He'd like to see over it."

See through/1. to discover a hidden attempt deceive; understand the real meaning of or a reason for, realize the falseness of; assess to be untrue: "He could see through most of their plays and ruses." "Father saw through Anthony's excuses not to go to bed on Christmas Eve." "He knew he wanted to stay up to see Santa Claus." 2. do (something) until finished; stay with until the end: "Once Jack started a job, he saw it through till it was finished." 3. help and encourage (a person) through trouble or difficulty; help through a difficult period: "They'll see this problem through together." "Mrs. Jones saw Jill through her sickness." 4. be enough for; last.

See to or look to/to make arrangements; put right; repair; attend to; take care of; do whatever needs to be done about: "While Sally bought the theatre ticket, I saw to the parking of the car." "Will she see to the children's lunch?" "He'll need to see to that cut on his leg." "If you can provide the beer, I'll see to the food." "The gas fire isn't safe. You should have it seen to." "Please see to it the windows are locked."

See you, see you later/ goodbye.

Seeing is believing/to want evidence of something before accepting that it really exists or is in fact the case.

Seem to be/to appear, look like.

Seize on/to make use of (a happening or idea.): "James seized on the rain as an excuse for missing school."

Sell like hot cakes/to sell very quickly or in large quantities; to be popular: "The toys are selling like hot cakes."

Sell off/to sell cheaply (what is left of a stock).

Sell out/1. to sell all of a certain type of article; sell all of a certain thing which a store has in stock: "In the store's February sale, the sheets and pillowcases sold out in two days." 2. sell all the stock and close the store; go out of business: "The local news agency sold out last month and was replaced by a café." 3. be unfaithful to one's family, community, position, or country for money or other reward; be disloyal; sell a secret; accept a bribe: "The dishonest boxer sold out to his opponent for a hundred dollars."

Sell the family silver/to part with a valuable resource for immediate for immediate advantage.

Send away for/to write and ask for: "This is the address he'll need if he wants to send away for his free gift." "If he wants a catalogue, I'll send away for one."

Send something back/to return.

Send for/to summon: "One of their water pipes has burst. They must send for the plumber."

Send in/to send to someone; submit: "You must send in your application before Wednesday."

Send off for/to write asking for something to be sent: "He is going to send off for that record."

Send on/to forward; send after a person: "If any letters come for him after he has gone, I will send them on."

Serve two masters/to take orders from two superiors or follow two conflicting or   opposing principles or policies at the same time.

Set a good example/to be a good example.

Set about/to commence; begin to do something; start: "James set about learning the printer's trade at an early age." "She set about filing documents in quite the wrong way."

Set aside/1. to separate from others in a group or collection: "He set aside the things in the old trunk which he wanted to keep." 2. select or choose from others for some purpose: "The President set aside a day for mourning the late President George Bush." 3. pay no attention to (something); leave out. 4. save: "Each month she set aside part of her salary for her son's education."

Set back/1. to cause to put off or get behind schedule; slow up; check; delay; hinder: "The fire has set back our plans for expansion." 2. cause to pay out or to lose (a sum of money); cost: "Her new car set her back well over $10,000."

Set down/to lay.

Set eyes on/to catch sight of something.

Set fire to/to cause to burn; start a fire in; ignite: Somebody may have set fire to the forest deliberately.

Set foot in/to have visited or gone to a particular place; to have entered.

Set in/to begin (a period, usually unpleasant).

Set in motion/to start something off.

Set in one's ways/to be fixed in one's habits.

Set off/1. to leave; begin to go; depart; start a journey; start out on a journey: "The bus set off at eight o'clock." "Early in the morning, we set off for the country." 2. enhance. 3. ignite: "The children have been setting off fireworks all night. 4. start (a series of events)."

Set on fire/to ignite.

Set one's hearts or sights on/to long to become; yearn; aspire; dream.

Set out/1. to arrange. 2. start a journey; leave on a journey or voyage: "We set out at six and hoped to arrive before dark." "We set out for Seoul." 3. to have an intention or goal; decide and begin to try; begin this undertaking; aim; attempt: "The teacher set out to show that most illnesses were avoidable." "He set out to become Prime Minister." 4. place; put.

Set sail/to begin a voyage.

Set (or put) the record straight/to make sure that any mistake has been rectified.

Set up/1. to achieve; establish (a record); produce: "She set up a new record for the 1,000 meters." 2. start it; start a new business: "When Victor married, he left his father's shop and set up on his own." 4. place in a position. 5. arrange.

Set upon/to attack someone.

Settle a score/to take revenge on someone for something damaging that they have done in the past.

Settle down/1. to become accustomed to; contented in a new place, job ,etc.; live more quietly and sensibly; have a regular place to live and a regular job; stop acting wildly or carelessly, especially by growing up: "Sam will settle down after he gets a job and gets married." "Anna soon settled down her new school." 2. become quiet, calm, or comfortable: "Mother settled down with the newspaper."

Settle up/to pay money owed.

Shake off/to get away from when followed; get rid of; escape from; let go of a burden: "Sam could not shake of his cold." "I told him to shake off his moody blues."

Shake one's head/to turn the head from side to side to show refusal, disapproval, disbelief, etc.

Shake up/to bother; worry; disturb.

Shape up/1. to begin to act or work right; get along satisfactorily: "If the new girl doesn't begin to shape up soon, she'll have to leave school." 2. show promise: "Plans for our dance party are shaping up very well."

Shape up or ship out/excl., to behave properly or leave.

Share out/to divide something into equal parts and give a part to each person in a group.

She's right/that will be all right; don't worry; shift one's ground/say or write something that contradicts something one has previously written or said.

Shoot off one's mouth/to express one's opinion loudly.

Shoot oneself in the foot/to bring about one's own downfall.

Shoot out/to fight with guns until one person or side is wounded or killed; a settle a fight by shooting.

Shoot the messenger/to treat the bearer of bad news as if they were to blame for it.

Shore up/to add support to (something) where weakness is shown; make (something) stronger where support is needed; support.

Shout down/to make a loud noise to prevent a speaker from being heard: "Dave tried to make a speech defending himself, but the crowd wouldn't listen to his explanation and shouted him down."

Shout to/to communicate, call to: "Mary shouted to us to come in and swim."

Show off/1. to try to make people think you do something very well; display something (skill, knowledge etc.) to win notice or applause; put out nicely for people to see; display oneself; boast; exhibit: "Children love to show off to adults." "The Science Fair gave Jill a chance to show off her shell collection." "Roger is always picking up very heavy things just to show off his strength." 2. attract attention; try to attract attention to: "Andrew hasn't missed a chance to show off his muscles since that pretty girl moved in next door." "He enjoyed showing off his girlfriend in public." 3. show one around or show one round/take somebody on a tour of a place: "They visited a factory yesterday." "The manager showed them around."

Show one's true colour/to reveal one's real character or intentions.

Show oneself in one's true colors/to make one's true opinion known, to show one's real self: "She showed me Boston in its true colors."

Show the door/to sack someone; tell person to leave the room; ask (someone) to go away: "Julia was upsetting the other children, so I showed her the door." "Our neighbors invited themselves to the party and stayed until Robert showed them the door."

Show up/to expose; come or bring out; become or make easy to see. 2. arrive; come to; appear: "We had agreed to meet at the gym, but Peter didn't show up." "Only six pupils showed up for the class meeting."

Shrug off or shrug away/to brush aside; take no notice of; act as if uninterested or apathetic about something; not mind; not let oneself be bothered or hurt by: "James shrugged off our suggestions; he would not tell us what had happened." "Maria shrugged off every attempt to comfort her." "Mother cut her hand but she tied a cloth around it and shrugged it off."

Shut down/to close down.

Shut off/1. to stop a machine, equipment, light etc; make (something like water or electricity) stop coming. 2. be apart; be separated from; separate from: "Their camp is so far away from the highway, they feel shut off from the world when they are there." "The pig is so bad-tempered they had to shut it off from its piglets."

Shut one's mouth/to be quiet.

Shut out/1. to prevent from coming in; block: "The boys were annoyed by Sam's telling club secrets and shut him out of their meeting." 2. prevent (an opposing team) from scoring throughout an entire game: "Their team hasn't been shut out once this season."

Shut up/1. to be quiet; stop talking. "'Shut up,' said the angry man to his barking dog." "Little Shirley told Father about his birthday surprise before Mother could shut her up." "Shut up and let Adam say something." 2. close the doors and windows: "They got the house shut up only minutes before the storm hit." 3. close and lock for a definite period: "The Browns always spend Labor Day shutting up their summer home for the year."

Shy away or shy off/to avoid; seem frightened or nervous: "The girls shied away from our questions." "The horse shied away when Mark tried to mount it."

Side against/to join or be on the side that is against; disagree with; oppose: "Sam and Tom sided against me in the argument." "They sided against the plan to go by plane."

Side with/to support; agree with; help: "Peter always sides with Bill in an argument." "Tom sided with the plan to move the club."

Sign in/to write one's name on a special list or in a record book to indicate presence or attendance: "Every boy must sign in when he comes back to the dormitory."

Sign out/to write one's name on a special list or in a record book to record a departure or official exit.

Sign up/1. to promise to do something by signing your name; join; sign an agreement; register: "They will not have the picnic unless more people sign up." "Adam wants to Sign up for the contest." 2. write the name of (a person or thing) to be in an activity; persuade (someone) to do something: "Maria decided to sign up her dog for obedience training."

Sing a different tune or sing a new tune/to talk or act in the opposite way; contradict something said before: "Thomas said that all smokers should be expelled from the team, but he sang a different tune after the coach him smoking."

Sink in/to be completely understood; be fully realized or felt: "Everybody laughed at the joke but Adam; it took a moment for it to sink in before he laughed too." "When Sam heard that war had started, it didn't sink in for a long time until his father was drafted into the army."

Sink or swim/to succeed or fail by personal efforts, without help or interference from anyone else; to fail or to succeed: "When Frank was fourteen, his parents died, and he was left by himself to sink or swim." "Sam's new job was confusing, and no one had time to help him learn, so he had to sink or swim."

Sit back/to take no action; do no more work; relax; rest, often while others are working; take time out: "He has worked hard all his life, and now he's going to sit back and watch other people working." 2. attend but not participate.

Sit down/to rest; take a seat: "Jackie sat down." "Sit down, Emily!"

Sit in/1. to be a member; participate: "They're having a conference and they'd like you to sit in." "He wants you to sit in on the meeting."

Sit on the fence/to refuse to take sides in a quarrel or argument; remain neutral; avoid a conflict; remain undecided: "Adam sat on the fence for a week last spring before he finally joined the track team instead of the baseball team."

Sit pretty/to be in an affluent position: "After my wealthy husband died, I found myself sitting pretty."

Sit tight/to take no action; bide one's time: "I'll sit tight till I know what the decision is"; make no move or change; stay as one is: "The nurse said to sit tight until she arrived."

Sit up/to stay awake instead of going to a bed: "Joshua sat up through the night listening to music." "Mrs. Smith will sit up until both of her daughters get home from the dance." "I was very worried when she didn't come in, and I sat up till 2 a.m. waiting for her." "He sat up all night with the sick child."

Sit up and take notice/to be surprised into noticing something: "Hannah had never impressed her teachers." "Hearing that she had won the essay contest made them sit up and take notice." "Daniel's sudden success made the town sit up and take notice."

Sit well (with)/to find favor with; please: "The reduced hospital budget did not sit well with the nurses."

Skip out/to intentionally miss lessons at school or college that one should attend.

Slap in the face/to insult; embarrass; make feel bad: "Tom slapped our club in the face by saying that everyone in it was stupid." "I don't want to slap him in the face by not coming to his party."

Slave away/to work extremely hard on something that one doesn't enjoy.

Sleep around/to be free with one's sexuality, to behave promiscuously: Edmund is a nice guy but he sleeps around an awful lot with all sorts of people.

Sleep like a log/to sleep very well, deeply.

Sleep out/1. to sleep outdoors: "The Scouts plan to sleep out next Sunday." 2. go home at night.

Sleep over/to sleep at another's home (may just imply a party involving sleeping at a friends place, esp. for younger children).

Sleep with/to have intercourse with; to stay in the same bed with someone else (platonically).

Slip by/when time passes without one noticing.

Slow down/to go more slowly than usual: "The road was slippery, so Mr. White slowed down the car." "Robert once could run a mile in five minutes, but now that he's older he's slowing down."

Smash into/to hit, run into, as in to have a car wreck.

Smell a rat/to be suspicious; suspect that something is wrong; be suspicious; feel that something is wrong: "Every time Bill visits me, one of my ask trays disappear. I'm beginning to smell a rat."

Smooth away/to remove (unpleasant feelings); take away: "Mr. Green's new job smoothed away his worry about money."

Snap up/to take or accept eagerly: "Potatoes were on sale cheap, and the shoppers snapped up the bargain"; sell out quickly: "Mr. Smith told Bill that he would take him skiing, and Bill snapped up the offer."

Someone's days are numbered/when someone will not survive or remain in the particular position for much longer.

Someone's star is rising/when someone is becoming ever more successful or popular.

Spare a thought/to remember.

Speak for/to speak in favor of or in support of: "At the meeting, Tom spoke for the change in the rules." "The other boys made jokes about James, but Tom spoke for him." 2. speak in support of or against someone or something: "Adam spoke for Bill as club president." "Pat spoke for not letting girls join the club."

Speak out or speak up/to speak more loudly; speak in a loud or clear voice: "The truckers told the shy girl to speak out." 2. speak forcefully: "She spoke out in favor of the disabled."

Speak the same language/to understand one another as a result of shared opinions, values, etc.

Speak tongue in cheek/to speak sarcastically, mockingly or insincerely.

Speak volumes/to be informative, emphasizing the relevance of the words.

Speed up/to go faster than before; make go faster; accelerate; speak more loudly.

Spell out/1. to say or read aloud the letters of a word, one by one; spell: "Ed could not understand the word the teacher was saying, so she spelled it out on the blackboard." 2. read slowly, have trouble in understanding: "The little girl spelled out the printed words." 3. explain something in very simple words; explain very clearly: "He spelled out the difficulties involved in moving house."

Spend money like water/to spend money carelessly.

Spill the beans/to tell a secret to someone who is not supposed to know about it: "Jacob's friend were going to have a surprise party for him, but Lachlan spilled the bean."

Spit the dummy/to give up or opt out of a contest or the like before there is reasonable cause to do so; lose self-control, display anger.

Split down to middle/divided into two equal halves

Sponge off/to obtain money or benefits from others instead of trying to support oneself.

Stab in the back/to say or do something unfair that harms (a friend or someone who trusts you): "Robert stabbed his friend Bill in the back by telling lies about him."

Stamp out/to destroy completely and make disappear.

Stand a chance/to have a possibility or opportunity; be likely to do or get something: "Donald doesn't stand a chance of being elected." We stand a good chance to dance with Deborah at the party."

Stand by/1. to be close beside or near: "Maria could not tell Anne the secret with her little brother standing by." 2. be near, waiting to do something when needed: "Frank stood by with a fire extinguisher while the trash was burning." 3. follow or keep (one's promise): "She is a girl who always stands by her promises." 4. be loyal to; support; help; continue to support and help one: "When three big boys attacked Pat, Bill stood by him." "They agreed to stand by the company and see its difficulties."

Stand for/1. to endure or tolerate: "I won't stand for any nonsense." 2. mean; to represent; be a sign of; make you think of; mean: "The symbol x stands for a known quantity." "The letters "U.K." stands for "United Kingdom." 3. speak in favor of something, or show that you support it: "The new Prime Minister stood for honest government." "Ed always stands for what is right." 4. be a candidate for Parliament; offer oneself for election; try to win an election: "Three men from Paris are standing for parliament." "Mr. White stood for Parliament three years ago but he wasn't elected." 5. allow to happen or to be done; permit; tolerate: "She won't stand for any nonsense."

Stand off/1. to stay at a distance; stay apart: "At parties, Mr. White goes around talking to
everyone, but Mrs. White is shy and stands off."
Stand on one's own feet/to be independent; not rely on other people.
Stand out/1. go further out than a nearby surface; project: "A mole stood out on his
cheek." 2. be easily seen; be conspicuous; be more noticeable in some way those around
you; be higher, bigger or better: "Max was very tall and stood out in the crowd." "Ed
stood out as a track star." "Angus stood out from the crowd because of his height and his
flaming red hair."
Stand over/1. to watch closely; keep checking all the time: "Fred's father had to stand over him
to get him to do his homework. 2. be held over for later action; be postponed; wait.
Stand up/1. to support: "Throughout the entire trial, the lawyer stood up for his client." 2.
be firm in one's attitude: "She asserted her rights and stood up to the boss." "Stand up for
your rights!" 3. rise to a standing position; get up on one's feet: "She stood up and left the
room." "When he came into the room, she stood up." 3. be strong enough to use hard or
for a long time.
Stand up and be counted/to state publicly one's support for someone or something.
Stand up for/to support; defend verbally; support: "You should stand up for your little sister."
"Stand up for your rights!" "She always stands up for the underdog."
Stand up to/to defend oneself against a person or force); resist: "Your boss is a bully. If you
don't stand up to her, she'll lead you a dog's life."
Stare at/to watch
Start from scratch/to start from the very beginning and with no help or advantage: "Nancy
already knew how to sew a little, but Rose had to start from scratch."
Start off on the wrong foot/to make a bad start when meeting someone new.
Start something over/to start again.
Start up/1. to begin operating. 2. to begin to play (music).
Stay in/to stay at home: "She's going to stay in this evening." "Can't we go out to a disco? I
don't want to stay in all night."
Stay in driver's seat/to stay in control.
Stay put/to remain where placed; not to move from a position.
Stay the course/1. to hold out to the end of a race or contest. 2. pursue a difficult task or
activity to the end.
Stay tuned/to keep listening
Stay up/to remain out of bed till later than usual, usually pleasure.
Steal a person's thunder/to take away the attention due to someone else by using his or her
words, ideas, etc.
Steal one's thunder/to use someone's ideas or methods without permission and without
giving credit.
Steal the show/to outshine other performances, especially unexpectedly; achieve great success,
as an actor in a play; act or do so well in a performance to receive most of the attention:
"Nancy was in only one scene of the play, but she stole the show from the stars."
Steer clear of /1. to steer a safe distance from; go around without touching. 2. stay away from;
keep from going near: "Ted was angry at Fred, and Fred was steering clear of him."
"Some words Anne spells wrong. She tries to steer clear of them."
Step down/1. to come down in one move from a higher position to a lower. 2. make go

slower little by little. 3. leave a job as an official or some other important position: "When the principal became ill, he had to step down."

Step in/to begin to take part in a continuing action or discussion, especially without being asked: "When the dogs began to fight, Sam stepped in to stop it before they were hurt." "When Ted had done as much as he was able to on his model plane, his father stepped in to help him."

Step into one's shoes/to do what someone else usually does after he has stopped doing it: "When Charles' father died, Joseph had to step into his father's shoes to support his mother."

Step up/1. to go from a lower to a higher place: "James stepped up onto the platform and began to speak." 2. increase rate of; increase speed of (to industrial production); go or to make (something) go faster or more actively: "After they had reached the outskirts of town, they stepped up the engine." 3. rise to a higher or more important position; be promoted: "This year Maria is secretary of the club, but I am sure she will step up to be president next year."

Stick around/to stay or wait nearby: "Pat's father told him to stick around and they would go fishing." "After work, Mr. Johnson stuck around to ride home with his friends."

Stick out/1. to stand out from a wall or other surface; project; extend. 2. be seen or noticed more easily or quickly than others; be noticeable: "His house is the only brick one on the street. It sticks out and you can't miss it." "Nancy plays basketball very well. The others on the team are good, but she really sticks out." 3. keep on doing until it is done, no matter how long, hard, or unpleasant: "Ted is not a fast runner, and he doesn't have a chance of winning the marathon, but he will stick out the race even if he finishes last."stick to one's game or guns or stand by one's guns maintain one's position/to hold to an aim or an opinion even though people try to stop or say one is wrong: "At first the boss would not give Nancy the rise in pay she wanted, but she stood by her guns and he gave it to her."

Stick to/to keep a promise even though the situation has changed.

Stick to one's guns/to refuse to compromise or change, despite criticism.

Stick to the point/to remain on the subject: "Let's stick to the point!"

Stick together/to remain close together in a situation: "Pat and Ed stick together in a game or in a fight."

Stick up for/to support someone who is in trouble: "I knew it wasn't Mark's fault, so I tried to stick up to him when the others blamed him."

Stick with/1. to continue doing; not quit: "Ed stayed with his homework until it was done." "Practicing is tiresome, but stick with it and some day you will be a good violinist." 2. stay with; not leave: "For two months John's boss could not pay his salary, but John stuck with him, because he thought the company would soon succeed." 3. leave (someone) with (something unpleasant); force to do or keep something because others cannot or will not: "When Ted and I went to the store to buy ice cream cones, Ted ran away with his cone without paying, and I was stuck with paying for it." "Sandra didn't wash the dishes before she left, so I'm stuck with it." "Mr. Green bought a house that is too big and expensive, but now he's stuck with it."

Still waters run deep/phr., a quiet manner may conceal a passionate nature.

Stir up/1. to bring (something) into being, often by great exertion or activity; cause: "It was a quiet afternoon, and Sam tried to stir up some excitement." "Robert stirred up a fight between Sam and Ted." 2. cause (someone) to act; incite to action or movement; rouse: "When Sandra heard that Anne said about her, she became stirred up."

Stitch up/1. to sew. 2. to close a wound with stitches.

Stop over/to stay at a place overnight or for some other short time while on a trip elsewhere: "When they came back from California, they stopped over one night near The Grand Canyon."

Stop working/to fail.

Strike it rich/to find a source of abundance or success.

Strike me as (something)/to seem or appear to me as (something).

Strike rich/1. to discover oil, or a large vein of minerals to be mined, or buried treasure. 2. become rich or successful suddenly or without expecting to: "James did not know he had a rich Uncle Bill in Canada." "Bill struck it rich when his uncle left his money to him."

Strike while the iron is hot/to act promptly at a good opportunity.

Sum up/to summarize: "The teacher summed up the lesson in five rules."

Swear by/1. to use as the support or authority of the truth; take an oath upon: "Adam swore by his honor he would return the bike." 2. to have complete confidence in; be sure of; trust completely: "When Sam has to go somewhere fast, he swears by his bike to get there."

Swear in or swear into/to admit to an office or organization, usually by a formal act or ceremony: "Nancy and Sandra will be sworn into the club tonight. Henry was sworn in as class president."

Sweep the board/to win all the points, medals or prizes.

Sweep under the rug or sweep something under the carpet/to hide or keep secret something unpleasant; dismiss casually (something one is ashamed of or does not know what to do about: "Around the world, drug abuse by school children is swept under the rug."

Switch off/to turn off: "Switch the kettle off." "Switch it off."

Switch on/to turn on a light; start a machine.

T

The tail wags the dog/phr. the less important or subsidiary factor or thing dominates a situation; the usual roles are reversed.

Take a back seat/to accept an inferior or lower position; be second to something or someone else: "He does not have to take a back seat to any singer alive."

Take a chance/to accept a risk of failure or loss: "They will take a chance on the weather and have the party outdoors."

Take a hammering/1. to be subjected to harsh punishment. 2. be heavily defeated.

Take a nap/to sleep.

Take a punt/to attempt at, have a go.

Take a risk or run a risk/to be open to danger or loss; put oneself in danger; be unprotected: "James takes a risk of being hit by a car when he runs into the street without looking." "He was afraid to run the risk of betting on the game."

Take a sickie/to have a day off.

Take a trip/to travel.

Take a trip down memory lane/deliberately to recall pleasant or sentimental memories.

Take advantage of/1. to make good use of: "Jill took advantage of the lunch hour to finish her homework." "We took advantage of our position." 2. use for one's own purposes; treat (someone) unfairly for gain or help; make unfair use of: "She took advantage of her friend's kindness." "The little children did not know how much to pay for the candy, and Robert took advantage of them."

Take after/to resemble (one's parents or grandparents, etc.); look or act similar to a family member; have the same looks and ways as (a parent or ancestor): "She takes after her grandmother; she had red hair too." "My mother was forgetful and I take after her; I forget everything."

Take aim/to get ready to hit, throw at, or shoot at by sighting carefully: "Before the hunter could take aim, the tiger jumped out of sight."

Take away/to subtract; remove: "A truck took all the bottles away." "Take them away."

Take back/1. to withdraw (remarks, accusations etc.): "He must take back what he said about our sales figures." 2. accept a return: "I'm going to take these trousers back to the shop; they're too small." "She took her new sweater back to the shop. It was too small for her."

Take by storm or by storm/1. to capture by a sudden or very bold attack: "The Marines did not hesitate. They took the city by storm." 2. to win the favor or liking of; make (a group of people) like or believe oneself: "Kenneth gave Susan so much attention that he took her by storm, and she said she would marry him."

Take care/to be useful; use wisdom or caution: "They must take care to let nobody hear about this."

Take care of/to watch; attend to; supply the needs of; look after: "You should take care of it." "If they can find somebody to take care of the children, they can have a week's holiday for themselves." "Anne stayed home to take care of the baby." 2. mind; deal with; do what is needed with: "I will take care of that parcel." "The coach told Robert to take care of the opposing player."

Take charge/to begin to lead or control; take control or responsibility; undertake the care or management: "With Mrs. Jones in the hospital, her sister took charge of the Jones children. "Bill was elected president of the club and took charge at the next meeting."

Take control/to start organizing; assume effective power in a situation.

Take cover/to hide, often from enemy fire, in a military or police situation.

Take crack/to make an attempt.

Take down/ 1. to write or record (usually from dictation): "Victor read out the names and his secretary took them down." 2. pull to pieces; take apart: "He'll take down those posters and put up some new ones."

Take effect/1. to have an expected or unintended result; cause a change: "It was nearly an hour before the cold pill took effect." 2. become lawfully right, operative: "The new tax law will not take effect until July."

Take for/to attribute the incorrect identity or qualities to someone: "I took her for her sister. They were extremely alike."

Take for granted/to assume; to suppose or understand to be true: "Mr. Johnson took for granted that the invitation included his wife." 2. accept or become used to (something) without noticing or saying anything: "John took for granted all that his parents did for him." "No boy likes to have his girlfriend take him for granted; instead she should always try to make him like her better."

Take in/1. to deceive somebody; be tricked; dupe: "I was taken in by what she said, but it was relay a lie." "She was plausible and took us all in." 2. believe; understand; receive into mind: "He couldn't take in the lecture at all. It was   too difficult for him." "It was such a surprise that we couldn't take it all in." 3. include. 4. receive as guests or lodgers; bring someone into one's home: "When our car broke down, the nearest neighbor very kindly took us in and gave us a bed for the night." 5. understand: "He's sorry, but he's quite taken in by what she said." 6. make something narrower; make less wide (clothes): "The skirt was too big, so she took it in at the waist." "He's getting much thinner; he'll have to take in his clothes." 6. follow.

Take into account/to consider; remember and understand while judging someone or something; consider: "How much time will we need to get to the mountain?" "You have to take the bad road into account." "Her acting in the play was remarkable, taking into account her youth and inexperience."

Take into consideration/to think about.

Take into custody/to arrest.

Take it easy/to rest; also a request to go more slowly or to control one's emotions; do no more than one must.

Take it or leave it/an expression of indifference or impatience about another's decision after making an offer.

Take its toll/to cause loss or damage: "The budget cut its toll of nurses."

Take me back/to make someone remember; to recall or recollect; to end a breakup (romantic).

Take my breath away/to be surprised.

Take no prisoners/to be ruthlessly aggressive or uncompromising in the pursuit of one's objective.

Take off/1. to rise into air; leave the ground; ascend; leave the ground; go into air; rise from the ground (used of aircraft); leave the ground (for planes; of aircrafts); leave fast; depart suddenly; run away: "The plane took off at 8 a.m." "The plane took off 10 minutes late but landed on time." 2. go away; leave: "The three girls got into the car and took off for the perfume store." 3. become successful: "The record took off as soon as it appeared." 4. take (time) to be absent from work: "You look so tired, Bernard. Take the day off." "When her husband became sick, she took off from work." 5. imitate; mimic: "She enjoys taking off Margaret Thatcher." 6. remove; the opposite of put on; remove; undress: "Sally took off her clothes." "It was so hot, she took off her coat."

Take on/1. to prove successful or gain traction: "Her new idea took on immediately." 2. adopt; accept as an opponent; engage in a fight or argument; challenge: "He'll take you on at tennis." "We took on a strong team from Japan." 3. receive for carrying; be loaded with: "The bus driver stopped at the curb to take the man on." 4. engage staff; give a job to; hire, employ: "They have to take on more staff next year." "They're taking on 30 new workers at the factory." 5. undertake work; accept: "He has taken on a directorship of IBM." "He was taken on as a laboratory assistant." 6. play. 7. challenge.

Take (something) on board/to consider (something) seriously.

Take one's breath away/to surprise greatly; impress very much; leave speechless with surprise or wonder or delight; astonish: "The beach is so beautiful it takes our breath away." "Her refusal was so unexpected it took my breath away."

Take one's word for/to believe.

Take out/1. to remove; extract: "The dentist took out one of his teeth." 2. take someone on a date, entertain one (usually at some public place): "His small boy is at boarding school quite near here." "I took him out every month for a meal."

Take over/1. to take control; assume control of; assume responsibility for, in succession; take control or possession of; gain control of; absorb: "Miss Jones is leaving to get married, and Miss Smith will be taking over the class." "James expects to take over the business when his father retires." 2. take charge or responsibility. 3. borrow, imitate, or adopt: "The Korean people have taken over many American ways of life."

Take part/to have a part or share; join: "Andrew saw the new boy watching the game and asked him to take part."

Take place/to happen; occur: "The accident took place only a block from her place." "The formal handover of the new school will take place on 13 October."

Take pleasure in/to enjoy.

Take pride in/to draw satisfaction from.

Take root/1. to become fixed or established: "Capitalism took root in China." 2. form roots so as to live and grow: "They hope the transplanted orange trees will take root." 3. be accepted; be adopted; live and succeed in a new place: "Many European customs failed to take root in Asia." "The immigrants to our country took root and began to think of themselves as native Australians."

Take someone at their word/to interpret a person's words literally or exactly by believing them or doing as they suggest.

Take someone's word for it/to believe what someone says without checking.

Take something for granted/to assume that something will take place without evidence that it will.

Take something to heart/to feel deeply pained about something.

Take stock/to review or make an assessment of a particular situation, typically as a prelude to making a decision.

Take the back seat of/to take or be given a less important position or role.

Take the easy way out/to find an easy solution.

Take the law into one's own hands/to punish someone for an offence according to one's own ideas of justice, especially in an illegal or violent way.

Take the plunge/to take a decision on something risky; resolve to do something and act straightaway.

Take the shine off/to spoil the brilliance or excitement of; overshadow.

Take things easy/to avoid hard work or worry; have an easy time; live in comfort: "The doctor said that John would have to take things easy for awhile after he had his tonsils cut."

Take to/1. to begin a habit: "She took to drink (began drinking too much)." 2. find likeable or agreeable, particularly at first meeting: "I was introduced to the new headmaster yesterday. I can't say I took to him." "Dave went to sea (became a sailor) and took to the life like a duck to water." 3. seek refuge or safety in.

Take to heart or take it to heart/to be seriously affected by; feel deeply; be deeply troubled: "When her friend deserted her, she took it to heart." "She took her sister's death very much to heart." "She took her friend's advice to heart."

Take to the road/to set out on a journey or series of journeys.

Take up/1. to begin a new activity; start doing something new; start doing; begin   some activity or occupation; begin a hobby, sport or kind of study: "She took up golf and became very keen on it." "To help improve her concentration, she took up yoga." 2. acquire land for farming: "He took up a soldier settlement block." 3. occupy (a position in time or space): "She has a very small room, and most of the space is taken by a grand piano."

Take up with somebody/to associate or form a friendship, especially a romance, with somebody: "Joshua took up with Hannah three years ago, and now they're engaged."

Take with a grain of salt/to accept or believe only in part; not accept too much: "We took Uncle Thomas's stories of the war with a grain of salt."

Talk back/to reply defiantly.

Talk big/to talk boastfully; brag: "Dave talks big about his pitching, but he hasn't won a game."

Talk back or answer back/to answer rudely; reply in a disrespectful way; be fresh: "When the teacher told the girl to sit down, she talked back to her and said she couldn't make her." "Anne talked back when her mother told her to stop watching television. She said, 'I don't have to if I don't want to.'"

Talk crap or talk shit/vulg., to insult someone or lie or both at the same time.

Talk into/1. to get (someone) to agree to; make (someone) decide on (doing something) by talking; persuade: "Robert talked us into walking home." She talked me into accepting the job." 2. cause to be in or to get into talking: "Mr. Brown lost the customer in his store by arguing with her."

Talk out of/1. to persuade not to; make agree or decide not to: "Jane's mother talked her out of quitting school." 2. allow to go or get out by talking; let escape by talking: "Bob is good at talking his way out of trouble."

Talk over/to talk together about; try to agree about or decide by talking; discuss: "Talk it over your husband and give me your answer tomorrow." "James talked his plan over with his father before he bought the car." 2. persuade; make agree or willing; talk and change the mind of: "Mark is trying to make Andrew over our side."

Talk turkey/to talk about something in a really businesslike way; talk with the aim of getting things done: "Robert said, 'Now, let's talk turkey about the bus trip. The fact is, it will cost each student $3.'" "The mother always spoke gently her son, but when the son broke the windshield of the car, the mother talked turkey with him about working to pay for the cost of the damage."

Talk up/1. to speak in favor or support of: "We should talk up the game to get a big crowd." 2. speak plainly or clearly: "The teacher asked John to talk up." 3. to boost the performance of (shares, the economy, etc.) by making confident assessments and predictions.

Tamper with/1. to meddle with (something); handle ignorantly or foolishly: she tampered with the insides of her watch and ruined it. 2. secretly get someone to do or say wrong things, especially by plying with money, or by threat: "A friend of the woman being tried in court tampered with a witness."

Teach a lesson/to show that bad behavior can be harmful: "When Peter pulled Anne's hair, she taught a lesson by breaking his toy car." "The burns Jack got from playing with matches taught him a lesson."

Teach someone a thing or two/to impart experience; to show someone the error of his way of thinking, perhaps at that person's expense due to ignorance and pride.

Tear apart/to destroy.

Tear down/1. to demolish; reduce to nothing; take all down in pieces; destroy: "He'll tear down those posters and paste up some good new ones." 2. take to pieces or parts: "The motor mechanics had to tear down the engine, fix it, and put it together again."

Tear up/to tear into pieces: "Jane tore up the old sheets and made costumes for the play out of the pieces." "Henry tore up his test paper so that his father wouldn't see his low grade."

Tell off/to speak angrily because another did something wrong: "His mother told him off for coming home so late." "At school, he was always being told off for talking in class."

Test the water/to check people's reaction to something.

There's no such thing as a free lunch/phr., one never gets something for nothing; any benefit received has eventually to be paid for..

There's safety in numbers/to be in a group of people typically creates more confidence or security in a line of thinking or course of action.

Think about (or of)/to plan: "She never thinks about (or of) other people." "Jacob is thinking of (or about) buying a new car."

Think back/to remember the past.

Think out/to reason; plan: "They will have to think out their next move very carefully."

Think over/to think carefully; consider; study: "When Bill asked Anne to marry him, she asked him for time to think it over."

Think twice/to consider a course of action carefully before embarking on it.

Think up/to invent.

Throw a party/to hold a party; have a part: "The club is throwing a party in the university gym on Friday night."

Throw a lifeline to/to provide someone with means of escaping from a difficult situation.

Throw a punch/to strike at someone with your fist; hit; punch: Bill became so mad at Frank that he threw a punch at him.

Throw away/1. to refuse. 2. discard; get rid of; put in the rubbish; get rid of as unwanted or not needed (rubbish, things you don't want); junk; trash: "These pears are bad. Shall I throw them away?" "Don't throw away that book. I want it." 2. to waste: "The congressman criticized the government for throwing away money on the space program." 3. fail to make use of: "He threw away a good chance for a better job."

Throw cold water on something or pour cold water on/to discourage an idea or suggestion; discourage; say or do something to discourage: "Peter's father threw cold water on his plans to go to college by saying he could not afford it."

Throw good money after bad/try to solve a problem by recklessly spending more money on it, without due consideration of what is required.

Throw in towel/to give in; to stop trying; admit defeat.

Throw one's hat in the ring/to indicate a willingness to take up the challenge or enter a contest.

Throw one's weight around or throw your weight about/to be domineering; exert influence or pressure; use one's influence or position in a showy or noisy manner: "James was the star of the class play, and he was throwing his weight around telling the director how the scene should be played." "Bill was stronger than the other boys, and he threw his weight around."

Throw out or toss out/1. to discard; get rid of; remove unwanted items; jettison (rubbish): "She didn't need the brush any more so she threw it out." 2. refuse to accept. 3. force to leave; dismiss: When the basketball manager complained too loudly, the umpires threw him out."

Throw the baby out with the bath (bath water)/illogically to reject all of something because part is faulty; to go overboard with a thought or (re-)action.

Throw up/1. to abandon suddenly (some work or plan): "She suddenly got tired of the job and threw it up." 2. vomit.

Thumb one's nose at/to show disdain or contempt for.

Tick off/to mention one after another; list: "The teacher ticked off the assignments that Anne had to do."

Tide over/to carry past a difficulty or danger; help in bad times or in trouble: "She was out of work last summer ,but she had saved enough money to tide her over until fall."

Tie in the knot/to marry, take one's marriage vows.

Tie up/1. to show or stop the movement or action of; hinder; tangle: "Ronald tied up his shoelaces." 2. take all the time of: "The meeting will tie the Prime Minister up until noon." "The Congress didn't vote because a debate on a small point kept it tied up all week." 3. limit or prevent the use of: "Her money is tied up in a trust fund and he can't take it out." "Their company has tied up with another firm to support the show." 4. bind one's hands and feet so that one cannot move.

Tighten one's belt/to carefully avoid spending money; live on less money than usual; use less food and other things: "When our father and mother lost their jobs, their family had to tighten their belts."

Tighten the screws/try to break someone by making a matter more and more difficult; apply pressure: "When many pupils still missed class after he began giving daily quizzes, the teacher tightened the screws by failing anyone absent four times."

Tighten your belt/to spend less in order to save money.

Time is money/phr., time is a valuable resource.

Tip off/to give private and secret information; tell something not generally known; tell secret facts to; warn: "Ethan tipped off the police."

Tip the balance/to have important or decisive influence; make a decision go for or against someone; decide: "Anthony's vote tipped the balance in our favor, and we won the election."

Tip the scales/1. to weigh: "James tips the scales at 80 kilograms." 2. to have important or decisive influence; make a decision go for or against; decide: "Peter's vote tipped the scales in our favor, and we won the election."

Tire out/to make very tired; weaken: "When Bill got home from the long walk, he was all tired out."

Tone down/to make softer or quieter; make less harsh or strong; moderate: "She toned down the sound of the TV." "He wanted the bright colors in his house toned down."

Toe the line/to do exactly as requested.

Tomorrow is another day/phr., the future will bring fresh opportunity.

Touch a nerve/to provoke a reaction by referring to a sensitive topic.

Tough it out/to maintain an unyielding or unrepentant attitude throughout an episode, despite all criticisms or blame.

Tough out/to withstand or see through (something) by showing endurance and tenacity.

Toy with/to play with.

Track down/to find; find by or as if by following tracks or a trail: "He spent weeks in the library tracking the reference down in all their books on the subject."

Trade in/to give something to a seller as part of payment for another thing of greater value: "The Greens traded their old car in on a new one."

Trade on/to use as a way of helping oneself: "The congressman's son traded on his father's fame when he ran for a mayor."

Transform into/to turn into.

Travel back in time/to return to an earlier period in history.

Travel light/to travel with very little luggage or with very little to carry: "Peter and Frank travelled light on their camping trip."

Trend up/to follow an upward trend.

Trip down in memory lane/to report past events; to recall; to have a reverie.

Trump up/to invent, fabricate.

Try hard/to strain.

Try on/to put on (an article of clothing) to see if it fits; put (clothing) on to see if it fits; put it on for fitting and appearance: "The tailor asked him to try on the suit." "He tried on several pairs of shoes before he found one he liked."

Try out/1. to test and evaluate; test by trial or by experimenting: "The company is trying out a telephone system." "She tried golf out to see if she would like it." 2. try for a place on a team or in a group: "John tried out for the baseball team." 3. audition for: "The actor tried out for the part of Hamlet."

Try to keep a straight face/to do one's best not to smile or laugh.

Tune in/to adjust a radio or television set to pick up a certain station: "James tuned in his portable radio to a record show." "John tuned in to Channel Seven to hear the news."

Tune up/1. to adjust (a musical instrument) to make the right sound: "Before she began to play, Anne tuned up her piano." 2. adjust many parts of (car engine) which must work together so that it will run properly: "She took her car to the garage to have the engine tuned up."

Turn a blind eye/to pretend not to notice.

Turn around or turn round/1. to reverse course; backtrack: "They went for a long walk. After six kilometers they turned round (or around) and went back." 2. to look behind or change one's posture to look behind oneself: "When I touched her on the shoulder, she turned around."

Turn away/ refuse admittance: "The woman at the door turned away anybody who hadn't an invitation card." "Australia was turning away from multiculturalism."

Turn a blind eye/to ignore an action or behavior; pretend not to see; not pay attention; pretend not to see something: "John turned a blind eye to the "No fishing" sign."

Turn down/1. to make quieter (TV, radio, music etc.); decrease the pressure, force, volume (of gas or oil, lights, fires, or of radios); reduce loudness, brightness, or force of: "The movie hall lights were turned down." "Anna turned down the radio." 2. reject something; say no to something; refuse an offer or ideas; refuse to accept; reject an offer, application, applicant: "I offered her $100, but she turned it down." "He applied for the job, but they turned down his application because I didn't know French." "She was offered $1,000 for the picture, but she turned down the offer."

Turn in or hand in/1. to give to someone; deliver to someone: "I want you to turn in a good English paper." "When the soccer season was over, they turned in their uniforms." 2. inform on; report: "He turned them in the police for breaking the street light." 3. go to bed (used chiefly by sailors or campers, etc.) 4. submit classwork.

Turn into/to become; convert into: "He's going to turn his garage into a playroom for the children."

Turn off/1. to switch off (machines, lights, gas, fires, radios, taps etc); stop by turning a knob or handle or by working a switch; cause to be off: "She turned the water off." "Before he went to bed, he turned off the lights." 2. disgust, bore, or repel (someone) by being

intellectually, emotionally, socially, or sexually unattractive: "I won't date Shirley any
more. She really turns me off." 3. extinguish: "He turned off all the lights which had been
left on."

Turn on/1. to start or switch on (machines; lights, gas, fires, radios, taps etc.); start by turning a
knob or handle or working a switch; cause to be on: "We wanted to watch TV, so I turned
it on immediately." "Bill turned on the water." 2. become greatly interested in an idea,
person, or undertaking; arouse the senses pleasantly; to enthuse others with one's own
interests or pleasures: "Beatles' music always turns me on." 3. attack suddenly: "Her
former allies turned on her." "The lioness turned on the trainer and struck him to the
ground." 4. arouse someone sexually.

Turn one's back on/to refuse to help (someone in trouble or need): "She turned her back on her
own family when they needed help." "We can't turn our back on poor nations."

Turn out/1. to evict; empty; 2. turn inside out; empty one's pockets, handbags or   drawers,
etc: "They turned out the bags." "John turned out his pockets looking for the money." 3.
develop; make; produce: "Anne can turn out a cake in no time." "Robert turns out a poem
each week for the school paper." 4. be revealed; prove to be; be in the end; be found out;
end; transpire: "She told him that she was a spinster, but it turned out that she was
married with five children." "The old boat turned out to be in good condition." "Her plan
has turned out very well." 5. clean a room thoroughly, first putting the furniture outside:
"She tries to turn out one room every month if she has time." 6. assemble; come out into
the street (usually in order to welcome somebody): "The whole city turned out to
welcome the winning soccer team when they came back with the Cup." 7. extinguish a
light; switch off: "We turned out the light."

Turn over/1. to give to someone for use or care; transfer: "He turned his account over to
another bank." "He turned his library books over to the librarian." 2. buy and then sell to
customers: "The store turned over $4,000 worth of skiing equipment in February." 3. be
bought in large amounts; sell. 4. turn something so that the side previously underneath is
exposed: "She turned over the stone." 5. turn upside down, upset; capsize: "The truck
struck the wall and turned over." "The boat turned over, throwing the girls into the
water."

Turn over a new leaf/to begin again, resolve to behave better; make a sudden change for the
better in conduit: "John turned over a new leaf and stopped disturbing the class." "Alice
decided to turn over a new leaf and study hard."

Turn the clock back/to return to an earlier period: "Father wished he could the clock back to the
days before the children grew up and left home."

Turn the corner/to begin a process of recovery from misfortune.

Turn the heat up on someone or something/to concentrate pressure or criticism on.

Turn the other cheek/to ignore an abuse or an insult; to let someone do and not do it in return; not
hit back when hit; be patient when injured or insulted by someone; not try to get even:
"Nathan turned the other cheek when he was hit with a snowball."

Turn the tables on/to reverse the position of two rivals.

Turn the tide/to change what looks like defeat into victory: "They were losing the game until
James arrived." "His coming turned the tide for them, and they prevailed."

Turn up/1. to find; discover. 2. come; arrive, usually unexpectedly; appear or be found
suddenly or unexpectedly: "She didn't turn up for work, so the meeting had to be

called off." "They had arranged to meet at the station, but he didn't turn up." 3. make
louder (TV, radio, music etc.); increase something by using a control: increase the
pressure, force, volume (of gas or oil, lights, fires, or of radios): "Can you turn the TV
up?" 4. appear.
Turn up the heat/to intensify pressure or criticism.
Turn upside down/to completely change or alter the situation or condition of a person, place or
thing..
Twist one's arm/to force someone; threaten someone to make him do something: "I had to
twist Robert's arm to make him eat the candy."
Two heads are better than one/phr., it's helpful to have the advice or opinion of a second person.

U
Use something up/to use all of it so that nothing is left: "He's going to take a few more
photographs." "He wants to use up the rest of the film."
Used to/acclimated, to find familiar or normal in one's experience; the way one did something
formerly: "He used to walk to school every day, but now he goes to school by bus."

V
Vanish into thin air/to disappear completely
Vote down/to defeat in a vote: "The Senate voted the bill down."
Vote with one's feet/to indicate an opinion by being present or absent or by some other
course of actions.

W
Wait on/to attend; serve (at home or restaurant): "The woman who was waiting on us seemed
very inexperienced; she got our orders mixed up."
Wake up/1. to stop sleeping. 2. to begin to appreciate a situation, especially a welcome or
threatening one that has been present for some time: "He didn't wake up to the situation
until our ammo depot was bombed in the middle of the night."
Walk away from/to refuse to be involved.
Walk back/to return from a destination: "After eating at a restaurant, they walked back to
their hotel."
Wake up/to stop sleeping: "She often wakes up in the middle of the night."
Walk away with or walk off with/1. to take and go away with; take away: "When John went
to work, he accidentally walked away with his wife's umbrella." 2. take, get, win easily:
"Robert walked away with all the honors on Class Night." "Their team walked away
with the championship."
Walk down the aisle/to marry; to accompany the bride down the aisle to a marriage
ceremony: "Prince Charles accompanied Meghan Markle down the aisle."
Walk in/to enter: "He opened the door and walked in."
Walk out/1. to go on strike: "When the factory would not give them higher pay, the
workers walked out." 2. leave suddenly, especially to desert: "He walked out on her."
"She didn't say she wasn't coming back; she just walked out." 3. march out in disgust
or indignation.
Ward off/to prevent something happening.

Warm up/1. to reheat cooked food: "Mr. Smith was so late that his dinner got cold; his wife had to warm it up." 2. become friendly or interested: "As she warmed up to her audience, Jill forgot her bashfulness." 3. get ready for a game or other event by exercising or practicing: "The fork dancers began to warm up fifteen minutes before the performance."

Wash one's hands of/to disclaim responsibility; decline responsibility; withdraw from or refuse to be responsible for: "They washed their hands of politics long ago." "The school washed its hands of the pupils' behavior during winter recess."

Wash out/to disappear by washing: "These stains won't wash out."

Wash up/to wash dishes; wash the plates after a meal: "When they have dinner very late, they don't wash up till the next morning."

Waste away/to become thinner and weaker every day: "Sally is wasting away with tuberculosis."

Watch for/to be on the alert for.

Watch out/to look out; be attentive.

Watch out for/to look out; be careful about: "If you're going barefoot, look out for dangerous spiders." "Watch out for kangaroos in the road here!"

Watch over/to guard, protect.

Water down/1. to clean a surface usually with water: "They washed down the paintwork before they started redecorating." 2. informally to have a drink with a meal: "She washed down her meal with a glass of beer." 3. to dilute, usually with a negative reference: "They watered down the whisky punch, since the juice cost $50 a pint!"

Wave back/to return a greeting or salutation: "I waved to him, and he waved back to me."

Wear away/gradually to reduce; make smooth or flat; hollow out.

Wear off/to lose power; disappear gradually: "When his first feelings of shyness had worn off, he started to enjoy himself." "She began to try to sit up, which showed us that the effects of the drug were wearing off."

Wear out/1. to use until no longer serviceable: "Students wear out their shoes very quickly." 2. exhaust (often in passive).

Weed out/1. to remove what is unwanted, harmful, or not good enough from: "Father weeded out the library because there were too many books." 2. take (what is not wanted) from a collection or group; remove (a part) for the purpose of improving a collection or group; get rid of: "The teacher told Jane to read over her English composition and weed out every sentence that was not about the subject."

Weigh in/1. to take the weight of; weigh: "A doctor weighed in the boxers." 2. to have something weighed: "He weighed in at 60 kg on the scale." 3. to be weighed as a boxer or wrestler by a doctor before a match: "The champion didn't want to weigh in at more than 120 kg."

Weigh up/to consider carefully (the available options): "Weigh up all the factors before making a decision."

Wheel and deal/to behave aggressively for one's own gain; make many big plans or schemes; especially with important people in government and business; in matters of money and influence; handle money or power for your own advantage; plan important matters in a smart or skillful way and sometimes in a tricky, not strictly honest way: "Mr. Jones made a fortune by wheeling and dealing on the stock market."

When pigs fly/phr. an expression that means never; something won't occur.

Where there's a will there's a way/phr., determination will overcome any obstacle.

Will do/enough, satisfactory: "That will do."

Win out/to be victorious or successful after hard work or difficulty; win or succeed; in the
    end: "Half way through the race James was last, but in the end he won out." "Mark was a
    poor boy, but he won out and became rich by hard work."
Win something hands down/to win easily.
Wind down/to terminate; to diminish; to finish off.
Wind up/1. to tighten the spring of a machine; make it work or run: "She doesn't have to
    wind up her watch because it is run by a battery." 2. bring or come to an end; finish; stop:
    "Before Peter knew it, he had spent all his money and he wound up broke." "The
    headmistress wound up the meeting by thanking the parents."
Wipe out/1. to remove or erase by wiping or rubbing: "The teacher wiped out with an eraser
    what he had written on the board." 2. remove, kill, or destroy completely: "Doctors are
    searching for a cure that will wipe out skin cancer."
Wipe something off the map/to obliterate something totally.
Wise up/to become aware, informed, or alerted; face the realities.
Work hard/to struggle.
Work like a dog/to work very hard.
Work out/1. to find an answer to, solve; find by calculation or study the solution to some
    problem; study and decide on the details; solve (a problem): "She used her calculator to
    work out the cost." "There was one clue he couldn't work out." 2. plan; progress;
    develop: "Jill worked out a beautiful design for a sweater." "Jane worked out a new hair-
    do." 3. accomplish; arrange: "The electrical engineers worked out a system for getting
    electricity to the factory." 4. be efficient; get results. 5. count. 6. do physical exercises:
    "Sally works out at the gym three times a week."
The world is one's oyster/phr., one is in a position to take the opportunities that life has to
    offer.
Write down/to write on paper for use later as information: "He wrote down the address." "Write
    down your name." "Write the formula on a piece of paper, and put it in the safe."
Write in/to enter text, and is associated with both word processing and handwriting.
Write off/1. to remove (an amount) from a business record; cancel (a debt); accept as a loss:
    "If a customer dies when she owes the store money, the store must often write it off." 2.
    accept (a loss or trouble) and not worry any more about it; forget: "Mr. Green had so
    much trouble with the new radio set that he finally wrote it off and bought a new one."
Write off for/to send a letter asking or ordering something, often something from an
    advertisement: "Anthony will write off for that chair."
Write up/1. to write the story of; describe in writing; give a full account of: "The magazine is
    writing up the life of the Prime Minister." 2. put something thought or talked about into
    writing; finish writing (something): "James took notes of what the teacher said in class,
    and he wrote them up when he got home."

Y
Yearn for/to want something so much that one feels sad without it.
You bet!/an expression meaning "Yes!"; an affirmation or statement of agreement.
You can't win them all/an expression that no one is invariably successful.

IV.   **Multi-Word Nouns, Adjectives, Prepositions and Adverbs**

i. Colloquialism: appropriate to or characteristic of conversational speech or writing in which the speaker or writer is under no particular constraint to choose standard, formal, conservative, deferential, polite, or grammatically unchallengeable words, but feels free to choose words as appropriate from the informal, slang, vulgar, or taboo elements of the lexicon. 2 conversational. 3. a figurative expression used in informal everyday speech, including slang. 4. language used in ordinary conversation; not formal or literary.

A colloquialism is a figurative expression used in informal everyday speech, including slang. Examples include: at a loose end; dead beat; face the music; smell a rat; under a cloud.

ii. Idioms: "Out of sight, out of mind" or "Seeing is believing" can be proverbs probably. However, two idiom experts feel that they can class them as idioms without, as they put it. "stretching the definition too far".

Idioms are normally phrases, whereas proverbs are entire sentences. Idioms are 1. a more or less fixed expression, such as "out of hand", "in spite of", "to come into one's own", or "a storm in a teacup", the meaning of which are distinct from the individual senses of the words they contain. 2. a form of expression peculiar to a language, esp. one having a significance other than its literal one. 3. a variety of form of a language; a dialect. 4. the language peculiar to a people. 5. the peculiar character or genius of a language. 5. a distinct style or character, as in music, art, etc.

Many idioms are used in only colloquial English as a sequence of words that is a unit of meaning (kick the bucket = die). Idioms are phrases and expressions in common usage. Most are very familiar, some are amusing, but the majority are not to be taken literally. Idioms trawl the language of colloquialism for some of their most memorable lines.

-- Opaque idioms: sacred cow; to jump the gun; to pass the buck; a shot in the arm.
-- Semi-opaque idioms: to lay down the law.
-- Transparent idioms: to stand shoulder to shoulder.

Idioms are group of words which people use together. They have become standard phrases which people tend to use in less formal situations. Example: "She always pokes her nose into other people's business." (To poke one's nose into something is an English idiom which means to interfere in it.) Idioms are very interesting but they are sometimes hard to understand. Idioms are used a lot by native speakers in informal situations. If people use the phrase a lot, idioms are very fixed and the phrase is always said in the same way.

There are a number of things to remember about idioms:
    a.   Idioms usually stay the same and don't change. This makes them easy to remember.
    b.   Their meaning is not always very clear.
    c.   The individual words do not always indicate what the whole group means.
       Treat idioms like single words because the meaning comes from the whole group.
    d.   One often can guess the meaning of idioms from how and when people use them.

e. We usually use idioms in informal language, so be careful when and where you use them.

f. The best way to find out what idioms is to ask someone who knows the language. There are also idiom dictionaries which can use.

V. Frequently Used Foreign Words, Phrases and Origin

5.1. Foreign Terms from European Countries that influenced English

Abbreviations:

Cel.: Celtic
Czec.: Czechoslovakia
D.: Dutch
F.: French
Ger.: German
Gr.: Greek

Hun: Hungarian
It.: Italian
L. Latin
Sp.: Spanish
W.: Welsh

a la carte/L. ordered separately from a menu
ad hoc/L. for a special purpose; for this (purpose); to this (specific purpose); done or set up
solely in response to a particular situation or problem and without considering wider
issues: ad hoc measures
adios/Sp. a word meaning, "Goodbye" or "Farewell".
anno domini or A.D./L. in the year of our Lord.
allegro/It. cheerful; bright (often used as a musical tempo)
alias/L. meaning "otherwise named" or "alternate", as in an alias name.
alma mater/L. a person's school or university.
alumna or alumnus/L. a pupil of a school or university, a graduate or former student.
ancient regime/F. the old regime.
ante meridiem or a.m./L. before noon.
ante mortem/L. made or done before one's death.
a priori /L. (of reasoning) not deductive; not derived from experience; known to be true, that it
does not need validation.
armadillo/Sp. armed man or little armoured one; an animal known by this name.
arbitrator/L. a person designated to resolve a dispute between two or more persons or parties.
attaché/F. diplomatic official.
autobahn/Ger. expressway.
avant-garde/F. innovators, especially in art or literature.

bambino/It. a baby; a child.
belle/F. beauty; a beautiful woman.
blitz/Ger. sudden attack; lightning attack.
bon voyage/F. a pleasant journey
bona fide/L. in good faith; of good faith; genuine and real or sincere: "He will accept any bona
fide offer."; good standing; evidence of good faith

cappuccino/ It. Original meaning: A hood or cowl. A coffee termed a cappuccino, because it
is topped with hot milk.
carpe diem/L. enjoy the moment.
carte blanche/F. full discretion to act; unconditional freedom; unrestricted power, access, or
privilege: "She was given carte blanche to do what she wanted."
chalet/F. Swiss cottage.

circa/L. about or around.
charge d'affaires/F. n. an official in charge during a temporary absence of the ambassador or
        minister.
cliché/F. stereotype.
client/L. a patron of someone or of a business.
clientele/F. clients
confer or cf./L. to compare.
confetti/It. small bits of paper thrown at festive occasions such as weddings or parades.
coup d'état/F. a sudden, often violent seizure of power; overthrow of a government by force.
cul-de-sac/F. a street or lane open at only one end; dead end.
curriculum vitae/L. a record of one's professional life; an account of one's education,
        qualifications, and career experience.
custody/L. having legal title or right to possess of property, often used with reference to children.

de facto/L. in fact, whether by right or not; as a matter of fact.; in actual fact.
déjà vu/F. a sense of having already experienced something before; the experience of
        seeming to have seen or experienced a present event at some time in the past.
ditto/It. copy of something, duplicate; an indication to repeat something.

El Niño/Sp. an irregularly occurring and complex series of climate changes affecting the
        equatorial Pacific region and beyond every few years, characterised by the appearance of
        unusually warm, nutrient-poor waters off northern Peru and Ecuador, typically in late
        December.
en masse/F. all together; in a body; adv. phr., together; in one body or group: "The
        university turned out en masse to cheer the returning astronaut."
en route/F. adv. on the way.
en suite/F. in sequence.
entourage/F. attendants.
entrée/F. main course (in dining); entrance, access or permission to enter.
errata/L. errors (in the plural).
erratum/L. an error.
espresso/It. the original meaning: express. a type of coffee in which hot water is used to brew
        a stronger, slightly denser coffee drink.
et alli or et al./L. and others (frequently used where several authors).
et cetera or etc./ L. and so forth; and so on; and the rest.
ex gratia/L.as a matter of choice and favor rather than legal requirement.
exempli gratia or e.g./L. for example.

fait accompli/F. something that has been done and is past altering; an accomplished fact;
        something completed; something that has already been done and that therefore cannot be
        changed.
frankfurter/Ger. hotdog, wiener, a casing filled with ground cuts of beef, pork, or other meats.

hamburger/Ger. ground beef; a patty made from ground beef.
homicide/L. the or an act of murder or killing.
homo sapiens/L. the human species; a human being.

ibidem or ibid./L. in the same place.
id est. or i.e./L. that is; that's to say; in other words.
in absentia/ L. in one's absence.
in situ/L. in its original situation; in its original place.
in status quo/L. in its original state; in position.
in vitro/L. (of biological processes) taking place in a living organism.

laissez-faire/F. non-interference in the affairs of others; let well enough alone!; the sense of
        economic non-interference (=roughly); connotes an economic system with minimal
        regulations.
legal/L. of or with reference to the law.
lingua franca/It. any language widely used as medium among speakers of other languages.

negative/L. F. a word expression denial or objection or absence of support; no.
noblesse oblige/F. privilege entails responsibility; nobility imposes obligations; the idea that
        people born into the nobility or upper social classes must behave in an honourable and
        generous way toward those less privileged.
nota bene or n.b./L. mark well; note well; take notice.

paparazzi/It. freelance photographers who aggressively pursue celebrities to take candid pictures
        to sell to newspapers and magazines.
per annum/L. per year; annually; for each year.
per capita/L. per person; for each person.
per se/L. by itself; for itself; by or in itself.
persona non grata/L. an unacceptable person; someone unwelcome or unacceptable: "After her
        book was published, she become persona non grata with certain foreign powers."
post meridiem or p.m./L. afternoon; the period of time falling in the last half of a twenty-four
        hour day.
post mortem/L. after death.
postscriptum or p.s./L. marks additional text in a letter or note, usually after the end.
prima donna/ It. n. lead female singer; principal female singer; principal female performer;
        female opera star; a leading female singer in an opera company.
prima facie/ L. at first appearance, immediately clear; at first sight without further examination
        (of evidence= immediately conclusive); on first appearance.
pro rata/L. proportionately; at the same rate; in proportion; in proportion to an amount: a part-
        time job paid pro rata at a salary of $40,000 per year.
prosecute/L. to pursue or aim for; to try a defendant in a court.

RSVP/F. please reply (to an invitation or call).

salvo/It. burst of applause; a round of gun or weapons fire.
Santa Claus/D. St. Nicholas.
status quo/L. the existing state of affairs; the existing situation; the present state; unchanged
        position.
suede/Fr. a clothing material of leather with a napped surface.

testify/L. to provide evidence or witness in a court; to profess a belief.

vice versa or v.v./L. in reverse order; the order having been reversed; the other way
    around.
vis-à-vis/F. with respect to; in relation to; compared with.
vox populi/L. public opinion

5.2 Origins

Austria: mesmerize
Belgian: saxophone
Celtic languages: ambassador, boycott, car, clan, galore, hooligan, peat, piece, slogan,
    trousers, truant, whisky
Dutch: bamboo, boss, buoy, cruise, decoy, easel, gas, yacht
Dutch or Afrikaans: apartheid, bluff, boss, brandy, bully, bumpkin, clamp, commando,
    cookie, cruise, dope, drill, drum, frolic, golf, kink, landscape, loiter, skipper, sledge, slim,
    smack, smuggle, snap, trek, waffle, yacht
Finland: sauna
French: ambush, attorney, avant-garde, ballet, bayonet, beg, biscuit, bouquet, boutique,
    buccaneer, buffet, burgundy, bureau, butler, cabaret, café, carol, cashier, chassis, chateau,
    chauffeur, chowder, connoisseur, cognac, corps., coup, coupe, courage, crèche, crime,
    crusade, cuisine, cul de sac, debacle, debris, debut, deluxe, denim, depot, détente, dinner,
    dossier, elite, esplanade, fillet, flour, flower, foreign, foyer, franchise, garage, genre,
    gopher, gourmet, Grand Prix, Grands Ecoles, grenade, grotesque grotesque, , guillotine,
    hazard, horde, host, hostel, impasse, jacket, lettuce, lingerie, limousine, madame,
    mansion, margarine, matinee, mayonnaise, migraine, mirage, morale, mount, moustache,
    niche, nicotine, ocean, omelette, ogre, paper, pawn, penchant, perspire, picnic, plateau,
    premiere, protégé, rapport, rebel, regime, rendezvous, repair, repertoire, republic,
    restaurant, resume, roulette, royal, sacred, sauté, scarlet, scout, seal, secure, seminar, sir,
    squat, syrup, tambourine, tennis, ticket, trait, vandal, venue, waltz, zest
German: automation, basis, blitz, dahlia, delicatessen, diesel, edelweiss, Fahrenheit, flak,
    frankfurter, Gestapo, horizon, hamburger, kindergarten, lager, neuron, neutron, poker,
    poodle, pretzel, proton, shuffle, slot, spell, swindle, wafer, worm
Greek: academy, anonymous, apostrophe, atlas, chameleon, church, dogma, drama, elastic,
    electricity, helicopter, hippopotamus, idiot, intoxicate, nostalgia, ozone, pseudonym,
    pygmy, rhinoceros, synopsis, synonym, theory, thesaurus, xylophone
Irish: whisky
Islandic: saga, mumps
Italian: aria, ballerina, bandit, broccoli, buffalo. Carnival, casino, coffee, concerto,
    confetti, domino, fiasco, galvanize, ghetto, gondola, graffiti, grotto, infantry,
    inferno, jeans, lava, macaroni, maestro, malaria, mascot, motto, pants, pasta, piano,
    salami, solo, soprano, spaghetti, supreme, tempo, terracotta, umbrella, vendetta, virtuoso,
    volcano, volt, zucchini
Latin: album, affidavit, alga, alibi, alligator, antenna, apex, appendix, apparatus, aquatic,
    area, ascend, aural, bacterium, barber, bovine, cactus, campus, canine, canopy, circus,
    exhilarate, explode, ferret, focus, index, insulate, interest, interim, interrogate, exit, focus,

font, formula, forum, fungus, humble, larva, lens, library, locus, map, marine, matrix, maximum, medium, mental, mob. monster, navy, nebula, omnibus, ounce, petrol, piano, placebo, podium, pope, pound, pram, prefix, premium, propaganda, quarantine, radius, referendum, salary, saucer, sinister, slave, sock, solar, soldier, spinach, stellar, stimulus, stupid, suffix, syllabus, tabernacle, terminus, union, vaccinate, vermin, vicinity, virus, vortex

Norse and the Scandinavian languages: anger, bleak, blink, bloom, blunder, blur, chamber, creek, crook, dahlia, die, dirt, doze, egg, fellow, flat, gasp, gaze, glitter, happen, harsh, husband, inkling, kick, krill, law, leg, lemming, meek, muck, nasty, odd, ombudsman, raise, reindeer, roof, saga, sauna, scalp, scant, scold, seat, ski, skid, skill, skin, skirt, skull, sky, smorgasbord, sniff, squeal, take, they, thrift, thrust, tungsten, ugly, want, weak, window

Norway: lemming, ski

Portuguese: cobra, commando, dodo, marmalade, turban

Scottish: bikie

Spanish: bonanza, cobra, embargo, guerrilla, iguana, indigo, junta, lasso, macho, marihuana, matador, mosquito, patio, plaza, que sera sera, siesta, tornado

Swedish: ombudsman

Welsh: penguins

5.3. Foreign terms from other regions or countries:

Crimea: balaclava

Czechoslovakia: robot

Hungary: biro, coach

Russia: Bolshevik, glasnost, gulag, intelligentsia, Kremlin, perestroika, Soviet, sputnik, troika, tzar or tsar

Turkey: caftan, coffee, jackal, kebab, kiosk, tulip, yoghurt

North American languages: cafeteria, coyote, igloo, jazz, kayak, kidnap, moose, persimmon, raccoon, shanty, shack, skunk., totem

American Indian: caribou, moccasin, tomahawk, wigwam

South American languages: alpaca, avocado, barbecue, buccaneer, condo, llama, Inca, jaguar, piranha, potato, puma, tango, tobacco, tomato

Caribbean languages: canoe, chimpanzee, impala, mumbo-jumbo, voodoo, zombie.

Africa: guinea pig, impala, safari, trek, voodoo

Hebrew: alphabet, camel, cinnamon, hallelujah, hosanna, Jehovah, jubilee, kibbutz, manna, messiah, rabbi, Sabbath, shalom

Eskimo: kayak, igloo

Arabic: admiral, alchemy, alcohol, algebra, alkali, almanac, apricot, assassin, bazaar, caravan, couscous, giraffe, harem, hazard, jackal, jasmine, jihad, jumper, Kebabs, Koran, lemon, magazine, mattress, monsoon, Muslim, safari, saffron, scarlet, shah, sofa, syrup. Talisman, tariff, zero

Persian: pagoda, shawl

Central Asia: lama, polo, shaman, yak

Sri Lanka: anaconda

Indian languages: anaconda, bungalow, cashmere, cheetah, crimson, curry, dinghy, guru, juggernaut, jungle, lacquer, mango, mantra, nirvana, pal, pyjamas, sapphire, shampoo, sugar, sutra, swastika, thug, yoga

Korean: ondol, kimchi, taekwondo

Chinese: chopsticks, chop suey, dim sum, feng-shui, ginseng, kaolin, ketchup, kung-fu, Mandarin, tea, tycoon, wok

Japanese: bonsai, futon, hara-kiri, geisha, haiku (Japanese style of poetry), judo, kamikaze, karaoke, karate, kimono, pachinko, samurai, shogun, sumo, sushi, tofu, yen, zen

Australian: kangaroo, koala, dingo, wombat, emu, boomerang

New Zealand: pakeha, kiwi

Polynesia: taboo, tattoo

Caribbean: barbecue, canoe, carnival, impala, potato

Aleutian: parka

Hawaii: aloha

VI. Nationality Vocabulary

For each country, one needs to know four words:

i.   the Adjective (the language is often the adjective: "Do you speak Japanese?")

American civilization   French perfume   Danish bacon

ii. the singular noun used for a person from the country

an American   a Frenchman   a Dane

iii.   the plural expression the used for the nation

the Americans   the French   the Danes

iv.   the name of the country

America or the United States   France   Denmark

Group 1 (Regular)

Adjective	Person	Nationality	Country
Afghan	an Afghan	the Afghans	Afghanistan
Algerian	an Algerian	the Algerians	Algeria
American	an American	the Americans	America
Argentine	an Argentine	the Argentines	Argentina
Australian	an Australian	the Australians	Australia
Austrian	an Austrian	the Austrian	Austria
Bangladeshi	a Bangladeshi	the Bangladeshis	Bangladesh
Belgian	a Belgian	the Belgians	Belgium
Brazilian	a Brazilian	the Brazilians	Brazil
Bruneian	a Bruneian	the Bruneians	Brunei
Burmese	a Burmese	the Burmese	Myanmar (Burma)
Canadian	a Canadian	the Canadians	Canada
Chilean	a Chilean	the Chileans	Chile
Chinese	a Chinese	the Chinese	China
Colombian	a Colombian	the Colombians	Colombia
Congolese	a Congolese	the Congolese	Congo
Cuban	a Cuban	the Cubans	Cuba
Egyptian	an Egyptian	the Egyptians	Egypt
Ethiopian	an Ethiopian	the Ethiopians	Ethiopia
German	a German	the Germans	Germany
Greek	a Greek	the Greeks	Greece
Hungarian	a Hungarian	the Hungarians	Hungary
Indian	a Indian	the Indians	India
Indonesian	an Indonesian	the Indonesians	Indonesia

Iraqi	an Iraqi	the Iraqis	Iraq
Italian	an Italian	the Italians	Italy
Japanese	a Japanese	the Japan	Japan
Kenyan	a Kenyan	the Kenyans	Kenya
Korean	a Korean	the Koreans	Korea
Kuwaiti	a Kuwaiti	the Kuwaitis	Kuwait
Lebanese	a Lebanese	the Lebanese	Lebanon
Liberian	a Liberian	the Liberians	Liberia
Libyan	a Libyan	the Libyans	Libya
Malaysian	a Malaysian	the Malaysians	Malaysia
Mexican	a Mexican	the Mexicans	Mexico
Moroccan	a Moroccan	the Moroccans	Morocco
Nigerian	a Nigerian	the Nigerians	Nigeria
Norwegian	a Norwegian	the Norwegians	Norway
Panamanian	a Panamanian	the Panamanians	Panama
Peruvian	a Peruvian	the Peruvians	Peru
Portuguese	a Portuguese	the Portuguese	Portugal
Romanian	a Romanian	the Romanians	Romania
Russian	a Russian	the Russians	Russia
Singaporean	a Singaporean	the Singaporeans	Singapore
Saudi Arabian	a Saudi	the Saudis	Saudi Arabia
South African	a South African	the South Africans	South Africa
Swiss	a Swiss	the Swiss	Switzerland
Syrian	a Syrian	the Syrians	Syria
Tanzanian	A Tanzanian	the Tanzanians	Tanzania
Thai	a Thai	the Thais	Thailand
Ukrainian	a Ukrainian	the Ukrainians	Ukraine
Uzbek	an Uzbek	the Uzbeks	Uzbekistan
Venezuelan	a Venezuelan	the Venezuelans	Venezuela
Vietnamese	a Vietnamese	the Vietnamese	Vietnam

Group 2 (Exceptions)

Adjective	Person	Nationality	Country
British	a Briton	the British	Britain
Danish	a Dane	the Danes	Denmark
Dutch	a Dutchman	the Dutch	Holland
English	an Englishman	the English	England
Finnish	a Finn	the Finns	Finland
French	a Frenchman	the French	France
Irish	an Irishman	the Irish	Ireland
Israeli	an Israelite	the Israelites	Israel
Mongolian	a Mongol	the Mongols	Mongolia
New Zealand	a New Zealander	the New Zealanders	New Zealand
Pakistani	a Pakistani	the Pakistanis	Pakistan
Philippine	a Filipino	the Filipinos	the Philippines

Polish	a Pole	the Poles	Poland
Scottish	a Scot	the Scots	Scotland
Spanish	a Spaniard	the Spaniards	Spain
Swedish	a Swede	the Swedes	Sweden
Turkish	a Turk	the Turks	Turkey
Welsh	a Welshman	the Welsh	Wales

VII. Abbreviations and Acronyms

7.1. Practices

7.1.1. Definitions

Abbreviation – a reduced version of a word, phrase, or sentence; cf. acronym; initial; ellipsis. An abbreviation is a shortened or contracted form of a word or phrase, used as a symbol for the whole. For example, the abbreviated form of 'I would' is 'I'd'. In the United States, they tend to use a period after an abbreviation.

Acronym- a word made up out of the initial letters of a phrase (laser, standing for light amplification by the stimulated emission of radiation). An acronym is a word formed from the initial letters (occasionally syllables) of other words. We usually say the word rather than the letters. It may be a made-up word (EFTPOS) or may coincide with a real word (BASIC). Most authorities use the term for such a letter group when it is pronounced as a word (CAT, laser, NATO, USA).

Clipping is a form of abbreviation and is a type of word formation that occurs when a word or group of words is abbreviated, i.e., ad for advertisement. Some words are abbreviated by using the first and last letters only. These are contractions of the original word, i.e., Dr. for Doctor.

Full stops are not usually written in a group of initial letters that is pronounced like a word (like NATO). In America, a full stop is often used after an abbreviated word, and after an initial letter that stands for a word or name: Mr. Lewis, T.S. Eliot, etc. e.g. U.S.A. S.E. Asia. In modern English (especially British English), abbreviations are often written without full stops: Mr Lewis TS Elliot etc e.g. USA SE Asia

Some words from abbreviations and acronyms start with capital letters, but they do not start with capital letters in other references.

Full stops are not usually written in a group of initial letters that is pronounced like a word (like NATO).

Webster's <u>New World Dictionary</u> in 1970 listed acronyms like USA or UN in two forms with or without a full stop. Consequently, the following lists will be provided without the full stop. All the abbreviations are printed without periods. Although this is a widespread trend, the practice is not without its critics.

7.1.2. Clipping or shortened words

Clipping is a type of word formation which occurs when a word or group of words is abbreviated. The resting terms are often colloquial, and found more often in spoken than in written English. Examples are:

advertisement   ad or advert

ampere   amp
bicycle   bike
blackboard   board
omnibus   bus
cabriolet   cab
suitcase   case
violoncello   cello
chimpanzee   chimp
demonstration   demo
discotheque   disco
examination   exam
facsimile   fax
influenza   flu
refrigerator   fridge
gentleman   gent
goalkeeper   goalie
gymnasium   gym
hippopotamus   hippo
laboratory   lab
mathematics   maths
mobile vulgus (the masses) (Lat.)   mob
pantaloons   pants
newspaper   a paper
telephone   phone
photograph   photo
pianoforte   piano
aeroplane   plane
perambulator   pram
professional   pro
representative   rep
revolutions   revs
specification   spec
taxi-meter cab   taxi
television   TV or telly
veterinary surgeon   vet
periwig   wig
zoological garden   zoo

7.1.3. Blending

From advertisement/editorial   advertorial
From Algo-language   Algol
From affluence/influenza   affluenza
From biologically degradable   biodegradable
From breakfast/lunch   brunch
From breath/analyzer   breathalyzer

From camera/recorder   camcorder
From Channel/Tunnel   Chunnel
From chocolate/-aholic   chocaholic
From electro-/execute   electrocute
From European/bureaucrat   Eurocrat
From European/television   Eurovision
From formula/translator   Fortran
From gleaming and glamour/Ritzy   glitzy
From guess/estimate   guesstimate
From helicopter/airport   heliport
From information/commercials   infomercials
From information/entertainment   infotainment
From motor/pedal bike   moped
From motor/hotel   motel
From motor/cavalcade   motorcade
From Oxford/Cambridge   Oxbridge
From Oxford/famine relief   Oxfam
From petroleum/dollar   petrodollar
From situation/comedy   sitcom
From smoke/fog   smog
From square/aerial   squaerial
From television/broadcast   telecast
From television/evangelism   televangelism
From teleprinter/exchange   telex
From toys/cartoons   toytoons

7.2. Measurement – New Metric and U.S. and British Standard

Metric Systems

Length	kilometer	km
	meter	m
	centimeter	cm
	millimeter	mm
Area	square kilometer	km2
	hectare	ha
	acre	a
	square centimeter	cm2
Mass &	Weightmetric ton	mt or T
	kilogram	kg
	gram	g
	milligram	mg
Volume	cubic centimeter	cc or cm3
Capacity	kiloliter	kl
	liter	l
	milliliter	ml

| Temperature | Celsius | C |
| | centigrade | c |

U.S. and British Standard

Length	mile	mi.
	Yard	yd
	Foot	ft or '
	Inch	in. or ''
	Square mile	sq. mi. or mi. 2
	Acre	a. or A
	Square feet	sq. ft. or ft2
	Square inch	sq. in. or in2
Volume	cubic yard	cu. Yd. or yd3
	Cubic foot	cu. Ft. or ft3
	Cubic inch	cu. In. or in3
Weight	ton	tn.
	Pound	lb.
	Ounce	oz. or oz
Capacity	barrel	bbl. Or bbl
(Liquid)	Gallon	gal,
	Quart	qt.
	Pint	pt.
Capacity	bushel	bu. Or bu
	Pint	pt.
Temperature	Fahrenheit	F

7.3   Countries, Continents and Cities

Africa, African	Afr.
American	Am.
Australia, Australian	Aus.
Bengali	Beng.
Brazil, Brazilian	Braz.
British	Brit.
Canada, Canadian	Ca. Canad.
China	Chin.
Dutch	Dut. Du.
Egypt, Egyptian	Egypt.
Eskimo	Esk.
Europe, European	E.
Finnish	Finn.
France, French	Fr.
Germany, German	G. Ger.
Great Britain	G.B.

Greece, Greek	Gr.
Hong Kong	HK
Hungary, Hungarian	Hung.
Iceland, Icelandic	Ice.
India, Indian	Ind.
Iranian	Iranian
Ireland, Irish	Ir.
Italy, Italian	It.
Japan, Japanese	Jap.
Javanese	Jav.
Korea, Korean	Kor.
Lithuania, Lithuanian	Lith.
London	LD
Los Angeles	L.A.
Mexico, Mexican	Mex.
Mongolic	Mong.
New York	N.Y.
New Zealand	N.Z.
Oxford and Cambridge	Oxbridge
Peruvian	Peruv.
Philippines, Philippine	Phil.
Poland, Polish	Pol.
Russian	Russ.
Scandinavian	Scand.
Scottish	Scott.
Serbian	Serb.
Slavic	Slav.
South Africa	S.A.
Spain, Spanish	Sp.
Tibetan	Tibet.
Turkey, Turkish	Turk.
West Indian	Wind.
United Kingdom	U.K.
United Arab Emirates	U.A.R.
United States of America	U.S.A. or USA

7.4   Postal Abbreviations

Arcade	arc
Avenue	Ave. AVE
Boulevard	Blvd. BLVD
Circle	Cir. CIR
Circuit	Cirt.
Court	Ct. CT
Crescent	Cr.

Drive   Dr.
Esplanade   Esp.
Lane   Ln. LN
Link   Lnk
Mount   Mt.
North   N
Parade   Pde.
Place   Pl.
Road   Rd. RD
South   S
Square   Sq. SQ
Street   St. ST
East   E
West   W

7.5.   Business and Technical Terms

A
Account current   a/c
Administration   admin.
Administrator   adm.
Advertisement   advt. , ad
Afternoon (post meridiem)   p.m. or P.M.
Alternating current   A.C.
American wire gauge   A.W.G.
Amplitude modulation   AM, am
Anonymous   anon.
Approved   appd.
Approximately   approx.
Arrival, arrived   arr.
Assistant   asst.
Association   assn., ass'n
Atomic weight   at. Wt.
Attorney   atty.
Audio frequency   AF
Average   av., avg.

B
Balance   bal.
Bank   bk.
Bank draft   BD
Bankrupt   bkpt.
Barrels   bbl. , bbl
Before Christ   B.C.
Before noon (ante meridiem)   a.m.
Bibliography   bibliog.

Bill of sale	B/S, BS
Biology	biol., bio
Book value	b/v
British thermal unit(s)	BTU
Brother	Bro.
Brothers	Bros.
Building	bldg.
Bulletin	bul., bull
Business manager	Bus. mgr.

C

Capital	cap.
Capital account	C/A
Capital letters	caps
Carat	K., kt.
Carried forward	C/F
Cash book	C/B
Cash on delivery	C.D.D., COD
Cash order	C.O.
Chapter(s)	ch., chap.
Chartered Accountant	C.A., c.a.
Committee	Comm
Company	co.
Cooperative	co-op
Credit, creditor	cr.
Cumulative	cum.
Currency	cur.
Current account	c/a

D

Dead freight	d.f.
Debenture	deb.
Decibel	dB
Delivered	dld
Department	dept.
Depreciation	depr.
Diameter	diam., Dia.
Direct current	DC, dc
Director	dir.
Discount	dis.
District	dist.
Ditto	do.
Dividend, division	div.
Dozen	doz.
Draft	dft.

E
Each	ea.
Editor, edition(s)	ed.
Enclose, enclosed, enclosure	enc.
Encyclopedia	ency.
Endorse, endorsement	end.
Engineer, engine	eng.
Equipment	equip.
Estate, estimate, established	est.
Et alii (and others)	et al.
Et cetera (and so forth)	etc.
Ex dividend	ex div. x-div.
Executive	exec
Executor	exr
Express, expenses, export	exp.

F
Facsimile	fac.
Facsimile transfer	fax
feet per minute	f.p.m., fpm
feet per second	f.p.s., fps
figure(s)	fig(s).
first class	A-1
folio, following	fol., ff.
for example (exempli gratia)	e.g.
forward	fwd.
for your information	FYI
free delivery	f.d.
freight	frt.
Frequency modulation	FM, fm

G
Gallons per minute	g.p.m.
Government	govt.
Gross.	Gro.
Gross weight	gr. wt.
Guaranteed	guar.

H
Hardware	hdwr.
Head	hd.
High technology	high tech.
High water, hot water	hw
Horsepower	hp
Hour(s)	hr

I
Id est (that is)   i.e.
Idem (the same)   id.
Incorporated   inc., Inc.
Institute, institution, instant   inst.
Intelligence quotient   IQ, I.Q.
Interest, interior   int.
Internal Revenue Service   IRS
In the same place (ibidem)   ibid., ib.
Invoice, invention   inv.
Italics   ital.

J
Joint account   JA
Joule   J
Journal, journalist   jour.
Judge, Justice   J.
Just-in-time   JIT
Justice of the Peace   J.P., JP
Juvenile   juv.

K
Kilocycles(s)   kc
Kilovolts   kv
Kilowatt-hour(s)   kWh
Knocked down   K.D.

L
Large   lge., lg.
Latitude   lat.
Leave   lv.
Letter of credit   L/C
Limited   Ltd.
Lire   l.
Logarithm   log.
Longitude   long.
Long tom   l.t.
Lower case   l.c., lc

M
Manager   mgr.
Manufacturer   mfg.
Manuscript(s)   ms(s)., ms(s), MS(s)
Margin   marg.
Married, male   m.
Master of ceremonies   M.C., m.c.

Mathematics, mathematical	math.
Maximum	max.
Megacycle	MC
Memorandum(s)	memo(s)
Merchandise	mdse.
Miles per hour	m.p.h., mph
Minute(s)	min., min(s)
Miscellaneous	misc.
Money order	M.O,, MO
Month(s)	mo., mos.
Morning (anti meridiam)	A.M., a.m.
Mountain	mt., mtn.

N

National	natl., nat.
Nautical	naut.
Net tons	n.t.
Net weight	nt. wt.
No good	N.G., NG
Nonvoting	n.v.
Number	No., no.

O

Old English	OE, O.E.
On account of, on or about	o/a
One way	ow
Out of stock	o/s

P

Package	pkg., pkge.
Page	p.
Pages	pp.
Pamphlet	pam.
Parcel post	p.p., p,p.
Passed, paid	pd.
Patent	pat.
Per annum (by the year)	p.a.
Percent	p.c., pct.
Post office	PO, p.o.
Postscript	P.S., ps
Premium	prm.
Prepaid, post-paid	ppd.
Prime minister	PM
Principal	prin.
Profit and loss	P.&L.
Promissory note	P/N, p.n.

Q
Quality   qlty.
Quarter   qr.
Question, query   q.

R
Radio frequency   r.f.
Railway   ry., rwy.
Real estate   R.E., RE
Received   recd., rec'd.
Referee, reference   ref.
Refund   rf.
Regarding   re
Registered, regulation   reg.
Report   rep., rept
Repondez s'il vous plait (please reply)   R.S.V.P., r.s.v.p.
Returned   retd.
Revolutions per minute   r.p.m., rpm
Revolutions per second   r.p.s, rps

S
Saint   St.
Secretary   secy., sec.
Section(s)   sec.
Share, sheet   sh.
Signed   sgd.
Society, social   soc.
Standard   std.
Sterling   stg.
Supplement   supp.

T
Telegram, telegraph, telephone   tel.
Telegraphic transfer   TT
Territory   ty., ter.
Thousand   M
Translated, transportation   trans.
Treasurer   treas.
Trial balance   t.b.

U
Ultimate   ult.
Ultra-high frequency   UHF, uhf
University   univ., U.

V
Value-added tax   VAT
Versus   vs.
Very high frequency   VHF, vhf
vice versa   v.v.
video frequency   V.F., VF
volume   vol.

W
Warranted   w/d
Waterproof paper packing   w.p.p.
Wavelength   w.l.
Week, work   wk.
Weight   wt.
Wholesale   whsle.
Words per minute   w.p.m., wpm

Y
Yard   yd.
Year, your   yr.
Yearbook   yb.

Z
Zero population growth   ZPG
Zone, zero   Z
Zoology, zoological   zool.

7.6.   Associations, Agencies and Organizations

A
African National Congress   ANC
American Broadcasting Company   ABC
Australia Broadcasting Corporation   ABC
American Federation of Labor and   AFL-CIO
        Congress of Industrial Organizations
American Medical Association   AMA
American Standards Association   ASA
Asia Pacific Economic Cooperation   APEC
Asian Pacific Council   ASPAC
Associated Press   AP
Association of South-East Asian Nations   ASEAN
Automated teller machine   ATM

B
British Broadcasting Corporation   BBC

C
Cable News Network	CNN
Central Intelligence Agency	CIA
Columbia Broadcasting System	CBS
Compact read only memory	CD-ROM

D
Digital versatile disk	DVD

E
European Free Trade Association	EFTA
European Parliament	EP
European Atomic Energy Community	EURATOM
European Union	EU

F
Federation Internationale de Football Association	FIFA
Federal Bureau of Investigation	FBI
Federal Reserve Bank or Federal Reserve Board	FRB
Federal Trade Commission	FTC
Food and Drug Administration	FDA
Football Association Cup	FA cup

G
General Agreement on Tariffs and Trade	GATT
Group of Eight	G8
Grand Old Party; US Republican Party	GOP
Gross National Products	GNP

I
International Air Transport Association	IATA
International Bank for Reconstruction and Development	IBRD
International Chamber of Commerce	ICC
International Committee of the Red Cross	ICRC
International Court of Justice	ICJ
International Energy Agency	IEA
International Labor Organization	ILO
International Monetary Fund	IMF
International Olympic Committee	IOC
International Red Cross	IRC
Irish Republican Army	IRA
International Whaling Commission	IWC

J
Japanese Air Line   JAL

K
Komitet Gosudarstvennoy Bezopanosti   KGB
Korean Advanced Institute of Science   KAIST
        and Technology
Korean Airlines   KAL
Korea Institute of Science and Technology KIST
Ku Klux Klan (US racialist organisation) KKK

L
Ladies Professional Golfers' Association LPGA
London Stock Exchange   LDSE

M
Massachusetts Institute of Technology   MIT
Ministry of International Trade and   MITI
        Industry (Japan)
Moral re-armament   MRA

N
National Aeronautics and Space   NASA
        Administration
National Broadcasting Company   NBC
National Basketball Association   NBA
        or National Boxing Association
National Rifle Association   NRA
New York Stock Exchange   NYSE
North America Free Trade Agreement   NAFTA
North Atlantic Treaty Organization   NATO

O
Organization for Economic Cooperation   OECD
        and Development
Organization of African Unity   OAU
Organization of Petroleum Exporting   OPEC
        Countries

P
Pacific Area Travel Association   PATA
Palestine Liberation Organization   PLO
Parent-Teacher Association   PTA
Pan American Union   PAN
Professional Golfers' Association   PGA

R
Royal Society for the Prevention of   RSPCA
     Cruelty to Animals
S
Securities and Exchange Commission   SEC
Search for Extraterrestrial Intelligence   SETI

T
Tennessee Valley Authority   TVA
Train a grande vitesse   TGB
     (French high speed train)

U
United Nations   UN
United Nations Conference on Trade   UNCTAD
     and Development
United Nations Development Program   UNDP
United Nations Educational, Social, and   UNESCO
     Cultural Organization
United Nations Food and Agriculture   UNFAO
     Organization
United Nations Industrial Development   UNIDO
     Organization
United Nations International Children's   UNICEF
     Emergency Fund
United Nations Security Council   UNSC
United Press International   UPI
United States of America   USA
United States Information Service   USIS
Universal Postal Union   UPU
University of the Third Age   U3A

V
Voice of America   VOA

W
World Boxing Association   WBA
World Boxing Council   WBS
World Food Program   WFB
World Health Organization   WHO
World Trade Organization   WTO

Y
Young Men's Christian Association   YMCA
Young Women's Christian Association   YWCA

7.7. Abbreviations of Negative and Auxiliary Verbs - Contractions

Short form	Full form
I'm	I am
I've	I have
I'll	I will or shall
I'd	I had, would or should
You're	you are
You've	you have
You'll	you will
You'd	you would or should
He's	he's or has
He'll	he will
He'd	he had or would
She's	she is or has
She'll	she will
She'd	she had or would
It's	it is or has
It'll	it will
It'd	it had or would
We're	we are
We've	we have
We'll	we will or shall
We'd	we had or would
They're	they are
They've	they have
They'll	they will
They'd	they had or would
Aren't	are not
Can't	cannot
Couldn't	could not
Doesn't	does not
Hasn't	has not
Haven't	have not
Hadn't	had not
Isn't	is not
Mightn't	might not
Mustn't	must not
Needn't	need not

Oughtn't	ought not
Shan't	shall not
Shouldn't	should not
Wasn't	was not
Weren't	were not
Won't	will not
Wouldn't	would not

Here's	here is or has
That'll	that will
That's	that is or has
There's	there is or has
What's	what is or has
Where's	where is or has
Who'd	who would or had
Who's	who is or has

N.B. irregular formation compared with above

I am not	I'm not
I will not	I won't
I cannot	I can't

Non-standard or slang short forms

Ain't	am not	I ain't coming till seven
Dunno	don't know	"Who's that?" "Dunno."
Gimme	give me	Gimme a cigarette, will you?
Gonna	going to	I'm gonna win this time.
Gotta	got to	I've gotta get out here.
Wanna	want to	He doesn't wanna go home.

7.8. Combined Abbreviations

If the first letter and only a part of the word is written, a full stop is used to show there is part of the word missing:

Reverend	Rev.
Tasmania	Tas.
Major	Maj.
Captain	Capt.
etcetera	etc.
Figure	Fig.
Crescent	Cres.

In the first letter and other letters including the last letter of the word are included in the abbreviation, no full stop is necessary:

Mister	Mr
Doctor	Dr
Father	Fr
Avenue	Ave
Road	Rd

If a name which is made up of more than one word is shortened, the first letter of each word is used without full stops in between:

United States of America	USA
Australian Labor Party	ALP
European Economic Community	EEC

7.9   Abbreviations and acronyms

A

AA	Alcoholics Anonymous
Ab. Abt.	about
Abb,. Abbr.	abbreviation
ABC	Australian Broadcasting Corporation
a/c	account current
A.C., AC	alternating current
ACCC	Australian Competition and Consumer Commission
ACF	Australian Conservation Commission
ACOSS	Australian Council of Social Service
ACTU	Australian Council of Trade Unions
Ad/advert	advertisement
ADD	attention deficit order
ADF	approved deposit fund
Adj.	adjective
admin.	administration
adm.	administrator
adv.	adverb
advt. , ad., advert.	advertisement
AEC	Australian Electoral Commission
AEU	Australian Education Union
AF	audio frequency
AFI	Australian Film Institute
AFK	away from keyboard
AFL	Australian Football League
AFP	Australian federal police
Aft.	after; afternoon

AGM	annual general meeting
Agric.	agriculture
a.h., AH	after hours
AI	artificial intelligence, artificial insemination, Amnesty International, avian influenza
AIDC	Australian Industry Development Corporation
AIS	Australian Institute of Sport
AIDS	Acquired Immune Deficiency Syndrome
AKA	also known as
Alg.	algebra
ALP	Australian Labor Party
AM, a.m.	amplitude modulation
AMA	Australian Medical Association
Amen.	amenities
Amt.	amount
ANC	African National Congress
Ann.	annual
Anniv.	anniversary
anon.	anonymous
ans.	answer
ANSTO	Australian Nuclear Science and Technology Organization
ANU	Australian National University
ANZ	Australia and New Zealand Banking Group, Ltd.
ANZAC	Australian and New Zealand Army Corps
AP	Associated Press (USA)
APEC	Asia-Pacific Economic Cooperation
App.	appended; appendix; appointed; approval
appd.	approved
approx.	approximately
APS	Australian Public Service
Arch.	architect; architecture; archipelago
Arith.	arithmetic
ARL	Australian Rugby League
arr.	arrival, arrived
ASAP, a.s.a.p.	as soon as possible
ASC	Australian Sports Commission
ASEAN	Association of Southeast Asian Nations
ASIO	Australian Security Intelligence Organization
ASIS	Australian Secret Intelligence Service
ass'n, assn.	association
Assoc.	associate; associated; association
Asst.	assistant
Astr., astron.	astronomy; astronomical; astrologer
asst.	assistant
ASX	Australian stock exchange

at. Wt.	atomic weight
atm	standard atmosphere
at. no.	atomic number
ATO	Australian tax office
Attrib.	attributed
At. wt.	atomic weight
atty.	attorney
AUD	Australian dollar
Aug.,	August
Aus., Aust.	Australia; Australian
av., avg, avge	average
av., Ave	avenue
AV	audio-visual
AWB	Australian wheat board
AWL	absent without leave
A.W.G.	American wire gauge

B

b.	born; bowled; breadth; blend of; blended; bedroom; billion
BA	Bachelor of Arts
bal.	balance
b & b	bread and breakfast
b & w	black and white
Bapt.	Baptist
BAS	business activity statement
BASIC	Beginner's All-Purpose Symbolic Instruction Code (computer terminology)
BBC	British Broadcasting Corporation
Bbl	barrels
BBQ	barbecue
BC, B.C.	before the birth of Christ
BCA	Business Council of Australia
Bcc	blind carbon copy
BD	bank draft
b/d	brought down
bde	brigade
b/e	bill of exchange
Benelux	Belgium, the Netherlands and Luxembourg
Beng	Bengali
b/f	brought forward
BH	business hours
Bi, b/I	built-in
Bib.	Bible; biblical
Bibi, bibliog..	bibliography
Bike	bicycle

Biochem	biochemistry
Biol.	biology; biological; biologist
Bir	built-in robe
BIOS	Basic Input/Output System (computer)
Bit, bit	binary digit
Bk	bank; book
bkpt.	bankrupt
bldg.	building
blvd, boul	boulevard
BMI	body mass index
B-movie	low-cost supporting movie
Bn	billion
Board	black board
BOD	biological oxygen demand (sewage treatment)
Bot.	botany; botanical; botanist; bottle
Bp	boiling point
BP	before present
Bpm	bits per minute
BPS	bits per second
Br.	brother
bra	brassiere
Braz	Brazil, Brazilian
Brig	brigadier
Brit.	Britain; British
Bro, bro	Brother; brother
Bros.	Brothers
B/S, BS	Bill of sale
BSc	bachelor of science
BTU	British Thermal Unit
BTW	by the way
Bull	bulletin
Bus	omnibus; bushel
bus. Mgr.	business manager
b/v	book value
BYO	bring your own (alcohol)
BYOB	bring your own beer/bottle
BYOG	bring your own grog
BYOW	bring your own wine

C	
C	caught; cent; centigrade; century
C	Celsius; centigrade; century; coulomb
Ca	about
Ca	Canada; Canadian
CA	cabin attendant
Cab	taxi (from cabinet); cabin; cabinet; cable

CAD	computer-aided design
CAE	computer-aided engineering; college of advanced education
Cal	calendar; calorie; calibre
CAM	computer-aided manufacturing
CAP	Common Agricultural Policy
Capt	captain
CAT	computerized axial tomography (a CAT scan is a form of high-speed layered X-ray.)
Cat	catalogue
CATV	cable television
Case	suitcase
CBD	Central Business District
CBS	Columbia Broadcasting Service (US)
Cc	cubic centimetre; carbon copy (of a letter)
CCTV	closed circuit television
CD	compact disc
c/o	care of
CD-R	compact disc that can be recorded on once
CD-ROM	computer disc – read–only memory
CD-RW	compact disc that can be recorded on over and over
Cent.	central; century
CEO	Chief Executive Officer
Cert.	certain; certificate; certified
Cf	compare; centre forward (football); centre fielder (baseball); confer
c/f	carried forward; carry forward
CFC	chlorofluorocarbon
CFL	compact fluorescent light bulb
CFO	Chief Financial Officer
CGA	color graphic adapter (computer term.)
CGT	capital gains tax
Ch., chap.	chapter; central heating
CHAP	chaplain
Chem.	chemistry
Chimp	chimpanzee
Chin	Chinese
CHOGM	commonwealth heads of government meeting
Chq.	cheque
CIA	Central Intelligence Agency (US)
Cif	cost, insurance, freight
Circ	circular
CIS	The Commonwealth of Independent States (former USSR)
Cit.	citation; cited
Cm	centimetre

CMT	cash management trust
Co	company
c/o	in the charge of; cash order; care of
COD	cash on delivery; collect on delivery
Co-ed	co-educational
Col	colonel; colour
Colloq.	colloquial
Comm.	commonwealth
Comp.	compiled; composition; compound
Compl.	complimentary
Condo	condominium
Conj.	conjunction
Cont., contd.	continued
Co-op	co-operative society or union
Corp	corporation; corporal
Cot	cotangent
CPI	Consumer Price Index
CPL	corporal
CPR	cardiopulmonary resuscitation, a newer and more inclusive form of artificial respiration
CPU	central processing unit (computers)
CRT	cathode-ray tube
Cr.	councillor
Cres.	crescent
CRO	cathode ray oscilloscope
CRT	cathode ray tube
CSIRO	Commonwealth Scientific and Industrial Organization
Ct.	caught
Cu.	cubic
CV, cv	curriculum vitae; a summary of a person's career and attainments
CWA	country women's association
D	
d	died; daughter; density; diameter
Dan	Danish
dB, db	decibel
dbl., dble	double
d.c.	direct current
DC	District of Columbia (Washington); direct current
DCF	discounted cash flow
D-day	Start of Allied invasion of mainland Europe; WW2
DDT	dichloro-diphenyl-trichloroethane (insecticide)
Deb.	debenture
Dec	deceased
Dec.	December

Deg.	degree
Deli	delicatessen
Dem	Democrat; member of American political party
Demo	demonstration
Dept, dept	department
d/g	double garage
dict.	dictionary
DINK	double income, no kids
DINKY	double income, no kids yet
Dip.	diploma
Disc.	discount
DJ	disk jockey
Dip. Dip	diploma
div	division
DIY, diy	do it yourself
DLUG	double lock-up garage
DMZ	demilitarized zone
DNA	deoxyribonucleic acid, the main constituent of chromosomes
Dob	date of birth
Doc	document
DOS	disk operating system (computer term.)
Doz	dozen
Dr	doctor
Dr.	drive
Dpt	department
DST	daylight saving time
DTP	desk-top publishing
Du	Dutch
Dup.	duplicate
DVD	digital video disk
d/w	dishwasher
dwt	dead weight tonnage
E	
E	East
Ea.	each
EC	European Community
Ecol.	ecology; ecological
Econ.	economy; economics; economist
Ed,. edit	editor; edition; edited by
EDT	Eastern Daylight Time
EEC	European Economic Community (now EU, European Union)
EEO	Equal employment Opportunity
EEZ	exclusive economic zone

EFL	English as a foreign language
EFTA	European Free Trade Association
EFTPOS	electronic funds transfer at point of sale
e.g.	exempli gratia = for example
Egypt	Egyptian
EIA	environmental impact assessment
EIS	environmental impact statement
E-mail	electronic mail
EMI	Electric and Musical Industries Limited
EMF, e.m.f.	electromotive force
Enc., encl.	enclosed; enclosure
Eng	English
Enl.	enlarged
Ens.	en suite
ENT	ear, nose and throat
ENTER	equivalent national tertiary entrance rank
EP	European Parliament
EPA	Environment Protection Agency
EQ	emotional quotient
Equiv.	equivalent
ESL	English as a second language
Esp.	especially
Esq.	esquire
EST	Eastern Standard Time
Est.	established; estimated
Estab.	established
et al.	et alia = and others (frequently used where several authors)
Etc	et cetera = and so on; and so forth
EU	European Union
EURATOM	European Atomic Energy Community
Exam	examination
Exc.	excellency; except; excellent
Exch.	exchange
Exel.	excluding; exclusive
Exec.	executive; executor
Exod.	exodus
Exp.	expenses; experienced; export; express
Ext.	external
EZ	easy

F

F	Fahrenheit; folio; following; franc
f., fem.	feminine; female
f/f	fully furnished

FA cup	Football Association Cup, open to all teams of the Association
Fac	facsimile (Fax, fax)
FAO	Food and Agricultural Organization (UN);
FAQ	Frequently asked question; fair average quality
Fr	Father
Fax	facsimile
FBI	Federal Bureau of Investigation (US)
FBT	fringe benefits tax
FDA	Food and Drug Administration (US)
Feb.	February
Fed	Federal; Federal Reserve Bank (US)
Ff	folios; following; fully furnished; fast foward
FIFA	Federation Internationale de Football Association (International Association Football Federation)
Fict.	fiction
FID	financial institution duty
Fig.	figure; figurative
Figs	figures
Fin	finis (the end)
Fl.	flourished
Flr	floor
Flu	influenza
FM	1. field marshal 2. Foreign minister 3. frequency modulation
FOB, fob	free on board
FOI	freedom of information
Fol.	folio; following
FORTRAN	Formula Translation (computer term.)
4WD	four wheel drive
Fr	Father; France, franc; Friday, French
FRB	Federal Reserve Board
Freq.	frequent; frequently
Fri., Frid.	Friday
Fridge	refrigerator
Ft	foot
f.t.	full time
FWD	four wheel drive
FYI	for your information

G

G	gram; gigabyte; general viewing
Gal.	gallon
GATT	General Agreement on Tariffs and Trade
GB	Great Britain; gigabyte
GBH	grievous bodily harm

GC   gas chromatograph
GDI   Gross Domestic Income
GDP   Gross Domestic Product
Gds   goods
GE.   genetic engineering; genetically engineered
Ge.   general; genius; gender
G8   Group of Eight (economic policy coordinating
                        committee of eight leading industrial nations:
                        Canada, France, Germany, Italy, Japan, Russia, UK
                        and US)

Geog.   geography; geographical; geographer
Geol   geology; geological; geologist
Geom   geometry
Ger   German
GFC   global financial crisis
G-G, GG   Governor-General
GM(O)   genetically modified (organism)
GI   Government Issue (US soldier)
GHQ   general headquarters
GI   glycaemic index
GMT   Greenwich Mean Time
GNP   Gross National Product
GOP   Grand Old Party; US Republican Party
Gov.   Governor
GP   General Practitioner (medical doctor); Grand Prix
GPO   General Post Office
GPS   global positioning system
Gr   Greek
Gr.   grains; grade; gross
Gr   gram
Gr. Wt   gross weight
Gram   grammar
GST   goods and services tax
Gym   gymnasium; gymnastics

H
h   height; hour
Ha   hectare(s)
Hanky   handkerchief (also hankie)
H-bomb   hydrogen (thermonuclear) bomb
Hcp   handicap
HD   hard disk (computer term.)
HDL   high-density lipoprotein
HDP   high-density polyethylene
Herb   herbarium; herbalist
h.f.   high frequency

hi-fi	high fidelity
Hind	Hindi
hippo	hippopotamus
hist.	history; historical
HIV	human immunodeficiency virus
HK	Hong Kong
HMAS	Her Majesty's Australian ship
HO	home office
homo	homosexual
Hon.	Honorable; honorary
hons	honors
hosp.	hospital
HP, hp	horse power; high pressure; high purchase
HQ, hq	headquarters
Hr	hour
HR	human resources
Hrs	hours
HRT	Hormone Replacement Therapy
HSC	high school certificate
Hts	heights
http	hypertext transfer protocol
hwy	highway
Hz	hertz (unit of frequency)

I

IATA	International Air Transport Association
IB	International Baccalaureate
Ibid.	ibidem = the same; in the same place; in the quoted reference
IBRD	International Bank for Reconstruction and Development
i/c	in charge; in command
IC	integrated circuit; industry commission
ICAC	Independent Commission Against Corruption
ICBM	intercontinental ballistic missile
ICC	International Chamber of Commerce
ICJ	International Court of Justice
ICRC	International Committee of the Red Cross
ICT	information and communication technology
i.e.	the same
ID	identification; identity (an identity card or passport)
i.e.	id est = that is; that's to say; in other words
IEA	International Energy Agency
ILO	International Labor Organization
Illus.	illustrated; illustration
IMF	International Monetary Fund

Imp.	emperor; empress
Imperf.	imperfect
In	inch
Inc	incorporated
Inc. Incl	included; including; increase; inclusive
Init.	initially
Ins.	insurance
Insp.	inspector
Int., intl	internal
Intro., introd,	introduced; introduction
I/O	input/output
IP	intellectual property; internet protocol
IQ	intellectual quotient
IRA	Irish Republican Army
Iran	Iranian
IRC	International Red Cross
IR	internal rate of return; industrial relations
Is, isl.	island
ISB	International Standard Book Number
ISD	international subscriber dialing
ISO	International Organization for Standardization
ISP	Internet Service Provider
ISBN	international standard book number
ISSN	International Standard Serial Number
IT	Information technology
It	Italian
Ital.	italics
IVF	in-vitro fertilization.
IWC	International Whaling Commission

J	
J	joule; journal; judge; justice
JAL	Japan Air Lines
Ja, Jan	Japan
Jan	January
Jap	Japan; Japanese
JC	Jesus Christ
JIT	just in time, just-in-time concept (Toyota production method)
Jn, Jun.	June
Jnr., jr	junior
JP	Justice of the Peace
Jud., judg	judges
Jul, Jl, Jy	July
Jun	June

K

K   kilometeres; kilobyte; thousand; kilometre; kelvin; king; knight

KAIST   Korea Advanced Institute of Science andTechnology

KAL   Korean Air Lines

Kb.   kilobit; kilobyte

Kbps   kilobits per second

Kbyte   kilobyte

Kd   killed

KFC   Kentucky Fried Chicken

Kg   kilogrammes

KGB   Komitet Gosudarstvennoy Bezopasnosti (the Soviet Committee of State Security (or secret police)

kHz   kilohertz

KISS   "Keep it simple, stupid!"

KIST   Korea Institute of Science and Technology

Kit.   kitchen

Kj   kilojoule

KKK   Ku Klux Klan, US anti-black organization

KL   Kuala Lumpur

Kl   kilolitre

Km   kilometres

Km/h   kilometres per hour

Knt, kt   knight

KO   knockout

Kor   Korean

kPa   kilopascal

k.p.h.   kilometres per hour

Kph   kilometers per hour

kW   kilowatt

kWh   kilowatt hour

L

l   liters; lire

l.   left; length; line

LA   legislative assembly

Lab   laboratory

LAN   local area network

Lang.   language

Laser   Light Amplification by Stimulated Emission of Radiation

Lat.   latitude

Lb   pound weight

LBM   lean body mass

Lbs   pounds

l.c.	lowercase
LC	legislative council
L/c	letter of credit
LCD	liquid crystal display
l.c.d.	lowest common denominator
LDC	less developed country
LDL	low-density lipoprotein
LDPE	low density polyethylene
LED	light-emiting diode
Lge	large
Lh.s.	left hand-side
Lieut	lieutenant
Limo	limousine
Lit	literally
Lm	lumen
LME	London Metals Exchange
LNG	liquefied natural gas
Log.	logarithm
LOL	laughing out loud
Long.	longitude
LOTE	languages other than English
LP	long playing (record)
LPG	liquid petroleum gas
LPGA	Ladies' Professional Golfers' Association
LSD	lysergic acid diethylamide (hallucinogenic drug)
LSE	London Stock Exchange
LSL	long service leave
Lt	lieutenant
Ltd, ltd	limited
LUG	lock-up garage
LWR	light water reactor (nuclear power generation)
lx.	lux
l.y.	light year

M	
M	marks
M	meter; married; masculine; married, mass, million, mile; minute; month; male
MA	Master of Arts
MAD	mutual assured destruction
Maj	Major
Mar., Mch	March
Masc.	masculine
MASH	Mobile Army Surgical Hospital (US)
Math, maths	mathematical; mathematics

Matric.	matriculation
Max.	maximum
Mb	milibar; megabit
MB	megabyte
MBA	Master of Business Administration
Mbps	megabits per second
m.c.	medical certificate
MC	master of ceremonies; Military Cross
MCG	Melbourne cricket ground
MD	Medical Doctor; managing director
Med.	medicine; medical; medium
Memo	memorandum
Messrs	messieurs; plural of "Mr."
Met.	metropolitan
methy.	methylated
m.f.	medium frequency
mfd	manufactured
mfg	manufacturing
MFN	most favoured nation
Mfr	manufacture; manufacturer
Mg	milligram
MITI	Ministry of International Trade and Industry (Japan)
Mid.	middle; midnight
Mil.	military
Mill.	million
Min.	minute; minimum
Misc	miscellaneous
MJ	megajoule
MKS	metre-kilogram-second
ML	megalitre
Mm	millimetre
Mo.	month
MO	money order; mail order; medical officer
Mod.	modern; moderate; moderately
Modem	modulator/ demodulator; device for connecting a computer to a telephone
Mon.	Monday
Mongol	Mongolian
Moped	motorized pedal cycle
Movie	moving picture
MP	Member of Parliament; Military Police
Mp	melting point
M.p.g	miles per second
M.p.h	miles per hour
M.p.s	metres per second
Mr	Mister

MOU	Memorandum of Understanding
MP	Member of Parliament
Mr	Mister
MRA	moral re-armament
MRI	magnetic resonance imaging (health sciences)
Mrs	missus; prefix for married woman
MS	multiple sclerosis; manuscript
Ms	Miz; a title of a mature woman not referencing marriageable status
MSF	Medecins Sans Frontieres (Doctors Without Borders)
MSG	monosodium glutamate (food flavor enhancer)
mt	mountain
MSS	manuscripts
Mt.	mount; mountain
MTBE	methyl tertiary butyl ether (motor fuel additive)
MTV	modified television version; music television
Mum	mother
Mus.	music; musical; musician; museum
MVP	most valuable player
MW	megawatt
MYOB	mind your own business
Myth	mythology; mythological

N	
N	North; northern
n/a, n.a.	not applicable; not available
NAB	National Australia Bank
NAFTA	North America Free Trade Agreement
NAM	non-aligned movement
NASA	National Aeronautic and Space Administration
Nat.	national; native; natural
NATO	North Atlantic Treaty Organization
Naut.	nautical; navigation; navy; naval
Navig.	navigation; navigator
NB	please note
NBA	1. National Basket Association 2. National Boxing Association
NBC	National Broadcasting Company (US)
NBT	next big thing
NDE	near-death experience
NDP	net domestic product
NE	northeast; negative
Net	after all deductions (also nett)
Neg.	negation; negative
NFF	National Farmers federation

NGA	National Gallery of Australia
NGO	non-government organisation
NIC	newly industrialized country
NIMBY	not in my back yard
NLA	National Library of Australia
NMA	National Museum of Australia
No.	number
Nos.	numbers
Nov	November
NPT	Nuclear Non-proliferation Treaty
Nr	near
NRA	National Rifle Association (US)
NRL	National Rugby League
NSW	New South Wales
NT	northern territory
NW	north-west; north-western
NY	New York
NYSE	New York Stock Exchange
NZ	New Zealand

O

OA	Order of Australia
OAU	Organization of African Unity
OBE	Order of British Empire
Obs.	observation; observatory; obsolete
Occas.	occasion
Oct.	October
O/D	overdraft; overdrawn; on demand
OECD	Organization for Economic Cooperation and Development
OED	Oxford English Dictionary
Off.	office; officer; official
OHMS	On His/Her Majesty's Service
OHS, OH & S	occupational health and safety
OK, ok	all right; alright; everything in order
OMG	oh my gosh
o.n.o.	or nearest offer
007	British Secret Service codename for Ian Fleming's fictional spy James Bond
o.p.	observation post; out of print
op.	operation
OP	out-of-print
OPEC	Organization of Petroleum Oil Exporting Countries
Opp.	opposite
Opt.	option
Orch.	orchestra

Ord.	order; ordinary
Orig	origin
O-ring	rubber oil seal ring used in machinery
o.s.	overseas
o/s	out of stock
OS	outsize; operating system
o/t	overtime
OT	Old Testament; occupational therapy; occupational therapist
Oxbridge	Oxford and Cambridge
Oxfam	Oxford Famine Relief
Oz.	ounce
P	
p	page; per ;pence
P	provisional (driver's licence)
p.a.	yearly
P & O	Peninsular and Oriental (steamship company)
P & P	packing and postage
PABX	private automatic branch exchange telephone system
Par., Para.	paragraph
Parl., parlt	Parliament
Partn.	partnership
Pass.	passenger; passive
PATA	Pacific Area Travel Association
PAU	Pan American Union
Pax	passengers
PAYE	pay-as-you-earn (income tax payment system).
PAYG	pay-as-you-go
PAX	private automatic exchange
PB	personal best
PBS	pharmaceutical benefits Scheme
PBX	private branch exchange
PC	personal computer; police constable; politically correct; personnel carrier
Pc, p.c.	per cent
PCB	printed circuit board
p.c.m	per calendar month
pd	paid
p.d.	per day; potential difference
PDA	personal digital assistant
PE	physical education
P/E	Price-Earnings ration
Pen.	peninsula
PEN	poets, playwrights, editors, essayists, novelists

Percent	percentum = of every hundred (i.e. six percent or 6% = six hundredths of the whole)
Perm.	permanent
Perq	perquisite
Pg., p.	page
PGA	Professional Golfers' Association
pH	potential of hydrogen = measurement scale of acidity and alkalinity
PhD	Doctor of Philosophy
Phil	Philippians
Philos	philosophy
Phone	telephone
Photo. Photog.	photograph; photography
Phr.	phrase
Phys. Edu	physical education
Phys.	physical; physics
Physio	physiotherapy
Physiol	physiology
PIN	personal identification number
PISA	program for international students assessment
Pixel	picture element (computers)
Pk	park
Pkt	packet
Pkg	package
pl., Pl.	place; plate
pl., plur.	plural
P/L	Proprietary Limited
plane	aeroplane
PLO	Palestine Liberation Organization
PM	Prime Minister
p.m. or P.M.	Afternoon (post meridiem = afternoon; post mortem)
PMG	Postmaster General
PMS	pre-menstrual syndrome
PMT	premenstrual tension
PND	postnatal depression
PNG	Papua New Guinea
PO	postal order; post office; petty officer
Pol	Polish
Polio	poliomyelitis
Pop.	population
Pop art	art with allusions to popular culture, launched in 1950s
Porn	pornography
Pos.	position
POW	prisoner of war
Pp.	pages

Ppm	parts per million
Ppp	purchasing power parity
PPP	public-private partnership
Pr	pair
PR	public relations; permanent residence; proportional representation
Pref.	preference; preferred
Prelim.	preliminary
Pres.	president
Prof	professional
Pram	perambulator (baby carriage)
Prep	preparatory; prep school = preparatory school
Pro	professional
Prof.	professor
Pronunc.	pronunciation
Prop.	proprietor
Ps, PS	postscriptum = postscript
Pseudo	pseudonym
Psi	pounds per square inch
Psychol.	psychology; psychological
Pt	point; pint
p.t.	part time
PT	physical training
PTE	private
PTA	parent-teacher association
PTO, p.t.o.	please turn over
Pty	proprietary = private limited company
Pub	public house; published by
Pv	present value
PVA	polyvinyl acetate
PVC	polyvinyl chloride (plastic)
Pvt	private
Pw, p.w., p/w	per week

Q

q.	question
Q, Qd, Qld	Queensland
Q&A	question and answer
QC	Queen's counsel
qq.	questions
qr.	quarter
qt.	quantity
qtr	quarter; quarterly
Qty	quantity
Qual.	qualified; quality
Quango	quasi-autonomous non-governmental organization

R

r.	radius; right
RAAF	Royal Australian Air Force
Rad	radian
Radar	Radio Detecting and Ranging
RAM	random access memory (computers)
RAN	Royal Australian Navy
R & B	rhythm and blues
R & D	research and development
RBA	Reserve Bank of Australia
RBL	reasonable benefit limit
RBT	random breath test
RC	Roman Catholic; Roman Catholic
Rd. rd	road
RDI	recommended dietary intake; recommended daily intake
RDT	random drug test
Rec.	receipt
Recd	received
Ref.	reference; referee
Reg.	registered; registration; regulation
Relig.	religion; religious
Rep.	business representative
Retd	retired
Rev., Revd	Reverend
Revs	revolutions
Rhino	rhinoceros
r.h.s.	right-hand side
RIP	rest in peace
riv.	river
rm	room
RN	Registered Nurse
RNA	ribonucleic acid
ROM	read-only memory
Roo	kangaroo
ROI	return on investment
Rom.	Roman; Romanic
ROTC	Reserve Officers Training Corps
ROW	right of way
R.p.m	revolutions per minute
RRP	recommended retail price
RSI	repetitive strain injury
RSL	returned and services league of Australia
RSPCA	Royal Society for the Prevention of Cruelty to Animals
RSVP	respondez s'il vous plait = please reply
Rt	route
Russ	Russia, Russian

S	
s.	singular; seconds; south; southern
S	South; section
SA	South Africa; South Australia; South America; Salvation Army
s.a.e, SAE	self-addressed, stamped envelope
SALT	Strategic Arms Limitation Talks (US and former USSR)
SAM	surface to air missile
SARS	severe acute respiratory syndrome
SAS	special air service
SAT	Scholastic Aptitude Test (US)
Sat.	Saturday
SBS	special broadcasting service
s/c	self-contained
Scand	Scandinavian
SCG	Sydney Cricket Ground
Sch.	School
Sci-fi, SF	science fiction
Script	scripture
SCUBA	Self-Contained Underwater Breathing Apparatus
SDI	Strategic Defense Initiative (US "Star Wars" project)
SE	southeast; southeastern
sec.	second; secondary; secretary; section; secure
Sec.	secretary
Sect.	section
Secy, sec.	secretary
Sen	Senator
Sen., snr, sr	senior
Sep., Sept	September
SES	State Emergency Service
SETI	Search for Extraterrestrial Intelligence
Sf	science fiction
S.g., sg	specific gravity
SGC	superannuation guarantee charge
Sgt	Sergeant
Shd	should
Shpt	shipment
Shr.	share
SI unit	Systeme International d'Unites = system of international units (e.g. ampere, metre, kilogram, second etc)
Sig.	signature
Sing.	singular
SMSF	self-managed superannuation fund
SLR	single lens reflex (camera)
Snr, snr, sr	senior
Soc.	society

SOHO	small office home office
Sonar	Sound Navigation and Ranging
Sop.	soprano
SOS	save our soul; the Morse code signal for distress
Sp	Spanish
Sp.	special; species
Sp.gr.	specific gravity
Spec.	specification; special
SPF	sun protection factor
Sq., sq	square
Sr	senior; sister
SRC	Students' Representative Council
SST	supersonic transport
St.	street; Saint; state; strait
Stat	statistic
STB	set-top box
STD	subscriber trunk dialing; sexually transmitted disease
Stereo	stereophonic sound; stereophonic record player
Stp	standard temperature and pressure
Sth	south
Sthn	southern
Stn	station
Sub.	subeditor; subject
Subj.	subject
Sun., Sund	Sunday
Super.	Superintendent
Surg.	surgery; surgical; surgeon
SUV	sports utility vehicle
SW	southwest; southwestern; short wave
Swatch	Swiss watch
Swed	Swedish
Sym.	symbol; symbolic; symmetrical; symphony
Sz.	size
T	
T	tonne
Tab	table; tabulate; tabulation; tablet
TAB	Totalisator Agency Board
TAFE	technical and further education
Tan	tangent
Tarmac	bituminous surfacing
Tas.	Tasmania
Tax	taxation
TB	tuberculosis
Tbs, tbsp..	table spoon
Tech.	technical; technology

TEFL	teaching English as a foreign language
Tel.	telephone
Telecom.	telecommunication
Telex	teleprinter exchange
Telly	television
Temp, temp.	temperature
TESOL	teaching English to speakers of other languages
TFN	tax file number
Theat.	theatre; theatrical
Thu, Thurs	Thursday
TGIF	Thank God It's Friday.
TGV	train a grande vitesse = French high speed passenger train
Thro, thro'	through
TKO, tko	technical knockout (boxing)
TLC	tender loving care
TM	transcendental medication
TNT	2-4-6 trinitrotoluene (explosive)
TO	technical officer
TPC	trade practices commission
TQM	Total Quality Management
Tr.	transitive; translate; translator; translated by
Trad.	traditional
Trans.	transcript; translated; translation; translator
Trig.	trigonometric; trigonometry
Trop.	tropical
Tsp., t.	teaspoon; teaspoonful
Tues., Tue., Tu.	Tuesday
Turk	Turkish
turps	turpentine
TV	television
TVA	Tennessee Valley Authority (US)
TWI	trade-weighted index
U	
U	you; union; united; university
UAE	United Arab Emirates
UAV	unmanned aerial vehicle
U-boat	unterseeboot = submarine
uc. u.c.	upper case
u/c	undercover
UCP	undercover parking
UFO	Unidentified Flying Object
UHF, uhf, u.h.f.	ultra-high frequency
UK	United Kingdom (Britain)
UN	United Nations
UNCTAD	United Nations Conference on Trade and Development

UNDP	United Nations Development Program
UNEF	United Nations Emergency Force
UNESCO	United Nations Educational Scientific and Cultural Organization
UNFAO	United Nations Food and Agriculture Organization
UNHCR	United Nations High Commission for Refugees
Uni.	university
UNICEF	United Nations Children's Emergency Fund
UNIDO	United Nations Industrial Development Organization
UNSC	United Nations Security Council
UK	United Kingdom
UPI	United Press International
UPU	Universal Postal Union
US	United States
USIS	United States Information Service
USA	United States of America
USD	US dollar
USSR	Union of Soviet Socialist Republics (dissolved 1991-92)
Usu.	usually
U3A	University of the Third Age
UV	ultraviolet
V	
v.	verb; verse; versus; volume; velocity
V	versus = against; volt
Vac.	vacancy; vacant; vacation
Var.	variant; variation; variety
VAT	Value Added Tax
Vb	verb
VC	Victoria Cross; vice-chairman; vice-chancellor
VCR	video cassette recorder
VD	venereal disease
V-Day	Victory Day
VDU	visual display unit
VE Day	Victory in Europe Day
Vel.	velocity
Ver	version
Vet	veterinary surgeon; veteran
VET	vocational education and training
VG	valuer-general
VHF, v.h.f.	very high frequency; very high fidelity
Vic.	Victoria
VIP	very important person
VJ Day	Victory over Japan day
VOA	Voice of America
VOD	video on demand

Vol, vol.	volume
VP	vice-president
VP Day	Victory in the Pacific Day
Vs	versus = against; opposite
VTR	videotape recorder/ recording
Vs.	versus; verse
vv.	verses; vice versa; very very

W	
w.	week; weight; west; western; wide; width; with
W	West; western; watt
WA	Washington; Western Australia
WAN	wide area network
WASP	White Anglo-Saxon Protestant
WBA	World Boxing Association
WBC	World Boxing Council
WBP	world's best practice
WC	water closet; toilet
w.c.	without charge
wd	word; would
Wed., Wed	Wednesday
WEL	women's electoral lobby
WFP	World Food Program
Wh	watt hour
WHO	World Health Organization
Wir	walk-in robe or closet
Wk	week; work
Wkly	weekly
WMD	weapon of mass destruction
w/o	without
wpm. W.p.m.	words per minute (keyboard typing speed)
wt	weight
WTO	World Trade Organization
Ww, w/w	wall-to wall (carpets)
WWF	world wildlife fund
WWW	World Wide Web
WYSIWYG	What You See is What You Get

X	
XL	extra large
Xmas	Christmas
XOXO	hugs and kisses
X-ray	short wavelength electromagnetic radiation
X ref.	cross-reference

Y

y.	year
Yd	yard
YHA	Youth Hostel Association
YMCA	Young Men's Christian Association
Yo, y/o	years old
yr	year
yuppie	young urban/upwardly mobile) professional
YWCAY	Young Women's Christian Association

Z

ZEV	zero emission vehicle
Zool.	zoology

VIII. Short Sentences

This section includes short sentences often used by native speakers.

Absolutely crackers!
Absolutely not.
Above all I need love.
Actions speak loudest.
Actions speak louder than words.
Advertising is total war.
After a storm comes the calm.
All feathers, no meat. (Christopher Pyne).
All bets are off.
All comes down to this.
All comes to fruition.
All hope is gone.
All I want is you.
All for one, one for all.
All go away.
All in all, I'm a lucky guy.
All in all, I could care a less.
All in one go.
All in a day's work.
All is not lost.
All is on its way.
All our eggs are in this basket.
All people can get into it.
All work and no play makes Jack a dull boy.
All's come to end.
All things are nonsense.
All will be well.
All wonderful things are over.
All yours.
Always think about others. (Dame Elizabeth Murdoch)
An apple a day keeps the doctor away.
Am I making myself clear?
Another disaster has hit again.
The answer is simple.
The answer is straightforward.
Answer me.
Answer my prayer.
Anybody here?
Any good?
Anybody can become somebody.
Anyone can do it.
Anyone can have a go.

Anything is possible.
Anything sharp will do.
Appearances are deceptive.
Are their concerns justified?
Are there any questions?
Are they coming?
Are they lucky

Are we alive, changing too far and too fast, falling behind, going in, starting, the lucky country, there yet, truly alone, trying to help them out?

Are you accusing me, alone, angry with me, crazy, a betting man, a philosophical person, a shock joke, being served, better off, coming, completely comfortable with that position, eating enough food, going to get married, going to hand it over, happy to be here, having a good time, hungry, in love with her, interested, leaving, keeping something from me, learning anything, making fun of me, man enough, okay, out of your mind, prepared to deny this, promised to him, ready, satisfied, serious, smiling all the time, speaking to me, still with me, sure, sure of it, talking to me, the manager, there, terribly angry?

Aren't you afraid, glad to see me, young?
Art is just fraud. (Paik Namjune)
Art is long, life is short.
Art tells me who I am.
As good as it gets. (Movie title)
As long as it takes.
As usual, I'm running a bit late.
Australia is in the right place at the right time.
Australian people should stand up together as one.
Australia will end up like Europe.
The atmosphere is great.
Attack is the best form of defence.
Australia can't get enough of him.
The axe will fall.

Back in business.
Back it up or shut up.
Back off.
Back to you.
Bad luck one day, good luck the next.
Bad news travels fast.
The ball is in your court.
The battle lines are clear.
Be a good boy.
Be a smarter consumer.
Be alert!
Be ambitious.
Be bold.
Be brave.
Be calm.

Be careful.
Be curious.
Be happy.
Be inspired.
Be it.
Be kind.
Be my guest.
Be on time.
Be quick.
Be respectful.
Be practical.
Be prepared to haggle.
Be quiet.
Be sensible.
Be serious.
Be there.
Be your best.
Be yourself.
Bear with me.
Beauty is skin deep.
Because it is there. (George Mallory, mountain climber)
Beg your pardon.
Behave yourself.
Being hungry makes you healthy.
Believe me.
The best is yet to come. (Hilsung Church and Obama)
Better late than never.
Better safe than sorry.
Better the devil you know than the devil you don't know.
Better safe than never.
A bird in hand is worth two in the bush.
Blind Freddie could see that.
The blind leading the blind.
Blood is thicker than water.
A boom time is over.
Boys, be ambitious! (William Clark)
Boys will be boys.
Brand new world needs a new party.
Brighten up your life.
Brighten your smile.
Bring another glass.
Bring him in.
Bring it back.
Bring it in.
Bring it on!
Bring me peace now.

Bring the world to your kitchen.
The bucks stops here. (Harry Truman)
Bugger off.
By all means.
Bye now until we meet again.

Caffeine makes me crazy.
Call me today to see how I can help you.
Call the doctor.
Call the police.
Can I ask you something, be in love, come in, deny everything I believe in, do anything, fix a drink, get you a drink, get you anything, give you a hand, go on, help you, keep them, look, say this, take another topic, take time off, talk about it later, talk to you for a minute?
Can it be true?
Can modern men have it all?
Can she make it?
Can they keep cool, keep the secret?
Can we have a win-win situation?
Can women have it all?
Can we beat the heat, do that, get it out economically, get out of it?
Can you answer me, be sure the kids are all right, believe it, believe that, blame me, buy happiness, continue, do it, imagine, escape your past, explain it, hear me, help me through, help us, imagine life without it, pick me up tomorrow, see that, sing like him, tell us which is which, think something, understand that?
Capitalism has lost its moral compass.
The caravan has moved on.
Carry on.
Carry out the order.
Case closed.
Cash is king.
The cast couldn't be better.
Cast not the first stone.
Catch it. Bin it. Kill it.
Catch me if you can. (movie title)
Celebrate our love.
Change your life.
Charity begins at home.
Cheaper than you think.
Check it out.
Check on him.
Cheer up.
Cherish that experience.
Chickens come home to roost.
Children make mistakes.
Chill out.

China is a force to be reckoned with.
The choice is yours.
Choose the lesser of two evils.
Christmas came early. (Is Christmas better than Easter?)
A child could do that.
The chips are down.
The choice has to be made.
The choice is yours.
Choose well.
The city meets farmers.
The city was a safe place.
Clear it up.
Cleanliness is next to godliness.
Clear some space.
Clear the way.
Clear your name.
Close your eyes.
Clothes do not make the man.
Cold enough for you?
Come along with me.
Come and get it, get me, join us, see me.
Come back, again, with us.
Come closer.
Come forward.
Come in.
Come inside,
Come on in.
Come out.
Come outside.
Come over.
Come over here,
Come straight back.
Come with me.
Coming.
Comparison doesn't fly.
Conditions have improved.
Consumers can't find any difference.
Cook something.
Correct me if I am wrong.
Could I have done more?
Could we start all over again?
Could you do me a favour, make it simpler, put it there?
Count us in.
The customer is always right. (Gordon Selfridge)
Culture changes.
Culture is important.

Culture makes all the difference.
Curiosity killed the cat.
Culture makes all the difference.
The customer is king.
Cut it down.
Cut it out.
Cut that out.
Cut the red tape.

Damned if you do, damned if you don't.
The danger is there.
Days of reckoning may come soon.
The deal is the deal.
The debate does matter.
Defend yourself.
The devil is in the details.
The devil you know is better than the devil you don't know.
Did I do that, get the address, hear something, see anyone?
Did she deliver?
Did she say anything about me?
Did they get away?
Did you enjoy the weekend, ever love me, fall out of love, feel for me, find it, get the ticket, hear
    that, grow up in a loving household, know, like it at all, see the end of it?
The die is cast.
Direct marketing gives me the opportunity.
Diversity doesn't end there.
Do any good.
Do as I say, I told you, you want, you were told.
Do get in.
Do go on.
Do I care what people think about me?
Do I feel lucky?
Do I have to eat it, know you too well, what?
Do it anyway, today not tomorrow, yourself.
Do not go anywhere.
Do something about it.
Do the right thing.
Do we really have to go?
Do whatever you want.
Do you think I'm sexy?
Do you believe in marriage, feel anything, find it attractive, follow that, have some time, hear,
    know anything about this, know him, know what I mean, know who I am, know who you
    are, love her, mean that, mind putting on your hat, need any help, need a hand, recognize
    me, remember, see that happening, speak English, think I can do this job, trust her, try to
    train them, understand, understand me?
Do you feel good, proud, vindicated?

Do you have a girl to go with, a good antennae, any new project in mind, any suggestions, any
    thought on this, to?
Do you hear me, something, that?
Do you like him, it?
Do you want me to leave, tell the truth, to get angry, to leave, to quit?
Do you really have to go, mean this, think so?
Do your best.
Does he promise the world to you?
Does it hurt, matter, work perfectly?
Does money buy happiness?
Does that answer you?
Don't apologize, argue with me, ask any questions, ask me, bet on it, betray me, blame them,
    blame yourself, block the street, bother, call me pretty, change the subject, count on it,
    cry, curse me, cut and run, damage the lawn, disappear too soon, do that, do it, drop it,
    embarrass me, even think about it, ever do that again, expect me to visit you, fear, fight,
    force it, forget, forget that, forget to have a laugh, give me a hard time, give up, go, go
    anywhere(TV presenter), go away (TV presenter), go near the water, hold back, interrupt
    me, leave me, look at me like that, look now, marry her, mention it, mess it up, mess with
    me, miss it, miss out, muck around, nag, overthink, park too close, pay debt with debt,
    pick on me, push me, put your head in the sand, put it off, risk it, raise your voice, rush
    me, say that, sit idly by, stop living life, strive desperately, take my word for it, tell the
    bride, throw away the medicine, touch anything, touch it again, touch that, trouble
    yourself, trust a man, try this at your home, turn away from him, underestimate the task,
    wait until it's too late, work too hard, worry about me.
Don't be a fool, afraid, crazy, embarrassed, fooled, too hard on yourself, insulting, mad, mean,
    nasty, out too late, in a panic, ridiculous, sad, scared, shy, silly, so stupid, sorry, upset.
Don't be afraid, of failure, to ask, to talk.
Don't cry over spilt (or spilled) milk.
Don't do it, it again, that, this, this to me, worry about him, worry about me.
Don't get carried away, excited, fresh with me, me wrong, too panicky, upset.
Don't just sit there.
Don't kill the goose that lays the golden egg.
Don't let anything happen to you, him get away, let me down.
Don't make a fool of me, a fool of yourself, fun of us, him angry.
Don't make me come again, do that, suffer any longer..
Don't put all your eggs in one basket.
Don't say anything, anything to her, it, that.
Don't talk too loudly, back, like that.
Don't throw out the baby with the bathwater .
Don't worry about a thing, about too much, be happy.
Don't you forget it, get it, know who I am, remember me, remember who I am, want to hear,
    you worry.
Draw your own conclusion.
Dreams are nothing if actions do not follow.
The dream of life time is about to come true.
A dream didn't come true.

The dream comes true.
Drive the change.
Drive your dollar further.
Drive your dream.
A drowning man will clutch at a straw.
Dying is a part of life. (Jack Thompson)

The early bird catches the worm.
The earth revolves around the sun.
Easier said than done.
Easy come, easy go!
Eat humble pie.
Eat fresh.
Eat well.
The economy is difficult.
The economy is going south.
It's the economy, stupid. (Bill Clinton)
Education is close to my heart.
Education is too important.
The education standard is going backward.
The Emperor has no clothes. (He must be very poor.)
The end justifies the means.
The end does not justify the means.
English people are cold.
Enjoy the evening.
Enjoy your life.
Enjoy yourself.
Empty vessels make most noise.
Enough is enough.
Enter the dragon. (Movie title)
The essence of attack is surprise.
Every house should have one.
Even rich Koreans feel less happy.
Even truth can hurt.
Everybody chips in.
Everybody dreams.
Everybody else is cracking up.
Everybody is blaming me for everything, on the line, crazy about her, a winner, doing it, entitled to his opinion, ok.
Everybody knows everybody.
Everybody understood what it is for.
Everybody wins.
Everyone deserves a small ride.
Everyone has a dream.
Everyone has to make up their own minds. .
Everyone owns their bodies.

Everyone's all right, happy, hard, too busy in listening to Psy.
Everything is political.
Everything is possible.
Everything looks good on paper.
The evidence is alarming.
Expect the unexpected.
Experience the wonder.
Explore your world.
Everybody chips in.
Everyone can say what they want.
Everyone is a winner.
Everything is under control.
Everything old is new again.
An eye for an eye, a tooth for a tooth.

Face the facts.
Factual knowledge must precede skill.
Fair enough.
Families are better off.
Farewell forever.
The fight goes on.
The fight isn't over yet.
Fight with me.
Figure it out.
Find out.
Find out what has happened.
Find the stone.
Find us.
Fine with me.
Find your ideal car.
Finish him.
The fire is out.
Fight fire with fire.
First come, first served.
Fix the debt.
Follow me.
Follow me around.
Follow music around Korea.
Follow the voice of your wisdom.
Follow your heart.
Food is a foundation for human relationships.
Food is poison.
Food remains safe.
For me, it's wrong.
For the Olympics, we'll be sleepless in Seoul.
Forge ahead.

Forget about this whole thing.
Forget it!
Forgive me.
Friends don't act like that.
The future has just begun.
The future is now.

The game has changed.
The game is up.
Get away.
Get back.
Get back here.
Get cracking.
Get fresh.
Get in.
Get in the car.
Get informed.
Get it.
Get out of here.
Get me out of here.
Get moving.
Get off my land.
Get on.
Get on board.
Get on with our lives.
Get out and get planting.
Get out of it, of my way, of the house, of the way, of this.
Get over it.
Get professional.
Get ready.
Get smart. (Movie title)
Get some sleep.
Get started.
Get the balance right.
Get the facts straight.
Get the hell out this time.
Get the idea.
Get the job done.
Get the light ready.
Get the picture? (Parent Trap)
Get the whole panel to dance.
Get them back if you can.
Get used to it.
Get yourself together.
Girls are all right.
Girls get to choose.

Give me it to me.
Give it back.
Give it up.
Give me a break, a kiss, the number, an example, the rope, the money.
Give the money back.
Give that back.
Give us a break.
Give your encouragement, goodwill, smile.
Give yourself up.
The glass is half empty or half full.
The glass is more than half full.
Go back to sleep, to where you came from, to your doctor.
Go ahead!
Go away!
Go easy.
Go easy on him.
Go for it.
Go in.
Go, Korea, Go!
Go on.
Go over there.
Go right ahead.
Go top free. (Slogan for women protestors)
God bless.
God helps those who help themselves.
God is dead. (Friedrich Nietzsche)
God is love.
Going, going, gone.
Golden geese are bent on fattening themselves.
Good luck.
Good luck to them.
Good on you.
A good question!
Good to be here.
Good to see you.
Goodness me!
The government is dying of shame. (Tony Abbott)
The government is everywhere.
The government is short-sighted.
The government makes too much money from it.
The government will come to the party.
The greatest moment is yet to come.
Greatness is measured by time.
Grow up.
Guess what?
Guns are doing all the talking.

Hands off.
Hang around.
Hang on a minute.
Hang out with friends.
Hang up.
Happiness is equality.
Has a lesson been learned?
Has anyone changed their minds?
Has he made the case?
Have a chat.
Have a wonderful trip.
Have a drink.
Have fun.
Have a go.
Have a good time.
Have a good hard look at it.
Have a great day.
Have a heart.
Have a look around.
Have a lovely day.
Have a rest.
Have a wonderful trip.
Have I forgotten something?
Have mercy on him.
Have they been overly aggressive?
Have we met before?
Have we no shame?
Have you anything to do with it, eaten, ever been here, forgotten something, found
      someone else, got the stomach for it, ruled out the plan?
Haven't you got a nerve, had one, seen the paper?
He asks for her hand in marriage.
He avoids me.
He beat the shark.
He belongs here.
He can take care of himself.
He can't be disturbed.
He can't handle women in authority. (Tony Abbott)
He comes to the party.
He could be anywhere.
He did everything right.
He did the wrong thing.
He didn't beat you.
He didn't see it coming.
He does a lot of driving.
He does what he does.

He doesn't do things by halves, get it, look like you, pull any punches.

He eats nothing but meat.

He gave me my life back.

He gets the balance right.

He's got to be specific.

He's got what it takes.

He has his whole life ahead of him.

He has a problem of his own, a tremendous potential, absolutely nothing, changed a lot, done
  it, dealt with the issue, everything he wants, never lied to me, to be himself.

He hasn't looked back.

He hit me.

He is always by my side, out of line.

He keeps shouting.

He lives by his words.

He lives on.

He'll be there.

He looks like you.

He loved the place.

He loves his job.

He loves what he does.

He lost the plot.

He makes me laugh.

He makes no bones about it.

He makes it up.

He must be crazy, on the run, sacked.

He nearly had a heart attack.

He never took him seriously.

He's a lucky man, a quiet man, an inspiring Australian, beginning to talk like a man, an
  expert, becoming a man quickly, caught out, completely humiliated by them, counting on
  you to take over, doing his job, done, done it, entitled to celebrate, entitled to do so,
  entitled to his view, finished, genuine, getting some help, learned a lesson, lucky to be
  around, my rock, not comfortable with a powerful woman, moving ahead, my
  responsibility, not in trouble, not taking responsibility, old enough to be your father,
  remarkably civilised, respectful of women, safe, the man to show how to do it, the one,
  travelling back to time, come to meet you, very good at cheating, well looked after, well.

He sees social media as a big leap forward.

He seems to be happy.

He seems to be fit.

He should be off the air. (Allan Jones)

He showed me some respect.

He stood down anyway.

He tells all.

He tells me.

He wants a credit.

He wants to win back his girlfriend.

He was delighted, framed, right in his predictions, holding it tight, looking for you, upfront about

his involvement, visionary.
He will not be silenced.
He will not walk away with it.
He wasn't feeling very well.
He who laughs last, laughs best.
He won't hurt a thing, leave, like it.
He would not have it any other way.
Heads will roll.
Hello there.
Help me.
Help yourself.
Her position is untenable.
Her record speaks for itself.
Her spirit will love on in him.
Her wish comes true.
Here comes the pain.
Here goes.
Here I am.
Here is the result.
Here's what's in store.
Here it is.
Here's a message to dad, a win-win situation, how it works, how to fit it in, the money, what's in
    store.
Here they are.
Here we are, go, go again.
Here you are.
Here you are again.
His day of reckoning is coming.
His influence is everywhere.
His legacy is stronger than ever.
History repeats itself.
His left hand doesn't know what his right hand is doing.
History can be made.
Hit the nail on the head.
Hold it.
Hold my breath,
Hold my hand.
Hold on.
Hold on tight.
Honesty is the best policy.
Honour your word.
Hope comes from strange places.
The horse has bolted.
Housing shows a glimmer.
How about a cup of tea, joining us tonight, you?
How am I supposed to know?

How am I supposed to make money?

How are people coping, things, we getting out of this?

How are you doing, feeling, feeling now, going to fill that gap, going to do it, keeping?

How can I turn my back on my faith?

How can you say that?

How come?

How can I be happy, help you, make sure it works out, put it?

How can it be, Korea ensure energy security, this be, we do this, we get in, you do that?

How cool is that?

How cool is this?

How could I marry him?

How could they do anything like that?

How could we ever forget?

How could you leave us?

How could you lose?

How could you not love that?

How cruel it is!

How dare you?

How did it all begin?

How did it all happen?

How did it go?

How did we get here?

How did you do that, find me, get here, get in there, get into sport, get this, live like that, manage, manage to get here?

How different is it going to be?

How do I get started, I get there, l look, we get back?

How do they do it?

How do they know about that, this?

How do you go about going home, feel, feel about it, handle all this, know, know that, like that, propose to get him back, respond to that?

How do you feel, about that, right now?

How do you make it happen, sense of it?

How does it change your life, make you feel, work?

How easy is that?

How far are you going?

How fortunate am I.

How good is that?

How happy would you be?

How has that happened?

How has the journey been so far?

How have you been?

How is it going to be different, that possible, your family holding up?

How is everything with you, the day, the trip, your health, your memory holding up?

How long are you going to keep me here, are you going to stay, have you been in Korea?

How lucky am I?

How lucky I am.

How low can you go?
How many times does a man have to win you?
How much flirting is too much, is enough, time have you done (jail), trouble are we in?
How nice.
How shall we live?
How should I know?
How simple is that?
How smart are you?
How was it for you?
How would you see?
How would you know?
The hungrier one will always win.
Hurry up.
Hygiene is really important.

I absolutely don't want to do it.
I absolutely loved that.
I accept the gift.
I accept your challenge.
I admire that.
I admire you.
I adore your honesty.
I adored your speech.
I advise you to leave.
I agree with that.
I always keep learning, loved you, said what I mean.
I am a great fan of Korean products, done, driven by dissatisfaction, going back to
Australia, here, here to help you, hoping for a miracle, impressed, a legend, not afraid
of you, not looking for the tax cut, on my way, only a human, seeing someone, still
seeking, the victim, who I am.
I apologize.
I appreciate that.
I appreciate your point.
I asked him to sing.
I believe in free speech, in you, that we are doing our best.
I came all the way to Seoul to see you, as fast I can, here to get gold, with nothing.
I can be anything, bring everyone back, buy him a drink, do it all over again, do
anything, do it, get him, hardly move, have a little business, hear you, help you with
anything, manage it, pay you back, see that, show them the way, stand up for myself, take
care of myself, see your heart breaking, understand that, wake you up, walk outside
safely
I can't accept it, answer that, beat my daughter's illness, believe how good they are, believe it,
change that, cope any more, do anything for you, imagine my life without her, enter,
explain it, feel it, finish it, fix it, get to sleep, have you back, hear you, help it, help
myself, let you do that, like you, marry him, marry you, please everyone, promise you
anything, really answer that, remember anything, see a thing, see anything, sleep, speak

more highly of him, stand it any longer, stay, stay with her any longer, stress it enough, stop loving you, take it anymore, tell you, tell you yet, understand that, wait, wait much longer.

I can't be around him, disappointed, held responsible, helped, stopped.

I can't get sleep.

I can't go back now, into details, with you.

I can't make you love me, you stay, a joke about this.

I can't stop.

I can't talk about that right now.

I care about you.

I came to a decision.

I could have a shower after all.

I couldn't agree more, argue with her, be careless, beat him, believe it at first, believe it, do that, figure it out, do that, get you out of my mind, help it, hold my tears back, let it happen, pass it up, see it any other way, stand it, stop her.

I'd better get back to work, get started, get you in, hit the road.

I'd like to apologise to you, have a few words with you, stay for a night, talk to you for a minute.

I'd like you to have it.

I never need anybody's help.

I'd rather finish my sentence, not talk about that.

I deserted her.

I did everything I could, it all for you, ok, nothing wrong, it my way, what I had to do.

I didn't aim to be a champion, do anything, do it, find it funny, know what I was doing, know where water comes from, mean it, mean to, mean to say that, order that one, recognize you, say anything, say that, see any difference, say that, see it coming, see the incident, want to see you fail.

I do have a place to stay, know, need to escape, not have to go back, the talking, the right thing.

I did not do this.

I do not plan to wait much longer.

I do not want that.

I don't accept that, agree with it, agree with that, argue with that, bite, believe in luck, blame anyone, buy it, doubt it, feel like it, get it, get lonely, give a damn, have the number, have to say any more, know what I'm doing, know why, mean that, mean to hurt you, mind telling you, need anyone, oppose coal seam gas, quite follow you, realize, recognize you, remember that, see any choice, share his diagnosis, share it, stay long, think it will work out between us, understand, understand the complexity at all, worry about other athletes..

I don't believe in luck, it, you.

I don't care about the money, what happened, what he said, whether you like me or not.

I don't feel a thing, any pain, better at all, hungry now, like it now, too good

I don't have a problem with women. (Tony Abbott)

I don't know about this, how, much about gardening, what else to do, what to do, how I'm going to get him back, what to say, why.

I don't like it, that, this, to waste anything.

I don't need all these, anyone, anything, anything else, to explain, special treatment, your advice.

I don't think it matters, we should relax, we can make it.
I don't want any trouble, anything to happen to you, my life inside out, that, to discuss this
    further, to elaborate on that, to go anywhere without you, to go with you, to hear this, to
    take advantage of it, to go to that school, to see that happen, to worry anyone, you to go,
    you to ring, you to take me home, you to do anything.
I encourage people to push the limit.
I enjoy good laughs. I enjoy that.
I expect so.
I fear the worst.
I feel all right, amazing, for everybody, good about myself, just great, like a new man, no
    comfort at all, sorry for you, the same, very hurt, your pain.
I felt sick.
I felt sick to my stomach.
I find it hard to believe that.
I forbid you.
I forgive you.
I gave absolutely everything.
I gave my best tonight.
I get the car.
I go no further.
I gotta go.
I guess so.
I had a good life, a good time, a wonderful time with her, my reason to pretend, a wonderful
    time.
I happen to love you.
I hardly know you.
I hate the issue, to tell you, you.
I have a better idea, a confession to make, a dream (Martin Luther King, Jr.), a little
    happiness, a lot of problems, a lot of things to do, a much better idea, a party, a problem,
    a secret, a venturesome spirit, already done so, an idea, come a long way, confidence in
    you, done that, found paradise, no choice, responsibility for them, some bad news,
    something for everyone, to temper myself, things to do, to really fight it, work to do,
I have been completely happy, beaten, looking for you everywhere.
I have done this before, learned from you, listened to you, met the boy, preached dishonesty,
    said that, seen anything like this.
I have failed him.
I have never been more happy, miserable, wrong, proud.
I have never expected anything like this, expected to see you, heard such a thing.
I have no idea, idea what you are talking about, ill feeling against him, intention to live here,
    need of it, objection, problem with you, time to waste.
I have nothing against you, but time, left, to do with it, to look forward to, to say.
I have to clean up, get away, go, go to upstairs, leave, think about it, wear that,
I haven't anything to do with this, been honest with you, introduced myself, invented this,
    regretted from that day to now, thought about it.
I hope I never wake up, not, so, you're right, you don't catch a cold.
I just can't do that.

I just can't do this.

I kept my word.

I know all of it, the tricks, better than you do, exactly what I'm doing, him, how to make it happen, that, who he is.

I know what I am doing, I am talking about, I want, you are, you are trying to help me, you mean.

I learned something.

I learned to be alone.

I'll let others make my decisions, you be the judge, you do the honour,

I like a good laugh, it, that, the way you are, this way, to see a comeback, to dance.

I'll be back (The Terminator.), in trouble, long gone, seeing you, straight back, there, with you.

I'll be right back, over.

I'll ask her, call you back, call you back tomorrow, change it, come back for you, explain it later, fetch them, fix this, get him back, get it, give it try, give you a ride, go along, handle this, help you, leave it to you, let him out, let you know, look after him, miss him for the rest of my life, never see you again, not marry you, open my heart to you, see what I can do about it, see you tonight, survive, take it, take the chance, teach you a lesson, try.

I'll come clean to that in a moment, with you.

I'll be back as soon as I can, in a moment, in a minute.

I'll be coming with you, down in a few minutes, famous, here, right back, seeing you soon, with you as soon as I can.

I'll do anything, anything you want, better next time, the talking.

I'll miss cheap public transportation, heated floors, my friends, public saunas and the food (An American leaving South Korea).

I'll take care of you, some holiday, that, the dress, you home.

I'll tell you a secret, one thing, the truth, what.

I lost concentration.

I look at it this way.

I love a happy ending, her, it, every minute of it, here, my time, that, this guy, this woman, to, what I do, your honesty.

I love you with all my heart, forever, too, very much,

I'm a failure, a home grown girl, a private person, a silent partner, afraid not, after you, ahead of myself, all ears, alone, always responsible, always with you, an emotional guy, an entirely modern man, as mad as hell, ashamed of all of you, ashamed of myself, asking you to be patient, asking you to come with me, coming, comfortable with it, deeply honoured, delighted to be here, delighted to hear, delighted to be here, done, embarrassed, eternally grateful, excited to be here, fed up, fed up with you, fine, freezing, getting coffee, getting late, getting out fast, glad to hear, glad you asked the question, going to settle down, glad you've brought up, gone, good at this, grateful to you, happy to be here, happy to hear it, having one, hoping for that, hungry, into you, involved just fine with that, just checking, living around here, loving it, lost forever, lucky to be here, lucky to be alive, madly in love with you, more motivated than ever, never leaving, nobody, nothing special, off to America, offering you a lift, on your side, out, proud that we are doing, ready to go with you, really pumped up for this Olympics, really in trouble, really tired, running away, serious, shocked, shy, sick of it, so glad, so lucky to come along,

somebody, sorry the way I treated you, speechless, still hungry. Gus Hiddink, still in
shock, struggling with that, sure that you are starving, talking on the phone, telling you
now, telling you this, the best, the greatest. Muhammad Ali, the happiest person on earth,
the king of the world. Titanic, the top of the world, thrilled to be here, through, tough,
under the thumb, very sorry, waiting, what I am. yours, who I am, wondering what's up,
yours for life.

I'm all wrong. You're all right.

I'm doing it for his own good, right, very good, you a favour,

I'm going back, back there, for a walk, to get changed, to get him, to play, to give it all I've got.

I'm going to do anything, do that, do this, to leave, leave you alone, to live forever, lose my
family again, muck around this anymore, take this anymore.

I'm in big trouble, danger, grief, hurry, love with him, love with you, no hurry, the chair, trouble
because of love, your hands.

I'm Joe Citizen. Average people.

I'm not a bad person, a born-again Christian, afraid, an activist, an expert on this, blaming
you, complaining, confident at all, funny, getting any younger, getting married, going
anywhere, happy, in hurry, holding anything back, kidding, looking forward to going
home, ruling in, ruling out, so sure, worrying about that.

I'm sorry, already, for all these, for everything, for making so much noise, for you, to
disappoint you.

I may be late.

I may hang out a little while longer.

I might be able to help you.

I make a change, easier for you, it very simple to you, no apology, own decision.

I manage to survive.

I may be wrong.

I mean to be here.

I met what I said.

I miss you.

I must ask you to leave, go, have it, help her, say it to you, see you again.

I need a holiday, help, your assistance.

I need to be more connected , catch this, get through, see her,

I never did it for the money, forget this, forgive you, hated you, like you, leave you, loved
anyone else, speak to you again.

I object to that.

I offer you my friendship.

I passed the test.

I pity you.

I pretend to be sleeping.

I really like this guy.

I really like you.

I reflect that.

I see no end, the poor, the rich.

I shall be waiting for him, come back, miss you, prove it, retire.

I share my sorrow.

I should have known it better, have come here alone, not attempt too much, think about it,

write something today.
I shouldn't be talking about this thing.
I simply can't choose.
I sing from the heart.
I stand by that.
I started small.
I step aside.
I still have a long way to go, have hope, think about him.
I suppose so.
I tell you this.
I think I love you.
I think so.
I thought you were gone.
I told you so.
I tried to copy you.
I try to forget.
I try to hide.
I understand how you feel.
I understand you.
I've been able to do it, changed my mind, come to watch, done nothing, done nothing wrong, finished for today, got a job, heard so much about you, never been bored in Seoul, told you a lie, tried to forget you.
I wait for you forever.
I want freedom to smoke.
I want it right now.
I want no nonsense here.
I want to be in it, your guest, left alone.
I want to apologize to you, build on this, contribute something, do something right, go back to Korea, go out, hang out with my friend, help, help you, hold on to you, leave, listen, play, please you, save him, see different people, show you something, spend the rest of my life with you, take time out, talk to you, tell you something.
I want you to meet somebody, to do something for me.
I wanted to be her friend.
I warned you.
I was amazed, away, completely devastated, hoping to find you here, invincible, not comfortable, shocked, so fortunate, stunned by that, that tired, young and naïve. I went too far.
I will ask her, be here doing it, be near you, come to that in a moment, do anything, do it, follow him, have a little get-together this Saturday, make up to you, make you cry, miss him for the rest of my life, never forget this moment, never forget that, not be silenced, not make fun of you, see what I can do, take you home, wait for you, wait outside.
I wish I could be that confident, them well, you a luck,
I wish to be back, be long, give up, go on forever, let you go, you well,
I wonder you care to come with me.
I won't be forever, bite you, do that, force you, hurt, part of it, shut up, stop at sewing my lips to bail out any companies, together.

I work here.

I would appreciate it**,** find the perfect guy, have done the same, like to see that, rather not
    say, say so.

I wouldn't deny that.

I wouldn't say that.

I wouldn't be here without mum's sacrifice, losing my sleep over it, brag about it, know, know
    where else to go, too much problem for you, trouble now.

I wouldn't want to upset your schedule.

Identify yourself.

If a crowd, choose easy food.

If Australia does something (plain packaging on cigarettes), the world listens. Michael
    Bloomberg

If enough people laugh, you don't care.

If one door shuts, another opens.

If that is not love, then what is love? *Fiddler on the Roof*

If that is not integration, then I don't know what is.

If there is a good idea, please tell me.

If they can do it, I can do it too.

If you are good to him, then he will be good to you.

If you can't beat them, join them.

If you can't take the heat, then get out of the kitchen.

If you have time again, you can do better.

If you look after the land, the land will look after you. Aborigines

If you can make it in New York, you can make it anywhere.

Ignore the propaganda.

Images say more than words.

Immerse yourself.

In the beginning, there was the Word. *The Bible*

In vain, you would be powerless.

The intervention is very effective.

Is everyone on board?

Is everything all right, ready, under control?

Is he all right?

Is he innocent or guilty?

Is it a proposal, convenient for you, for better or for worse, fun, good or bad, right, right or
    wrong?

Is she ok?

Is she out of line?

Is something wrong?

Is technology driving us crazy?

Is that all, clear, easy, enough, fair, it, simple, so, the way, too much to ask for, true, what you
    wanted, understood, you?

Is the problem too big?

Is there a problem?

Is there anything I can do for you, I can do, else I can do for you?

Is there something wrong?

Is this a bad luck?
Is this the last straw?
Is your car ready for summer?
Is your muscle ready?
Isn't it lovely, obvious, amazing, enough time to give up, wonderful.
It all comes down to education.
It appears that way.
It applies to the entire system.
It belongs to me.
It breaks my heart.
It can be done.
It can happen in Korea.
It can happen to anybody.
It can only help.
It can't be that big.
It certainly is not for lack of trying.
It could be anyone of us.
It could be worse.
It could happen to anyone.
It couldn't come quick enough.
It depends on what you like.
It did change my life.
It does not always need to be that way.
It doesn't change a thing, cost anything, cost anything to be friendly, explain the whole
       thing, feel real to me, get any better than this, have to be that way, get any better than
       that, help, hurt, make sense, matter, matter at all, mean a thing to me, mean anything, sit
       too well, worry me, yet exist.
It failed to catch a fire.
It feels like flying.
It feels like home.
It gave me hope.
It gives me a bit of strength.
It gives me great pleasure to introduce Mr. Jung.
It had a massive impact.
It has been a long time.
It has no place in Australia.
It hasn't been easy, happened, helped it.
It hurts.
It hurts us too long.
It goes much deeper than that.
It is a fact, a good price, a state of fact, by partnership, me, always better late than never, painful
       to face the truth, time for change, true.
It is not always an easy relationship, my area, as simple as that.
It isn't working.
It just gets worse.
It leaves me no choice.

It looks great.

It looks like you are in a very tough situation.

It looks that way.

It makes me feel live, me proud. no difference, me smile every time.

It matters a great deal.

It may come as a surprise.

It must be wonderful to be a doctor.

It never happens.

It pays.

It's a big mistake, family life, game, great to be different, lot of hard work, journey for all of us, little bit early to tell, matter of honour, matter of thinking, miserable life, more human way of doing it, new country, real issue, ridiculous idea, significant success, simple thing to do, step in the right direction, tough place to live, unique part of Korea, very cherished value, wonderland, world away from Korea, world of his own, worry.

It's about growing the community, about the standard, almost here, almost over, all happened too fast, amazing, an easy plant to grow, an issue for Korea, away, back to you, beautiful, better that way, closed, called choice, dangerously dumb, entirely your choice, fabulous, free, full, full on, funny, game on, going ok, going to get worse, great, good enough for me, hard to say now, hardly a runaway success, incredible, Korea's time to shine, late, magical to watch, me, much worse before it gets better, new to me, nice to be here, no use, none your business, normal, not the end of the world, nothing short of extraordinary, a once in life time opportunity, one of those magical moments, only getting worse, only natural, over, personal, ready, phenomenal, pretty clear, reckless, ridiculous, showtime, simple, simply not true, sink and swim, so difficult to do anything, as simple as that, something we prepare to consider, such good fun, that easy, that simple, the hardest part of my job, the main game, the right thing to do, totally feasible, totally possible, tough as it can be, true, up to us to get life rolling, up to you, what you think that matters, your call, really counts, wonderful to be here, your call, your choice, your turn.

It's getting better, better all the time, worse by the day.

It's all about family, about love, over, yours.

It's a long expensive mistake, story, time coming.

It's all about fun, sports, for you, over.

It's good to be back, be young, chat with you.

It's hard to deal with fame, silence him, sustain, talk about.

It's my fault, pleasure, turn.

It's a once-in-a lifetime thing. Psy fan

It's not about you, going to be easy, like that, quite easy, real, that easy.

It's time. (The ALP election slogan in 1972), to get something done, to call it off, to get to work, for peace, for women to be kind to each other, to change, to leave Korea, to look after my health.

It's too good to be true, late, sensitive to talk about, sour to eat.

It's very beautiful, hard for people to stomach, hard to keep doing.

It's not a good look, a main focus, about dollars and cents, going away, fair, good enough, my business, my cup of tea, over, over yet, that easy, that simple, the case, the end of the world, to work, up to us.

It's your call, health, life, party.

It scared me to death.
It seems like yesterday.
It seems that way.
It served a very good purpose.
It smells great.
It sounds better, cleaner, interesting, marvellous, nice, odd, romantic.
It takes commitment and effort.
It takes two to tango.
It tastes good.
It tastes like real food.
It turned out that way.
It used to be a good life.
It was a key to victory, healing, inevitable, like magic, spectacular, the accident, very tough,
    what I knew, wonderful.
It wasn't all bad news, for the money, me, a pushover, on, that simple, too bad.
It will all dry up, be all right, be a lot of fun, close, bring in more money, happen, never get
    off the ground, not be the end of the world, work out.
It won't be easy, happen, hurt, too bad, work.
It would have been easy to do.

A Jack of all trades is master of none.
Japan is trying to spoil the party.
Join our community.
Join the fight.
Join the fight back.
Join the front line.
Judgement is not gender-specific.
The jury is out.
Just-in-time. Toyota
Just like that.
Just look at that man.
Just process them.
Just put it right here.
Just relax and enjoy yourself.
Justice must prevail.
Justin Bieber steals the show.

Keep active.
Keep calm.
Keep going.
Keep him warm.
Keep informed.
Keep in touch.
Keep it simple, stupid! (KISS) Good design principle by Kelly Johnson
Keep it clean, going, short and snappy, steady, up.
Keep moving.

Keep an eye on.
Keep on fighting,
Keep on keeping on.
Keep out of trouble.
Keep on pushing.
Keep our options open.
Keep out.
Keep out of it.
Keep quiet.
Keep rocking.
Keep safe.
Keep talking.
Keep the change.
Keep the channel open.
Keep them healthy.
Keep together.
Keep up the good work.
Keep well.
Keep your mind calm.
Keep your mouth shut.
Kids should be kids.
Kill two birds with one stone. Kim Yu-na makes the Koreans proud.
Know why.
Knowing is half the battle.
Knowledge is our experience.
Knowledge is power. Socrates
Korea came back.
Korea can't go back.
Korea comes of age.
Korea has a good story to tell.
Korea is a wonderful place.
Korea is now at a crossroads between East and West.
Korea is proud of you.
Korea learns a lesson.
Korean cosmetics are selling like hotcakes abroad.
Korean frustration is growing.
The Koreans are coming.
The Koreans want to work.

Laughing all the way to the bank.
Laughter brings happiness.
Learn from our mistakes.
Leave a message.
Leave him alone.
Leave it to me.
Leave it with me.

Leave me alone.
Leave that to me.
The left hand doesn't know what the right hand is doing.
Legalization is not the answer.
Lend me your ears. Annabel Crabb
Less is more.
The lesser of two evils.
Let's be frank.
Let bygones be bygones.
Let go of me.
Let go of my arms.
Let her recover.
Let him go in.
Let him win once.
Let it all go on Tasmania, be, go, slide.
Let me ask another question, be alone, be blunt, be honest with you, call you back, clarify that, clear about this, get through, give you a hand, give a lift home, give guidance, go, have it, help you, in, know, listen, look at you, out, put it that way, put it this way, remind you, say this, see what you get, show you around, speak, take you home, tell you, think about it, think over, try, watch.
Let natural light into your home.
Let's be blunt, frank about that, happy, honest here.
Let's begin, break it down, bring you into the discussion, build it again, celebrate, clean you up, do it, face it, fix the system, flee, forget about that, go forward together, keep that way, make another call, move, move on, not forget, see some intellectual debate, see what's inside, sit down, start, take a break, the game begin, get this party started, try to be serious, wait for the details, watch.
Let's get into it, on with it, started, to work, away, down to the fact, going, it started, on and get it done, on board, on with it, out of here, physical, the science right.
Let's go around this way, out shopping, home, shopping.
Let's have a chat, a drink, a free kick, a fun, a look, a word.
Let's see what I can do about your mother, your face.
Let the fun begin.
Let the sunshine in.
Let there be light.
Let them come.
Let them do the talk.
Let there be light.
Let us down badly.
Let us in.
Life doesn't get any better than this.
Life has not been always like this.
Life is a precious gift, a series of cycles, difficult, not a movie, not fair, quiet, good. (LG adv.), not that bad, not too bad, short, unfair.
Life will be better one day.
Life will not be the same.

Life will go on.
Lighten up.
Like father like son.
The line has to be drawn.
The list goes on.
Listen to me.
Listen to the music.
Live a great life.
Live as one. London Olympics
Live one day at a time.
Live your passion. Rio Olympics
Living alone is a new norm. *Time* article
Location! Location! Location! Real Estate
Lock the doors.
Look after yourself.
Look around the world.
Look at me, that, the crowd, the outcome, them, this, you, yourself.
Look before you leap.
Look how easy it is.
Look no further.
Looks can be deceiving.
Look out!
Look what I've found.
Look what we have got.
A lot of people are not pleased about that, have bought it, didn't make it.
A lot of works have to be done.
Love at first sight.
Love conquers all.
Love has many faces.
Love is all you need.
Love is blind.
Love is gender blind.
Love is love.
Love is the most dangerous idea.
Love makes the world go round.
Love thy enemy.
Love your neighbour.
Lucky you.

Make a stand.
Make a wish.
Make him well.
Make it happen.
Make it quick.
Make hay while the sun shines.
Make my day. Clint Eastwood

Make no mistake.
Make your mouth water.
Make your move.
Make yourself at home.
Man does not live by bread alone.
Man needs a job more than money.
Man shall not live by bread alone.
Man shall not live on bread alone.
Many agree with him.
Many people are happy about it.
Many took up the challenge.
Marry me.
The math doesn't add up.
Maybe we agree on this.
Maybe you can help me.
Meet the challenge.
Meet the change.
Meet the man behind the idea.
Men and women can't be friends.
Memories are short.
Money makes people blind.
Money does not grow on trees.
Money is all the matters to you.
Money is freedom. Robert Kiyosaki
Money is not important to me.
Money is power.
Money means nothing to me.
Money never sleeps (Working too hard?).
The money runs out.
Money spending now is money well spent.
Money talks.
More can be done.
The more I learn, the more I was humbled.
More should be done.
More than all right.
Most of us believe in the mission.
The mother nature is the mother nature.
Move it.
Mud sticks.
Music is her medicine.
Music stops in 2007. (financial meltdown)
My conscience is clear.
My defence has always been good.
My hands are tied.
My heart goes out to her.
My heart's broken.

My home is my castle.
My job is done today.
My life is never the same.
My love will keep you alive.
My mum will kill me.
My place is here.
My time has come. A song title
My work is fun.
My work is my life.

Nature is over. Time article
Necessity is the mother of invention.
Never be forgotten.
Never do that again
Never give up.
Never give up. Do it today not tomorrow.
Never give up giving up.
Never go away.
Never mind.
Never mind about that.
Never say never.
Never tell me never.
Never too old to learn.
The news came from a friend of mine.
Nice to meet you.
No big deal!
No free lunch.
No go!
No harm done.
No ifs or buts.
No is no.
No laughing matter.
No man serve two masters .
No means no.
No mercy!
No mercy in life.
No news is a good news.
No one has a husband like him, owes Australians a living, questioned things, is suggesting
that, walked out, will know.
No one is going to take away from you., laughing now, standing over you. Train driver,
No other way out.
No pain, no gain!
No problem.
No sex please. We're the British.
No stones unturned (Then one will find plenty of earthworms.)
No trouble at all.

Nobody knows everything.
Nobody wanted to do anything to do with him.
Nothing ventured, nothing gained.
No worries.
Nobody asked you.
Nobody is coming to me.
Nobody knows anything.
Nobody pushes me around.
Nobody will do anything about it.
None of your business.
No one bothers us, can predict the future, has ever raised the issue, is listening, was hurt, will
    be disappointed, will miss out.
No way.
None of these are new.
None of your business.
Not again.
Not bad at all.
Not everyone is convinced.
Not funny!
Not in my backyard!
Not enough.
Not much hope is there.
Not my cup of tea.
Not quite.
Nothing can defeat you.
Nothing has worked.
Nothing is a foregone conclusion, impossible, missing.
Nothing has been achieved in Iraq.
Nothing has been set in stone.
Nothing is going to happen.
Nothing is impossible.
Nothing much stands out.
Nothing to say each other.
Nothing to worry about it.
Nothing serious.
Nothing will happen to us.
Now is a good time to buy.
Now is the right time to get started.
Now is the time.
Now it's time to catch up.
Now or never.

Of course not.
Off you go.
Oh, my God (OMG).
Oh, no! Jackie Kennedy

Old habits die hard.
Once bitten and twice shy .
Once in your life, do something bright.
One cannot live by bread alone.
One apple per day will keep doctors away.
One person can make a difference.
One person can't do everything.
One size does not fit all.
One size fits all.
Only weak me want weak wives.
The order is the order.
Out of sight, out of mind.
Open the door.
Open up.
The operation is fine.
The orders are the orders.
Ordinary becomes extraordinary. CSIRO TV show
Our economy is healthy.
Our eyes are looking the north.
Our home is broken up.
Our story begins.
Out of question.
Out of sight. Out of mind.
The outcome is never guaranteed.
The outcome is the same.
Over my dead body.
Own it outright.

The pacific is big enough for all of us. Hilary Clinton
Parents want a normal child.
The party's over.
Passion drives me.
Pay attention.
Peace be with you.
The pen is mightier than the sword.
People are really getting hurt.
People are the same.
People can't eat sands.
People don't know where we are going.
People get to see them
People love me or hate me.
People know what is good and what is bad.
Piano is my best friend. Lang Lang
Pick it up.
Pick up the jacket.
Pick up the phone.

A picture is worth a thousand words.
People are grateful of that.
People are milking the opportunity.
People have to be respectful of each other.
Pig can fly. (Yes, on the Show Day).
The plan seems to be good.
Please explain. Pauline Hanson
Please save our life.
Please stop crying.
Pleased to meet you.
Politics is a team sport. Malcolm Turnbull
Poor blokes can't get ahead.
Poverty depresses me.
The price is right.
The power's back.
Practice makes.
Prevention is better than the cure.
The price of wheat is doing well.
The problem is the way that it has been done.
Protect what is here.
Prove it to yourself.
Push harder.
Put her down.
Put him on.
Put it back, in this way, on, this way.
Put me down.
Put money where your mouth is.
Put pressure on him.
Put that down.
Put the cart before the horse.
Put up or shut up!
Put up with a good fight.
Put yourself in good hands.

The race is on.
Raise your voice.
Read between the lines.
Read my lips. No new taxes. (How can anyone read lips?). George HW Bush
Real heroes walk away.
Realise the potential.
Reduce, reuse, recycle.
The reduction target is on.
Relax and enjoy it.
Relax and take it easy
Remember, you are not alone.
Remember me.

Repeat after me.
The report is too late.
The rest is history.
The rest of the world is going to toilet.
Results speak themselves.
Retire is young. Retire rich. Robert Kiyosaki
Retirement isn't in the air.
Revenge is sweet.
Ride your way to work, health and happiness.
Robbing Peter to pay Paul .
Rome wasn't built in a day.
A rooster one day, a feather duster next.
Rub your hands together now.
Rules stimulate.
The rule is the rule.
The rules of the game have changed.

Save the best for last
Say again.
Say it.
Say no more.
Say something.
Say that again.
Say what you like.
The secret is out.
See eye-to-eye
See it, feel it, get it, touch it. Latrobe University
See it first.
See monkey, do monkey.
See that through.
See the big picture.
See what has happened, I mean, is going on there.
See **you** around, back in Korea, later, there.
Seeing is believing.
Send a hero message.
Set me free.
Settle down.
Settle for less.
Sex sells.
Shall I ever be free?
Shall I let him go?
Shall I take away?
Shall we go in?
Shall we talk later?
Shape up.
Share the moment.

She asked for it.
She cannot believe.
She couldn't be happier.
She couldn't let it go.
She doesn't say a word to me.
She doesn't feel comfortable.
She fell in love.
She felt about him.
She gave me a purpose.
She has been caught with this scandal, done no harm, found happiness again, gone back what she said, got what she came for, to deal with it, to make up her mind, to overcome the past.
She hasn't got the money.
She hit the glass ceiling.
She is rock for family.
She knew nothing.
She leave a significant hole in Australian life. Jeff Kennett about Dame Murdoch
She made up the story.
She managed to pull it off.
She means the world to me.
She missed the point.
She nearly had a heart attack.
She never thinks about you.
She never turns off the light.
She pressed on.
She pulled it off.
She put her hand up.
She remains a formidable politician.
She's a cracker, fighter, a real collector, cleaned up everybody, coming in, cool and calm, going to get better, gone, gorgeous, incredible, mature at her age, my favourite to win, never coming back, not happy with him, passionate about education, reasonable, right about this,
She set to tell all.
She should have been aware of that.
She turned the tables.
She wanted to do in her way.
She was depressed.
She will be missed by many
She will go for it. .
She will sleep through this morning.
She won't be silenced.
She won't let you down. She wouldn't be able find us.
Should birth control be banned?
Should I get out of bed tomorrow?
Should I go on?
Should there be the limits on free speech?

Should we shut up?
Shouldn't that be the focus?
The shows are off.
The show is over.
Show me mercy.
Show me the money. Jerry Maguire
The show must go on.
Show us your tricks.
Shut up!
The sign is very clear.
Simple as that.
Simply call the number.
Simply eat well.
Simply the best.
Single mothers are raising future leaders.
Sit back and relax.
Sit down.
The situation is fluid.
The sky is the limit (There is no limit in sky).
Sky opens (No such thing as open and close in sky.)
Silence is golden.
Sleep well.
Small business does well in Korea.
A smile from you brightens the sky.
So be it.
So do I.
So long.
So what!
The sole explanation is a desire of people.
Some are not holding breath.
Some argued with that.
Some days you win. Some days you lose.
Somebody asked you out.
Somebody else made that happen.
Somebody had to do it.
Somebody is coming.
Somebody must have put it there
Someone get curious.
Someone is hard at work, innocent until proven guilty, more equal than others. George Orwell,
        watching, wrong.
Someone should mention to her.
Some people make a living by talking.
Something actually happened.
Some had to give.
Something has happened to you.
Something has to be done.

Something is going on here.
Something is missing.
Something is wrong.
Something miserable happened.
Something needs to be done.
Something never changes.
Something terrible happened.
Sound familiar?
Sorry for the interruption.
South Korea needs to chill out.
South Korea went from rags to riches.
Sounds wonderful.
Spare me this pain.
Spare the rod. Spoil the child.
Speak up!
Speech is silver, silence is golden.
Spend your life well.
Spice up.
Spot on.
Spring is around the corner.
Spring turns nasty.
The stage is set.
Stand by.
Stand by to be blown away.
Stand clear.
Stand up, for a clean future, to be counted.
Start talking.
Stay active.
Stay and play.
Stay away from her.
Stay away from him.
Stay away from it.
Stay behind.
Stay cool.
Stay foolish. Stay hungry. Steve Jobs
Stay here.
Stay home.
Stay in tune. TV
Stay out of this.
Stay safe.
Stay strong.
Stay tuned. TV
Stay where you are.
Stay with me.
Steady as she goes.
Stealing isn't right. Apple

Step back.
Step back in time.
Step forward.
Step outside.
Stick around. TV presenter
Stick with it.
Stick with us. TV presenter
Stop here.
Stop it.
Stop resisting.
Stop smoking today.
Stop staring at me.
Stop taking us for granted.
Stop talking nonsense.
Stop that.
Stop the rot.
The story gets better.
The story is over.
A strange is going on here.
Suit yourself.
Sure does.
Support the cause.
The system is rotten.

The tables are turned.
Take a cold shower.
Take a deep breath.
Take a good hard look at myself.
Take a good care of her.
Take a listen.
Take a look.
Take a look around.
Take a stand.
Take care of yourself.
Take it away, down, or leave it, easy, off.
Take off your shirts.
Take the guesswork out of your decisions.
Take the money and run.
Take my advice.
Take no prisoners.
Taekwondo is no stranger to foreigners.
Take a break.
Take control of yourself.
Take it away.
Take it back.
Take the challenge.

Take your time.

Talk fast.

Talk is cheap.

Talk it over calmly.

Talk things over.

Talk to me.

Tear down that wall. (the church and the government)

Technology is a double edge sword.

Tell him how sorry I am.

Tell me a secret, a story, something, about that, about the farm, why, why you are
    leaving.

Tell me what you think, you want, you want me to do.

Tell me where you are?

Tell us a bit about that, what has happened, what you think, where we are.

Thanks for having me.

Thank god It's Friday. (TGIF)

That doesn't matter.

That didn't go down well.

That explained a lot.

That has changed now.

That is a proper cause, not true, the history now.

That is then. This is now. Tony Abbott

That'll be all, fantastic, hard, nice, not go down well.

That (cloud) looks like you. adv. From daughter to her dad

That makes life a lot easier.

That may not happen.

That's a bad idea, a beautiful smile, a big ask, a curious question, a fabulous piece of drama, a
    good thing, a long way down the track, a real challenge for us, a real mystery, a terrific
    shot, a tough question, a very good point, absolutely breath taking, all, amazing, better,
    big, cool, correct, enough, exactly what I am thinking, exciting, exactly right, fantastic,
    fine, for me to decide, for sure, good, hard to say, how I feel, how it should be,
    impossible, just perfect, laughable, life, marvellous, news to me, no business like show
    business, no going back to past, normal range, our view, really a good question, $64,000
    question, something I haven't tried before, stupid, that, the best friend for, the fact, the
    idea, the record, the spirit we are going for, too bad, up to you, up to you to prove, very
    cruel, very kind of you, very nice of you, very sweet, your problem.

That's all, I can say, I need, over, over now, we can do, we have time today, we're looking for

That's further down the track.

That's not a positive thing to do, a smart thing to do all, always the case, expected, funny, going
    to happen, my word, on, possible, right, the capitalism, the point, too difficult, what we
    want.

That's the answer for Korea, bargain, best audition I have had, dream, best thing I can
    describe it, end of story, fact, final, idea, next, news today, one, order, point, process,
    program tonight, question, question for her, reason, show,   trick, truth, way you wanted.

That's what education is, happened, he has done, I am concentrating on, I do, I got me
    through, I want, they say, matters, we'll do, we want, why I left home, you want.

That's why, I am here, it matters, people are concerned about, this house doesn't want you, we
ended up here,
That sounds bad, great, like funny, like much.
That was his style.
That was lovely.
That will do.
That will not be necessary.
That won't do good.
The friend is you.
The list goes on.
The only international language is a child's cry. Eglantyne Jebb
The sooner you act, the better.
There are never dull moments.
There are similarities that run deep.
There are winners.
There is.
There's no way.
There's no place like home.
There's nothing I can do, wrong with growing up here. you can do about it.
There's safety in numbers.
There isn't a leader any more.
There isn't time.
There'll be another update, dance, no fight, problems.
There's a battle of ideas, a difference, a good news, a natural law, a problem, a simple
explanation, a track, a way, enormous rush, always help out there, always the value for
money , less work, little common ground, more we can do, never a dull moment, not
much we can do, one thing we can do, nothing better, nothing you can't do, nothing she
can answer, one small problem, racism in my school.
There's nothing coming in, more you can do, we can do, you can do about,
There's no answer, control over it, doubt about that, greater shock, incentive to work hard,
love lost between them, other way for you, more time, place like home. The Wizard of
Oz, place to hide , room for an error, shame in being yourself, sympathy for John
Lennon's killer, system in place, time for loneliness, turning back, way I would stop, way
you have a cheap wedding,
There was guilt, fear, anger, shame.
There was no time to lose.
There you are, go. Go again, see.
These steps look stopgap.
They are a number of big surprises, absolutely thrilled. Desperate, dreaming all the time,
engineers in 10 years' time, exploiting children's naivety, fighting back, full of dreams,
going to do again, going to find it, off the mark, proved wrong, similar reductions in
income, too many problems here, used to humans, winning.
They are not allowed to answer, many takers, taking the journey lightly.
They can afford it.
They beat themselves. The Russians
They can't do anything about it.

They can't see that.
They didn't get on very well.
They don't get it.
They exceeded all expectations.
They have listened to her.
They learn everything.
They mean no harm.
They normally get on.
They seem to be fond of each other.
They set out to destroy people.
They decided to do something about it.
They didn't see eye to eye.
They don't know what they are doing.
They got it wrong.
They had fun.
They have been shots.
They have a special room for us, done the time. Pensioners, gone back to basics, made it, no
    right to do that, the right to do so, to compete with each other.
They have not been cooperative.
They jammed through the parliament.
They'll be easily trained, come to nothing, get him out, keep coming back.
They made a really stupid decision.
They must enjoy time like this.
They never stop.
They should see what is coming.
They want to make him an example.
They waste no time.
They won't get away.
A thing happen.
Things are looking up.
Things could be worse.
Things got out of control.
Think about it.
Think again.
Think before you speak.
Think differently.
Think globally, act locally.
Think harder
Think how I feel.
Think it over.
Think laterally.
Think of me.
Think out of the box.
Think outside the box.
This campaign is too close to your heart.
This certainly won't happen again.

This couldn't be further from reality.
This fire is finally under control.
This house was built last.
This is a good time for him to come, a great achievement, a great moment of my life, a little trickier than expected, a matter of pride, a nation of immigrants, a new idea, a profound question, a real problem, a sensitive issue, a step in the right direction, a turning point, an amazing night, an utter lie, as far as you go, an important bit, anybody's race, completely out of order, completely unnecessary, crazy, extraordinary, fine, for everyone, for you, going to be your home as long as you live, going to blow your mind, for me, home, how it will ends, it, just beginning, my only hope, no other hand, not quite what I expected, progress, ridiculous, so wrong, the century for austerity, the circus, the fountain of youth, the game for everyone, the hardest day in my life, the house, the man I know, the next best thing, the party I like, what you eat, where it happened, why we are weak, your land.
This is on the world, our mark, time, time to leave,
This is not a good idea, a laughing matter, amusing, ok, the case, the case for Korea, your house.
This is the best idea, in the world, thing has happened to me,
This issue is not going away.
This is not Madonna. Who is?
This is nothing unusual about that.
This is what happened, I do, you have to do,
This lesson is more relevant today than ever.
This must be a letter.
This offer can't last long.
This parliament died of shame.
This place is very close paradise.
This question has a simple answer.
This thing has to be tried first.
This time he might have gone too far.
This wasn't a good idea.
This will be interesting.
Throw enough mud until some sticks.
The threat is real.
Three cheers.
The tides have turned.
Time can heal.
Time flies like an arrow.
Time for a break.
The time has come for Koreans to shout.
The time is excellent.
Time is everything, money, now, ripe, running out, up.
Time no doubt heal.
Time to move on.
Time to say goodbye. Song title
Time will tell.
The timing is not important.
The timing is wrong.

The timing could not have been better
To be, not to be: That's the Question. William Shakespeare
Together we can save lives on our roads.
Together we stand.
Tomorrow is another day.
Too good to be true.
Too many cooks spoil the broth.
Treat her right.
The trial is about to start.
The truth never lies.
Trust me.
Try it on.
Try me.
Try not to be conspicuous.
Try not to think too much.
Turn around.
Turn up the heat.
Two's company. Three's a crowd.
Two wrongs do not make a right.
Two steps forward, one step back.
Two steps forward. One step backward.
Two Wongs don't make a white. Arthur Calwell
Two wrongs don't make a right.

Unfortunately I did not get in.
United we stand, divided we fall.
Upgrade your life.

Very much so.
Victory is smiling on us.
Vote so that your voice is heard.

Wait a moment.
Wait for me.
Wait here.
The wait is over.
Wake up.
Walk the talk.
Walk with me.
The war is over.
Wash your hands thoroughly.
Wasn't it enough?
Waste not, want not.
Watch out!
Water is life.
The way to happiness is lowering your standards.

We all are in the same boat, do that, have a role to play, have to live, make mistakes, needed that, played an instrument, want to be loved by our parents.

We are a country of migrants, a little bit ahead of ourselves, a part of the real world, a wealthy society, about common sense, almost out of time, destroying the planet, doing it now, engaged, expecting him in a minute, expecting you, free, full, getting fatter, having fun, here for you, here not to fight, home, in good shape, in your hands, invincible, just good friends, leaving, living in complex world, looking for you everywhere, lucky, lucky to be alive, making history, moving in, off, on a roll, on the run, open for business, ordinary people, pricing ourselves out, serious about each other, still growing together, still working on it, the light of world, the people, too busy moving forward, two of a kind, upfront, very grateful, very sorry, wasting our time, who we are, with you, worthy of that trust,

We're all equal, for you, winners, working on it.

We are crazy about each other, going home, not there yet, on a trip, to keep it that way.

We are not allowed to say too much, as bad as the Koreans, asking your permission, doing enough, far from the closing ceremony, going to see you until next year, talking about people.

We balance the budget.

We bounce back.

We came to say goodbye.

We can do better. Mitt Romney, do better than that, do it in an orderly way, manage it and protect it better, manage that, travel up together.

We cannot live by bread alone.

We cannot refuse.

We can't be certain about anything, do it alone, escape one another.

We continue to improve every day.

We all want to fit in.

We are not welcome.

We can do it.

We can do that.

We can take our car.

We can't do it alone.

We can't let that happen.

We chose not to have a car.

We couldn't be prouder.

We couldn't think about anything else.

We complete the circle.

We'd better cracking.

We'd better get started.

We'd like your blessing.

We did it right, it right when our time came, not sleep together, the wrong thing.

We didn't do that, expect anything like this, get out our message,

We do open our door.

We don't do anything, do that in Australia, go overboard, have to live like this, know what to do next, live in vacuum, see that coming, slash jobs, want anything to change. Want you to fall behind.

We figure it out.

We forgive but we shall never forget. Korea to Japanese colonization

We gave each other the pledge.

We get expertise, nowhere, on very well, used to it.

We got out before that happened, so much to do, stuck, to get them out.

We had the deal.

We hardly think about that.

We have a choice to make, a good future, a long way to go, a lot of work to do, a lot to do, a package for you, a surprise for you, a very serious work to do, been leading by example, come a long way, come so far, everything to gain, known about this, learned a lot from Korea, made it, no choice, no money ,not made a good start, nothing further to discuss, nothing to fear, overcome, responsibility to do that, the solution, time to think,

We have to be up to the task, do something about it, eat to survive, face up to that, find money, get going, get out of here, hide, leave, make it up, wait, walk.

We hope that you have enjoyed it.

We ignore it at our peril.

We just wait.

We know how important it is.

We learn to love each other.

We leave there.

We like to impress.

We like to see Korea's leadership.

We look after each other.

We must create it together.

We lit the flame.

We lit up the world.

We live in a complex world, a dangerous world, a real world, an interesting time, your world.

We'll be home by 10, be right down, beat any price, come to that, come with you, die, do it again, do it our way, do that again, drive on, figure something out, find a way, leave it there, live like a king, look after you, meet again. A song title, part, see what happens, start ground, want that, take care of everything, welcome without judgement, win,

We'll get him back, out, some advice,

We'll never do it again, manage it, see again,

We love each other.

We love your imagination.

We make dream homes come true.

We manage it.

We may come to regret.

We might ask ourselves.

We minimize risk.

We miss you.

We must be true to ourselves, carry on hard, find that woman, get moving, make Korea proud, stay the course, stick together, travel back in time.

We mustn't despair.

We mustn't do it.

We need publicity, that, the cash, to change mind on Korea, to have more information, to implement, to know, to know who they are and what they are , to move on, to stop this happening,

We never do that. Oz advertising in other languages.

We opened it up.

We paid the price.

We ran away.

We really haven't come a long way.

We reap what we saw.

We refused to give it up.

We remind ourselves what we can do it.

We should not be part of it, expect anything else. lose heart.

We simply don't know what went wrong.

We still have a long way to go.

We understand that.

We will do it.

We won't sit idle.

We would like to catch up.

Who said I cannot have a business?

We screwed up this planet.

We see you as person not as number. American Express

We should be backing them, defend ourselves, do better, doing a lot more, respect that, stick to the time table, take a step further, try that.

We shouldn't take dogs so much for granted.

We speak many languages in Australia.

We split the right down the middle.

We spoke to him.

We stick together.

We still have a chance.

Wc took ovcr him.

We've all done it.

We waited long enough.

We've been sold out.

We've got more work to do.

We've never been more in love.

We want consultation, mutual understanding, to know about it, to understand each other better, you to know that.

We were instant stars.

We will never surrender.

We will not be moved.

We won't be beaten on price, be long, bother you, write off America, worry about it.

Welcome back.

Welcome on board.

Welcome people and don't judge them.

Well done.

West meets East.

What a bargain, beauty, champion, chance, combination, cracker, day, dream, fantastic thing, joke, line up, lovely man, lucky man I am, mess, moment, nice surprise, picture, pleasant surprise, relief, sensational performance, sensational start, shame, shock, standout, surprise, the difficulty, tremendous performance, turnaround, woman, wonderful name, wonderful world. A song title, world.

What about me, others, our backyard, tonight, you?

What am I doing, doing here, going to do, going to do with you, hearing, saying, supposed to do?

What an honour, amazing performance, incredible change!

What are making news, their beliefs, they about, they fleeing?

What are we? Paul Gauguin

What are we going to achieve?

What are you asking me, complaining about, having, hoping for, looking at, looking for, referring to, saying, suggesting, talking about, thinking, thinking about, trying to do, waiting for?

What are you doing, around here?

What are you going to do, about it, about that, next year?

What can be done, boost the economy, I say, I say to him, we do, you tell us?

What can I do, about this, for you?

What can I do, I do to help, we do, you do?

What can Korea do?

What can you tell us?

What captures your imagination?

What comes in must go out.

What comes to mind?;

What could be sweater?

What could you do here in Sydney?

What did he say, I go wrong, you do, they say, they want to know about you, you do this to us, you say?

What do I do, next, wrong?

What do I have to do?

What do they stand for?

What do you do, that for, when friends repeat themselves, with the snake,

What do you for a living, feed next week, get out of this, know about me, like him, make it, make of that, mean, mean by that, reckon, say, suggest, take on that, think, want from me?

What do you know, about him, about that, about this guy?

What do think, about the response, we can do with,

What do we do next, do now, do with what we got, get to lose, know, want?

What do we do about it?

What do you do for work?

What do you do now?

What do you want now?

What do you get out of this?

What do you mean by that?

What do you recommend?

What do you want, for your future, for your life, me to do, to do?

What does it mean, that do the catchment, that mean?

What drives you?

What else do I need, can you say, do you want, is in play here?

What gave that idea?

What goes around comes around.

What goes up must come down.

What happens here?

What happens next?

What happens when you fall out of love?

What happens with that?

What happened?

What happened with my money?

What has been achieved in Korea, gone wrong, he said?

What have I done?

What have we done wrong?

What have we proved?

What have you been up to, done to him, got, got to lose, got there?

What have your two been up to?

What he has done is great.

What is done is done, it, it like, made from, made of, that for? (When someone stole one's kiss
    suddenly), that, the matter with you, wrong with that, your home worth?

What kind of business do I do, doctor are you, father are you, friend are you, hospitality is
    that, talk is that, trick is this?

What lies beneath?

What limitations have you found?

What made you stop playing?

What makes Australia great, Korea tick, news, powerful men act like pigs, you say that, you so
    sure, you think so?

What matters?

What more can we ask, can we do, can you do, do we know?

What more can you tell us?

What now?

What really happened?

What's a friend for, all about it, done is done, downside, exciting about, funny, going on
    here, got to do with it, happened, he look like, in your mind, it all about, made change
    your mind, making news, next, next step, so funny, special about modern world,
    supposed to mean, that for, the best way to bring it to the end, that, that for, that rebel us,
    the difference between can and may, the problem, this, this for, up, up with her, wrong
    with us, your take?

What's your problem, response to that, thought on that?

What's happened there?

What's happening, here, there,?

What's the deal, the difference between Bono and God, feeling down there, idea, ideal world,
latest, law, matter, matter with you, point, position in Korea, problem,
    proof, prospect, question, road forward, situation, situation now, story, time limit, trouble,
    verdict?

What's wrong with being rich, dreaming large, it, that

What's your answer, background, goal, opinion, position, solution?

What's your emotion right now, feeling about that aspect of policy, name, plan B, vision for
your school?

What seems to be a trouble?

What sets a god medallist apart?

What shall I do next?

What shall I do with him?

What shall we do?

What should they do?

What sort of impact do you see?

What the devil is going on?

What the hell are you doing here?

What the hell is all this, going on, that?

What time will they be back.

What we are doing is making a difference.

What was that dream, the answer, the mission again, the secret?

What went wrong?

What will happen to you, we do, they produce, you do about that, you have?

What would I do without you, that be, you do, you like to do?

What you are telling us is far from the truth.

Wheels come off.

When America sneezes, Australia catches a cold.

When are they coming back?

When are you coming?

When Australia does something, the world listen. Michael Bloomberg.

When did you find out?

When do we start?

When do we want it?

When in Rome, do as the Romans do.

When is that going to happen?

When was the last time you felt the life?

When will it be ready?

When will they ever learn?

When will we get there?

Where am I?

Where am I from?

Where are all the women, from, to grow our food, the rest of you, you?

Where are we going? Paul Gauguin

Where are you?

Where are you going?

W here did it all begin?

Where did our money go?

Where did you get this?

Where did you get the idea?

Where did you get the story?

Where do they come from?
Where do we come from? Paul Gauguin
Where do we begin?
Where do we go from here?
Where do you begin, draw the line, take them, want to go?
Where does he get from, it stop, that come from, the ambition come from, the money come
        from?
Where have all the kids gone?
Where have you been?
Where is accountability, everybody, food coming from, love, the popular one, the justice, the
        money coming from?
Where is everybody?
Where is the limit?
Where shall I begin?
Where there's a will, there's a way.
Where to from here?
Where to next?
Where were you?
Where were you were when Kennedy was assassinated?
White people never understand that.
Who are these people?
Who are they?
Who are we?
Who asked you?
Who brought them up?
Who can?
Who can do that?
Who cares?
Who copied who?
Who could be the next?
Who did you trust?
Who do you think you are?
Who do you trust? John Howard
Who else live here?
Who is at faulty, going to do it, it, me, next, that, that man, the money, there, winning?
Who do you pick?
Who do you think you are?
Who else could have done that?
Who goes into the big brother house?
Who has the power?
Who is looking after you, meaning what, most at risk, this, telling the truth, to blame, up
        there, winning arguments?
Who knows?
Who knows what will happen next week?
Who lets you in?
Who likes to be a loser?

Who remembers the budget?

Who's at risk, going to look after me, got the cash, next, first, on first, that, there, this,
     wearing what?

Who said so?

Who said that?

Who said what?

Who sent you?

Should own this?

Who the hell is that?

Who told you?

Who told you about the island?

Who wants more?

Who wants to be him?

Who wants to try first?

Who will beat you, crash the party, go next, lead the Asian century, save him, speak for
     Korea, win?

Who would you like to give to?

Whole thing is impossible.

Whole trip will be like a dream.

Whose idea is it?

Whose is this?

Why are people deserting the Greens?

Why are we here?

Why are people so unkind, we discussing this, you crying, you doing it, you laughing, telling
     me?

Why aren't you happy?

Why can't I stop watching this, we be better, we get them?

Why can't women be more like men? you enjoy the journey? you get along with her?

Why did you come back for, come to see me, run away,

Why did you do it, that, this, this to me?

Why did that happen, you do it, you do that, you do this to me?

Why didn't you call me, come, come with us tonight, fight for me, help me, stand up to him,
     stay with us, tell me before?

Why do I say that?

Why do men cheat?

Why do people wear make-up?

Why do we do this?

Why do you do all these, live like this, say now, say that, think so, want to buy that?

Why don't you come to my office tomorrow, come up here, do something about that, go
     back where you came from, grow up, kiss me again, leave, let me the talking?

Why go for good when you go for best?

Why haven't you?

Why is that? this so?

Why not?

Why not the best?

Why should I feel guilty?

Why should I be upset?
Why should we care, care about, trust them?
Why should you care about super?
Will do.
Will history repeat itself?
Will this make you cry?
Will you all sit down, come back, come with me, do it, go with me, have dinner with me,
    help me, help me out, let me do that for you, let me know, marry me, mind your own
    business, stop that, wait for me?
The winner takes it all.
Winning is everything.
Winning is not everything.
Winning isn't everything, but wanting to win is. Posco's motto (the largest steel maker in SK)
Women are the 2nd banana.
Won't you be seated, come in, join us, sit down?
Work doesn't stop there. on that one.
The world is confusing to me. is flat (Thomas Friedman). is wide. has changed. sits up and
    notices. has turned upside down. will be a better place.
Would I lie to you?
Would you do me a favour?
Would you like to see my collections.
Would you care for dance, consider selling it $100, drink this, like to dance, like to work for me,
    mind my smoking, say nothing, write to me?
Wouldn't it be nice? that be good?

Yes from me.
Yes, we can. Barack Obama
You act like hogs.
You eat like hogs.
You agree to do this.
You ain't gonna need it.
You almost feel like home.
You and I need something straight.
You are a failure, a dynamite, a failure fine man, a fool, a little earlier, a lucky man, a national
    hero, a special girl, a wonderful cook, a wonderful man, absolutely fabulous, absolutely
    right, all alone, always doing this, an angel, back, back to square 1, behind the time,
    disqualified, doing fine, doing great, dressed up today, driving too fast, extremely
    generous to me, free to speak, full of doubts, going too far, hurt, in, in love with me,
    jealous, judged on your merit, kidding, letting hot air in, legend, looking well, lovely
    tonight, magnificent, making a big mistake, making that up, naughty, nervous, nice
    looking too, nobody, not going to give up, not out of woods, on your own, one of us,
    quite safe, a resourceful young man, so smart, speaking humanity, stuck with me, taking
    advantage of me, talking nonsense, terrible, the best friend I have had, the best friend I've
    ever had, the centre of universe, the man, the sweetest man, too serious, wasting your
    time, welcome, what you eat.
You are here once.

You are all the boat people. Geoffrey Gurrumul Yunupingu (indigenous singer from Oz)
You are the most famous man in the world. Psy
You are great, nervous, welcome, very kind.
You are not alone, going out with him, right for me, serious, stopping, telling the truth, well.
You asked for it.
You be judge.
You behave yourself.
You believe in a miracle.
You blow my mind.
You broke my heart.
You can be different, judge, trusted, yourself,
You can come back later, come up now, depend on me, do it, do what you want, get out
    of this, get through this, go back to sleep, go home, have anything you want, help us,
    knock off now, only try, pull it off, rely on it, say that, see by yourself, tell, think about
    that tomorrow, try, understand my problem.
You can't argue with that, ask more than that, ask more than this, be serious, be a half
    virgin, be trusted, behave like that, buy happiness, come in, deny that, fool me, go, go
    anywhere, go on, go on like this, handle the truth. A few good men, have both ways,
    ignore the convention, lose if you don't play, mean that, miss it, put a price on health, put
    a price on people, put it under the carpet, sleep here spend the money you haven't got,
    talk like that, talk me like that, too careful, touch my heart, turn it off, use it, win them all.
You can't do it by yourself, that, this, this to me.
You can't get away from your past, enough of it, clearer than that, win victory forever.
You clearly respect the law.
You come over.
You complete me. Jerry Maguire
You cook very nice.
You could do better than that. say that.
You couldn't care less, help yourself, make it up, pick better time.
You'd better believe it, believe that, get rest, stay where you are, tell them.
You decide.
You didn't have to tell me that. say anything. didn't tell me this.
You do it.
You do what you wish.
You don't belong here, care about the truth, got to be active, know me, know what you are
    doing, look like sick, make up your mind now, mean that, need money, owe me anything,
    pay attention to me, seem to know much, think much of me, want to get mixed up with
    me. worry about me.
You don't have the money, to apologize, to be over the top, to buy a thing, to go through it,
    to make up your mind now, to worry about me.
You didn't tell me that.
You expect me so much.
You gave up alcohol.
You get healed, it, one shot in your life, paid almost nothing, sick of it, the benefit there.
You go extinct.
You got a clean bill of health, it, to try.

You guessed it.

You hate me.

You hated me so much.

You have a bit of sunshine, a good chance, a good point, asked for, been under great strains, been with us in every step of the way, changed your mind, come a long way, done all you can do, done so much, everything to live for, finished with me, found the voice, made a good point, made it, lovely home, my word, never seen anything like this, not made anybody's life easier, one more apology to make, our admiration, our congratulations, shown the world the best Korean hospitality, surprised me, the great chance, whole life ahead of you.

You have no control on when you live or die, idea, need to be frightened, right, right to sell it.

You have to be aware of that, be in to win, be kidding, believe me, do more time (jail),give a full account of your past, help me ,help us now, keep going, make judgement, make a choice, own your future, pay for it, pretend, start from somewhere trust me.

You haven't got a chance.

You hear me.

You get right out here.

You got the deals.

You just can't make up your mind.

You just want to get thin.

You keep it that way.

You know better than I would, how to fight, nothing, something, something is going to happen, that, what I am thinking, what I mean.

You learn from mistakes.

You learn nothing.

You lied to me.

You lifted me the whole way. Obama

You light up my life. Movie title

You'll be fine, free, in trouble, late, ok,

You'll change your mind, do what I say, get used to me, never walk alone.

You look amazing, beautiful, different, gorgeous, so bad, tired.

You made mess.

You make me crazy, me sick, my day, yourself comfortable,

You matter to me.

You may fool yourself.

You mean it.

You missed the journey.

You must be crazy, come again, forget it, freezing outside, give me time, go at once, go back, have a special feeling, live with your means, pay, sure.

You mustn't be heard, interfere, too serious, trust anyone.

You need calm over your break-up with your girlfriend, it, this, to fix the problem, to set a goal.

You needn't be jealous of any man.

You never forget that, forget your first love, get it back, get there, know, know what you are going to get, know what's going to happen, know what's in store for you, stop smiling, stop working, your vision for granted.

You only live once.

You ought to be ashamed.
You pay the price.
You planned the whole thing.
You push too hard.
You're a good man, barking up the wrong tree, beautiful, changing your reality, doing it for
 me, expelled from this school, full of love, going to love it, in trouble, joking, just my
 type, kidding, loved, much too lovely, my kind, my pride, not alone, not to blame for it.
 on my level, on your own, only the one, out of line, punishing yourself, right, so bored,
 talking loudly, talking too loudly, tearing me apart. Rebel without a clause, the boss, the
 one, the reason we fly. Qantas, there to do the job, very attractive, very generous with
 your time, wasting your time, welcome, what you do, who you are.
You're never too old to learn.
You said enough.
You scared me.
You scratch my back and I'll scratch yours (Clever?).
You see that.
You see the end product.
You seemed to be happy.
You send it back.
You should leave everything to me, never delete the message, never let him do it, relax, told me
 earlier.
You shouldn't be out in bed.
You smell good.
You sound like my sister.
You stay right where you are.
You stay here where you belong.
You stuffed it up.
You take it.
You talk too much.
You think this is a good system.
You've brought what it is today, come to the right place, got to understand the resources boom is
 over (Martin Ferguson), made the right choice, maintained your cool, proposed me.
You want me to do it.
You want to be somebody.
You will see what I mean.
You won't be sorry.
You wouldn't believe it, dare, have any choice, understand it.
Your boss makes or breaks your career.
Your best is not good enough.
Your days are numbered.
Your food (Eddy Kwon) is better than sex. Madonna
Your guess is as good as mine.
Your headache goes away.
Your heart starts beating.
Your money is no good here. Giant
Your time will come.

IX. Quotations

9.1   General quotations

All animals are equal, but some animals are more equal than others. (George Orwell in
      Animal Farm)
All South Korea has is 50 million people, water and mountains. However, South Korea was
      the No. 7 exporter in 2010, No. 6 in 2011, No. 6 in 2012, No. 7 in 2013, No. 5 in 2014
      and No. 6 in 2016. (Kujong Jung)
All you need is love. (Paul McCartney)
And so, my fellow Americans, ask not what your country can do for you. Ask what you can
      do for your country. My fellow citizens of the world: ask not what America will do for
      you, but what together we can do for the freedom of man. (John F. Kennedy, 1961
      Inaugural Address)
Art is fraud. (Namjune Paik)
Bad artists copy; great artists steal. (Pablo Picasso)
The Beatles are bigger than the Catholic Church. (John Lennon)
Because it is there. (George Mallory in 1924 when asked why he wanted to climb Mount
      Everest)
Better the bitter truth than junk food's sweet lies. (Anonymous)
Boys, be ambitious! (William S. Clark)
The buck stops here! (Harry S. Truman)
But I say to you: love your enemies and pray for those who persecute you. (Jesus Christ,
      Matthew 5:44)
But man is not made for defeat. A man can be destroyed but not defeated. (Ernest Hemingway)
But this long run is a misleading guide to current affairs. In the long run we are all dead. (John
      Maynard Keynes, *A Tract on Monetary Reform*)
But in this world, nothing is certain but death and taxes. (Benjamin Franklin)
Cleopatra's nose, had it been shorter, the whole face of the world would have been changed.
      (Blaise Pascal)
Complacency is death in politics. (Anonymous)
Crossed the Rubicon. (Julius Caesar)
The customer is always right. (H. Gordon Selfridge)
Darkness cannot drive out darkness; only light can do that. Hate cannot drive out hate; only love
      can do that. (Martin Luther King, Jr.)
Discard the boat after crossing a river. (A quote from Buddhism)
Eat to live, don't live to eat. (Benjamin Franklin in *Poor Richard's Almanac*)
The end justifies the means. (Niccolo Machiavelli)
Even from my sick bed, even if you are going to lower me into the grave and I feel something is
      going wrong, I will get up. Lee Kuan Yew, Prime Minister of Singapore in 1988)
Even if the end of the world were tomorrow, I will plant an apple tree. (Benedict de Spinoza)
Everyone over forty is responsible for his face. (President Abraham Lincoln)
Everything is the creation of the mind. (Wonhyo, leading Korean Buddhist thinker)
Expecting democracy to flourish in South Korea would amount to expecting a rose to bloom in a
      trash can. (A British journalist in the Korea Times commenting on the South's military
      dictatorship)

Frailty, thy name is woman. (William Shakespeare)

Genius is one per cent inspiration and nine-nine per cent perspiration. (Thomas A. Edison)

God doesn't play dice. (Albert Einstein)

God is dead. (Friedrich Nietzsche)

God never closes one door without opening another. (The Sound of Music)

Government of the people, by the people, for the people, shall not perish from this earth.
    (Abraham Lincoln in the Gettysburg Address).

Han must be a main driving force for SK to shine in the economy, sports and culture since the
60s. Kujong Jung (referring to the concept of *han*).

Happy are the poor in spirit; theirs is the kingdom of heaven. (Jesus Christ)

Have no friends not equal to yourself. (Confucius, *The Analects*)

Hey, have you tried it ? (Chung Ju Yung, Hyundai group Chairman)

How can a rose bloom from a rubbish dump? (V.K. Krishna Menon)

Human beings are curious animals. They often ask questions like these: where do we come from,
    what are we, and where do we go? (Kujong Jung)

I am the greatest. (Muhammad Ali)

I am the light of the world; whoever follows me will not walk in darkness but will have the light
    of life. (Jesus Christ, John 8:12)

History is an unending dialogue between the past and the present. (E.H. Carr)

I am the state. (Louis XIV)

I am the way, the truth and the life. (Jesus Christ, John 14:6)

I did it my way. (Paul Anka; popularized by Frank Sinatra in the song, "My Way")

I do not know how to cook food, but I know how to eat it. (A famous Greek pianist)

I do not wish my country to be a military or a political power, rather I wish it were a cultural
    power. (Kim Koo, Korean freedom fighter)

I enjoy being the centre of attention. (Usain Bolt)

I give you a new commandment: love one another as I have loved you. (Jesus Christ, John 13:34)

I have a dream that my four little children will one day live in a nation where they will not be
    judged by the color of their skin but by the content of their character. I have a dream
    today. (Martin Luther King, Jr.)

I have a dream that one day this nation will rise up and live out the true meaning of its creed,
"We hold these truths to be self-evident, that all men are created equal." (Martin Luther King,
    Jr.)

I have no use for money. (Bill Gates on the campaign against polio)

I have nothing to offer but blood, toil, tears and sweat. (Winston Churchill)

I knew if I stayed around long enough, something like this would happen! (George
    Bernard Shaw's epitaph)

I love Jesus Christ but don't like Christianity. (Mahatma Gandhi)

I'm still hungry. (Gus Hiddink)

I think; therefore I am. (Descartes, *Discourse on Method*)

I want to discard time and space. (Korean Monk Beoupjung on his deathbed)

If there is a strong general, there will be no weak soldiers. (Chinese proverb)

If winter comes, can spring be far behind? (Percy Bysshe Shelley)

If you always do what you have always done, you'll always get what you've always got.

If you cannot love the person you see, how can you love God, Whom we cannot see. (Mother
    Teresa)

If you know the enemy and know yourself, you need not fear the result of a hundred battles. If you know yourself but not the enemy, for every victory gained you will also suffer a defeat. If you know neither the enemy nor yourself, you will succumb in every battle. (Sun Tzu)

If you want to go fast, go alone. If you want to go far, go together. (African proverb)

In a crisis, be aware of the danger, but recognize the opportunity. (John F. Kennedy)

The interview is the honeymoon; publication is the divorce. (Sinae Chun)

Is Google making us stupid? (Nicholas Carr)

It does not matter whether a cat is black or white so long as it catches mice. (Deng Xiaoping)

It features seven common social phenomena, characteristics of a nation on the brink of collapse: politics without principles, wealth without sweat, pleasure without scruples, education without character, science without humanity, commerce without morals and religion without sacrifice. (Mahatma Gandhi)

It's the economy, stupid. (Bill Clinton)

A journey of a thousand miles begins with a single step. (Confucius and Mao)

Keep it simple, stupid! (Kelly Johnson)

Kimchi and Korea are a match made in heaven. (Jon Huer)

Know thyself. (Socrates)

Knowledge is power. (Socrates)

Korea is a dolphin instead of a shrimp. (Daniel Tudor)

Korea is like Britain, while Japan is like America. One cannot imagine that America invades Britain to colonize it. (Kujong Jung)

Koreans are the only people who believe they can beat the Japanese. (Mahathir Mohamad, former Prime Minister of Malaysia)

The lady is not for turning. (Margaret Thatcher)

Lee Sun-sin is the person who I am afraid of the most, hate the most, love the most, admire and respect the most, wish to kill the most, and want to have tea together the most. (General Wakizaka Yasuhara of the Japanese Army)

The left hand doesn't know what the right hand is doing. (Matthew 6:3)

Let them eat cake. (Marie Antoinette)

Life is short, live it. Love is rare, grab it. Anger is bad, dump it. Fear is awful, face it. Memory is sweet, cherish it. (Anonymous)

Life wasn't meant to be easy. (Malcolm Fraser, Prime Minister of Australia . meaning one must work for one's keep)

Love is a many-splendored thing. (Han Suyin)

Love is patient, love is kind. It does not envy, it does not boast, it is not proud. It is not rude, it is not self-seeking, it is not easily angered, it keeps no record of wrongs. Love does not delight in evil but rejoices with the truth, always hopes, always perseveres. Love never fails. (Paul: I Corinthians 13)

Man is a social animal (Baruch Spinoza)

Man is but a reed, the feeblest thing in nature, but he is a thinking reed. (Blaise Pascal)

Man shall not live by bread alone. (Jesus Christ)

Men are from Mars. Women are from Venus. (John Gray)

More die in the United States of too much food than of too little. (John Kenneth Galbraith, *The Affluent Society*)

Mountain is mountain. Water is water. (Korean monk Seongcheol)

A nation that forgets its past has no future. (Winston Churchill)

Nature is your friend. Treat it with reverence and affection. It is not an object to conquer. (Lao-Tzu)

Never, never, never give up. (Winston Churchill)

No foreigner would ever understand Russia. (Alexander Pushkin)

Old soldiers never die. They just fade away. (General Douglas Macarthur)

One of life's eternal mysteries is why she ever married me in the first place. (Kevin Rudd, former Prime Minister of Australia)

The only international language is a child's cry. (Eglantyne Jebb)

The only thing we have to fear is fear itself. (Franklin D. Roosevelt)

Piano is my best friend. (Lang Lang)

Poetry should be expressive of enjoyment without being licentious, and expressive of sadness without grieving. (Confucius)

Political power grows out the barrel of a gun. (Mao Zedong)

Power tends to corrupt, and absolute power corrupts absolutely. (John Dalberg-Acton)

Should this life sometime deceive you, don't be sad or mad at it! (Alexander Pushkin)

Small is beautiful. (E.F. Schumacher)

Spit on my grave. (Park Chung-hee)

Stay hungry. Stay foolish. (Steve Jobs)

There's no business like show business. (Irving Berlin)

That's one small step for man, one giant leap for mankind. (Neil Armstrong after landing on the moon in 1968)

There are three kinds of lies: lies, damned lies and statistics. (Mark Twain)

There are known knowns; there are things we know we know. We also know there are known unknowns; that is to say we know there are some things we do not know. But there are also unknown unknowns – the ones we don't know we don't know. (Donald Rumsfeld, Former US Secretary of Defense)

There's no such thing as a free lunch. (Robert Heinlein)

Think different. (Steve Jobs)

To be, or not to be. That is the question. (William Shakespeare)

To see the world in a grain of sand. And heaven in a wild flower. (William Blake)

Tomorrow is another day. (Vivien Leigh in Gone with Wind)

Two wrongs don't make a right, but they make a good excuse. (Thomas Szasz)

United we stand, divided we die. (Syngman Rhee, first Korean president)

A virtuous man likes a mountain while a wise man likes water. (Chinese proverb)

Water is water and a mountain is the mountain. Great Korean monk Seongcheol.

We are given our body, skin and hair from our parents, which we ought not to damage. (Confucius)

We make a living by what we get. We make a life by what we give. (Winston Churchill)

We're more popular than Jesus now. (John Lennon)

Well, there is no question that we have evidence and information that Iraq has Weapons of Mass Destruction. (George Bush, 2003)

When you know a thing, to hold that you know it, and when you do not know a thing, to allow that you do not know it: this is knowledge. Confucius, *Analects*)

Where do we come from? What are we? Where are we going? (Paul Gauguin)

Who never eats with tears his bread? (Johann Wolfgang von Goethe)

Why can't a woman be more like a man? (Rex Harrison, My Fair Lady)
Will a female Socrates, Shakespeare, Einstein, Picasso, Mozart, Michelangelo, Kant, Keynes, Gandhi, Lincoln, Freud, Da Vinci, Darwin, Jobs or Edison emerge? (Kujong Jung)
Women are the biggest mystery. Women are a complete mystery. (Stephen Hawking)
Women hold up half the sky. (Mao Zedong)
The word " impossible" is not in my dictionary. (Napoleon Bonaparte)
The world is flat. (Thomas L. Friedman)
Yes, we can. (Barack Obama)
You are all the boat people. (Geoffrey Gurrumul Yunupingu, indigenous singer from Oz)
You are what you eat. (Ludwig Andreas)
You may compare me with Lord Nelson, but not with Lee Sun-sin. Japanese Admiral Togo Heihachiro who defeated the Russian fleet in 1905
You may fool all the people some of the time; you can even fool some of the people all the time; but you can't fool all of the people all the time. (Abraham Lincoln)
You thrive to die, you will live. (Great Korean Admiral Yi (Lee) Sun-sin)
Your food is better than sex. Madonna on Chef Eddy Kwon)

9.2　Some Whoppers (as predictions or statements of permanent fact)

Everything that can be invented has been invented. (Charles H. Duell, Commissioner, U.S. Patents Office, 1899)
I think there is a world market for about five computers. (Tom Watson, IBM Chairman, 1958)
There is no reason anyone would want a computer in their home. (Ken Olson, President, Chairman and Founder of Digital Equipment Corp., 1977)
We will never make a 32-bit operating system. (Bill Gates, Microsoft Corp., 1983)
A rocket will never be able to leave the Earth's atmosphere. (*New York Times*, 1936)
There is the biggest fool thing we have done. The bomb (atomic) will never go off, and I speak as an expert in explosives. (Admiral William D. Leahy, 1945)
The cinema is little more than a fad. It's canned drama. What audiences really want to see is flesh and blood on the stage. (Charlie Chaplin, 1916)
The Americans have need of the telephone, but we do not. We have plenty of messenger boys. (William Preece, British Post Office, 1871)
Fooling around with alternative current is just a waste of time. Nobody will use it ever. (Thomas Edison, 1889)
Television won't last. It's a flash in the pan. (Mary Summerville, Pioneer of Radio Educational Broadcasts, 1948)
When the Paris Exhibition (1878) closes, electric light will close it and no more will be heard of it. (Oxford Professor Erasmus Wilson)
(Television) won't be able to hold on to any market it captures after the first six months. People will soon get tired of staring at a plywood box every night. (Darryl Zanuck, 20th Century Fox, 1946)
Heavier-than-air flying machines are impossible. (Lord Kevin, British physicist, 1895)
Nuclear-powered vacuum cleaners will probably be a reality in 10 years. (Alex Lewyt, President of Lewyt Corp, 1955)
There is not the slightest indication that nuclear energy will ever be obtainable. It would mean the atom would be shattered at will. (Albert Einstein, 1932)

The X-ray will prove to be a hoax. (Lord Kelvin, President of Royal Society, 1883) The horse
is here to stay, but the automobile is only a novelty – a fad. (Horace Rackham, Henry Ford's
lawyer, 1903)

9.3   Movie Quotes

"All men are islands." Will in *About a Boy*.

"Old business is old business and new business is new business." *The Addams Family*

"Winter must be cold for those with no warm memories."
"You don't belong in a place like this."
"France needs men.' So he has seven daughters. Charming, witty ---- and irresistible?
     All I could say was, 'hello"
"Don't look at me like that. If one of us didn't show up, it would be for a darn good reason."
"If you can paint, you can walk, anything can happen, don't you think?" *An Affair to Remember*

"I don't date teenagers."
"Why did you marry him?" "Because he was a good kisser." *Alice Doesn't Live Here Anymore*

"Fasten your seatbelts, it's going to be a bumpy night." *All About Eve*

"I have one rule. There are no rules." *Alvin and the Chipmunks*

"Today is tomorrow." *Andre*

"We have the whole house to ourselves."
"You don't get to tell me what to do ever again."
"You have nothing to be sorry about."
"You've got the wrong idea."
"Your wife is with another man and you don't care." *American Beauty*

"I'm a girl."
"Hey, mister . . .? Don't you like girls?" Annie Oakley from *Annie Get Your Gun*.

"Don't fall in love with me I'm married."
"What's the size of the engine? This much."
"Did you hear what I said, Miss Kubelik? I absolutely adore you." *The Apartment*

"I love the smell of napalm in the morning… smells like…victory." *Apocalypse Now*

"Houston, we have a problem." *Apollo 13*

"I'm your sponge!"
"Life is a banquet, and most poor suckers are starving to death." *Auntie Mame*

"You've gotta come with me!" *Back to the Future*

"As far as I'm concerned, you are not human beings anymore." *Battle Cry*

"Your eyes are full of hate." *Ben Hur*
"Don't disappoint me, Messala."
Forgiveness is greater and love more powerful than hatred.
"I see no enemy, Messala."
"The race is not over."

Burma is a land of monks and soldiers. *Beyond Rangoon*
In Burma, everything is illegal.

"How many times does a man have to win you?" *The Big Country*
You don't like a school mom.

"Kitchen staff doesn't have an age." *Chef*
"I think that asshole might be our new partner."

"We rob banks." *Bonnie and Clyde*

"We didn't pick you. You picked us." *The Bourne Ultimatum*

"What have I done?" *The Bridge Over The River Kwai*

"East is east, and West is west." *Carlton-Browne of the F.O.*

"Here's looking at you, kid." *Casablanca*
"Louis, I think this is the beginning of a beautiful friendship." Humphrey Bogart
"Play it, Sam. Play 'As Time Goes By'."

"I don't have to do anything I don't want to!" Brick *Cat On A Hot Tin Roof.*
"I feel all the time like a cat on a hot tin roof." Maggie
"I'm not living with you! We occupy the same cage, that's all."
"I've got the guts to die. What I want to know is, have you got the guts to live?" Big Daddy
Not everybody makes as much noise about love as you do. Brick
"But how in hell on earth can you imagine you're gonna have a child with a man who cannot
     stand you." Brick
"The human animal is a beast that dies, and if he's got money he buys and busy and buys and I
     think the reason he buys . . . is the crazy hope that one of his purchases will be life
     everlasting! – Which it can never be." Big Daddy
"You don't know what love means! To you, it's just another four-letter word." Brick
"You can be young without money, but you can't be old without it." Maggie

"Can you give my time back to me?" *Changing Lanes*
"I don't want champagne. I am champagne." Doyle

"I don't bite you know unless it's called for." Audrey Hepburn in *Charade*

"I am an Englishman, first and last." *Chariots of Fire*

"Forget it, Jake. It's Chinatown." *Chinatown*

"Friendship is friendship. Business is business." *Cimarron*

"You are a virgin, who can't drive." *Clueless*

"What we've got here is a failure to communicate." *Cool Hand Luke*

"Who do you think you are? God?" *Crying Freedom*

"Are you afraid of burning?" *Dark Victory*

"Anything you can do, I can do better." *The Day The Earth Caught Fire*

"Do we understand each other?" Scorpion Killer from *Dirty Harry*

"Did I ruin your life? I ruined your life." *Divine Secrets of the Ya-Ya Sisterhood*

"A man's gotta do what a man's gotta do." *Doc Hollywood*
"I don't want Los Angeles. I want you."

"Bond, James Bond." *Dr. No*

"Don't go too far, hon! It will be over in sixty minutes." Bruce Lee to Linda Lee, *The Dragon Bruce Lee Story*.

I don't have to explain anything to anybody. *East of Eden*

"If we don't know the past, we will not have a future." *The Education of Little Tree*

"Get out of my life." *Elf*

"I am no man's Elizabeth." *Elizabeth*

"Nurse! I can't sleep. Would you kiss me?" *The English Patient*

"Mother, what's wrong with me?" *The Exorcist*

"Americans don't eat anything smaller than turkeys." *Everlasting Moments*

"You want the truth? You can't handle the truth!" *A Few Good Men*

And how do we keep our balance? That I can tell in a word: Tradition! Without our traditions,
         our lives would be as shaky as a fiddler on the roof.” *Fiddler on the Roof*
“Because of our traditions, every one of us knows who he is and what God expects him to do.”

“If you build it, he will come.” *Field of Dreams*

“Winner takes all, my friends.” *First Knight*

“Mama always said life was like a box of chocolates. You never know what you’re gonna get.”
Forrest Gump

“If it’s peace three wants, three won’t get it chopping wood.” *Friendly Persuasion*

“Ladies don’t run.” *The Getting of Wisdom*

“I was refused, rejected, rebuffed and --- reputed!” Gaston in *Gigi*
“I would rather be miserable with you than without you.”
“To ‘take care of me beautifully’ means I shall go away with you--- and that I shall sleep in your
         bed.”
“I don’t understand the Parisians.”
“Making love every time they get the chance.”
“Wasting every lovely night on romance.”

“I’m gonna make him an offer he can’t refuse.” *The Godfather*
“I’ll make him an offer he can’t refuse.”
“It’s not personal, Sonny. It’s strictly business.”

“I know it was you, Fredo. You broke my heart! You broke my heart!” *Godfather, Part II*
“Keep your friends close, but your enemies closer.”
“We’re bigger than US steel.”

“Do quickly what you have to do”. *Godspell*
“No man can serve God and money.”

“After all, tomorrow is another day.” *Gone With the Wind*
“As God is my witness, I’ll never be hungry again.”
“Oh, my darling, if you go, what shall I do?” “Frankly, my dear. I don’t give a damn.”

“Unleash hell.” *Gladiator*

“Mrs. Robinson, you’re trying to seduce me. Aren’t you?” *The Graduate*

“I wanted the money.” *The Great Train Robbery*

If you had one day to live, what would you do with it? *Groundhog Day*

"I love you. You don't even know me."
"I'm a god."
"You'll not love anyone but yourself."

"Who will protect you?" Pitch in *Rise of the Guardians*
"I will. I will. I will."

"I could never love someone like you because you'll never love anyone except yourself." "I'm a
    god, Phil."
"Today is tomorrow."
"You're God?" Rita

"Tess, get into the god damn chair." *Guarding Tess*

"To be or not to be." *Hamlet*

"I don't want to be worshiped, I want to be loved." Grace Kelly in *High Society*
"You're too good for me. George." Grace Kelly

"I wasn't a monster to work with. Was I?" *Hitchcock*
"What would I be without you?"

"I'm not going to fall in love with you, I promise." *The Holiday*

"You are the man of the house." *A Home of Our Own*

"Always the years between us. Always the years. Always the love. Always the hours." *The
    Hours*

"Divorce is out of the question as she is Italian." *How to Murder Your Wife*
"Either she goes or I goes."

"I'm not going to eat you." *Hue and Cry*

"Be a man." *The In-laws*

"Whatever you do, don't dance." *In and Out*

"I, not small! You, big." *The Indians in the Cupboard*

"You're gonna need a bigger boat." *Jaws*

"Show me the money." *Jerry Maguire*
"You complete me."

"You are the butter to my bread, and the breath to my life." *Julia and Julia*

"It was Beauty killed the Beast." *King Kong*

"The last thing you need is another mouth to feed." *Kit Kittredge*

"I'm afraid his last meal (tiger) would be a skinny vegetarian boy." *Life of Pi*
"Why would he send his son to suffer from the sins of ordinary people?"

"There's two kinds of people in this world, there's winners and there's losers." *Little Miss
        Sunshine*

"But I have nothing to give you. My hands are empty." Friedrich Bhaer from *Little Women*
"Not empty now." Louisa May Alcott

"I don't care if it's illegal. It's wrong." *Lord of War*
"Selling guns is like selling vacuum cleaners."

"Sex, to me, is not a spectator sport." *Lost in America*

"Love means never having to say you're sorry." *Love Story*

"Sometimes the wrong train will get you to the right station." *The Lunchbox*

"Don't chase rainbows." *Magic Man*

"I am a young king, but I am king." *The Man in the Iron Mask*
"One for all. All for one."

"I'm smart; you 're dumb; I'm big, you're little; I'm right; you're wrong, and there's nothing you
        can do about it." *Matilda*
"People don't buy a car. They buy me."

"I'm not a girl. I'm your research assistant." *Medicine Man*
"I'm not proposing you for marriage."
"Don't cry. Listen, when this is over, you can cry all you want."
"Unbutton your shirt."

"If we can through during the last 48 hours, we can get through anything." Greg Focker from
        Meet the Parents
"Bomb bomb bomb, bomb bomb bomb bomb bomb bomb bomb. You gonna arrest me? Bomb
        bomb bomb bomb!" Greg Focker

"I'm walking here!" *Midnight Cowboy*

"Because if I die, you die." *Misery*
"Please help me help you."

"We are meant to be together."
"Did I do good?"

"Go away. I'm busy." Harrison Ford from *Morning Glory*
"Go away, go away." Rachel McAdams

"You didn't bring my sandwiches." From the *Mouse that Roared*

"I am not laughing. I'm crying." *Monkey Trouble*

"I'm kind of a celebrity." Kermit the Frog from *The Muppets*
"I'm who I am." Miss Piggy.

"Damn! Damn! Damn!" from *My Fair Lady*
"I can do without you." Eliza Doolittle
"I sold flowers; I didn't sell myself. Now you've made a lady of me. I'm not fit to sell anything."
     Eliza Doolittle
"I've grown accustomed to her face." Professor Henry Higgins
"The rain in Spain falls mainly on the plain."
"Why can't a woman be more like a man?" Professor Henry Higgins from *My Fair Lady*

"I didn't marry any of them. They married me." *My Favorite Year*
"I'm not an actor. I'm a movie star!"

"If he ever tries to take Shelley's camper again, I'm gonna bury him in my front yard." *My Girl*
"But life isn't just death. Harry! Don't ignore the living--- especially your daughter."

"Human first, black second." *Not Easily Broken*
"I feel like Humpty Dumpty."
"These flowers don't mean I'm stalking you."

"I'm also a girl, standing in front of a boy, asking him to love her." *Notting Hill*

"I'm trying to clear up my ears." *The Odd Couple*

"Maybe that's the monster in your head." *Oranges and Sunshine*
"I'm nobody now."

"Eat the dogs." *The Patriot*

"Your baby loves you." *Precious*
"I love you."

"I'd like to marry her. Not today!" *Pretty in Pink*

"I never joke about money." *Pretty Woman*

"She's not a spy. She's a hooker."
"Remember me. Big mistakes."
"Your hurt me. Don't do it again."
"I want the fairy tale."

"I felt that you were the last man in the world whom I could ever be prepared upon to marry."
          Pride & Prejudice

Today, I consider myself the luckiest man on the face of the earth." *The Pride of Yankees*

"I feel about you." *Prom*
"A lot of people are wrong about you."
"You are about to kiss me."

"A boy's best friend is his mother." *Psycho*

"In my first year of law school, everybody loved everybody else." *The Rainmaker*
"What's the difference between a lawyer and a hooker?"

"I want you to fight for me, that is all I ever wanted." Son. *Real Steel*
"What do you want from me?" Father

"You're tearing me apart." *Rebel Without a Cause*

"It's a dictatorship. I am the law." *Remember the Titans*

"Here's a kiss from David." Humphrey Bogart on behalf William Holden to Audrey Hepburn.
          Sabrina
"The rest of the message from David." Linus Larrabee

"I work on my hair a long time, and you hit it." *Saturday Night Fever*
 "You want a dream girl? Then go to sleep and have a nightmare."

"Say 'hello' to my little friend." *Scarface*

"We want rock." *School of Rock*

"Let's go home, Debbie." *The Searchers*

"Me, not shut up." *Secret Agent*

"Life is a journey." *The Sessions*
"This is your body."

"If you're gonna act like hogs, you can eat like them." *Seven Brides for Seven Brothers*

"I forbid you to go out with that guy." "Who do you think you are, my father?" *Seventeen Again*

"Shane. Shane. Come back! Bye." *Shane*

"I am the law." *The Siege*

"You're either a thief or a hero." *Sinbad: Legend of the Seven Seas*
"A ship is no place for a woman."

"Can I borrow your underpants for ten minutes?" *Sixteen Candles*

"I see dead people!" *The Sixth Sense*

"You are the wisest of the wise or the fool of fools." *Solomon and Sheba*
"My love is not a lie."

"Well, nobody's perfect." *Some Like It Hot*

"If you love this man, it doesn't mean you love God less." from *The Sound of Music*
"These walls were not meant to shut out problems."
"When the Lord closes a door, somewhere he opens a window." Maria
"You brought music back into the house. I had forgotten."
"Captain, you have to face them."
"You have to live the life you were born to live." Mother Abbess

"I am Spartacus." *Spartacus*

"With great power comes great responsibility." *Spiderman*

"When necessary, share bodily warmth." *The Spy Who Loved Me*

"I have always depended on the kindness of strangers." *A Streetcar Named Desire*
"Stella! Hey, Stella!"

"Go ahead, make my day." *Sudden Impact*

"You used to be big. I am big. It's the pictures that got small." *Sunset Boulevard*

"You talkin' to me." *Taxi Driver*

"When you kill a worm, you kill a friend." *The Teahouse of Autumn Moon*

"Would you think about marrying me?" *Tender Mercies*
"Yes, I will."
"Don't you understand English?"

"I'll be back." *The Terminator*

"Don't talk about love." *Three Sisters*
"I love. I love. I love."

"But it would be no paradise if it was mine alone." *The Time Machine*
"There is no past and no future."

"I'm the king of the world." *Titanic*

"You kissed me back." *Trial and Error*

"Turbo proves that no dream is too big and no dreamer is too small." *Turbo*

"Crime is crime." *Two Way Stretch*

"Dave, this conservation can serve no purpose anymore. Goodbye." *2001: A Space Odyssey*
"I'm sorry, Dave. I'm afraid I can't do that."

"I'll go to your room, but you'll have to seduce me." Vicky Cristina *Barcelona*

"Saints are boring." *Two Weeks' Notice*

"Greed, for lack of a better word, is good. Greed is right. Greed works. Greed clarifies, cuts
through, and captures the essence of the evolutionary spirit. Greed, in all of its forms."
Wall Street

"Before a battle, there is nothing more important than to have a good sleep." General Kutuzov
War and Peace.
"The only important battle is the last." General Kutuzov
"I have loved you from the first moment I saw you."

"I can't die as I am engaged." *Waterloo Bridge*

"There's a time for us. Someday a time for us." Maria from *West Side Story*
"There's a place for us. Somewhere a place for us." Tony from *West Side Story*
"We never had the love that every child ought to get."
"When do you kids stop? You make this world lousy." Doc
"You hoodlums don't own these streets." Schrank
"One hand, one heart, even death won't part us now." Tony and Maria
"Get cool, boys. Get cool, boys."
"Girls here are free to have fun. She is in America now." Anita
"Get your hands off, American--- Stay away from my sister." Bernardo
"Someday, when you're an old married woman with five children, then you can tell me what to
do. Right now, it's the other way around." Bernardo

From *West Side Story*

I like to be in America!
O.K. by me in America!
Everything free in America
For a small fee in America!

Anita: Life can be bright in America.
Boys: If you can fight in America.
Girls: Life is all bright in America.
Boys: If you're all white in America.

"You son of a bitch. You yellow bastard." *White Hunter, Black Heart*

"If they move, kill 'em'." *The Wild Bunch*

"Your opinion is my opinion. My opinion is my opinion." *Wildcats*

"Life without whisky is just not worth living." *Whisky Galore*
"I'm not good enough to marry you."

"There's no place like home." Dorothy in *The Wizard of Oz*

"How many kids do you have?" "I have 8." "I have 10." *Yours, Mine and Ours*

9.4. Quotes from The Bible[1]

New Testament

"And when Jesus was baptized, he went up immediately from the water, and behold, the heavens were opened, and he saw the Spirit of God, descending like a dove, and alighting on Him." (Matthew 3:16)
"Follow me, and I will make you fishers of men." (Matthew 4:19)
"Blessed are the peacemakers, for they shall be called sons of God." (Matthew 5:9)
"You are the light of the world. "Let your light shine before men, that they may see your good works and give glory to your Father who is in heaven." (Matthew 5:14,16)
"But seek first his kingdom and his righteousness, and all these things will be yours as well." (Matthew 6:33)
"Another parable he put before them, saying, 'The kingdom of heaven may be compared to a man who sowed good seed in his field." (Matthew 13:24)
"Jesus immediately reached out his hand and caught him, saying to him, "O man of little faith, why did you doubt?" (Matthew 14:31)
"This is My beloved son, with whom I am well pleased; listen to Him." (Matthew 17:5)

---

[1] Quotations taken from the Revised Standard Version, accessed online at
http://www.biblestudytools.com/rsv .

"Unless you turn and become like children, you will never enter the kingdom of heaven."
        (Matthew 18:3)
"He was still speaking, when lo, a bright cloud overshadowed them, and a voice from the
        cloud said, 'This is my beloved Son, with whom I am well pleased; listen to him!"
        (Matthew 17:5)
 "---- and lo, I am with you always---" (Matthew 28:20)
"The earth produces of itself, first the blade, then the ear, then the full grain in the ear." (Mark
        4:28)
"'If you can?' said Jesus. 'All things are possible for him who believes." (Mark 9:23)
"Let the children to come to me; do not hinder them; for to such belongs the kingdom of God."
        (Mark 10:14)
"And this will be a sign for you: you will find a babe wrapped in swaddling clothes, and lying
        in a manger." (Luke 2:12)
"But love your enemies, and do good, and lend, and expecting nothing in return; and your reward
        will be great, and you will be sons of the Most High; for he is kind to the ungrateful and
        the selfish." (Luke 6:35)
 "Which of these three, do you think, proved neighbor to the man who fell among the robbers?"
        HE said, 'The one who showed mercy on him.' And Jesus said to him, "Go and do
        likewise." (Luke 10:36-37).
 "What man of you, having a hundred sheep, if he has lost one of them, does not leave the
        ninety-nine in the wilderness, and go after the one which is lost, until he finds it?" (Luke
        15:4)
"'Father, if thou art willing, remove this cup from me; nevertheless not my will, but thine be
        done.'" (Luke 22:42)
They said to each other, "Did not our hearts burn within us while He talked to us on the road,
        while he opened to us to us the scriptures?" (Luke 24:32)
"Beloved, I pray that all may go well with you and that you may be in health; I know that is
        well with your soul." (3 John 1:2)
For God sent the Son into the world, not to condemn the world, but that the world might be
        saved through Him. (John 3:17)
 "Go, wash in the pool of Silo'am" (which means Sent). So he went and washed and came back
        seeing. (John 9:7)
"Truly, truly, I say to you, unless a grain of wheat falls into the earth and dies, it remains
        alone; but if it dies, it bears much fruit." (John 12:24)
"I have come as light into the world, that whoever believes in me should not remain in
        darkness." (John 12: 46)
"Let not your hearts be troubled; believe in God; believe also in me. In my Father's house are
        many rooms." (John 14: 1-2)
"I am the way, and the truth, and the life; no one comes to the Father but by me." (John 14:6)
"Peace I leave with you; my peace I give to you; not as the world gives do I give to you. Let your
        hearts be troubled, neither let them be afraid." (John 14:27)
"A new commandment I give to you, that you love one another; even as I have loved you." (John
        13:34)
"I am the vine, you are the branches. He who abides in me, and I in him, he it is that bears much
        fruit." (John 15:5)
"If you abide in me, and my words abide in you, ask whatever you will, and it shall be done

for you." (John 15:7)

"If you keep My commandments, you will abide in my love, just as I have kept my Father's commandments and abide in his love." (John 15: 10)

Greater love has no one than this, that a man lay down his life for his friends. You are my friends if you do what I command you. (John 15: 13-14)

So you have sorrow now, but I will see you again and your hearts will rejoice, and no one will take your joy from you." (John 16: 22)

But you shall receive power when the Holy Spirit has come upon you; and you shall be my witnesses in Jerusalem and in all Judea and Samaria and to the end of the earth.. (Acts 1: 8)

. . who was put to death for our trespasses and raised for our justification. (Romans 4: 25)

Rejoice with those who rejoice; weep with those who weep. Live in harmony with one another; do not be haughty but associate with the lowly; never be   conceited. (Romans 12: 15-16)

May the God of hope fill you with all joy and peace in believing, so that by the power of the Holy Spirit you may abound in hope. (Romans 15: 13)

But in fact Christ has been raised from dead, the first fruits of those who have fallen asleep. (1 Corinthians 15: 20)

But I say, walk by the Spirit, and do not gratify the desires of the flesh. (Galatians 5: 16)

But the fruit of the Spirit is love, joy, peace, patience, kindness, goodness, faithfulness, gentleness, self-control; against such things there is no law. (Galatians 5: 22-23)

And let us not grow weary in well-doing, for in due season we shall reap, if we do not lose heart. (Galatians 6: 9)

For by Grace you have been saved through faith; and that not of yourselves, it is the Gift of God. (Ephesians 2: 8)

For the fruit of Light is found in all that is good and right and true. (Ephesians 5: 9)

Have no anxiety about anything, but in everything by prayer and supplication with thanksgiving; let your requests be made known to God. (Philippians 4: 6)

I can do all things in him who strengthens me. (Philippians 4: 13)

Give thanks in all circumstances;, for this is the will of God in Christ Jesus for you. (1 Thessalonians 5: 18)

Preach the Word; be urgent in season and out of season; convince, rebuke and exhort—be unfailing in patience and in teaching. (2 Timothy 4: 2)

To the pure, all things are pure, but to the corrupt and unbelieving nothing is pure; their very minds and consciences are corrupted. (Titus 1: 15)

Therefore, holy brethren, who share in a heavenly call, consider Jesus, the apostle and high priest of our confession. (Hebrews 3: 1)

Looking to Jesus the pioneer and perfecter of our faith, who for the joy that was set before him endured the cross, despising the shame, and is seated at the right hand of the throne of God. (Hebrews 12: 2)

Jesus Christ is the same yesterday and today and forever. (Hebrews 13: 8)

Through Him then let us continually offer up a sacrifice of praise to God, that is, the fruit of lips that acknowledge His name. (Hebrews 13: 15)

And the harvest of righteousness is sown in peace by those who make peace. (James 3: 18)

Is anyone among you suffering? Let him pray. Is any cheerful? Let him sing praise. (James 5:13)

Beloved, I pray that all may go well with you and that you may be in health; I know that it is well with your soul. (3 John 1: 2)

Old Testament

Is not the whole land before you? Separate yourself from me. If you take the left hand, then I
        will go to the right; or if you take the right hand, then I will go to the left. (Genesis 13: 9)
And you shall love the LORD your God with all your heart, and with all your soul, and with
        all your might. (Deuteronomy 6: 5)
Have I not commanded you? Be strong and of good courage; be not frightened, neither be
        dismayed; for the LORD your God is with you wherever you go.(Joshua 1: 9)
And she vowed a vow and said, "O LORD of hosts, if thou wilt indeed look on the affliction of
        thy maidservant, and remember me, and not forget thy maidservant but wilt give to thy
        maidservant a son, then I will give him to the LORD all the days of his life, and no razor
        shall touch his head." (1 Samuel 1: 11)
And now, O Lord GOD, thou art God, and thy words are true, and thou hast promised this
        good thing to thy servant; now therefore may it please thee to bless the house of thy
        servant, that it may continue forever before thee; for thou, O Lord GOD, hast spoken, and
        with thy blessing shall the house of thy servant be blessed forever. (2 Samuel 7: 28-29)
And at the time of the offering of the oblation, Elijah the prophet came near and said, "O
        LORD, God of Abraham, Isaac, and Israel, let it be known this day that thou art God in
        Israel, and that I am thy servant, and that I have done all these things at thy
        word. Answer me, O LORD, answer me, that this people may know that thou, O LORD,
        art God, and that thou hast turned their hearts back." (1 Kings 18: 36-37)
But he knows the way that I take; when he has tried me, I shall come forth as gold. (Job 23: 10
He is like a tree planted by streams of water, that yields its fruit in its season, and its leaf does
        not wither. In all that he does, he prospers. (Psalms 1: 3)
Thou has put more joy in my heart than they have when their grain and wine abound. (Psalms 4:
        7)
For the LORD is righteous, he loves righteous deeds; the upright shall behold his face. (Psalms
        11: 7)
Thou dost show me the path of life; in thy presence there is fullness of joy, in thy right hand
        are pleasures for evermore. (Psalms 16: 11)
I love thee, O LORD, my strength. (Psalms 18: 1)
Surely goodness and mercy shall follow me all the days of my life; and I shall dwell in the
        house of the LORD forever. (Psalms 23: 6)
Teach me thy way, O LORD; and lead me on a level path…. (Psalms 27: 11)
God is our refuge and strength, a very present help in trouble. (Psalms 46: 1)
Create in me a clean heart, O God, and put a new word and right spirit within me. (Psalms 51:
        10)
For God alone my soul waits in silence; from him comes my salvation. (Psalms 62: 1)
He only is my rock and my salvation, my fortress; I shall not be shaken. (Psalms 62: 6)
For the LORD is a great God, and a great King above all gods. In his hand are the depths of
        the earth; the heights of the mountains are his also. (Psalms 95: 3-4)
For he is our God, and we are the people of His pasture, and the sheep of his hand. O that today
        you would harken to his voice (Psalms 95: 7)
O give thanks unto the LORD, for he is good. (Psalms 106: 1)

The fear of the LORD is the beginning of wisdom; a good understanding have all those who
        practice it. His praise endures forever. (Psalms 111: 10)
For great is his steadfast love toward us; and the faithfulness of the LORD endures forever.
        (Psalms 117: 2)
Give thanks to the LORD, for he is good; his love endures forever. (Psalms 118: 29)
Forever, O LORD, thy word is firmly fixed in the heavens. Thy word is a lamp to my feet and
        a light to my path. (Psalms 119: 89, 105)
He will not let your foot be moved, he who keeps you will not slumber. (Psalms 121: 3)
The LORD is your keeper, The Lord is your shade on your right hand. (Psalms 121: 5)
He that goes forth weeping, bearing the seed for sowing, shall come home with shouts of joy,
        bringing his sheaves with him. (Psalms 126: 6)
I lift up my eyes to the hills. From whence does my help come? (Psalms 421: 1)
He stores up sound wisdom for the upright; he is a shield to those who walk in integrity.
        (Proverbs 2: 7)
Honor the Lord with your substance, and with the first fruits of all your produce; then your barns
        will be filled with plenty, and your vats will be bursting with wine. (Proverbs 3: 9-10)
I love those who love me, and those who seek me diligently find me. (Proverbs 8: 17)
The fear of the LORD is the beginning of wisdom, and the knowledge of the Holy One is insight.
        (Proverbs 9: 10)
The fruit of the righteous is a tree of life, but lawlessness takes away lives. (Proverbs 11: 30)
Commit your work to the LORD. and your plans will be established. (Proverbs 16: 3)
Righteous lips are the delight of a king, and he loves him who speaks what is right. (Proverbs 16:
        13)
Train up a child in the way he should go, and when he is old he will not depart from it. (Proverbs
        22: 6)
In the morning sow your seed, and at evening withhold not your hand; for you do not know
        which will prosper, this or that, or whether both alike will be good. (Ecclesiastes 11: 6)
Remember the former things, those of old; I am God, and there is no other; I am God, and
        there is none like me. (Isaiah 46: 9)
Let the wicked forsake his way and the unrighteous man his thoughts; let him return to the
LORD, that he may have mercy on him, and to our God, for he will abundantly pardon.
        (Isaiah 55: 7)
Arise, shine; for your light has come, and the glory of the LORD has risen upon you. (Isaiah 60:
        1)
And this city shall be to me a name of joy, a praise, and a glory before all nations of the earth,
        who shall hear of all the good that I do for them; they shall fear and tremble for all the
        goodness and all the prosperity that I provide for it. (Jeremiah 33: 9)
They shall be mine, says the LORD of hosts, my special possession on the day when I act,
        and I will spare them as a man spares his son who serves him. (Malachi 3: 17)

9.5   Quotes from Confucius (Kung Fu Tzu or Kung Tzu)

Jesus is known everywhere in Oz. Nonetheless, Confucius is one of the four saints of the world (with Jesus, Buddha, and Socrates), but he is not well known here. My late father was a Chinese scholar and poet. I learned about Confucius from him. These quotes are just the tip of iceberg:

Clever talk and a neat appearance are signs of benevolence.

Do not impose on others what you yourself do not desire.

If a man the morning hears the right way, he may die in the evening without regret.

Isn't it a joy to study and regularly practice? (Is it not pleasant to learn with constant perseverance and application?) Opening words from *The Analects*

A journey of a thousand miles begins with a single step. (Records say that this is a quote from another great Chinese philosopher, Lao-tzu, the founder of Taoism.)

The noble man seeks what is right; the inferior one seeks what is profitable.

One is quick and fond of learning, and is not ashamed to ask those beneath oneself.

Poetry should be expressive of enjoyment without being licentious and expressive of sadness without grieving.

Real knowledge is to know the extent of one's ignorance.

Reviewing the old and deducing the new makes a teacher.

To see what is right and not to do it is want of courage. (To know what is right and not to do it is the worst cowardice.)

What is more, isn't it a joy to meet comrades from afar? (Is it not delightful to meet friends coming from distant quarters?)

When I was fifteen years old, my entire will was devoted toward learning. At thirty, I took a stand. At forty, I no longer had doubts. At fifty, I knew the will of the heavens. In my sixties, everything sounded pleasant to my ears. At seventy, I follow all the desire of my heart without breaking any rules.

When three people travel together, one must be the teacher.

Worry not that no one knows of you; seek to be worth knowing.

X. Proverbs

It is a short, rhythmical saying expressing a general belief? Proverbs are pithy sayings that contain wisdom or observations about life and people. Some sound profound, but beware of always believing the wisdom of a proverb or taking it literally. Proverbs are not always right or true!

Proverbs can be defined as "memorable short sayings of the people, containing wise words of advice or warnings".

Some come from the Bible.

Proverbs exist in all languages and written collections of them date back to the earliest times. Proverbs are generally held in high esteem, whereas idioms have had to struggle for recognition. Perhaps this is a little surprising, as there's some overlap between idioms and proverbs.

Absolute power corrupts absolutely./Power requires checks and balances.
Actions speak louder than words/People's actions are more convincing than their words. What you do shows your character better and is more important than what you say.
After a storm comes a calm/When things are bad, you can nevertheless look forward to better times.
All in a day's work./Good, bad, whatever happens is all a part of life.
All roads lead to Rome. / There are many different ways of reaching the same goal or conclusion.
All work and no play will make Jack a dull boy/Too much hard work without time out for play or enjoyment is not good for anyone. It is good to combine work and play instead of work only.
All you need is love. (Paul McCartney)
Another day, another dollar.
Appearances are deceptive/Never judge by appearances.
Appearances can be deceiving (are deceiving).
An apple a day keeps the doctor away./Eating healthy food will keep you in good health. Eating an apple every day helps a person to stay healthy.
April is the cruelest month.
Art is long, life is short./1. There is so much to learn in life but only a short time in which to learn it. 2. Art lasts longer than the artist who created it.
As you sow, so shall you reap (so you reap.)./Your eventual reward will be based on how you lived your life. (Expresses the idea of karma.)
Attack is the best form of defense/It is better to take the initiative than to wait for something to happen.

Bad news travels fast./Bad news reaches you more quickly than good news.
A bargain's a bargain./You should stick by your agreements, no matter how things turn out.
A barking dog never bites./Displays of anger may mean nothing further.
Beauty is only skin deep./Physical beauty is fleeting, of secondary importance.
Beggars can't be choosers./Accept what is offered when in need and without alternatives.

Behind every great man there's a great woman./Men depend upon women.
The best defence is a good offense./Take the initiative instead of responding.
Better late than never/It's better to arrive late than not at all. It's better to do something late
       than not to do it at all.
Better the devil you know than the devil you don't./ Something unknown is more frightening
       than something already experienced.
Better to be safe than sorry./It's better to choose a safe path than to take a dangerous one
       unnecessarily.
A bird in hand is worth two in the bush./ Hold on to what you have rather than waiting for
       something better.
The blind leading the blind./a situation in which the ignorant or inexperienced are instructed
       or guided by someone equally ignorant or inexperienced.
Blood is thicker than water./Members of the same family share stronger ties with each other than
       they do with others Persons of the same family are closer to one another than others;
       relatives are favored or chosen over outsiders.
Boys will be boys./Typical behaviour for boys or men, often pejorative in meaning.
Burnt child dreads the fire or once bitten and twice shy/A person who has suffered from doing
       something has learned to avoid doing it again.
Business is business./Doing business requires cold reasoning or going by the numbers.

Cannot see the wood for the trees./Overly immersed in details, failing to see the bigger picture.
Cast not the first stone/ Before you criticize others, make sure you are not guilty yourself. The
       Bible
Charity begins at home/You may need help, but I must help myself. One should take care of
       one's own family, friends, or fellow citizens before helping other people.
Chickens come home to roost./Words or acts come back to cause trouble for a person; something
       bad you said or did receive punishment; you get the punishment that you deserve:
       Edward's chickens finally came home to roost today. He was late so often that the teacher
       made him to go to the principal. Susan's selfishness will come home to roost someday.
Choose the lesser of two evils/ If you have to choose between two bad choices, choose the least
       bad.
Cleanliness is next to godliness./A clean person is likely to be a moral person.
Clothes do not make the man./Don't judge by external appearances. (However, many people do!)
Cross the Rubicon./Take an irrevocable step.
Curiosity killed the cat./Avoid being nosy, as it can cause harm.
Custom is a second nature./The common is normal.
The customer is always right./Businesses should value their customers' interests and opinions,
       even when they complain.

Damned if one does and damned if one doesn't./In some situations whatever one does is
       likely to attract criticism or lead to an undesirable outcome; catch-22.
Dead men tell no tales./Better kill an enemy than let him live to talk about your acts.
Do unto others as you would have them do unto you./The Golden Rule; treat others as you
       would want to be treated in a similar situation or circumstance. The Bible
A dog is man's best friend./Dogs care about humans often better than other people.
Don't bite off more than you can chew./Be measured in your actions and aims.

Don't count your chickens before they are hatched. Don't count one's chickens before they
        are hatched. /Don't anticipate the future too much.
Don't cry over spilt (or spilled) milk./Don't grieve about having done something that
        cannot be undone.
Don't judge a book by its cover./Appearances can be deceiving.
Don't kill the goose that lays the golden eggs/Don't cut off the source of your success or
        profit.
Don't put all your eggs in one basket./Don't invest all your efforts, or attention in just one
        thing.
Don't put new wine into old bottles./Better to make a fresh start.
Don't put the cart before the horse./Proceed in logical fashion; don't leap ahead or rush.
Don't shoot the messenger./Someone telling you information is not necessarily the enemy.
Don't scapegoat the informer.
Don't throw out the baby with the bathwater/In an effort to achieve your aim, don't overlook
        important details on the way.
Don't put all your eggs in one basket/Don't risk losing everything at once.
A drowning man will clutch at a straw./The desperate will try anything.

The early bird catches the worm./A person who gets up early in the morning has the best chance
        of succeeding; if you arrive early or quicker, you get ahead of others. Arriving early gives
        one an advantage. Act quickly and in good time.
Easier said than done./Many things are more difficult to do than to talk about doing.
East is east and West is west./Two things that fundamentally differ.
Easy come, easy go./What was easily won is easily lost; Something you get quickly and
        easily may be lost or spent just as easily.
Empty vessels make most voice.(noise; sound)/A big talker may be a bigger fool.
The end justifies the means/ If the result is good, it doesn't matter what methods were used to
        achieve it.
An Englishman's home is his castle./There is no place like home.
Enough is enough./No more will be tolerated.
Even a worm will turn./Everyone, including the timid, will react when pushed too far.
Every Jack has his Jill./In time, we all find our love.
Everything old is new again./There is nothing new on earth.
An eye for an eye, a tooth for a tooth./ This refers to revenge, getting exact justice for crimes
        committed. Return to others the same action they give you. The Bible

Faint heart never won fair lady./Be direct and forthcoming in matters of the heart.
Fight fire with fire./Use weapons or tactics of one's enemy or opponent even if one finds them
        distasteful.
Fine clothes make the man./People pay attention to appearances; people judge by appearances.
First come, first served/The first to arrive will be the first to receive attention. Be early or
        lose out.
First things first./Important matters should be attended to before anything else.
A friend in need is a friend indeed/Someone who helps you when you are in trouble is a true
        friend. A true friend will help you in time of trouble.

Give credit where credit is due./Acknowledge one's debts and the contributions of others.

God helps those who help themselves./Take care of yourself first and foremost to do better in life.

The grass is always greener on the other side of the fence./Another place or situation always appears to be better than your own. We are often not satisfied and wants to be somewhere else; a place that is far away or different seems better than where we are. Discontent with what you have leads you to believe that others are more fortune.

Half a loaf is better than no bread./Be grateful (for what one has, even if it's little.)

Haste makes waste. Hurry makes waste./Rushing is imprudent or foolish.

He who laughs last laughs best(longest)./The person who succeeds in making the last move has the most fun or succeeds.

He who lives by the sword shall die by the sword./Those who commit violent acts must expect to suffer violence themselves. What we do to others will be done to us.

Heaven helps those who help themselves./Help oneself; make effort for one's goal instead of looking to others.

History repeats itself./If it has happened once, it will happen again.

Hit the nail on the head./Expressed the point exactly; on point.

Home is where the heart is./We all yearn for our home and family life.

Honesty is the best policy./You will always gain the trust of people by being honest.

If anything can go wrong, it will. (Murphy's law)/Possible bad things tend to happen.

If one door shuts, another opens/ If you fail, try again; there will be other opportunities. Don't give up.

If there is a strong general, there will be no weak soldiers. (Chinese proverb)/A leader or virtuous person inspires others to heroic acts or better performance.

If you can't beat them, join them./ If what you suggest is totally opposed, join the majority. If you can't defeat your opponents, join forces with them.

If you can't stand the heat or If you don't like the heat, get out of the kitchen./If the pace is too fast for you, then step aside and allow others more capable to take over. if you can't tolerate the pressure of a particular situation, remove yourself from that situation. (Harry S. Truman)

It never rains but it pours./Bad times can snowball.

It's never too late./Look for the positive and try again.

It's no good (use) crying over spilt milk./What has happened has happened; accept things and move forward.

It's the empty can that makes the most noise./Big talkers make little sense.

It takes two to tango./When two people work as a team, they are both responsible for the team's successes and failures.

A jack of all trades is master of none. (Jack of all trades and master of none.)/ Someone who tries their hand at too many things will never be expert in any.

A journey of a thousand miles begins with a single step./Take action; see change as a process that begins with something small and grows.

Judge not, that ye be not judged./Think of others more as you would want them to think of you if they were in your position.

Kill the goose that lays the golden eggs./Destroy a reliable and valuable source of income.

Kill two birds with one stone./Maximum effect with minimum effort; one course of action leads to two desirable outcomes; to succeed in doing two things by only one action; get two results from one effort.

Knowledge is power./The basis for effective behaviour is knowledge.

Laughter is the best medicine./We need to laugh.

Leave no stone unturned./Try every course of action in order to achieve something.

Less is more./Real things do not need artifice or adornment.

The lesser evil./The less or unpleasant of two bad choices or possibilities.

Let bygones be bygones/ Forget past quarrels and forgive; let the past be forgotten to agree to forget past quarrels.

Like father, like son./A child often behaves like his parents. A son is usually like his father in the way he acts.

The longest journey begins (starts) with a single step (Confucius)./Incremental effort makes sense; make a beginning no matter the journey.

Look before you leap./Think carefully before you act.

Love is blind./Those in love cannot see faults in their partners; one sees no faults in the person one loves.

Love makes the world go round/When people show respect and consideration for one another, the world is a better place.

Love thy neighbor as thyself. (The Bible)/We live well by treating others as we want to be treated.

Make hay while the sun shines./Take advantage of something while it is available.

Man cannot or does not live by bread alone./People's psychological needs as well as their physical needs must be satisfied if they are to live.

A man is known by the company he keeps./One's friends reveal who one is.

Money can't buy happiness./There's more to life than money; money isn't everything.

Money does not grow on trees. /Money is not easily obtained; don't act like money is always available.

Money is power./Having money means we can buy our way.

Money isn't everything./There's more to life than money; life requires more than attention to money.

Money talks./Money is power; money is king.

More haste, less speed. /One makes better progress with a task if one doesn't try to do it too quickly; slow and steady wins the race; a deliberate pace is best.

A necessary evil./Something that is undesirable but must be accepted.

Necessity is the mother of invention./When faced with a difficult problem, one can think of an ingenious way out. Most inventions are created to solve a problem.

Never count your chickens before they hatch./Don't overreach or overstep in haste; jumping to conclusions can lose something of value.

Never judge a book by its cover./Don't judge people or things by their outward appearance.

Never put off till tomorrow what may be done today./ If something needs to be done, don't delay by putting it off until another day.

Never too old to learn./No one is too old usefully to learn new things.

New wine in old bottles./Something new or innovative added to an existing or established system or organization.

No man is an island./We are social beings; avoid self-centered thinking; community is necessary for humanity.

No man serve two masters./One can't be totally loyal to two people or two ideas at the same time.

No news is good news./News can be good or bad; the fact that there is no news means that all could be well. if one does not hear the outcome of a situation, that outcome must be positive.

No pain, no gain or No pains, no gains/ One won't gain anything without some trouble. nothing can be accomplished without effort.

Nothing is certain but death and taxes./Everyone dies, and we all face a bill for public services; taxes are bad (a burden).

Nothing ventured, nothing gained./ If one never tries, s/he gains nothing.

Oil and water don't mix./Two opposites; two contradictory things.

Old habits die hard/ It's very difficult to change an established pattern of behavior.

Old soldiers never die, they just fade away. (General Douglas MacArthur); some roles in life mark the man/person.

Once bitten, twice shy./A bad experience makes one avoid a second one. An unfortunate experience makes one cautious in similar situations.

An apple a day keeps the doctor away/Good habits keep a person healthy (including eating fruit).

One law for the rich another law for the poor/Class (socioeconomic status) matters.

One man's trash is another man's treasure./What one doesn't want, another can use (needs or wants).

One swallow doesn't make a summer./ A single instance or indicator of something is not necessarily significant.

Out of sight, out of mind./If something is not seen, it is soon forgotten.

Patience is a virtue./ Bearing with others (with life, with bad things or times) leads to greater good.

Patience opens all doors./Good things come to pass with time and sometimes through waiting or enduring in the meantime.

Patience is a virtue./Forbearance is queen.

The pen is mightier than the sword./ What is written can often have more power than brute force. the written word is more powerful than physical force. Words can inflict more pain than physical actions.

A penny saved is a penny earned/gained./Happiness comes from earning one's way; everything counts in making an effort; saving small leads to big gains overtime.

A picture is worth a thousand words./Pictures say a lot; pictures mean more than what they appear on the surface.

Pigs might fly./The impossible; an impossibility.

Poor as a church mouse./Extremely poor.

Practice makes perfect./Regular exercise of an activity or skill leads to proficiency.

Practice what you preach. /Do what one advises others to do.

Prevention is better than cure/ It's always better to stop something bad from happening rather than put it right after it has taken place; be proactive.

A prophet is not recognized in his own land. (The Bible)/People consider their geniuses to be fools; pay attention to all persons.

Put the cart before the horse./Reverse the proper order or procedure of something; rush ahead before accomplishing first things; trying to jump to the end and failing in an action.

The right hand doesn't know what the left hand's doing./A state of confusion or a failure or a failure of communication within a group or organization.

Robbing Peter to pay Paul./Take something away from one person to pay another, leaving the former at a disadvantage; discharge one debt only to incur another; money is too scarce.

A rolling stone gathers no moss./Someone who frequently moves from place to place will not pick up habits and ways, good or bad.

Rome wasn't built in a day./Important things cannot be done in a short time; important things do not happen overnight.

A rooster one day, a feather duster the next./Popularity or celebrity is fleeting; build them up to knock them down.

Save your pennies for a rainy day./It's best to have money in reserve for an unexpected need. (Some experts say everyone needs to have savings to amount to six months of living expenses in the present day.)

See no evil, hear no evil, speak no evil./Avoid bad things, people, etc.

Seeing is believing./Seeing an object is proof of its existence. If one sees something, one will believe it. You have to accept the evidence of your own eyes. You are likely to believe what you see with your own eyes. Seeing something is good proof: Sam told Mark he had passed his test, but Mark said, "Seeing is believing."

Silence is golden./It's not necessary always to talk or to be heard; learn by listening.

The sky is the limit./There is practically no limit; we can accomplish all things.

Small is beautiful./The belief that something small scale is better than a large scale equivalent; size is not the same thing as excellence.

Sour grapes./An attitude in which someone disparages or affects to despise something because they cannot have it themselves; having a dour or bad attitude.

Spare the rod and spoil the child./If punishment is not meted out to a bad child, he or she will suffer in the long run; we must discipline our own.

Speech is silver, silence is golden/Sometimes it is better and more eloquent to remain silent.

Still waters run deep./A quiet or placid manner may conceal a passionate nature.

Talk is cheap./Don't believe everything people say; much talk is much nonsense.

That's further down the track/That's to come; wait; be patient.

There's no place like home./Home is the best place to be; a person is happiest with his or her family and friends.

There's no pleasure without pain./Every good thing requires work; all good things require effort.

There's no smoke without fire. Where there's smoke, there's fire./Rumours are usually based on some degree of truth.

There's no such thing as a free lunch./We pay for everything in the end; the hand that feeds
        requires something in return.
There's safety in numbers/ If many other people are doing or thinking as you do, then
        you are probably safer or more likely to survive, succeed
Time flies./Things move so fast, often said in retrospect.
Time heals all wounds or sorrows./With time, balance returns or perspective is regained.
Time is money./Time is a valuable resource; we can express value in terms of time.
Time will tell./Wait and see; find out the result later.
To bite off more than one can chew./To overstep or exhibit hubris in a small way; to
        attempt what one cannot achieve.
Tomorrow is another day./Get a fresh start after resting or taking stock of things.
Tomorrow never comes./We may lose a chance or experience a disappointment that cannot be
        reversed.
Too many cooks spoil the broth./Something can be ruined if too many people try to do the
        same job at the same time. Too many people trying to take care of something can ruin it.
Turn over a new leaf./Make a change; make a new beginning; change one's stripes or adopt a
        different (usually better) attitude, frame of mind, or behaviour.
Two heads are better than one./In a difficulty it's better to seek advice rather than carrying on
        alone.
Two's company, but three's a crowd. /Couples often enjoy their privacy and dislike having a
        third person around.
Two wrongs don't make a right./ If someone does you a wrong, then having your revenge will
        not make things right.

United we stand, divided we fall/If people work together, they have a stronger chance of
        winning.

Walls have ears./Be careful of what one says, take care not to be overheard (may imply that
        someone is listening or a related fear).
Waste not, want not./If you're careful with what you have, you'll not go hungry.
What goes around comes around./The consequences of one's actions will have to be dealt with
        eventually.
What goes up must come down./All things end; gravity is a law of nature (so nature governs
        human life); man cannot best nature.
When the cat's away, the mice will play/People will take advantage of someone else's absence to
        behave more freely.
When in Rome, do as the Romans do./Behave like the locals; people must respect the customs of
        where they find themselves.
Where there's a will, there's a way./If you are determined to do something, you will find a way
        of doing it.

You are never too old to learn. You're never too old to learn./A person can learn at any age;
        learning expresses life.
You can choose your friends, but you can't choose your family./We must see the
        difference between the given and the chosen; we must accept from where we come.
You can lead a horse to water, but you can't make him drink./You can't force someone to do

something they don't want to do; a person must make his/her own decisions.
You can't judge a book by its cover./Don't go by appearances; there's more to a person or thing than what is on the surface.
You can't please everyone./It's a trap to want everyone to like you; leadership or genuine action may not be universally admired or accepted.
You can't teach an old dog new tricks. (A leopard doesn't change his spots.)/We are who we are; praise or a criticism of ingrained habit; an acknowledgement of the ways of the aged or those set in their ways.
You reap what you sow./What we do comes back to us; expression of karma
You scratch my back and I'll scratch yours./ If you do me a favour , I will return it; *do ut des*; expresses reciprocity as the basis of cooperation.

XI. Unusual Expressions in a Grammatical Sense

i. There are a number of adverbs which are both adjective and adverb and cannot add the adverbial ending –ly, e.g. alone, fast, low, early, further, much, enough, little, still far, long, straight.

ii. Some other adjectives can be used as both with and without –ly. The two forms have different meanings, e.g. deep, high, near, hard, late

iii. The forms without –ly are adverbs more closely similar in meaning to the adjectives, as the following examples illustrate:

Big/Borrowing up big. Spend up big (Could be adverb – quantifies the verb) Shoppers spend big. Think big. Talk big.
Clean/She clean forgot.
Close/Nothing comes so close.
Dead/He was dead cool.
Deep/Still waters run deep. She read deep into the night.
Easy/Take it easy. Do it easy.
Fair/Play fair.
Far and wide/Bats spread seeds far and wide.
Fast and slow/Fast is better than slow/
Fine/You are doing fine.
Free/Feel free. Born free. Walk free.
Hard/He hit me hard in the chest. She lost her hard-earned money./They will be hard put to be ready by Christmas.
High/It soared high above them. Don't fix your hopes too high. Live high. Fly high.
High and dry/Left high and dry.
Late/He will stay up late to finish it. A drawing dated as late as 1960
Light:/Travel light.
Loud/Laughing out loud.
Low/Stay low. How low can you go?
Near/She won't come near me. As near as makes no difference. Near-famine conditions
Pretty/Be sitting pretty.
Quick/We have to get out quick.
Strong and healthy/Please help me to grow up strong and healthy with regular medical check-ups.
Supreme/Rule supreme.
Sure/Make sure.
Tall/Stand tall.
Tight/Hold tight. Sit tight.
Tough/Do it tough. Farmers doing it tough.
Wild/Go wild.
Wrong/You can't go wrong.

iv. Some forms with –ly have meanings more remote from those of adjectives:

deeply is chiefly figurative, e.g. Deeply in love.
hardly/scarcely. E.g. She hardly earned her money.
highly is chiefly figurative, e.g. Don't value possessions too highly.
lately/ recently, e.g. She has been tired lately.
nearly/almost, e.g. The conditions were nearly those of a famine.

Non-native speakers (NNS) tend to be dogmatic about grammar. Some expressions like the above examples are unusual to NNS. The following expressions have been taken from English newspapers and books. They are not broken English. People in the non-English speaking world should not forget that many words are used for several different functions as nouns, adjectives, verbs and adverbs.

Adverbs and adjectives with the same form: back, deep, direct, early, far, fast, hard, high, ill, just, kindly, late, left, little, long, low, much/more/most, near, north/east etc., pretty, right, short, still, straight, well, wrong

Used as adverbs: **Used as adjectives**

Come back soon.   the back door

You can dial Seoul direct   the most direct route

The bus went fast.   a fast bus

We worked hard. (energetically)   The work is hard.

An ill-made road   You look ill.

Turn right here.   The right answer

He went straight home.   A straight line

She led us wrong.   This is the wrong way.

v. The following words are usually used as adjectives but sometimes as nouns in the following examples:

Big/Track down Mr. Bigs.
Build/Medium-build
Clear/Mum's in the clear.
Cold/No one is left out in the cold.
Cool/Cool is cool (the 1st cool).
Dry/The big dry
Empty/Running on empty
Enough/Enough is enough. The first enough is a noun.
Fast and slow/Fast is better than slow.
Free/Far from free. (I think 'free' could be an adjective here if being before free is omitted.)
Full/He lived life to the full.
Good/Water bans are here for good. It's all for your own good. For good becomes adverb phrase.
Green/Endless sea of green
Handful/Handfuls
High/Fuel prices at new high. Hit a high in sales.

High and low/A lot of highs and a lot of lows. Famous faces reveal the highs and lows of their
        school report cards. Highs and lows for outgoing Turkish envoy. Wonderful highs and
        difficult lows
Hopeful/Former Seoul Mayor leads presidential hopefuls. Meet presidential hopefuls.
Less/Why settle for less?
Lifeless/Deserts are far from lifeless.
Middle/Children caught in the middle
New/Big guys rely on new.
New and old/ Creating new from old; new for old
Nuclear/Nobel goes nuclear (The Nobel Peace prize goes to the head of the International Atomic
        Agency.)
Rich and famous/Rubbing shoulders with the rich and famous
Right/I can't find Mrs. Right. A Bill of Rights
Small/Small is beautiful
Spoonful/spoonfuls
Traditional/I want a white and kind of traditional (wedding).
Wet/big wet
Wrong/A bill of wrongs. There are a few ways to right the wrongs of Kim Jong-il's dictatorship.
Young/Most mammals give birth to live young.
Young and old/The young and old gather.

vi. The following words are usually verbs, but they are used as nouns here:

Ask/Big ask. Tough ask.
Buy/Good buy Buy/Good buy. Impulse buy.
Come and go/Easy come, easy go.
Dip/Double dip
Divide/Digital divide
Fight and kill/Give up her kill without a fight.
Finish and start/From start to finish.
Go/Give another go. Give it a go. No go. Make a go of it. No go.
Kill/Lions are built for the kill.
Look/Looks can be deceiving.
Must/Fewer young women believe marriage is a must in life. This is a must. Must-see movie.
        Must-see experience. Must-win situation.
Sell/Hard sell
Start/Flying start A great start. For a start, we'd like get our hands dirty.

vii. Adjectives usually do not describe pronouns, but there are exceptions:

New/New me or new you. Usually adjectives do not describe pronouns, but new may describe
me or you when you or I were injured, and your or my appearance has changed.
Old/Old me.

viii. The following words are normally used as adverbs, but they are used as nouns:

up and down/ ups and downs

ix. Some words are normally used as conjunctions, but they are used as nouns in the following example:

No ifs, ands, or buts.

x. This word is usually used as a noun or verb, but it may be used as adverb: Wonder/Work wonders.

xi. This word is usually used as a verb but may be used as an adverb:

Put/Stay put. Cash in super stays put.

xii. The following words are usually used as adjectives, but here they may be used as verbs:

Right/There are a few ways to right the wrongs.

XII. Funny Expressions, Quotes, Idioms and Proverbs

Aussie salute (to humble flies?)
Baby (What kind of baby do you mean? There are several different meanings.)
back of envelope calculation (not enough paper to write on?)
Banana republic (Good to eat a lot of bananas.)
Bangkok Hilton (5 star jail?)
Big Apple (New York)
Big smokes (not a lot of smokes in big cities these days.)
blood boil (Boil means above 100 C.)
Bollywood (It sounds familiar.)
Born with a silver spoon (should have been "born with a gold spoon")
Boys are boys (Obvious!)
Carrots and sticks (Giraffes will love carrots. for sure)
Cash cow (should have been "cash horse" due to racing money)
Chicken game (Why not bull?)
Comeback kid (should have been comeback man as Bill Clinton is not a kid.)
Con artist (should have been "con technician")
Dead meat (Meat is already dead, cannot be dead twice.)
Deep pocket (Good to carry a sweet potato.)
Dead man walking (Impossible!)
Dig deep (to try to find water?)
Dirty dogs (not dogs but people)
Dirty dancing (sexier than clean dancing?)
Dying to see you (Why dye?)
Emperor has no clothes (He must be very poor.).
Down Under (Australia; Is there UP Above?),
The 11th hour (What is special about this hour?),
End of story (More story please!),
Faceless men (how to be faceless?),
Fat cat (should have been "fat pig"),
Good drink (good rain in Australia),
Hair cut (shearing sheep in Australia),
Half pregnant (Is it possible?)
Have a bad hair day/(someone's hair is in a mess; everything is going wrong),
Hen's teeth (Who is after hen's teeth?)
Hot dog (Is there food called 'cold dog'?)
Hot potato (easier to swallow it if you immerse it into cold water)
Hot property (Jessica Watson)
Hollywood action (cheating in soccer games)
Indians (Indians in India, American Indians or low paid workers)
Jail bird (So many have fallen.)
Jumping ship (One will be drowned to do so.)
Little emperor (a son under China's one child policy)
The little red dot (Singapore)
Missile (Being hit by eggs will not kill people.)

Money never sleeps (Is money an animal? Money will be too tired to do so.)
Not in my backyard (Then can I plant my broccoli in your front yard?)
New kid on the block (South Korea by Jon Huer)
A new Roman empire (America)
No meat in sandwich (no substance)
No more petrol in tank (no resource)
No stone unturned (one will find ants)
Rain cats and dogs (should have been "rain elephants and whales" as they are heavier
     than cats and dogs)
Rainy days (Farmers will welcome them.)
The rat pack (Why not the cat pack?),
Read my lips (How can anyone read lips?)
Rocket scientist (There must be smarter people than rocket scientist.)
Sandbagging (pork barrel?)
Sardines (passengers in subway in Tokyo or Seoul)
Sea change (Why not land change?)
Sex strike (unworkable in large scale)
Sick to stomach (must have eaten too much food.)
Silver bullet (How about gold bullet?)
Sitting on fence (The fence must be low enough to sit on.)
Solongos (Mongolians call Korea like that (rainbow country)
Song pub, with no beer by slim dusty (In this case, it is not a pub)
Super fish (Can I gobble it up?)
This guy (this animal or insect)
Sky is the limit (There is no limit in sky)
Sky opens (No such thing as open and close in sky.)
Straight shooter (direct talker),
TLC (tender loving care)
To bite bullet (How?)
To bring home the bacon (why not bread?)
To cost me an arm and a leg (should have been "two arms and legs")
To draw a line in the sand (Only a finger is necessary to do that.)
To face the music (what kind of music, classic or popular?)
To fall on one's sword (Sword is now out-dated.)
To have a cold shower (nice to have one during hot summer months.)
To hold one's breath (Do so for too long, and it will kill you!)
To kill time (Is it possible?)
To put his foot in his mouth (Impossible!)
To run out of steam (Steam power has gone except Puffing Billy.)
To sleep like a baby (not all the babies sleep well.)
To sweep under the carpet (Is there only the area to hide something?),
To take no prisoners (Kill them all?)
Top dollars (Are there bottom dollars?)
Top dog (top man)
Train wreck (Why not shipwreck?)

Two and a half men (TV drama from America; How is it possible to be a half men ?) We've got
to zip it! (shut the mouth)
Wild goose dads (Korean invention?)
You are dynamite (Chilling?)
You scratch my back and I'll scratch yours (Clever?)

The funniest idioms:
Barking up the wrong tree
Black sheep
Bottom fell out
Bottomless pit
Change goalposts
Cheating death
Couch potato
Crocodile tear
Dog's breakfast
Elephant in the room
The eleventh hour
Filthy rich
Finger lickin' good
Gate crasher
Get rich quick
Go out the window
Helicopter parents
Kangaroo court
Laughing all the way to the bank
Lift a finger
No stone unturned
The old bomb (cars)
Over my dead body
Over the moon
Party animal
The $64,000 or 64 million dollar question
Sin bin
Smiling assassin
Spring chicken
Stone dead
Storm in a teacup (or tempest in a teapot)
Sunday school picnic
Tiger mom
Wolf in sheep's clothing

Good short sentences, quotes and proverbs:
All work and no play makes Jack a dull boy.
Art is fraud. (Paik Namjune)
Are you ready?

Because it is there. (George Mallory, Mountain climber)
Better late than never.
Better to be safer than never.
Blind Freddie could see that.
Blood is thicker than water.
Boys, be ambitious! (William Clark)
Boys will be boys.
The buck stops here. (Harry Truman)
Christmas came early. (Is Christmas better than Easter?)
Chickens come home to roost.
Customer is always right. (Gordon Selfridge)
Damned if you do, damned if you don't.
The devil is in the details.
The devil you know is better than the devil you don't know.
Do not say anything.
Don't try this at home.
Easy come, easy go!
Eat humble pie.
Emperor has no clothes (He must be very poor.).
Enough is enough.
Glass is half empty or half full.
He is my rock.
His left hand doesn't know what his right hand's doing.
Hit the nail on the head.
It's not my cup of tea.
It takes two to tango.
It's the economy, stupid. (Bill Clinton)
The jury is still out.
Laughing all the way to the bank.
Looks can be deceiving.
Love conquers all.
Love is blind.
Make my day. (Clint Eastwood)
Make your mouth water.
Money does not grow on trees.
Money never sleeps. (Working too hard?)
Mud sticks.
Never say never.
No pain, no gain!
No stone unturned (Then one will find plenty of earthworms.)
Not funny!
Not in my backyard!
Nothing is impossible.
One cannot live by bread alone.
One size does not fit all.
The party's over.

Pigs can fly. (Yes, on the Show Day).
Put up or shut up!
Read my lips. (How can anyone read lips?) (George Bush)
Rebel without a cause.
A rooster one day, a feather duster next.
Show me the money. (Jerry Maguire)
The show must go on.
The sky's the limit. (There is no limit in sky.)
Sky opens. (No such thing as open and close in sky.)
So what!
Some are more equal than others. (George Orwell)
Stay foolish. Stay hungry. (Steve Jobs)
Take no prisoners.
Talk is cheap.
There's no love lost between them.
There's no place like home. (The Wizard of Oz)
Waste not, want not.
We can do better.
What goes up must come down.
What have I done?
What is that for? (When someone stole kiss suddenly.)
What makes Australia great?
What's so funny?
What's up?
What would I do without you?
When America sneezes, Australia catches a cold.
The world is your oyster.
Yes, we can. (Barack Obama)
You are dynamite.
You are nobody.
You're tearing me apart.
You are what you eat.
You broke my heart.
You can't handle the truth. (A Few Good Men)
You complete me. (Jerry Maguire)
You scratch my back, and I'll scratch yours. (Clever?)
Your guess is as good as mine.

XIII. Konglish

Only India has contributed more English words than the Japanese in Asia. e.g. karaoke, tsunami, origami, bonsai, hara-kiri, geisha, haiku (Japanese style of poetry), kamikaze, karate, kimono, pachinko, samurai, shogun, Sudoku, sumo, ninja, sushi, Tamagotchi, tofu, yen, Walkman, Zen. China has 10 times the population of Japan. However, it has contributed fewer English words than Japan. Korea has donated seven English words e.g. Hangul, Kimchi, Chaebol, Korea, Moonies, Ondol, Soju, and Taekwondo.

As far as proper pronunciation of English is concerned, the Japanese may be among the worst in the world. The Japanese language is short on pronunciation. For instance, the Japanese might say 'lice' instead of 'rice'. Many Jenglish words became Konglish as Japan ruled Korea from 1910 to 1945.

Jenglish	**English**
air con	air conditioner
ankooru	encore
ansa	answer
arapo	around forty
arasa	around thirty
apato	apartment building
bakkumira	back mirror, rear-vision mirror
bajin rodo	virgin road
batderi	battery
bbanggi	paint
bbanku	puncture
bbantsu	pant
bibinpa	bibimbap
biru	beer
bodi con	body conscious
burashi	brush
Burugogi	bulgogi
buruusu	Blues
chaumupointo	charm point
chickan	chicken
choggoletddo	chocolate
churining	sports wear
combina	convenience store
cooler	air conditioner
cunning	cheating
dakusi	taxi
daseu	dozen
Datdo is a hatdo	That is a hat
defle	deflation
depa	department store
depart	department store

dlive	drive
dokuta stoppu	doctor stop
doracku	truck
doransforma	transformer
dorotdo	trot
ekgiseu	extract
garubi	galbi
gene kon	general contractor
gohi	coffee
gulabu	club
gurumun	cream
hambak stek	hamburg steak
Hoddo ddoggu	hot dog
icekeki	ice cake
infle	inflation
jaggu	zipper, chuck
joggi	jug
keoning	cunning; cheating at exams
kimuchi	kimchi
klav	club
kombini	convenient store
kurakbu	club
kurumun	cream
labu hoteru	love hotel
leja	leathe
lemicon	ready-mixed - concrete
lice	rice
libiggurum	living room
loli con	Lolita complex
makudonarudo	McDonald
mammoseu	mammoth
masisoyo	matileouyo
mas pro	mass production
masukomi	mass communication
matkori or makori	makgeolli (rice wine from Korea)
meriyaseu	madias in Spanish
mishing	sewing machine
morninggu	morning
nanningu	running
nanning shatsu	running shirts
Nixon shocku	Nixon shock
Oba	over coat
OL	office lady meaning female office worker
Olympicku	Olympic
pama	permanent wave

paso com	personal computer
projecto	project
pureigaido	play guide
pureste	playstation
rajio	radio
remo con	remote controller
ristoappu	list up
roman	romance?
rub	love
rubu hoteru	love hotel
sabis	service
salada	salad
sarariiman or salary man	a white-collar worker or male salaried employee
sekuhara	sexual harassment
supa com	super computer
starba	star bus
salada	salad
sekuhara	sexual harassment
sten	stainless
supa com	super computer
taggusi	taxi
tarento	talent
terebi	television
vent	ventilate
waishyeochu	white shirt
wapuro or wapro	word processor
y syatsu	white shirts

British English expert Tim Alper commented that native speakers have great difficulty understanding Korean English.

Konglish	**English**
accessory	jewellery
Agree!	I agree
audio	audio system
back	connection (to powerful people)
back music	background music
back number	number on the back of your sports shirts
back mirror	rear-view mirror
ball pen	ball point pen or biro
band	band aid
boarding passes (KTX)	ticket
boiler	heating
bond	super glue

booking	making reservation
cash corner	ATM or cash machine
chorus	choir
cider	a soft drink similar to 7 Up
claim	complaint
classic	classical (music)
claxon	horn
clip	paper clip
cloak	cloakroom
close	closed
cola	coke
consent	electrical outlet, socket
cooler	air conditioner
cunning	cheating in an exam
cutline	cut off point
depart	department store
dead ball	pitched ball
dessert	a hot drink after a meal
do	do it
Don't waste wastes	Cut down on waste
driver	screwdriver
Dutch pay	going Dutch, splitting the bill, Dutch treat
eye shopping	window shopping
febook	Facebook
fighting, paiting or hwaiting	Don't give up (to cheer someone on). Victory! Come on! Cheer! Let's Go, Go!
fine play	fair play
flash	flashlight or electric torch
for lady	for ladies
four balls	a walk
free-size	one size fits all
free-ticket	all day ticket
gagman	comedian
gargle	mouthwash
goal ceremony	goal celebration
golden time	precious time
gonna/wanna	going to/want to
gown	dressing gown
hand phone	mobile phone, cell phone
handle	a steering wheel
Hangang Park	Hangang Riverside Walk
Health	a health club
health centre	fitness centre
hearing	listening comprehension

hip | buttocks
home-in | reaching home
hotcake | pancake
How are you? | What's up?
I will do. | I will do it.
I am doing arbeit. | I have a part-time job
I am playing with friends. | I am hanging out with friends.
ice bar | ice lolly
ice skate | ice skates, ice skating
interphone | intercom
It's my mind. | That is what I want.
It's service. | It's free or It's on the house.
Japan people | Japanese people
Japanese dining bar | Japanese restaurant and bar
Jeju Island | the Isle of Jeju
Korean traditional foods | Korean traditional food
light coke | diet coke
line | managerial staff
liner | lining (of a coat)
long leg | long legged
Let's Dutch pay. | Let's split the bill.
line | managerial staff
magic | magic marker
manicure | nail polish
mansion | luxury apartment a luxury building

marker pen | (board marker)
mart | shop, corner store or store
a meeting | a blind date
melodrama | romantic drama
miko | Miss Korea
Member ID | user name on the internet
mission | transmission
morning call | wake-up call
mug cup | mug
name card | business card
My/our company | work/the office
My company's location is in Suwon. | My office is in Suwon.
My condition is not good. | I don't feel well.
narrow-minded | oversensitive
neck flesh | neck meat
necktie | tie
night | nightclub
no in | No entry
no mark chance | unmarked chance
not touch | Do not touch

note   notebook

oil   petrol

oil bank   gas station

Our nation   this country

overeat   vomit

pop song   an English-language song

one room   a bachelor-style studio apartment

one shot   a form of toast, "Bottoms up!"

open car   convertible

opener   corkscrew, can opener

panel   panelist

panties   underwear

panty stockings   tights, panty hose

polifessor   political academics

potato fry   French fries

President Kim   just "Kim" (or "Mr. Kim)

quiz   word puzzle

reception   a backstage party

rebate   bribe, kickback

rent car   hire car

revival   cover version

ribbon   bow

rinse   conditioner

running machine   treadmill

sack   backpack

sand   sandwich

self   self service

service   bonus, freebee, free of charge; complimentary

sharp   mechanical pencil

short leg   short-legged

sign   autograph

skin   toner

skinship   physical contact between a pair of lovers or mother and child, body contact or touch or close relationship

sofa   a sofa or armchair

solo   single

speaker   loudspeaker

sports dancing   competition ballroom dancing

stainless   stainless steel

stamp   land

sunglass   sunglasses

surfing board   surfboard

syndrome	fever
The Han River	the River Han
talent	a TV star, celebrity
To gain weight	to put on weight
To lose one's weight	to lose weight
To raise children	to bring up children
To raise pets	to have pets
toilet-men	men's toilet
training	sweat suit, tracksuit
vacance	vacation, holiday
villa	small block of flats
vinyl	any kind of plastic
walkers	jump boots
We go to company MT (membership training; company outing).	We are having a company get-together (or a party)
well-being	healthy products
wrap	plastic wrap, cellophane
yacht	any size of boat with a sail
yoghurt	drinking, liquid yoghurt
You're in good shape.	You look fit.

Koreans are not far behind the Japanese as far as broken English is concerned. Japan ruled Korea from 1910 to 1945. Many Konglish words came from Jenglish!

accel	accelerator
Air con	air conditioner
alba	arbeit
ama	amateur
ana	announcer
apatu or aparteu	apartment, flat
alba or arbeit or areubaiteu	part-time, casual job
AS (after service)	after sales service, repair
auto-bi	motorbike
backkumira	back mirror
babarikoteu (Barberry coat)	trench coat
B/D	building
benest	best nest
capa	capacity
centi	cm
CF or commercial film	television advertisement, commercial or advertising
condo	time share apartment
D/B	database
DC or D/C	discount, low price, money off
dasu	dozen
defle	deflation

dica	digital camera
dis	disrespect people
docu	documentary
ekisu	extract
ero	erotic
geulleimeo (glamour)	a buxom woman
gyps	(plaster) cast
hair pin	hair clip
hendeupon (hand phone)	mobile phone, cell phone
handi	handicap (golf)
heli	helicopter
handple	hand play
hof	draft beer
hojikiseu (Hotchkiss)	stapler
homepi	homepage
hwaiting or paiting (fighting)	used to cheer a player or team in sports, or anyone doing something difficult
IC	interchange
icekeki	ice cake
infle	inflation
infra	infrastructure
inteli	intelligentsia
kalay	curry
keoning	cunning; cheating at exams
klaxon	(car) horn
kopi	coffee
le-ports	leisure sports
gurumun	cream
L.T.	leadership training
ment	mention
mira	mummy
mishing	sewing machine
momdents	mother and students
MT(membership training)	club initiation
navisatellite	navigation
nodaji (no touch)	gold
O/D	owner-driver
Officetel	office hotel
ollari	all right – only used when backing up a car
old miss	spinster
O/T	orientation
officetel	office and hotel, a bedsit, studio apartment
opi	officetel

ova   overcoat

otobai   autobicycle

pama   permanent wave

PD (producers)   program directors

peeja   pizza

penshi   (fancy) stationery

ppakku   back up

perma   permanent wave

polifessors   politicians and professors

pro   program/professional

punk   tyre puncture

remokeon (remocon)   remo con

remote controller   remote control

saida (cider)   lemon-lime soda, Sprite, 7-up

salada   salad

sarariiman or salary man   a white-collar worker or male salaried employee

saladents   salaried person and students

selca   self-camera, amateur video or a selfie

Sinchon Rot   Sinchon Rotary

S-line   an attractive woman's body

seukin seukubeo   skin scuba , scuba-diving

SF   science fiction, sci fi

ski   skis, skiing

spec   specifications (a job applicant's qualifications)

spo-lex   sports complex

ssiko   a psycho

sundae   black pudding (black sausage)

t   T-shirt

terebi   television

trans   transformer

waishyeochu   white shirt

wedding ceremony   wedding

wonroom (one room)   studio apartment

Key References

Atchison, J., Cassell Dictionary of English Grammar, Cassell Wellington House, London, 1996, 301 p.
Allen, R., Allen's English phrases, Penguin Books, London, 2006, 805 p.
Alexander, L.G., Longman English Grammar, Longman, London, 1988, 374 p.
Anon, Australian Almanac, Hardie Grant Books, South Yarra, 2003, 546-557 p.
Anon, Longman Elementary Dictionary, Longman., 124 p.
Anon, Macmillan Australian Primary Dictionary, Macquarie University NSW, South Yarra, 2005, 282 p.
Anon, The Macquarie Office Manual, The Macquarie Library, McMahons Point, 1984, 1009 p.
Anon, common abbreviations, Macquarie Dictionary, Macmillan, Australia, 2015.
Anon, Work on your vocabulary, Harper Collins, London, 2013, 127 p.
Ashton, C., Words can tell, Julian Messner, Englewood Cliffs, 1988, 141 p.
Axtell R. E., Do's and Taboos of English Using English around the World, John Wiley & Sons, Inc., New York, 1995, 206 p.
Bauer, L. An Introduction to International Varieties, Edinburgh University Press, Edinburgh, 2002, 135 p.
Beal, G., Book of Words, Kingfisher Books, London, 1991, 200 p.
Beckett, R., The Dinkum Aussie Dictionary, Child & Associates Publishing, Frenchs Forest, 1986, 59 p.
Blackman, J., Aussie Slang Dictionary for Old and New Australians, Pan Macmillan, Sydney, 1990, 115 p.
Blackman, J, Aussie Slang, , Pan Macmillan, Sydney, Indianapolis, 1998, 214 p.
Blamires, H., The Penguin Guide to Plain English, Penguin Books, London, 2000, 360 p.
Blaxwell G. and Winch, G., The English Language Users Guide, Phonex Education, Albert Park, 1995, 135 p.
Boyer, S., Understanding Spoken English, Boyer Educational Resources, Glenbrook, 2003, 133 p.
Brett, R., The Dinkum Aussie Dictionary, Child & Associates, French Forest, 1986, 59 p.
Butler, S. (Editor), The Macquarie Children's Dictionary, Macquarie Library, Ryde, 1983, 108 p.
Butler, S., The Macquarie Dictionary (Third Edition), Ryde, Macquarie Library, 1997, 2504 p.
Butler, S., The Macquarie Dictionary of New Words, The Macquarie Library, NSW, 1990, 406 p.
Clark, S. & Pointon. G., Word for Word, Oxford University Press, Oxford, 2003, 250 p.
Cindy Leaney, Junior Dictionary & Thesaurus, Bardfield Press, Essex, 2004,
Clutterbuck, P. M., Improve Your English – A Resource Book, Macmillan, South Melbourne, 1985, 115 p.
Collins, C., 101 American English Idioms, Passport Books, Chicago, 1987, 104 p.
Collins, C., 101 American English Proverbs, Passport Books, Chicago, 1992, 105 p.
Collins P. & Hollo, C., English Grammar – an Introduction, Palgrave, , New York, 2000, 268 p.
Cowie, A.P., English Dictionaries for Foreign Learners: A History, Oxford University Press, Oxford, 1999, 232 p.
Craig, R.P. & Hopper, V. F., Barron's 1001 Pitfalls in English Grammar, Barron's Educational Series. Inc., New York, 1986, 376 p.
Crystal D., The Cambridge Encyclopedia of The English Language, Cambridge University Press,

Cambridge, 1995, 489 p.

Cullup, M., Brush Up Your Grammar, Elliot Right Way Books, Surrey, 160 p.

Delbridge, A. (Editor-in- Chief), The Macquarie Dictionary, Macquarie Library, Ryde, 1981, 2062p.

DeVinne, P. B., (Coordinating Editors), Webster's Illustrated Encyclopedic Dictionary, Tormont Publications Inc., East Montreal, 1990, 1920 p.

Downing, A. and Locke, P., A University Course in English Grammar, Prentice Hill, London, 2002, 652 p.

Doyle, M. The A-Z of Non-Sexist Language, The Women's Press, 1995, 112 p.

Eastwood, J.& Macklin, A Basic English Grammar, Oxford University Press, Oxford, 1982, 160 p.

Eastwood, J., Oxford Practice Grammar with Answers, Oxford University Press, Oxford, 1992, 334 p.

Ender, A. Times Illustrated Dictionary, Earlybird Books, Singapore, 1994, 123 p.

Factor, J., Kidsspeak, Melbourne University Press, Melbourne, 2000, 244 p.

Fieldhouse, H., Everyman's Good English Guide, JM Dent & Son, London, 1982, 270 p.

Flavell, L. and R., Dictionary of Idioms and their Origins, Kyle Cathie, London, 2000, 216 p.

Flavell, L. and R, Dictionary of Word Origins, Kyle Cathie, London, 2000, 277 p.

Foster, J., Oxford Junior Rhyming Dictionary, Oxford University Press, Oxford, 2005, 160 p.

Fuller, N. and Gardener P., Book 1 – English for Everyone, Macmillan, Crows Nest, 1979, 186 p.

Gard, S. Fantastic Australians, Kangaroo Press, Kenthurst, 1994, 108 p.

Goldsmith, E.(Compiler), Collins Junior Thesaurus, Collins, London, 2004, 240 p.

Gooden, P., The Guide to Better English, Peter Collin Publishing, London, 2001, 194 p.

Goodman, B., English, Yes!, Jamestown, Chicago, 1996, 184 p.

Goodman, M., (illustrator), Let's learn English Picture Dictionary, McGraw-Hill, New York, 1991, 42 p.

Granger, M., English as a New Language – A Handbook for Students, Phoenix Education, Albert Park, 1995, 104 p.

Green, J., Dictionary of New Words, Bloomsbury, London, 1991, 339 p.

Grisewood, J., Children's Illustrated Dictionary, RD Press, Surry Hills, 1991, 320 p.

Grygel, J.A. (Project Editor), The World Book of Word Power, Vol. 1, World Book, Chicago, 194 p

Guralnik, D.B. (editor), Webster's New World Dictionary, Nelson, Foster & Scott, Toronto, 1970, 1092 p.

Gutierrez, L., English is not easy, Square Peg, 2015, 328 p.

Hamilton, E., Dictionary Power, Melbourne Oxford University Press, Oxford, 1984, 66 p.

Hamilton, E., How to Use Australian Pocket Oxford Dictionary, Oxford University Press, Oxford, 1984, 63 p.

Hayance B., Spark! Words and Pictures for Activating English, Actual Enterprises, Glebe, 2003, 128 p.

Hochstatter, D.J. (Illustrator), Just Look'n Learn English Picture Dictionary, McGraw-Hill, New York, 1997, 95 p.

The Bible (New International Version), Hodder & Stoughton, London, 1973, 1272 p.

Howard, P., Oz Slang, Jim Coroneos Publication, Rose Bay, 1997, 64 p.

Hudson, N., Modern Australian Usage, Oxford University Press, Oxford, 1993, 440 p.

Hughes, B.(General Editor), The Penguin Working Words, Viking, Ringwood, 1993, 570 p.

Jarvie, G., Bloomsbury Grammar Guide Grammar Made Easy, Bloomsbury, London, 1993, 216 p.

Jeans, P. My Word, St George Books, Perth, 1993, 278 p.

Joyce, H., Words for Living – A vocabulary Wordbook for Social English, Macquarie University, 1998, 71 p.

Keighery, Kath (compiled), Planned Progress in Word Study – an Approach to Spelling Skills, ATC Publishing, Mornington, 1990, 113 p.

King, G., Collins Wordpower - Abbreviations, Harper Collins, Glasgow, 2000, 233 p.

King, G. Collins. Wordpower - Good Grammar, Harper Collins, Glasgow, 2000, 240 p.

King, G. Collins. Wordpower – Super Speller, Harper Collins, Glasgow, 2000, 178 p.

Knowles E. and Elliott J., The Oxford Dictionary of New Words, Oxford University Press, Oxford, 1997, 356 p.

Lambert, J.(general editor), Macquarie Australian Dictionary, The Macquarie Library , NSW, 2004, 223 p.

Makkai, A., A Dictionary of American Idioms, Barron's, New York, 1987, 398 p.

Manser, M.H. (editor), Bloomsbury Good Word Guide, Bloomsbury, London,1988, 291 p.

McCarthy, M, and O'Dell, F, English Vocabulary in Use, Advanced, Cambridge University Press, Cambridge, 2002, 315 p.

McCarthy, M, and O'Dell, F, English Vocabulary in Use, Upper-intermediate, Cambridge University Press, Cambridge, 2001, 307 p.

McCarthy, M, and O'Dell, F., Test your English Vocabulary in Use, Advanced, Cambridge University Press, Cambridge, 2005, 165 p.

McFedries P., The Complete Idiot's Guide to A Smart Vocabulary, Logophilia, Indianapolis, 2001, 363 p.

McGough, R. My Oxford ABC and 123 Picture Rhyme Book, Oxford University Press, Oxford, 1990, 76 p.

Mellonie, B., Bruce's Aussie Dictionary, Puffin Books, 2003, 96 p.

Moore, B. (Editor), The Australian Concise Oxford Dictionary (4th Edition), Oxford University Press, South Melbourne, 2004, 1679 p.

Morris, E., The Word Detective, Algonquin Books, Chapel Hill, 2000, 228 p.

Morison, J., Correct English Spelling, Golden Books, Kuala Lumpur, 2001, 291 p.

Morwood J. and Warman, M., Our Greek and Latin Roots, Cambridge University Press, Cambridge, 1990, 56 p.

Murphy, R., Essential Grammar in Use, Cambridge University Press, 1997, 300 p.

Murphy, R., English Grammar in Use, Cambridge University Press, Cambridge, 2004, 379 p.

Murray-Smith. S., Right Words – A guide to English Usage in Australia, Penguin Books, Ringwood, 1989, 439 p.

Neaman, J. & Silver, C., In Other Words – A Thesaurus of Euphemisms, Angus & Robertson, London, 1990, 409 p.

Nelson, G., English an Essential Grammar, Routledge, London, 2001, 176 p.

O'Dell, F. and Head, K., Games for Vocabulary Practice, Cambridge University Press, Cambridge, 2003, 120 p.

Olsen, D., The Words You Should Know, Bob Adams, Holbrook, 1991, 235 p.

Peters, P., The Cambridge Australian English Style Guide, Cambridge University Press, Cambridge, 1995, 848 p.

Peters, P., The Cambridge Guide to English Usage, Cambridge University Press, Cambridge, 2004, 608 p.

Procter, P.(Editor-in-Chief), Cambridge International Dictionary of English, Cambridge University Press, Cambridge, 1995, 1773 p.

Raimes, A., Grammar Troublespots – A guide for Student Writers, Cambridge University Press, Cambridge, 2004, 186 p.

Reader's Digest Services Pty Ltd, Sydney (edited), How to Write and Speak Better, Surry Hills, 1989, 535 p.

Redman, S., English Vocabulary in Use, Cambridge University Press, Cambridge, 2003, 263 p.

Richards, K., Word Map, ABC Books, Sydney, 2005, 223 p.

Rinvolucri, M., Grammar Games – Cognitive, affective and drama activities for EFL students, Cambridge University Press, Cambridge, 1984, 138 p.

Rolton, G., The Macmillan Book of Neologisms, Macmillan, South Yarra, 1999. 96 p.

Root, B., Picture Pocket Dictionary, Kingfisher, London, 1991, 96 p.

Seuss, Dr. The Cat in the Hat Dictionary, Random House, New York, 1964, 95 p.

Seely, J. Oxford Everyday Grammar, Oxford University Press, Oxford, 2001, 219 p.

Sinclair, J.M. (General Consultant), Wilkes, G.A (For Australian Edition). Krebs, W.A. (For Australian Edition), Collins English Dictionary, 4th Australian Edition, 1998, Harper Collins Publishers, Aylesbury, 1998, 1785 p.

Sinclair, John (editor), Collins Cobuild Idioms Dictionary, HarperCollins, 2002, 497 p.

Smith, D. and Cassin S., Young Readers' Dictionary, HarperCollins, London, 1984, 192 p.

Speake, Jennifer (edited), The Oxford Dictionary of Idioms, Oxford University Press, Oxford, 1999, 395 p.

Sutherland, Lisa (Project manager). Collins Easy Learning English Idioms, HarperCollins, Glasgow, 2010, 315 p.

Swan, D., The Usbourne Guide to English Grammar, Usbourne Publishing, London, 1983, 48 p.

Swan, M., Basic English Usage, Oxford University Press, Oxford, 1984, 382 p.

Swan, M., Practical English Usage, Oxford University Press, Oxford, 1980, 664 p.

Swan, M. & Walter, C., The Good Grammar Book., Oxford University Press, Oxford, 2001, 324 p.

Taylor. J.G., A Handbook for Writers of English, How to Book Ltd., Oxford, 2002, 242 p.

Tardif, R. (editor), My Macquarie Picture Dictionary, The Jacaranda Press, 1990, 164 p.

Thompson, A.J. & Martinet, A.V., A Practical English Grammar, Oxford University Press, Oxford, 1986, 383 p.

Umstatter. J., Grammar Grabbers!, The Center for Applied Research in Education, Paramus, 2001, 328 p.

Umstatter, J., 201 Ready-to-Use Word Games for the English Classroom, The Center for Applied Research in Education, Paramus, 1994, 310 p.

Vermes, J.C. and Barnum, C.M., Secretary's Guide to Modern English Usage, Prentice Hall, Englewood Cliffs, 1991, 246 p.

Wardhaugh, R., Understanding English Grammar – A Linguistic Approach, Blackwell Publishing, Oxford, 2003, 279 p.

Weiner, E.S.C. and Delahunty, A., The Oxford Guide to English Usage, Oxford University Press, Oxford, 1994, 306 p.

Whitcut, J., Better Wordpower, Oxford University Press, Oxford, 1998, 329 p.